JUDAS *of* NAZARETH

"Combining some of my ideas—such as Paul as Herodian and Josephus's "Sadduk" as John the Baptist—with his own theory, Dan Unterbrink suggests a new and much earlier timeframe for Christian origins, claiming that the historical Jesus was actually Judas the Galilean, a rebel leader who came on the scene in 4 BC with the beginning of the Zealot movement.

"As he sees it, Christian scholarship as a whole has been searching for characters such as Jesus and Paul in the wrong places. Not only does he claim that Jesus was a literary stand-in for Judas the Galilean, but that Paul may have been an active participant in the composition of the Gospel of Mark.

"Detailing the similarities between the gospel Jesus and Paul's own life and teachings, Unterbrink claims the former to have been simply a clever blend of Judas the Galilean and Paul. In so doing, he gives his readers much to consider while at the same time challenging what they have always taken to be 'the Gospel Truth' and their traditional views."

ROBERT EISENMAN, PROFESSOR EMERITUS AT CALIFORNIA STATE UNIVERSITY–LONG BEACH AND AUTHOR *OF JAMES THE BROTHER OF JESUS* AND *THE NEW TESTAMENT CODE*

JUDAS *of* NAZARETH

How the Greatest Teacher
of First-Century Israel
Was Replaced by a Literary Creation

DANIEL T. UNTERBRINK

Bear & Company
Rochester, Vermont • Toronto, Canada

Bear & Company
One Park Street
Rochester, Vermont 05767
www.BearandCompanyBooks.com

Text stock is SFI certified

Bear & Company is a division of Inner Traditions International

Library of Congress Cataloging-in-Publication Data
Unterbrink, Daniel T., 1957–
  Judas of Nazareth : how the greatest teacher of first-century Israel was replaced
by a literary creation / Daniel T. Unterbrink.
      pages cm
  Includes bibliographical references and index.
  Summary: "An investigation into the historical Jesus and the veracity of the
Gospels" — Provided by publisher.
  ISBN 978-1-59143-182-4 (pbk.) — ISBN 978-1-59143-760-4 (e-book)
  1. Jesus Christ—Historicity. I. Title.
  BT303.2.U58 2014
  232.9'08—dc23

                                                          2013034252

Printed and bound in the United States by Lake Book Manufacturing, Inc.
The text stock is SFI certified. The Sustainable Forestry Initiative® program
promotes sustainable forest management.

10 9 8 7 6 5 4 3 2 1

Text design by Priscilla Baker and layout by Brian Boynton
This book was typeset in Garamond Premier Pro with Futura used as a display
typeface

To send correspondence to the author of this book, mail a first-class letter to the
author c/o Inner Traditions • Bear & Company, One Park Street, Rochester, VT
05767, and we will forward the communication, or contact the author directly at
www.danielunterbrink.com.

Contents

◄ PART THREE ►

The Creation of Jesus of Nazareth

PAUL'S HAND IN THE GOSPELS

Foreword

By Barrie Wilson

Professor Emeritus and Senior Scholar,
Religious Studies, York University, Toronto

Scholars have spent years investigating the problem of the historical Jesus. That is, how can we now reliably know what the Jesus of history said and did when Jesus himself wrote nothing, and the gospels were written at least forty to seventy years after his death, composed in light of Paul's mythologized Christ of faith? The problem becomes compounded when we also realize that the gospels themselves disagree on key elements: What was Jesus's genealogy? Did he undergo John's baptism for the remission of sin? Did he teach strict Torah observance? What were the charges against him? Who was responsible for his execution? What were his last words on the cross? Moreover, there are also gospels not included in the New Testament, those from the Gnostic as well as the Ebionite Christian traditions.

Dan Unterbrink's insightful book argues that scholars have been looking for Jesus in all the wrong places. Jesus really is a composite figure, a strategic blend of the historical, revolutionary Judas the Galilean with the Christ figure, a divine-human who spoke in and through Paul. This reimagined figure, "Jesus of Nazareth," was created for polemical purposes in the late first century CE as Judaism faced the task of

n after 70 CE; as Jewish revolutionary messianic move-
; and as Paul's religion of faith in the Christ succeeded.
from a Jewish milieu, the gospel authors needed to paint a
sus more relevant to potential Roman, non-Jewish converts
than a ɪoɪah-observant Jewish freedom fighter. Many of these would
have ventured into Gentile Christianity from pagan backgrounds, from
the worship of Mithras, Dionysus, or Isis, for instance. For them Paul's
Christ figure would have been immediately recognizable. So the Jesus of
the New Testament is a real person, rooted in early first-century messianic fervor, but covered over with a mystery-religion veneer. No wonder
the historical Jesus has been so difficult to uncover.

Follow Unterbrink's skillful detective work, honed as a forensic
auditor for many years. He is experienced in looking behind complex
and sometimes confusing documents to the truth they cover over. Just
like financial records the real meaning of the historical Jesus lies hidden
beneath the writings of the gospels, the book of Acts, and Paul's letters.
All it takes is a suspicious investigator with a nose for the truth—and
for documents that deceive or deflect. Consider the independent testimony of Unterbrink's outside expert, the Jewish-Roman historian of
antiquity, Josephus, whose writings are often overlooked by students
of the New Testament. Dan Unterbrink's block-by-block building of
evidence will take you on an exciting intellectual journey into the real
identity of Jesus.

If Jesus is modeled, in part, on the Jewish revolutionary Judas the
Galilean, then an earlier dating is required than the one presented in
the gospels. Instead of the conventional birth of Jesus around 5 or 4
BCE, before the death of Herod the Great, and a death around 30 CE,
this book argues that the dating has to be backtracked by more than a
decade. This would place Judas the Galilean/Jesus within the 25 BCE
to 19 CE time frame and would position him alongside other messianic
figures, such as Simon of Perea and Athronges. Clearly these were troubled times and Jews everywhere longed for the overthrow of the Roman
regime and the establishment of the kingdom of God. That yearning
built upon ancient Jewish hopes for a better world, one in which God

would be worshipped by all humanity, the Messiah king would rule over Jerusalem, peace would be enjoyed, and the righteous rewarded with everlasting life. That was the dream, and many Jewish leaders emerged to help God bring about this new world order.

Judas of Nazareth starts by orienting the reader in the political and revolutionary world of Judea in the early first century CE, tracing what we can reliably know about Judas the Galilean and his revolutionary movements from Jewish and Roman sources. It is within this context that we can now understand what Josephus calls the Fourth Philosophy, the complex mix of radicals who went by different names—Zealots, Sicarii, members of the Dead Sea Scroll community, and the Essenes, and, yes, the first Jewish followers of Jesus, the group some scholars call the Jesus Movement. All these groups hoped for—and worked toward—a transformed world, one in which they'd enjoy freedom from Roman rule and colonization, liberated from Roman taxation. It would be a time when the worship of the one true God could be carried out without fear of compromise.

The book then moves to Paul's perspective, his political connections and his pro-Roman stance. Paul's was a different religion from that fostered by the Jewish revolutionaries. Just how different Paul's Christ Movement was from Jesus/Judas the Galilean and his radical followers, Unterbrink makes clear. The thoughtful reader will wonder how and why these two quite different movements ever became associated with each other in the minds of subsequent generations.

Most importantly *Judas of Nazareth* shows *for the first time* the extent to which the four gospels in the New Testament were written in light of the success of Paul's Gentile religion. While this has been recognized for some time now, no one has demonstrated where and how each gospel is dependent upon Paul's perspective, his theology, and, to some extent, his experiences. This sleuthing clearly establishes that the gospels cannot be treated as transcripts or as actual history but should be viewed as creative works of historical fiction. They are products of Paul's mythologized Christ theology and their agenda is intended to serve the interests of the fledgling Gentile Christian communities. Not only is Jesus's Jewish heritage muted, but these writings are at pains to distance him from fierce anti-Roman messianic fervor. Gone is the messianic excitement, replaced by a perspective that sees Jesus as the savior of all humanity.

So, according to Unterbrink, Jesus is not just Judas the Galilean but Judas rewritten. He is a messianic pretender, at odds with Rome, a strong advocate of Torah observance, and a revolutionary bent on overthrowing the Roman government. He is presented in the gospels, however, as the anti-Torah, pro-Roman Christ of faith, along the lines envisioned by Paul, with only a thin substratum of the revolutionary, political Judas the Galilean/Jesus of history lurking underneath. The composite figure in the gospels gives us a sanitized hero fit for Gentile consumption. It's a remarkable creation, but one that the historically oriented reader should treat with extreme caution and skepticism.

Simultaneously this portrait of the gospel Jesus both complicates and simplifies the quest for the historical Jesus. It complicates the task by rendering the gospels themselves suspect documents in reconstructing the actual sayings of Jesus. They have been overwritten by the Pauline perspective of the Christ as a divine being, a savior come to rescue humanity, so a large portion of what they say can be dismissed as nonhistorical or even antihistorical. On the other hand this portrait simplifies the task of searching for the historical Jesus by allowing us to discount this whitewashed perspective as alien to the Jesus/Judas of history, who attempted to galvanize the Jewish people behind his vision of the coming kingdom of God.

Unterbrink's argument proceeds by way of similarities: X is similar to Y. This methodology represents interesting logical analysis. If there were only a few similarities, we could say with confidence that these are coincidences, X being *sort of similar* to Y. But when the similarities begin to multiply, then a pattern emerges. And that's where the intrigue of the argument lies. What are we to make of these compounded similarities? Perhaps we will say, X and Y are *somewhat the same*. Even more radically, perhaps we will agree with Unterbrink and contend that X and Y are, in fact, not just somewhat the same but actually *the same*.

Judas of Nazareth is a catalyst for discussion. Some readers will agree with Unterbrink that the problem of the historical Jesus has been solved . . . finally! Others may find that Unterbrink has overstated the case. But even these readers will discover some insightful parallels and a wealth of history. At the very least readers will come to see how radically different Paul was from anything resembling the Jesus of history and his revolutionary movement. Agree or disagree, the reader who investigates alongside Unterbrink will discover much that is new and worth pondering.

Those who like to explore, who value quests, who enjoy discovery, and who want an evidence-based faith—these are the readers who will find this book engaging and beneficial.

Acknowledgments

I would like to thank Margaret Starbird for her continued support on this project. She has encouraged me, shared my work with others and even helped proofread the manuscript. Her contribution has been invaluable.

Margaret introduced me to Professor Barrie Wilson of York University. Professor Wilson took an interest in this project and commented on each chapter, giving his feedback and impressions. He was even so kind as to write a foreword. His contribution has helped shape the final contents of the book.

And finally, I would like to thank Mari Young for setting up my website. As a college student she had many other things to do, but she still found time to design an appropriate platform for my ideas.

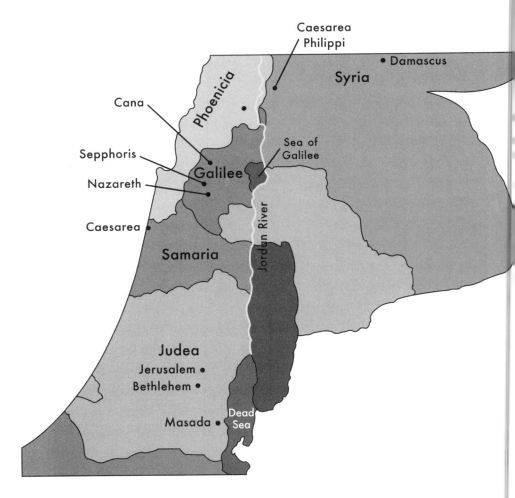

Map of Judea in the first century.

A Brief Explanation of the Major Political-Religious Movements

Herodians—This ruling family in Israel collaborated with the Roman occupation. It was founded by Herod the Great in 37 BCE. Paul is a member of this family.

Fourth Philosophy*—An anti-Roman religious and political movement, founded in 4 BCE by nationalistic Pharisees Matthias and Judas the Galilean. The movement is also referred to by Josephus as the Zealots, the Sicarii, and the Wonder Workers. They breathe their last at Masada in 73 CE, when Eleazar, the grandson of Judas the Galilean, leads a mass suicide, cheating the Romans of a great slaughter. (See time line in appendix A.)

Jewish Jesus Movement*—This first-century religious movement of so-called "Jewish Christians" is led by a Jewish Messiah figure. Its leaders include Peter (Cephas)† and James the Just. They are Torah-observant

---

*I argue that the Fourth Philosophy and the Jewish Jesus Movement are one in the same. Josephus coined the term Fourth Philosophy (*Antiquities* 18.4–10) (the other three philosophies were the Pharisees, Sadducees, and Essenes), while some modern scholars use the term Jewish Jesus Movement as a description of the Jewish Christians of that time.
†In the gospels Peter is used throughout, but Paul uses the Aramaic name Cephas, both meaning rock. This is explained in John 1:42 when Jesus said to Simon: "You are Simon son of John. You will be called Cephas" (which, when translated, is Peter).

and perish during the Jewish war with Rome (66–73 CE). The Jewish Jesus Movement is also known as the Way of Righteousness, or the Way.

Christ Movement—This Gentile movement springs from the imagination of Paul, through revelations from the Risen Christ. It was antinomian, stressing faith over the Law. Paul's Christ Movement is ousted from the Jewish Jesus Movement at Antioch, around 44 CE. (See the time line in appendix A.) Paul, the apostle to the Gentiles, is also known as Saul. He was the cousin of King Agrippa I and probably experienced his "revelations" in response to Agrippa's great successes. This is detailed in part two.

Jesus of Nazareth Movement—Through this post–70 CE movement, the actual Jewish Messiah is shaped into the likeness of Paul. It evolves from the Christ Movement and survives to this day. (See time line in appendix A.)

The Scholarly Mistake

Misinformation and improper use of sources have long hampered the search for the historical "Jesus." I intend to address these scholarly shortcomings by presenting a new thesis about the historical Jesus, focusing primarily on the writings of Josephus, which are often overlooked by scholars who favor the gospel time line.

I am not trained as a religious scholar and am therefore independent of the scholarly biases. In fact, I spent most of my life as a Medicare auditor. That outsider background may provide an important advantage for me over the religious community of scholars. A good auditor independently assesses information, ferreting out what makes sense and what does not, seeing through purposeful smoke screens. A mediocre auditor simply follows the work of previous auditors. If the previous auditor made a mistake, then the mediocre auditor will make the same mistake. Isn't this a pitfall of modern scholarship as well? What if earlier scholars are wrong? Should we blindly follow them, just as the mediocre auditor follows his predecessors?

ABOUT THE SOURCES

Much of the confusion over the historical Jesus stems from which sources scholars consider most reliable. For the purpose of this book I returned to the primary sources (as noted on the following page), identifying secondary and tertiary sources as such and recognizing these as sources of supplementary information, not historical record.

Primary

Josephus—*Antiquities of the Jews* (abbreviated as *Antiquities*), *The War of the Jews* (abbreviated as *War*), *The Life of Flavius Josephus,* and *Testimonium Flavianum* (abbreviated as TF)

Tacitus—*The Annals* and *The Histories*

Suetonius—*The Twelve Caesars*

Pliny the Younger—*Letter of Pliny the Younger to Trajan*

Paul's Letters*

Epistle of James

Philo of Alexandria—*The Works of Philo*

The Dead Sea Scrolls

In part one we examine the histories of Josephus, Tacitus, Suetonius, and Pliny and even touch on the Dead Sea Scrolls. In part two the emphasis is on the letters of Paul and the letter of James. These primary sources all point toward two separate movements: the Jewish Jesus Movement, centered in Judea with James in control, and the Christ Movement, centered on the teachings of Paul throughout the Roman Empire.

These primary documents are also used to ascertain the accuracy and reliability of the secondary and tertiary sources. This represents an important methodological shift from those who would use the canonical gospels as primary. The rationale for this decision rests on the fact these sources were written by historians with nothing to gain from promoting Christianity.

Secondary Sources

Gospel of Mark†

Gospel of Matthew†

Gospel of Luke†

Gospel of John†

---

*Paul's authentic letters (Romans, 1 and 2 Corinthians, and Galatians) are undoubtedly written by Paul while a member of the Jewish Jesus Movement and thus considered a primary source. These letters contain information that confirms the conflict between his teachings and that of the Jewish Jesus Movement led by James. Although the letters are biased in Paul's favor, historical truth is available. However, the gospels are written at a much later date by individuals with an agenda to rewrite history and are therefore secondary sources.

†Most quotes from these sources are from the New International Version (NIV).

Book of Acts*
Pseudoclementine *Recognitions*
Book of Revelation
Slavonic Josephus, *War* (distinguished from the primary source version as SJ *War*†)

In part three we will dissect the gospels and Acts, using information gleaned from the primary sources. The picture of Jesus of Nazareth must be compared to the one that emerges from the messianic movement described by Josephus, called the Fourth Philosophy, as well as that depicted by Paul. Any secondary source material that conflicts with the primary source material may indicate that the stories being told are more fiction than history.

The secondary sources flesh out the picture of Jesus of Nazareth (while the Jesus of Nazareth Movement is not cited at all in the primary sources). In the earliest phase of what became Christianity the Jewish Jesus and Christ Movements vie with each other, the Jewish Jesus Movement being one of many Jewish messianic movements. As we shall see out of Paul's Christ Movement emerges the Jesus of Nazareth Movement, a creation of the late first century CE.

Tertiary Sources

Justin Martyr (100–165 CE)—as cited by Eusebius in *The History of the Church, from Christ to Constantine*
Hegesippus (90–180 CE)—as cited by Eusebius in *The History of the Church, from Christ to Constantine*
Irenaeus (130–200 CE)—*Against Heresies*
Origen (185–254 CE)—as cited by Eusebius in *The History of the Church, from Christ to Constantine*
Eusebius (260–340 CE)—*The History of the Church: From Christ to Constantine*

---

*Most quotes from these sources are from the New International Version (NIV).
†This text is a copy of Josephus's *War* with several "Christian" passages added; throughout this book I will indicate when material comes from these additional passages.

Epiphanius (320–403 CE)—*Panarion*
Sulpicius Severus (363–425 CE)—*Chronica*

The majority of the tertiary sources support the gospels and Acts (secondary sources). However, even these supporters of the gospel time lines sometimes supply information helpful in constructing the true picture of events in the earliest days of the Messianic Movement.

The tertiary sources are used sparingly, but they may help clarify and expand on the primary sources. For example, Sulpicius Severus quotes a passage that may have come from a lost chapter of Tacitus. If so, then this tertiary source may provide real information concerning the early Jewish Jesus Movement.

THE CONTROVERSY SURROUNDING THE SLAVONIC JOSEPHUS

The Slavonic Josephus is a Reader's Digest version of Josephus's *War.* The controversy concerns thirteen passages that relate to the early church, which are not included in *War*'s original, Greek version. These passages have been labeled as late forgeries by most scholars as they tell a very different story of Christian origins.

For example, in the traditional Christian story, John the Baptist comes on to the scene in 29 CE. However, the Slavonic Josephus introduces John in 6 CE, right before the introduction of Judas the Galilean. If one believes the traditional story without question, then the Slavonic Josephus version must be wrong. However, if the thirteen passages in the Slavonic Josephus are matched with Josephus's *Antiquities,* then we can deduce that the Slavonic Josephus's John the Baptist matches a figure known as Sadduc, the second-in-command to Judas the Galilean.

I contend that the thirteen passages are not written by Josephus but by a very early follower of the Jewish Jesus Movement. No medieval scribe would have conceived a different dating for the life of John the Baptist or that Jesus, not Barabbas, is released or that the chief priests give thirty talents of silver to Pilate, not even mentioning Judas Iscariot.

In short the Slavonic Josephus has many elements that appear more historical than the gospel accounts. For more on this see appendix D.

BUILDING ON PREVIOUS SCHOLARSHIP

In my study I have been most impressed by the work of Robert Eisenman, Hyam Maccoby, and S. G. F. Brandon. These scholars worked outside the consensus box. Their viewpoints have been largely ignored, not due to any flaws in their arguments but rather because their arguments rock the boat. I have used their amazing command of the facts in arriving at my own conclusions.

Robert Eisenman published *James the Brother of Jesus* in 1997. In that book Eisenman argues that whatever James was, so was "Jesus." He then meticulously examines the life of James. The conclusion he arrives at is diametrically opposed to the traditional scholarly viewpoint. "Jesus" did not preach against the law of Moses, but, like James, vehemently upheld the Law. In a later book, *The New Testament Code,* Eisenman connects the Dead Sea Scroll concepts to early Christianity, another scholarly "off-limits" zone.

The late Hyam Maccoby envisioned a nationalistic "Jesus" who sided with the Pharisees. His 1973 book, *Revolution in Judaea,* presents excellent background material and attempts to make sense of the "Jesus story" using the historical constraints mixed with common sense. He even makes sense of the Transfiguration and Barabbas episodes, hardly easy subjects to tackle. In 1986 he wrote *The Mythmaker,* in which Paul is credited with the invention of Christianity.

In the 1950s and 1960s S. G. F. Brandon published *Jesus and the Zealots* and *The Trial of Jesus of Nazareth,* closely connecting the Jewish Jesus Movement with that of the Zealots. He emphasizes that the two groups have much in common. Why more scholars did not follow his lead is beyond comprehension.

Other current scholars are also working outside the box. Professor James Tabor, author of *The Jesus Dynasty,* has revisited the Messiah's family background, so maligned by the gospels. He claims that "Jesus" was not a lone actor but was part of a larger family movement, including his cousin John the Baptist. In this seminal work he traces Jesus's lineage through several generations: Jesus, James, Simeon, and some later family members. Tabor is chair of the Religious Studies Department at the University of North Carolina, Charlotte, and has participated in some high-profile archaeological digs in Israel relating to early Christianity.

Professor Barrie Wilson outlines his viewpoint of early Christianity in *How Jesus Became Christian,* tracing how a Jewish, human teacher and possible Messiah became a Gentile, divine-human savior, all within the space of some one hundred years. He argues that not one church existed in the early years, but rather two: the Jewish Jesus Movement, led by James and Peter, and the Christ Movement, championed by Paul. This insight helps explain much in Paul's letters, presenting potential answers to very difficult questions about why Paul and James were so much at odds with each other. Wilson also acknowledges that there may be more forms of early Christianity—the Gnostic Movement, for instance—whose existence is difficult to discern today. These might be groups associated with Thomas, John, and Mary Magdalene.

Independent scholar Margaret Starbird has written many books on Mary Magdalene, including *Mary Magdalene: Bride in Exile.* According to her the evidence within the Bible points to a married Jesus and that his marriage represents a sacred union. Her research dovetails nicely with Professor Tabor's theory of Jesus's family dynasty. If Jesus was married and had children, then the Messiah's story may be much more complicated than the gospel picture. Barrie Wilson, along with the investigative reporter and acclaimed filmmaker Simcha Jacobovici, has written a new book, *The Lost Gospel,* that investigates ancient manuscript evidence for a married Jesus and his political connections to the power brokers of his time, including those in Rome itself, the capital of the Roman Empire.

Finally, Bart Ehrman, a highly respected professor of New Testament at the University of North Carolina, Chapel Hill, says the following in his latest book, *Did Jesus Exist?:*

1. The gospels are filled with discrepancies and contradictions (pp. 182–183).
2. The gospels contain nonhistorical materials, such as the stories about Barabbas and the census (pp. 184–185).
3. Many traditions about Jesus were colored by legend, showing a Christian bias (pp. 185–190).
4. Ehrman believes that Jesus came from Nazareth but even if he did not, that does not prove his existence or nonexistence (p. 191).
5. Many details of Jesus's life were shaped by Hebrew scripture* heroes. For example, the birth of Jesus bears a striking resemblance to the birth of Moses (pp. 198–204).
6. Christians did indeed shape their stories about Jesus in light of other figures similar to him, such as Apollonius of Tyana (pp. 207–209).

Many contemporary scholars of the New Testament would agree with Ehrman. This represents standard teaching in many North American colleges and universities, where the teaching of religion and the Bible are not hampered by faculty bound by denominational faith oaths.

Ehrman does not deny that a "Jesus" actually existed. His point is that it is difficult now to know what the Jesus of history actually said and did because of the numerous portraits of him developed by later authors for polemical purposes. It is hard to move beyond the mythical Jesus back to the real Jesus who roamed the Galilee and who met a tragic end in Jerusalem.

I agree with the above-cited scholars on many points. Like Ehrman

---

*When the term Hebrew scriptures is used it denotes the language used in the Old Testament documents (Hebrew), while the term Jewish scriptures, which you will also see in this book, is a much broader term, including Old Testament documents written in both Hebrew and Greek (the Septuagint). For example, Philo used the Septuagint as did Paul and the gospel writers. The Jewish Jesus Movement used the Hebrew scriptures. So, when talking about Paul's and the gospel writers' use of the Old Testament, we use the term Jewish scriptures since they exclusively used the Greek version. Their use of the Greek version helped shape the New Testament. For example, when Matthew stated that the virgin will be with child, he was modeling after the Septuagint, in which the woman in Isaiah was a virgin. In the Hebrew version this woman was simply a young woman, not a virgin.

I contend that the Jesus of history was reinvented by the Christ of Paul and, as we shall see, by much more. Jesus, as portrayed in the New Testament, is really a composite figure, an individual shaped by many differing agendas, combining the actual life of Judas the Galilean with Paul's life and theology. I also concur that the historical Jesus was married and had important family ties. He followed the Law—the Torah—just like his brother James, and would not have condoned the teachings of Paul. He was an apocalyptic teacher, but was not the Jesus of the gospels. In short we all believe that "Jesus" was a human being and not a god.

Where do I disagree with most scholars? *The fundamental scholarly mistake assigns a primary role to the gospels and Acts.* For example, if one believes the chronology of Luke, then Jesus and John the Baptist must have come on to the scene around 29 CE. Since Josephus mentions no Jesus figure in writing about events in 29 CE, scholars claim that Jesus was not an extraordinary figure, excusing Josephus's omission. However, if we examine the writings of Josephus without being prejudiced by the gospels and Acts, a messianic movement emerges much different from the one found in the traditional picture.

By placing the emphasis of New Testament scholarship on the gospels and Acts, most scholars have assumed that one uniform brand of Christianity existed in the first century. Sure, problems existed, but any disagreements were resolved according to the account of Acts. However, the primary sources (Josephus, Paul, and the Roman historians) suggest that two early "Christian" movements coexisted, one led by James and the other by Paul. Without understanding this any attempt to find Jesus in actual history is impossible. I suggest that many scholars will never find the historical Jesus due to their inherently flawed methodology.

So did Jesus really exist? In his latest book, *Did Jesus Exist?,* Ehrman clearly proves that a Messiah figure existed in the first century CE. However, mythicists* can rightly argue that the gospel Jesus did not exist. Even

---

*Mythicists do not believe in historical Jesus but that the story of Jesus of Nazareth is derived from many individuals, such as Moses and Elijah, as well as characters from Josephus's writings. As such Jesus is a composite of others, not a historical being.

Ehrman admits that much of the gospel Jesus cannot be accepted as fact.

My viewpoint, which will be argued throughout this book, is that a Messiah did preach the kingdom of heaven to the Jews. So, yes, there was a historical Messiah, but his teachings were absorbed into what we now know as Jesus of Nazareth, reconstructed along lines that would resonate with a late first-century Gentile audience. So, in a sense, my viewpoint is a middle ground between the extremes, between the historical Jesus promoted by the above-mentioned scholars and the nonhistorical savior-god envisioned by mythicists.

This "Jesus" was the Messiah known to the earliest disciples. He was not part of Paul's fertile imagination. Ready yourself for the discovery of *Judas of Nazareth.*

◄ PART ONE ►

The Life and Times of Judas the Galilean and Jesus of Nazareth

THE ROAD TO THE FOURTH PHILOSOPHY

1 ➤ Hellenistic and Roman Influences

Throughout Israel's history, other larger powers invaded and conquered the Holy Land to secure trade routes and to extract great sums of money through taxation. Some individuals welcomed this as a means of procuring wealth for themselves, while others petitioned God to eradicate the foreign influence. This is the world where we must search for the Jesus of history, concentrating on the period from 200 BCE to 70 CE. Before tracing this history an example of Jewish resistance may be enlightening.

In 2 Maccabees, written in the second century BCE, a powerful story is told concerning a woman and her seven sons. Antiochus Epiphanes, a Greek king wishing to impose his authority on the locals, asks a woman and her sons to eat pork to show their allegiance to the new order. They refuse to disobey the food purity laws given to them by God through Moses. The first son says, "We are ready to die rather than to transgress the laws of God, received from our fathers" (2 Maccabees 7:2).

In response to their refusal and the first son's impertinent tone, the king orders that the first son should have his tongue cut out and his extremities chopped off. He then commands that the young man be fried alive in a frying pan. The other brothers and his mother say, "The Lord God will look upon the truth and will take pleasure in us" (2 Maccabees 7:6).

One by one the first six sons are put to death in front of their mother. To the seventh and last son Antiochus offers great wealth and happiness if only he will turn from the laws of his fathers and eat the forbidden pork. When the last son does not yield to the bribe Antiochus asks the mother to intercede. She responds, "My son, have pity upon me that bore thee nine months in my womb, and gave thee suck three years, and nourished thee, and brought thee up unto this age. I beseech thee, my son, look upon heaven and earth and all that is in them and consider that God made them out of nothing, and mankind also, so thou shalt not fear this tormentor, but being made a worthy partner with thy brethren, receive death, that in that mercy I may receive thee again with thy brethren" (2 Maccabees 7:27–29). The last son stands steadfast, as does the mother, and they die a noble death.

Seven sons and a mother all die because of the purity laws; they refuse to eat pork. To us this seems absurd, but the Law is not something to be so easily dismissed.

A SHORT HISTORY OF HELLENISM

To place the people and events from the first century CE in perspective, we must understand the social and cultural milieu in the Middle East in the first two centuries BCE. Jesus, Paul, and James all fit into a broader context and a preoccupation with Jewish identity and survival within a colonized society. Some of this history may be unfamiliar to many readers, but without this background, much of the impact of the New Testament is lost.

From 196 to 142 BCE Israel is occupied in varying degrees by the Seleucid Kingdoms, Greek in culture and ruled by absolute monarchs. The most famous of the Seleucid kings is Antiochus Epiphanes, who in 167 BCE installs an idol in the Temple and orders all Jews to follow Greek customs. A rebel, named Mattathias, organizes a resistance movement to this Greek presence, and he and his five sons successfully drive the Greeks out of Israel. Mattathias's five sons are Judas, Simon, John, Jonathan, and Eleazar, of whom the most famous is Judas Maccabee, responsible for the cleansing of the Temple, an act still celebrated by Jews today in the festival of Hanukkah. Maccabean rule lasts until 37 BCE, when Herod the Great assumes power.

At the very beginning of the Maccabean rule, holy men of that time, known as Hasidim (meaning "godly ones"), support the movement. Many of those supporting the rebellion are poor, creating class warfare that ultimately leads to sectarian division.[1]

After the rise of the Maccabees three distinct sects arise across Israel. The first, the Sadducees, originating around 160 BCE, are a small group of aristocratic priests who oppose Maccabean rule. They are much more comfortable with the Greek rulers than with the Maccabean usurpers. However, in time, the Sadducees align themselves with the Maccabean movement, where they can better influence public policy.[2] While this may not have been a principled stance it does keep these aristocrats near the center of power. In short the rich co-opt a movement that originally represents the poorer elements of society.

A second sect arises in opposition to the Sadducees. Called Pharisees this group is of middle-class origin and represents the masses. Their rise dates from the Hasidim's break with the Maccabean regime because of its secular character around 150 BCE.[3]

Pharisees believe in an evolving relationship between God and humanity and are much more likely to be nationalists and social critics of their time. Many early Jewish "Christians" come from the ranks of the Pharisees

A third sect, known as Essenes, may have been born of a reactionary opposition to Jonathan, who rules after his brother, Judas Maccabee, from 160 to 143 BCE. Many Dead Sea Scroll scholars claim that the Essenes frame this Jonathan as the wicked priest. There may be some truth in this, since Jonathan is constantly forging alliances with different kings and may have been seen as untrustworthy. Even if it were true the purpose of the Essenes is to place Israel on the right path before God, back to the time when the Hasidim supported Mattathias and Judas Maccabee.

As an offshoot of the Hasidim the Essenes have contempt for the

Hellenistic and worldly Sadducees. The Essenes feel that they alone are the true representatives of the high-priestly tradition.[4] They hold as their prime goal the pursuit of righteousness. According to Josephus two types of Essenes survive to his time: the main group does not marry and chooses a chaste lifestyle, while a smaller group prefers marriage, arguing that without reproduction the group will soon perish.

ROMANS, HERODIANS, AND THE FOURTH PHILOSOPHY

These three groups—the Sadducees, the Pharisees, and the Essenes—grapple with the political realities that seem to be constantly changing. Shifting alliances are part of the Maccabean strategy to stay in power. Their final alliance is with Rome in 63 BCE. Once allied with Rome a client kingdom does not easily stray to another power. Israel chooses Rome, and Israel suffers the long-term consequences of that decision.

Rome views client states as a tax resource. In the case of Israel it is deemed prudent to install a client king, who will collect taxes and be a buffer between the people and Rome, the power behind the king. This puppet king is Herod the Great, who rises to power in 37 BCE. One of Herod's first acts is to capture and execute Hezekiah, the grandfather of Judas the Galilean. From this early time the Herodian family and the family of Judas the Galilean struggle for control of Israel.

With Herod comes the end of the Maccabean reign.* According to Josephus Herod introduces foreign (Greek and Roman) ways to Israel and is vehemently opposed by more Law-abiding citizens. The whole Maccabean movement is swept aside by Herod. While the Maccabees were successful in preventing the encroaching Greek culture from overtaking the law of Moses, Herod was now intent on reintroducing Greek culture to the Jews. Athletic contests and theater productions are

---

*Herod does marry a Maccabean princess, Mariamme, to help consolidate his power. Although Josephus claims that Herod loves this Mariamme he nevertheless has her killed in 29 BCE because of a supposed affair with his brother Joseph (*Antiquities* 15.68–70).

just part of this Hellenizing process. What is viewed positively by the Romans (and by modern-day standards) is anathema to religious Jews around the turn of the first century.

So, with the arrival of the new power, Rome, a new dynasty emerges. The Herodian family works with Rome to gather tax revenues and to bring "civilization" to Israel. Herod the Great builds new cities and even rebuilds the Temple. One would think that the new Temple would pacify the opponents of change, but Herod's Golden Eagle on the Temple gate (a sign of fealty to Rome) enrages the fanatics and cannot be allowed to stand. Shortly before Herod's death in 4 BCE two freedom fighters, Matthias and Judas, convince their followers to tear down the Golden Eagle. Herod captures the leaders of this opposition and has Matthias put to death while Judas languishes in prison, awaiting his own death sentence.

Herod the Great has been in power for thirty-three years (37–4 BCE) and his paranoia borders on psychopathic. He has important men arrested throughout Israel and plans to have them executed on the day of his own death. In that way all Israel will mourn the death of Herod.

On the day of Herod's death the insane plan is not carried out. Herod's advisors know that the murder of good, honest men will forever taint the Herodian family and would probably prompt an uprising. So, at the crowd's request, Herod's son, Archelaus, grants tax relief and also releases Herod's prisoners.

This may have been the origin of the Barabbas legend: In Mark 15:6–15 Pilate offers to release a prisoner to the crowd, either Jesus or Barabbas, a man connected with an earlier insurrection. The Jewish crowd prefers Barabbas over the gospel Jesus. After the Golden Eagle Temple Cleansing Archelaus releases insurrectionists to the crowd, including Judas the Galilean, to the joy of his followers. Also, in the Slavonic Josephus, the wonder worker is released, not someone named Barabbas. And in some manuscripts Barabbas is known as Jesus Barabbas, which points to Barabbas and Jesus/Judas being one in the same. So the Barabbas legend had a historical background: the release of

Judas the Galilean in 4 BCE. This prisoner release is integral to Judas's story and is invariably woven into the story of the gospel Jesus.

During the shaky reign of Archelaus (4 BCE–7 CE) many Messiah figures attempt to capitalize on Archelaus's unstable government. However, backed by the power of Rome, Archelaus captures most of these self-styled Messiahs and has them put to death. Only Judas the Galilean survives (*Antiquities* 17.269–285).

In 7 CE Archelaus is stripped of power and the Romans appoint their own man as governor. Coponius arrives in Israel, along with the tax census of Cyrenius, the tax census Luke refers to in his birth scenario for Jesus of Nazareth. Two men, Judas the Galilean and John the Baptist (whom Josephus calls Sadduc), rally the Jews against the tax census, preaching a message of nationalism, where only God would be their Lord and Ruler. As such the rule of Rome cannot be tolerated.

According to the book of Acts (5:37) Judas the Galilean's tax revolt ends in total defeat. But according to Josephus Judas's anti-Roman message resonates with the people and eventually leads to the Jewish war against Rome (*Antiquities* 18.9–10). So does Judas die in 7 CE, as suggested by Acts, or does he continue his war against Rome for many years? Since Judas's movement continues to grow, his death at the very beginning of his resistance against Rome does not appear credible. Certainly Judas and John the Baptist continue their resistance movement for many years after the census.

In 18 CE Pontius Pilate becomes governor. (Josephus places Pilate's accession to the governor's office among many events that occur in 18–19 CE.) Pilate does many things to enrage the Jews: he brings his standards, Roman banners or flags bearing Caesar's effigy, into Jerusalem and also uses Temple funds to underwrite projects (*Antiquities* 18.55–62). Immediately after these inflammatory acts by Pilate the text of *Antiquities* describes the death of Jesus of Nazareth. Most scholars reject this *Testimonium Flavianum* (TF) as a later Christian insertion into Josephus's text. However, I contend that the passage by Josephus was originally about the death of Judas the Galilean. Earlier in his eighteenth book of *Antiquities*, Josephus goes to great lengths to explain the importance of Judas the Galilean and his movement. But, according to our current text, Josephus fails to record the death of Judas the Galilean, the greatest of all Jewish resistance fighters. To give Josephus some credit, he must have recorded the death of Judas. This death was simply rewritten as the death of Jesus of Nazareth, a person not previously mentioned in Josephus's narrative.

With the death of Judas the Galilean (19–21 CE) Sadduc seizes control of the Jewish Jesus Movement against Rome. Little is known about Sadduc; *Antiquities* introduces him as Judas's second-in-command but fails to detail his death. However, noted in appendix B, the Slavonic Josephus equates Sadduc with John the Baptist. If Sadduc is really another name for John the Baptist, then we know that he dies in 36 CE at the hands of Herod Antipas. Afraid of John's great influence over the masses Antipas puts John to death, hoping to stem any rebellion against his rule. Josephus states that John practiced righteousness and that his baptism was not for the forgiveness of sins, but rather for the purification of the body, as the soul had already been cleansed by righteousness (*Antiquities* 18.117). This attitude concerning righteousness is consistent with the Fourth Philosophy and mirrored in the Dead Sea Scrolls.

Shortly after the death of John the Baptist in 36 CE Agrippa I is appointed king over Israel by his close friend, the emperor Caligula. In fact, Agrippa I is a trusted advisor to both Caligula and to Claudius. This tie to the Roman emperors gives Agrippa I great influence, power not wielded by the Herodians since the death of Herod the Great in 4 BCE.

For many Jews Agrippa I appears as a Messiah figure and is accorded the title "king of the Jews." In 40–41 CE he tries to persuade Caligula to forgo plans to install a statue of himself in the Temple. Agrippa knows that that would incite a rebellion among the Jews, led by the radical Fourth Philosophy. He fails to convince Caligula to abandon this policy, but shortly thereafter, Caligula is assassinated and the plan is scrapped. Agrippa I then helps install Claudius as the next emperor and becomes Claudius's trusted advisor. All this time Agrippa amasses more and more power.

In 44 CE Agrippa I is assassinated with poison. Who is behind this plot to kill the king of the Jews? Certainly the Fourth Philosophy has much to gain by the power vacuum created by his death. Just as Matthias and Judas orchestrated the Golden Eagle Temple Cleansing on rumors of Herod the Great's imminent death, the Fourth Philosophy now pushes its own agenda. Theudas, a miracle worker who leads his followers out into the countryside and promises to part the River Jordan, is captured and beheaded (44–46 CE). Shortly thereafter James and Simon, the sons of Judas the Galilean, are crucified under Tiberius Alexander (46–48 CE).

After the death of Agrippa I in 44 CE conditions deteriorate in Israel. Since Agrippa's son, Agrippa II, is only a child, Rome sends its governors to collect the taxes, and their rule often rankles the native population. It was one thing to be ruled by a client-king, quite another to be ruled directly by Rome. Roman soldiers burn the Torah (*Antiquities* 20.115–117) and some make lewd gestures to the most religious of the Jews (*Antiquities* 20.105–112).

In response to Roman rule the Fourth Philosophy's tactics change. Instead of peacefully awaiting the return of their Messiah, they take up arms. Some renamed Sicarii by Josephus, so described because they carry a short knife, or sica, under their garments, to be used in assassination attempts.

By 62 CE the Fourth Philosophy is splintering. Many hope to defeat Rome with arms while others, led by James, the brother of Judas the Galilean, insist on waiting for the Messiah's return. In 62 CE James is stoned to death on accusations made by the high priest, Ananus, son of the gospel Annas. Enraged by the death of James the Sicarii exact revenge upon Ananus. Interestingly, in his entire chronicle of this period of Jewish history, Josephus never mentions a Jesus of Nazareth Movement.

With the death of James conditions quickly deteriorate. Within four years war breaks out with Rome. And as one would expect Rome wins the war and the insurgents are summarily slaughtered.

In this short history we must recognize the major players or groups.

The Herodians place their trust in Rome and help rule Israel from 37 BCE to 70 CE, a dynasty lasting over a century. This was a party and a political movement composed of forceful leaders, such as Herod the Great and Agrippa I. For them, Rome represents civilization, advancement, and modernity, and they see Jewish life as compatible with Roman rule.

Aligned against the Herodians are the followers of Judas the Galilean and John the Baptist, a movement called the "Fourth Philosophy" by Josephus. This group had its beginnings around 40 BCE and survives until its last gasp at Masada, in 73 CE. Eleazar, the leader at Masada, is the grandson of Judas the Galilean. So the Fourth Philosophy is a dynasty and includes Judas the Galilean's brothers, sons, and grandchildren. Put simply Josephus's Fourth Philosophy is just another name for the Jewish Jesus Movement.

The battle between the stalwart Jewish supporters of Rome—the Herodians—and the political activists or extremists—the Fourth Philosophy—dominates the political landscape of first-century CE Israel. The individuals and events in this period cannot be understood without reference to this political dynamic.

THE FOURTH PHILOSOPHY'S PLAN OF ACTION

The Fourth Philosophy does not create new beliefs, but rather incorporates existing ones. As mentioned earlier three other philosophies predate it in Jewish society—the Essenes, the Pharisees, and the Sadducees. Judas the Galilean shows his genius by combining the best of competing movements to his own advantage. Of the three earlier philosophies Judas intertwines the beliefs of the Pharisees with the practices of the Essenes. Since the Sadducees are few in number, oppose the belief system of the Pharisees, and support foreign invaders (Rome), they are left out of this strange mixture.

The Fourth Philosophy of Judas the Galilean may have had its beginnings prior to the Golden Eagle Temple Cleansing (4 BCE). Before Judas the Galilean teams up with John the Baptist in 6 CE, he is an important and well-respected political activist working with Matthias; their message and struggles parallel those of the earlier freedom fighters Judas Maccabee and his father, Mattathias. Based on their actions, Judas and Matthias may have been associated with either the Essenes or the Pharisees. And a later passage by Josephus concerning the census of Cyrenius (6–7 CE) also leaves us with a mixed picture of Judas's movement. To pinpoint the exact date of the Fourth Philosophy's birth may be impossible, but to examine the beliefs and practices is well within our abilities.

The Essenes have several practices in common with the Fourth Philosophy. Josephus claims that the Essenes are "despisers of riches . . . [with no one among them that] hath more than another" (*War* 2.122). This dovetails perfectly with the picture of Judas fighting Roman taxation and with later Sicarii burning the debt records to "enable the poor to rise with impunity against the rich" (*War* 2.427). This love of perfect, communal living is also found in the Dead Sea Scrolls (*Community Rule*). Jesus preaches a similar message and his disciples practice this in Acts 2:44: "All the believers were together and had everything in common."

Although the Essenes are not a majority party, having only four thousand followers (*Antiquities* 18.20), they have colonies in every city (*War* 2.124). This seems to be a contradiction, since the number of Essenes cited in *War* appears much larger than the mere four thousand noted in *Antiquities*. Josephus possibly conflates the Essene and Fourth Philosophy movements, attributing the popularity of Judas's movement to the Essenes. But even if the Essenes do have colonies in every city, this would have supplied the Fourth Philosophy with a large pool of possible adherents throughout Israel. When Jesus sends the Twelve Apostles out to proclaim his kingdom (Mark 6:7–13), surely each city has an Essene or Fourth Philosophy community that either supports him or holds him in high esteem. So the spread of the Fourth Philosophy may have been made possible by an existing network of like-minded communities.

Joining the Essenes is no easy task. In the first year the initiate is excluded from the group, his temperance tested. If he passes the test, two more years of character testing occur within the community. Only when he is deemed worthy, is he then accepted into the fold (*War* 2.137–138). This is consistent with the Dead Sea Scrolls book *Community Rule*, which also bears some similarities to early Christian practice. In addition, Paul claims a three-year gap between his conversion and his first meeting with the pillar apostles. This three-year absence may have been his testing period (Galatians 1:18).

To the Essenes, "Obedience to older men and to the majority is a matter of principle" (*War* 2.146). I mention this point because it emphasizes the place of high regard held by elders in first-century Jewish society. Unlike our own society, where the elderly are often shunted aside or placed in nursing homes, apart from the everyday troubles of this world, the elders of first-century Jewish society are the teachers and well respected by all. I think it very unlikely that the Messiah was only thirty-three by the end of his career. Judas the Galilean may have been the junior partner with Matthias, but this coupling with an older, wiser mentor would have added to his prestige. By the time of his final push to Jerusalem, Judas would have been in his mid-forties, respected by the masses for his long fight against Rome.

Of the Essenes Josephus states: "They neglect wedlock, but choose out other people's children, while they are pliable and fit for learning; and esteem them to be of their kindred, and from them according to their own manners" (*War* 2.120). The Essenes were so dedicated to following the Law that they viewed sex and marriage as a stumbling block to Torah observance. However, to perpetuate their own views, they had to indoctrinate other people's children and raise them as Essenes. This may explain why Judas and Matthias teach young men at the Temple. These students are eventually convinced to help tear down the Golden Eagle. This may be a case where the Fourth Philosophy copies a trait from the Essenes, but in pursuit of a different agenda, wishing to build an army of Torah-observant fanatics.

In many ways the Fourth Philosophy resembles the Essenes. However, in describing the Fourth Philosophy, Josephus compares them with the Pharisees, writing that they "agree with the Pharisaic notions"

(*Antiquities* 18.23) and that Judas the Galilean's co-teacher Sadduc is a Pharisee (*Antiquities* 18.4).

The main thrust of Josephus's description of the Fourth Philosophy is their insistence on freedom from Roman rule. This thirst for liberty is not the sole province of any one group. Members of both the Pharisees and the Essenes could have been attracted to this freedom message. So, in that sense, Judas's message may have played quite well with both groups. But Josephus is clear in his identification of Judas and Sadduc with Pharisaic notions. What exactly does that mean?

> [The Pharisees were] esteemed most skillful in the exact explica-
> tion of their laws. . . . [They] ascribe all to fate, and to God, and
> yet allow, that to act what is right, or the contrary, is principally
> in the power of men, although fate does cooperate in every action
> . . . [and] the souls of good men are only removed into other bodies,
> but the souls of bad men are subject to eternal punishment. (*War*
> 2.162–163)

When Jesus prays in the garden he believes it is within the power of men to assist God in His triumph over Rome. Although God is the ultimate force in the universe, men are not mere pawns to be moved against their free will. For example, if Jesus believes that humanity cannot assist God, then he and his disciples would not have been fervently praying in the garden. Certainly Moses believes that he can bargain with God. After the people cast a golden calf and anger God, Moses says, "But now I will go up to the Lord; perhaps I can make atonement for your sin" (Exodus 32:30). Certainly the Fourth Philosophy (much like the Jewish Jesus Movement) owes much to the Pharisees concerning these beliefs.

> [The Pharisees] live meanly, and despise delicacies in diet; . . . and
> what they prescribe to them as good for them, they do. . . . They
> also pay respect to such as are in years; nor are they so bold as to
> contradict them in anything which they have introduced. . . . [They

believe that] souls have an immortal vigor in them, and that under the earth there will be rewards and punishments, according as they have lived virtuously or viciously in this life, and the latter are to be detained in an everlasting prison, but the former shall have power to revive and live again. (*Antiquities* 18.12–14)

The diet prescribed by James and his followers is very strict, as noted by Paul in 1 Corinthians 8. In this respect Jesus's followers adhere to the dietary laws, as opposed to Paul's more liberal (non-Jewish) stance. So we have specific teachings that tie together the Fourth Philosophy, Pharisaic teachings, and the Jewish Jesus Movement. In addition, these groups all respect their elders and hold similar views concerning the rewards and punishments accorded to the good and evil. Unlike Paul's concept of grace, Pharisees and the Fourth Philosophy count heavily on one's righteousness. As James writes, "Faith without deeds is dead" (2:26). To top it off, the early disciples of Jesus are known as the Way (Acts 24:14) or the Way of Righteousness.

It is important to realize that this community represents a faction within Judaism. A solid link connects the Pharisees, the Fourth Philosophy, and the Jewish Jesus Movement. Note that both Judas the Galilean and Jesus are called *rabbi* or "teacher," a Pharisaic designation. Josephus calls Judas the Galilean a *clever rabbi* (*War* 2.433) and Peter refers to Jesus as *rabbi* in Mark 9:5 (the Transfiguration) and Mark 11:21 (the withered fig tree). We also know that Jesus teaches using parables, as do many other Pharisees. And Judas the Galilean's second-in-command (Sadduc) is denoted as a Pharisee by Josephus. Thus, the tie between the teachings of Judas and Jesus becomes more evident.

An interesting passage in the New Testament may help clarify this strange mix of beliefs and practices.

"Master," said John, "we saw a man driving out demons in your name and we tried to stop him, because he is not one of us."

"Do not stop him," Jesus said, "for whoever is not against you is for you." (Luke 9:45–50)

Such a saying by Jesus is *not* consistent with traditional Christian beliefs espoused by Paul. "But even if we or an angel from heaven should preach a gospel other than the one we preached to you, let him be eternally condemned" (Galatians 1:18). Yet the attitude by Jesus dovetails perfectly with that of Judas the Galilean, the teacher who brings all types of men together. In terms of the Fourth Philosophy, anyone who shares a desire for freedom from Rome constitutes an ally.

The unifying factor of foreign occupation makes the Fourth Philosophy powerful and widely embraced. Both Essenes and Pharisees are drawn to this belief system because it takes the best of their practices and adds a touch of hatred for Rome, popular among the masses and among the teachers as well. Judas the Galilean must have been a very charismatic teacher to keep these disparate groups together, but he is helped in this effort by continual Herodian and Roman oppression. Every time the Romans step near the Temple or display their standards, Judas had a ready-made disturbance at hand, reinforcing his new philosophy among the masses. In Acts 21:20, James and the elders say, "You see, brother, how many thousands of Jews have believed, and all of them are zealous for the Law." Are these followers of James part of the Fourth Philosophy? If so, then the historical Jesus is really the founder of the Fourth Philosophy, or, rather, he is none other than Judas the Galilean, and Judas's second-in-command, Sadduc, is John the Baptist.

2 ▶ Primary Text References to Jesus

In the quest for the historical Jesus, we must first examine the primary sources for any evidence of his existence, seeking out independent witnesses to the Jesus of history, rather than relying on Paul's Christ of faith, created by the four gospels. To be honest, only a few primary source passages point toward this messianic figure. But any mention is important. Critics of the historical "Jesus" concept confidently state that no such Messiah roamed the Earth during the reign of Pontius Pilate. In their minds the paucity of primary source materials proves their point.

But how much primary source material should we expect to find concerning this Messiah? Certainly, Josephus should have had extensive knowledge of this Messianic Movement. He is born in the 30s and eventually fights for the insurgents against Rome in the 60s. Josephus would not have excluded "Jesus" from his history of the Jewish nation. After all "Jesus" is a very important first-century religious leader. As such we should expect much from Josephus in our search.

On the other hand the Roman historians Tacitus and Suetonius, as well as Pliny the Younger, would have had no firsthand information about the early years of the Jewish Jesus Movement. In addition, the Jesus Movement would have held little importance in their worldviews. Rome is the center of the universe, while Judea is a lonely outpost in the vast Roman Empire. At best any mention of the Messiah would have been woven into the narrative, but only as an aside. The "Christian" movement has no hold on them and is not central to their thinking. Anything we can glean from these Roman historians should be considered golden, as their biases are very different from the gospel perspective.

In addition to these historians, we have the Dead Sea Scrolls. Do the Scrolls mention Jesus of Nazareth or do they point to another messianic movement?

In our search for the historical Messiah, we will first look to Josephus, then to the Roman historians, and finally to the Dead Sea Scrolls.

JOSEPHUS

Three passages from Josephus help determine the identity of the elusive Jesus when analyzed in light of Josephus's surrounding passages and his time line.

Passage 1: *The Testimonium Flavianum (TF)*

> Now, there was about this time Jesus, a wise man, *if it be lawful to call him a man,* for he was a doer of wonderful works—a teacher of such men as *receive the truth with pleasure.* He drew over to him both many of the Jews, and many of the Gentiles. *He was [the] Christ;* and when Pilate, at the suggestion of the principal men amongst us, had condemned him to the cross, those that loved him at the first did not forsake him, for he *appeared to them alive again the third day,* as the divine prophets had foretold these and ten thousand other wonderful things concerning him; and the tribe of Christians, so named from him, are not extinct at this day. (*Antiquities* 18.63–64) (Emphasis mine)

In the TF, Josephus supposedly calls Jesus a "wise man" and "a doer of wonderful works," the "Christ," and nearly calls him a god by saying, "if it be lawful to call him a man." In fact, the TF also attests to the resurrection and to the fulfillment of scripture. Did Josephus really write this or was this added by a later Christian? If Josephus actually wrote this, then he was a closet Christian.

Most scholars dismiss this passage as a later interpolation, not coming from the pen of Josephus himself. First, the tone of the TF is unlike other writings by Josephus; the TF praises Jesus as a doer of wonderful works. By contrast, later in *Antiquities,* Josephus claims that Wonder Workers are the most dangerous of all the insurgents. This utter disdain for Wonder Workers is absent in the TF.

Second, Josephus never mentions Jesus before this passage and only once afterward, and this later reference is most likely an interpolation as well. If Josephus considers Jesus to be the Christ, then why does he ignore him completely, aside from this passage? You would think that the Messiah, or Christ, would merit much more attention.

Very possibly Josephus does mention a Messiah figure at this point in his narrative. He attributes the founding of the Fourth Philosophy to Judas the Galilean, confirming that Judas's movement thrives in the early first century. Would Josephus have forgotten to relate the death of this great Jewish teacher? Perhaps the TF is simply a later rewrite of an original passage about the death of Judas the Galilean.

Third, according to Origen (185–254 CE), Josephus "did not receive Jesus for Christ."[1] By the early third century Christian historians know that Josephus never wrote the pro-Jesus TF. However, the TF becomes accepted Christian propaganda by the time of Eusebius in the fourth century.

And finally, the TF is situated among passages discussing events that occur in 19 CE. This certainly does not accord with Christian traditions, but it does ring true concerning the death of Judas the Galilean.

In short, when searching for the historical Messiah, we can only conclude that the TF is a rewrite of material relating to a real messianic contender, Judas the Galilean. Other than that nothing in this passage supports the gospel Jesus of Nazareth.

Passage 2: The Stoning of James, the Messiah's Brother

> And now Caesar, upon hearing the death of Festus, sent Albinus into Judea, as procurator; but the king deprived Joseph of the high priesthood, and bestowed the succession to that dignity on the son of Ananus [Annas], who was also himself called Ananus. Now the

report goes, that *this elder Ananus [Annas] proved a most fortunate man; for he had five sons, who had all performed the office of the high priest to God, and he had himself enjoyed that dignity a long time formerly, which had never happened to any other of our high priests.*

This younger Ananas . . . was also of the sect of the Sadducees, who are very rigid in judging offenders. . . . [Ananus] thought he now had a proper opportunity [to exercise his authority]. Festus was now dead, and Albinus was but upon the road; so he assembled the Sanhedrin of judges, and *brought before them the brother of Jesus, who was called Christ, whose name was James, and some others, [or, some of his companions]; and when he had formed an accusation against them as breakers of the Law, he delivered them to be stoned.*

. . . But now the Sicarii went into the city by night, just before the festival, which was now at hand, and took the scribe belonging to the governor of the temple, whose name was Eleazar, who was the son of Ananus the high priest, and bound him, and carried him away with them; after which they sent to Ananus, and said they would send the scribe to him, if he would persuade Albinus to *release ten of those prisoners which he had caught of their party.*

. . . Costobarus also, and *Saulus,* did themselves get together a multitude of wicked wretches, and this because they were of the royal family . . . but still they used violence with the people, and were ready to plunder those that were weaker than themselves. (*Antiquities* 20.197–200, 208–209, 214) (Emphasis mine)

Only the most ardent mythicists claim that James is not the brother of a Jewish Messiah figure. After all Paul twice mentions James as the brother of the Lord (1 Corinthians 9:5 and Galatians 1:19). In addition, many early traditions praise James, which goes counter to the gospel treatment of James and the family of the Messiah. And finally, the book of Acts uses this passage to frame its own version of the stoning of Stephen.

James, the brother of "Jesus," actually existed and died. In Josephus's account, several pieces of information help further our understanding about the Jewish Jesus Movement. First, Ananus, the son of Annas, leads the charge against James. The elder Annas has been chief priest from 7 to 15 CE and directs the arrest and questioning of Jesus, according to the Gospel of John.* In addition, this Annas has five sons and a son-in-law who also claim the title of chief priest. That a son of Annas has James put to death is most revealing. The families of the Messiah and of Annas have been enemies from the census of Cyrenius in 6–7 CE. If the elder Annas is behind the crucifixion of the Messiah figure, then Ananus's attack on the brother (James) can now be fully appreciated.

Second, after the stoning of James, the Sicarii begin attacking Ananus's family, kidnapping Ananus's son and offering him in exchange for ten of their members held in prison by Albinus. Josephus mentions Sicarii and not "Christians" as those avenging the stoning of James. This is important because it helps identify the Jewish Jesus Movement as fanatical nationalists, a far cry from the traditional gospel picture.

Third, Paul† attacks the poorer priests in the Temple after the stoning of James. This too is incorporated into the story of Paul in the book of Acts. However, in Acts, Paul's attacks are pre–Jewish Jesus Movement, while Josephus has Paul attacking the poor in 62 CE, long after Paul's ouster from the Jesus Movement at Antioch in 44 CE.‡

The passage in question surely depicts the death of James, the brother of the Lord. However, two points must be questioned. First, the passage states that James is the brother of Jesus. This reference to Jesus can only be seriously entertained if Josephus had written about Jesus in an earlier account. As noted above, the TF is a later interpolation.

---

*Upon arrest, Jesus is brought first to Annas (John 18:12–14), the father-in-law of Caiaphas. Annas has five sons who become chief priests, so Caiaphas may have been chief priest due to his association with the powerful Annas.

†Paul is also called Saul in the book of Acts. In fact, the name Saul is used before, and even shortly after, his conversion on the road to Damascus. Saul does not become Paul until after his meeting with Sergius Paulus in Acts 13:4–9.

‡Paul describes his confrontation with Peter at Antioch in Galatians. While Paul starts his own Christ Movement several years earlier, he nevertheless tries to stay within the bounds of the Jewish Jesus Movement, located in Jerusalem and Galilee. He does this by deceit, assuring James and Peter that his ministry to the Gentiles will be in accord with other Jewish outreaches. Unknown to James, Paul teaches that the Law is unnecessary. When his true ministry is unmasked, Paul is summarily ousted from the Jewish Jesus Movement.

Josephus would not have described James's lineage by using a totally unknown person (Jesus). Josephus probably does write that James is the brother of someone, replaced by the name *Jesus* by a later interpolator.

The second questionable reference relates to this "Jesus, who was called Christ." Josephus may have written that James's brother had messianic followers. That would explain why Ananus took action against James, trumping up charges that the Torah-observant James broke the Law. The murder of James is clearly illegal, part of Jewish infighting. However, nothing suggests that James's Messiah is Jesus of Nazareth. Any such connection is made by a later interpolator.

Passage 3: The Conversion of King Izates

And when he [King Izates] perceived that his mother was highly pleased with the Jewish customs, he made haste to change, and to embrace them entirely; and *as he supposed that he could not be thoroughly a Jew unless he were circumcised,* he was ready to have it done. But when his mother understood what he was about, she endeavored to hinder him from doing it, and said to him that this thing would bring him into danger; and that as he were a king he would thereby bring himself into great odium among his subject, when they would understand that he was so fond of rites that were to them strange and foreign; and that they would never bear to be ruled over by a Jew.

. . . [Ananias, a Jewish teacher, said *that King Izates] might worship God without being circumcised, even though he did resolve to follow the Jewish Law entirely; which worship of God was of a superior nature to circumcision.* He added that God would forgive him, though he did not perform the operation, while it was omitted out of necessity. So the king at that time complied with these persuasions of Ananias.

But afterwards, as he had not quite left off his desire of doing this thing, *a certain other Jew that came out of Galilee, whose name was Eleazar, and who was esteemed very skillful in the learning of his country,* persuaded him to do the thing; for as he entered into his palace to salute him, and found him reading the law of Moses, he said to him, "Thou dost not consider, O king, that thou unjustly break the principle of those laws, and art injurious to God himself [by neglecting to be circumcised]; for thou ought not only to read them, but chiefly to practice what they enjoin thee. How long will thou continue uncircumcised? But, if thou hast not yet read the Law about circumcision, and does not know how great impiety thou art guilty of by neglecting it, read it now."

When the king had heard what he said, he delayed the thing no longer, but retired to another room, and sent for a surgeon, and did what he was commanded to do. (*Antiquities* 20.38–46) (Emphasis mine)

This is the most important passage in Josephus, even though most scholars fail to recognize it as such. As noted above, the TF is an interpolation and the passage on James does not actually mention Jesus of Nazareth. From those two passages, we know that a messianic group does exist in Israel. This third passage suggests that two separate movements are at war with each other.

King Izates admires the Jewish religion but knows that conversion requires circumcision, a rite both painful and foreign. How would his subjects react to such a procedure? A Jewish teacher by the name of Ananias answers this question. He simply states that circumcision is unnecessary, claiming a superior method of worshipping God. Does this sound familiar?

Paul preaches the same message as Ananias, contending that his gospel is supposedly superior to the one taught by Peter and James. And Paul's religion downplays circumcision. To Paul the Gentiles can inherit the covenant between humans and God without undergoing circumcision. In short one can become reconciled with God by disobeying God's command concerning circumcision.

A clash of movements ensues. Eleazar is sent from Galilee to confront the teachings of Ananias. Eleazar persuades King Izates to undergo circumcision in order to fulfill the Law. The king dutifully obeys and becomes fully Jewish.

Note that Eleazar comes from Galilee, a stronghold of the Jewish Jesus Movement. Ananias represents the Christ Movement, headed by Paul. In this passage Josephus confirms the two movements consistent with the writings of Paul. In Galatians, Paul claims to have a superior gospel, but his gospel is repudiated by representatives of James. In both the King Izates conversion and the conflict at Antioch between Peter and Paul, the Jewish Jesus Movement aggressively pursues the Christ Movement, seeking to eradicate the Christ Movement's false teachings.

The conversion of King Izates occurs in 44 CE, a time marker that helps date the confrontation between Peter and Paul. It can be argued that Paul's gospel is repudiated and Paul himself ousted from the Jewish Jesus Movement in 44 CE.

This scenario may seem radical, but it does make sense. Josephus does not use the term *Christian* in his story of Ananias, Izates, and Eleazar. However, the earliest members of the Jewish Jesus Movement are fully Jewish and follow the law of Moses. Josephus's reference to Eleazar, and his ties to Galilee, certainly describe this messianic movement. Josephus also perfectly characterizes the Christ Movement, where the Jewish law is downplayed and circumcision considered inferior to this new form of worship. While not using the term *Christian,* Josephus paints a wonderful picture of two separate movements vying for supremacy.

Some might claim that Josephus's story of Ananias has no connection to the early Christian Church. But why would Acts include an Ananias in its own story of Paul's life (Acts 9:9–19)? As we will see in chapter 11, Acts incorporates much of Josephus's narrative in its fictionalized account. The very use of Ananias in Acts proves that Ananias is an important part of the story. And we should accept the primary source (Josephus) over the secondary source (Acts) in our understanding of Ananias's role in Christian history.

SUETONIUS AND TACITUS

Suetonius writes his book, *The Twelve Caesars,* around 120 CE. His writings are often critical of the Claudian emperors, painting unflattering pictures of both Caligula and Nero. In these pages Suetonius also makes two references to Christians:

. . . Since the Jews were continually making disturbances at the instigation of Chrestus, he [Claudius] expelled them from Rome.[2]

. . . Punishment was inflicted on the Christians, a set of men
adhering to a novel and mischievous superstition.[3]

The first quote can be dated to the early reign of Claudius, when
Agrippa I is advising him. Claudius would not have been able to distinguish one sect of Jews from another, but the troublemaking Jews are quite
familiar to Agrippa I. They are his opposition in Judea.[4] Note that the
book of Acts also includes this episode, where it is noted that "Claudius
had ordered *all the Jews* to leave Rome" (Acts 18:2).* The Acts account
changes Claudius's order from the Jews who followed "Chrestus" to all
the Jews, effectively shielding the Christian movement from any negative
associations with being expelled from Rome by the emperor.

Suetonius clearly writes that the Jews are continually causing disturbances in Rome, and these Jews follow "Chrestus" or Christ. This flies
in the face of the traditional story, where Christians are model citizens.
After all, Paul exhorts his followers to obey the government and to pay
all their taxes (Romans 13:1–7), so we would expect his followers to
be law-abiding individuals. Therefore, Suetonius's statement points to
another group, one not enamored of Rome and not law abiding. This
group is fully Jewish, not members of Paul's Gentile Christ Movement.

Why were the Jewish Christians (the Jewish Jesus Movement) continually in a state of rebellion during this time? This is shortly after
the assassination of Caligula, whose plans for the Temple have nearly
ignited a war between the Jews and the Romans. The Jesus Movement
does not trust the Romans and refuses to accept Rome as a partner.
Their official king, Agrippa I, has close ties to Claudius; this must have
been particularly painful to these most observant followers of the Law.

---

*Note that most scholars place this episode at the end of Claudius's reign, sometime
between 48 and 52 CE, because they hold on to the traditional time line. However, they
do not explain how Claudius could have distinguished one Jewish sect from another.
Also, according to Dio Cassius, ordering all the Jews from Rome would have been very
disruptive. (See Dio Cassius 60.6.6–7.)

The second passage by Suetonius states that the Christians suffer persecution under Nero. Suetonius characterizes Christians as "men adhering to a novel and mischievous superstition," wording consistent with Tacitus's description and certainly applied to Jewish messianic disciples.[5] However, this derogatory opinion of "Christians" does not account for why Nero persecutes them. In fact, Suetonius does not tie this persecution to the Great Fire of Rome. Why does Suetonius ignore the Great Fire as the reason for the persecution? Suetonius places full blame for the fire on Nero and wants no other possible suspects.[6]

Tacitus writes of the Christians once, regarding the Great Fire of Rome, in 64 CE.

But all the endeavors of men, all the emperor's largess and the propitiations of the gods, did not suffice to allay the scandal or banish the belief that the fire had been ordered. And so, to get rid of this rumor, Nero set up as the culprits and punished with the utmost refinement of cruelty *a class hated for their abominations, who are commonly called Christians. Christus, from whom their name is derived, was executed at the hands of the procurator Pontius Pilate in the reign of Tiberius* [14–37 CE]. Checked for the moment, *this pernicious superstition again broke out, not only in Judea, the source of the evil, but even in Rome,* that receptacle for everything that is sordid and degrading from every quarter of the globe, which there finds a following. Accordingly, arrest was first made of those who confessed [to being Christian]; then, on their evidence, an immense multitude was convicted, not so much on the charge of arson as because of hatred of the human race. Besides being put to death they were made to serve as objects of amusement; they were clad in the hides of beasts and torn to death by dogs; others were crucified, others set on fire to serve to illuminate the night when daylight failed. . . . All this gave rise to a feeling of pity, even toward *men whose guilt merited the most exemplary punishment;* for it was felt that they were being destroyed not for the public good but to gratify the cruelty of an individual.[7] (Emphasis mine)

Three important points can be gleaned from this passage. First, Tacitus associates the Christians with the Jewish state. He states that the movement starts in Judea during the administration of Pontius Pilate and that the 64 CE movement breaks out again in Judea and in Rome. Therefore, it can be argued that these Roman Christians are Jewish and not Gentile; they are members of the Jesus Movement, not the Christ Movement of Paul.

Second, these Jewish Christians receive punishment for their hatred of Roman ways. The Jesus Movement refuses to worship Caesar or to have anything to do with foods dedicated to the gods. Paul urges his Gentile disciples to mix with the population, telling them to obey the government and to pay all their taxes and allowing them to eat food sacrificed to idols (Romans 13:1–7 and 1 Corinthians 8:4–8). Paul writes that the weak-minded Christians (that is, Jewish Christians) do not understand this freedom in Christ. So Tacitus is surely writing about the Jewish Jesus Movement when speaking about their hatred of the human race.

The differences between the Jewish Jesus Movement and the Gentile Christ Movement are not well understood by most Christian scholars. However, one Christian scholar, Edward Gibbon, does apply logic to the passage by Tacitus, conjecturing that the Christians mentioned by Tacitus are really the followers of Judas the Galilean. Gibbon does not see how the traditional Christian movement, supposedly led by Saint Paul and Saint Peter, could be so maligned by Tacitus. According to the story chronicled in Acts, the Christian movement would have been insignificant in 64 CE, and would have flown under Nero's radar. Therefore, he reasons, those being punished are a different set of Galileans, the Zealots.[8]

Third, Tacitus states that many of these Christians confess and that on their evidence others are arrested and punished. Certainly, these Christians do not disassociate themselves from the movement, but rather chose to die for it. This fanaticism corresponds with that of Judas the Galilean's Fourth Philosophy, of whom Josephus writes, "They also do not value dying any kind of death, nor indeed do they heed the deaths of their relations and friends, nor can any such fear make them call any man Lord" (*Antiquities* 18.23).

But why would members of the Zealot party (Jewish Jesus Movement) present evidence against other members of their movement? Possibly, the Jewish community singles out members of the Jewish Jesus Movement in an attempt to save themselves. This happens in Alexandria, shortly after the fall of Jerusalem in 70 CE. A remnant of Sicarii escape from Jerusalem, travel to Alexandria, and try to whip up support among the Alexandrian Jews for revolt against Rome. The sober-minded Jews of Alexandria, having heard reports concerning the destruction of Jerusalem, turn the Sicarii in to the authorities (*War* 7.413–416). Six hundred Sicarii (men, women, and children) are tortured and put to death. Their deaths in Alexandria correspond to those Christians who die under Nero in Rome. Josephus writes this concerning the Sicarii in Alexandria:

> . . . whose courage, or whether we ought to call it madness, or hardiness of their opinions, everybody was amazed at; for when all sorts of torments and vexations of their bodies that could be devised were made use of them, they could not get any one of them to comply so far as to confess or seem to confess, that Caesar was their lord; but they preserved their own opinion, in spite of all the distress they were brought to, as if they received these torments and the fire itself with bodies insensible of pain, and with a soul that in a manner rejoiced under them. But what was most of all astonishing to the beholders, was the courage of the children; for not one of these children was so far overcome by these torments as to name Caesar for their lord. (*War* 7.417–419)

THE LETTER OF PLINY THE YOUNGER TO TRAJAN

The letter of Pliny the Younger to Trajan, concerning the fate of Christians under his jurisdiction, has long been used by Christians to support the existence of Christianity at a very early date. The letter is sent around 112 CE when Pliny is proconsul of Bithynia Pontus.* Pliny is a friend of both Tacitus and Suetonius, historians who also mention the existence of Christians in the mid-first century.† Needless to say, the opinions of Tacitus and Suetonius concerning early Christians may help in deciphering the meaning of Pliny's letter to Trajan. So we need to keep in mind the picture of Christianity described by Tacitus and Suetonius when reading Pliny's account.

In this letter Pliny the Younger describes a Christian movement that differs from that of Suetonius and Tacitus. After questioning members of this movement about their beliefs, Pliny condemns those who admit to being Christian. However, the majority of those questioned denounce their faith.

> Thereupon the usual result followed; the very fact of my dealing with the question led to a wider spread of the charge, and a great variety of cases were brought before me. An anonymous pamphlet was issued, containing many names. All who denied that they were or had been Christians I considered should be discharged, because they called upon the gods at my dictation and did reverence, with incense and wine, to your image which I had ordered to be brought forward for this purpose, together with the statues of the deities; and especially *because they cursed Christ, a thing which, it is said, genuine Christians cannot be induced to do.* Others named by the informer first said that they were Christians and then denied it; declaring that they had been but were so no longer, some having recanted three years or more before and one or two as long as twenty years [earlier]. *They all worshipped your image and the statues of the gods and cursed Christ.* But they declared that the sum of their guilt or error had amounted only to this, that on the appointed day they had been accustomed to meet before daybreak, and to *recite a hymn*

---

*Bithynia Pontus was in northern Asia Minor, a good distance from Rome.
†Pliny the Younger sends letters to Tacitus detailing the death of his uncle, Pliny the Elder, at the time of the Mount Vesuvius eruption of 79 CE.

antiphonally to Christ, as to a god, and to bind themselves by an oath, not for the commission of any crime but to abstain from theft, robbery, adultery, and breach of faith.[9] (Emphasis mine)

Pliny interrogates those charged with the crime of being Christian, and most recant. These particular Christians worship Caesar's image just as, earlier, they worshipped Christ as a god. The Christians described by Tacitus and Suetonius undergo tortures and hold steadfast to their beliefs. Since they are Jews, their practices would have included following the Law and undergoing circumcision, certainly practices not followed by those interviewed by Pliny.

Pliny does mention the Jewish Jesus Movement when he states, "because they [adherents of the Gentile Christ Movement] curse Christ, a thing which, it is said, genuine Christians [adherents of the Jewish Jesus Movement] cannot be induced to do." Before the destruction of Jerusalem in 70 CE, the Jewish Jesus Movement dominates any discussion concerning Christians. They are the genuine Christians—those who undergo all types of torture rather than worship another lord, such as Caesar. Suetonius's troublemaking Jewish Christians can be dated to 41–44 CE, while Tacitus's Christians are blamed for the Great Fire of Rome, in 64 CE. These events occur before the destruction of Jerusalem and the deaths of many Jewish patriots during the Jewish war. After 70 CE, the Gentile Christ Movement of Paul fills the void left by the annihilation of the original Jesus Movement. Pliny recalls the past when referring to the genuine Christians, but he is dealing with the Gentile Christians of 112 CE, some forty years after the Jewish Jesus Movement has been crushed.

THE DEAD SEA SCROLLS

Several credible explanations exist concerning the authorship of the Dead Sea Scrolls. The most popular, called the Standard model, credits the Scrolls to the Essenes, a first-century sect cited by Josephus in *War* as one of three Jewish philosophies flourishing at the time. In

Antiquities Josephus adds the Fourth Philosophy to those already noted in *War*. Some of the attributes assigned to the Essenes in *War* really belong to the Fourth Philosophy. Two of those attributes are marrying and the willingness to undergo torture for their God.

In *War* Josephus mentions another order of Essenes, who live according to the customs and laws of the other Essenes but are allowed to marry. They reason that "by not marrying they cut off the principal part of the human life, which is the prospect of succession" (*War* 2.160). These marrying Essenes are not included in the shorter version of the Essenes in *Antiquities,* but we know that adherents of the Fourth Philosophy practice marriage, since Judas himself has several sons, as noted by Josephus.

This merging of movements by Josephus can be best illustrated by the willingness to die. In *War* 2.152–153, the Essenes undergo all sorts of torture during the Jewish war with Rome. Surprisingly, in *Antiquities* 18.23–24, Josephus fails to attribute this willingness to die to the Essenes, instead assigning this trait to the Fourth Philosophy.

The possibility exists that both the Essenes and members of Judas's movement undergo torture during the Roman war. However, Josephus must have realized that he had ascribed this unusual trait to two separate "philosophies" in his two histories. He may have hidden the truth concerning torture in *War* for political reasons. *War* is written shortly after the conflict (75 CE), while *Antiquities* is not published until 93 CE. Josephus may have felt more at ease relating the true nature of things at a later date.

Thus, our understanding of the Essenes may be a bit distorted. Do they really marry and undergo torture? Even though Josephus ascribes these traits to the Essenes, they definitely characterize the Fourth Philosophy, as described in *Antiquities*. This is all the more interesting since Pliny the Younger and the Jewish philosopher Philo describe the Essenes as celibate, but many passages in the Scrolls presuppose that the members are married.[10] If the Essenes are truly celibate, then the passages must be referring to some other group, possibly the Fourth Philosophy. In addition, the Scrolls contain other information not characteristic of the Essenes but in conformity with the Fourth Philosophy.

Philo states that the Essenes are peaceful in nature, but the *War* Scroll warns of a future armed conflict with the forces of darkness.[11] Again, this appears to be more in line with Judas's movement; the *forces of darkness* most likely refer to Rome and its hirelings, the Herodians.

So the Essene Standard model may have some very real weaknesses. According to Michael Wise, Martin Abegg Jr., and Edward Cook, many of the Scrolls have pro-Hasmonean leanings, pointing to a later dating of some of the Scrolls. They cite *In Praise of King Jonathon* as an example in which Hasmoneans are highly regarded, unlike the picture painted by the Standard model.[12] This is important, as I have suggested that the Fourth Philosophy modeled itself after the Maccabees. It appears that those who followed the Scrolls also emulated the Maccabees.

Although the Dead Sea Scrolls may have been written before the advent of the Fourth Philosophy, it is almost certain that members of the Fourth Philosophy utilized the documents. The Scrolls' documents detail certain characters who may have been exemplars for later movements, including the Righteous Teacher, the Wicked Priest, the Liar, and the Root of Planting. A movement that styled itself as at war with an evil power could easily incorporate these archetypes into its own teachings. According to Wise, Abegg, and Cook, these archetypes are called "carrier groups" by sociologists.[13] The Fourth Philosophy may have been a carrier group, with Judas, and later James, as the Righteous Teacher; the Wicked Priest could have been Annas; the Liar was no doubt Paul; and the Root of Planting could have been Matthias.[14] (Labels such as Righteous Teacher, Liar, and Wicked Priest could have been applied to various individuals at various times, just as *pope* refers to various individuals, depending on the date.)

There is positive proof that the Fourth Philosophy did use the Scrolls. As noted by Wise, Abegg, and Cook, a Dead Sea Scroll called *A List of Buried Treasure* was created to hide the Temple treasures in case the Temple fell to the Romans. At this time, the Zealots controlled the Temple and presumably wrote the list.[15] In addition, Dead Sea Scroll materials were found at Masada, where in 73 CE the Sicarii commit suicide to avoid being slaughtered by the Roman army.[16]

This brings us to the Dead Sea Scroll theory posited by Robert Eisenman. Eisenman asserts that the internal evidence of the Scrolls points toward the first century CE, and that the Righteous Teacher is none other than James the Just, the brother of Jesus. He also presents a solid case citing Paul as the Liar. This theory has been criticized by mainstream scholars because the external evidence, carbon dating, and paleography *supposedly* point toward the second and first century BCE. Since the external evidence does not coincide with first-century CE dating, mainstream scholars confidently dismiss Eisenman's theory. In his latest book, *The New Testament Code,* Eisenman questions the validity of the Dead Sea Scrolls carbon dating, claiming that the initial reports were based on the wrong dating curve. (Carbon dating cannot prove an absolute dating but rather a relative dating or range of possible dates.) Thus, with the new and more accurate dating curve, the results move closer to first century CE.[17]

In addition, Eisenman meticulously compares the Dead Sea Scroll language to that used in the gospels and even in Paul's letters. Many of the same Dead Sea Scroll concepts and terms (that is, internal evidence) are used playfully in the composition of these later documents, often reversing their original meanings.[18]

If Eisenman is right—and I think he is—then Paul and the later gospel writers have knowledge of the Scrolls' language. This is very important in determining who wrote the Gospels of Mark and Matthew. Even though Paul's letters and these later gospels are meant for Gentile consumption, they nevertheless include Dead Sea Scroll concepts and wording, now used to justify Gentile faith over following the law of Moses.

From the five primary sources previously cited—Josephus, Tacitus, Suetonius, Pliny the Younger, and the Dead Sea Scrolls—we know that the Jewish Jesus Movement is obsessed with the law of Moses, and its adherents are willing to undergo any torture in defense of the Law. From Josephus and Pliny, we also glimpse the Christ Movement, founded by Paul. This Christ Movement, which is antinomian in nature, appeals to Gentiles but is wholly rejected by the Jewish Jesus Movement.

PART TWO

Paul, Apostle to the Gentiles

❖

THE MAKING OF A MESSIAH

3 ► Traditional versus Historical Paul

THE TRADITIONAL PAUL

Paul's life is conveniently encapsulated in one document, the book of Acts, the blueprint used by church authorities and scholars to present a seamless picture of the early church.

According to Acts, which we view as a secondary source for the purpose of this examination, Paul's gospel of the Holy Spirit and grace to the Gentiles is first preached by the twelve apostles (Acts 2). Philip, one of the Seven, teaches the Ethiopian eunuch about Jesus and baptizes him without any mention of the law of Moses (Acts 8:26–40). Shortly thereafter, Peter brings the gospel of faith to Cornelius, a Roman centurion (Acts 10). He explains his actions to the Jewish leadership: "As I began to speak, the Holy Spirit came on them as he had come on us at the beginning. Then I remembered what the Lord had said, 'John baptized with water, but you will be baptized with the Holy Spirit.' So if God gave them [the Gentiles] the same gift as he gave us, who believed in the Lord Jesus Christ, who was I to think that I could oppose God?" (Acts 11:15–17). So before Paul has any influence in the church, his message is already being preached.

The evil Saul (later renamed Paul) is introduced after the stoning of Stephen, one of the Seven (Acts 7–8:1). "And Saul was there, giving approval to his death." The young Saul begins to destroy the church, arresting and imprisoning the disciples. He asks the high priest for letters to the synagogues in Damascus, so that he can arrest members of the Way and bring them back to Jerusalem as prisoners (Acts 9:1–2). If one man could have destroyed the Church of God, it would have been the young Saul.

But God has other plans for Saul. On the road to Damascus a light from heaven blinds Saul, bringing him to his knees. The heavenly Jesus speaks, telling Saul that he must obey God's will. Saul meekly follows his traveling companions into Damascus and there is met by Ananias, the disciple who presents the gospel to him. Within days Saul fearlessly proclaims the message of Jesus (Acts 9:3–22).

Saul grows more powerful as he proves that Jesus is the Christ (that is, the Messiah). The Jews conspire to kill Saul, but he miraculously escapes, going to Jerusalem to join the other disciples who understandably do not trust him, since he has recently persecuted them. Barnabas vouches for Saul, explaining that the Lord Jesus has spoken to him. After that Saul moves around Jerusalem and boldly proclaims the message of Jesus. But once again the Jews try to kill him. When hearing of the plot, the Jewish leadership sends Saul to safety, to his birthplace Tarsus (Acts 9:19–31).

While Saul is in Tarsus followers of Stephen travel to Antioch, telling the Greeks "the good news about the Lord Jesus . . . and a great number of people believed and turned to the Lord" (Acts 11:19–21). When the apostles in Jerusalem hear about the Gentile conversions, they send Barnabas to Antioch where he encourages the new converts and helps bring even more to the Lord (Acts 11:19–24).

Barnabas must have remembered Saul's zeal, for he travels to Tarsus to look for him. He takes Saul back to Antioch, and the two teach the disciples for a year. It is in Antioch that the disciples are first named Christians (Acts 11:25–26). During this time a great famine spreads over the Roman Empire. Saul and Barnabas are sent to Jerusalem with a monetary gift to help the Jewish brothers in Judea (Acts 11:27–30). After finishing their mission they return to Antioch with another supporter, John Mark (Acts 12:25).

Later, Saul and Barnabas are sent to Cyprus. There they meet the proconsul, Sergius Paulus, and the false prophet, Elymas the sorcerer. Saul converts Sergius Paulus by overcoming the powers of Elymas. From this point on in the story, Saul is known as Paul, taking this name from the proconsul (Acts 13:4–12).

After many travels Barnabas and Paul return to Antioch and stay there for a long time. While there they are confronted by men from Judea who teach that Gentiles cannot be saved unless "circumcised according to the custom taught by Moses." Barnabas and Paul bitterly oppose this new teaching and are sent by the Antioch Church to Jerusalem to settle the dispute once and for all. Once in Jerusalem the two are welcomed by all the disciples (Acts 14:21–15:4).

After hearing Paul's testimony James agrees with Paul that the Gentiles should not be burdened with following the Law. He then sends his decision back to Antioch with his own delegation, along with Paul and Barnabas. Shortly thereafter Paul and Barnabas have a sharp disagreement concerning John Mark. They cannot be reconciled and go their separate ways (Acts 15:5–41).

Acts' account suddenly shifts from third person to first person. The *we* passages describe Paul's activities after the Council of Jerusalem up to his final return to Jerusalem (Acts 16–21:16).

When Paul arrives in Jerusalem he goes directly to James and the elders and reports on his mission to the Gentiles. The Jewish leadership is thankful but sees problems ahead, saying, "You see, brother, how many thousands of Jews have believed, and all of them are zealous for the Law. They have been informed that you teach all the Jews who live among the Gentiles to turn away from Moses, telling them not to circumcise their children or live according to our customs. What shall we do?" It is then decided that Paul should go to the Temple and join in the purification rites. Paul obeys, but the Jews seize Paul and try to kill him. The Roman commander rescues Paul and has him arrested (Acts 21:17–36).

Like Pilate in the story of Jesus of Nazareth the Roman commander orders Paul to be flogged and then questioned to find out why the Jews hate him. Here Paul gives the startling news that he was born with

Roman citizenship (Acts 22:22–29). The Roman commander releases Paul but has him sent to the Sanhedrin (the Jewish high court) for questioning. The next day the Jews conspire to kill Paul. Luckily for Paul his nephew is privy to this information and informs Paul (Acts 23:1–22). For safety he is sent with an armed escort to Caesarea, to trials before Felix and Festus, during which Paul appeals to Caesar and sets the stage for his trip to Rome (Acts 23:23–25:12).

Before traveling to Rome Paul has one more meeting with authority, this time before Agrippa II and his sister, Bernice. Paul recounts his conversion, claiming that he was once a Pharisee. His speech convinces Agrippa to say, "This man could have been set free, if he had not appealed to Caesar" (Acts 25:23–26:32).

Paul is then sent to Rome. On the way a storm overtakes his party and they are shipwrecked on Malta. Paul is the hero of the day, saving a great number of crew members. On Malta Paul is bitten by a poisonous snake but shows no ill effects, prompting the people to compare him to a god (Acts 27–28:10).

When Paul finally reaches Rome he wastes no time in calling on the Jewish leaders. He presents his gospel to them, but some refuse to listen to him. Paul then says to the Jews, "I want you to know that God's salvation has been sent to the Gentiles, and they will listen!" Paul stays in Rome for two years and boldly preaches his gospel of the Lord Jesus Christ (Acts 28:11–31).

QUESTIONS CONCERNING THE TRADITIONAL PAUL

While most scholars consider Acts as the basis for church chronology, a few obvious questions should illuminate the problems surrounding the story of the traditional Paul. Read each question thoughtfully, attempting to resolve the issues with nothing more than the knowledge put forth in the New Testament. You might discover why scholars steer clear of these questions: they cannot be adequately answered by Paul's traditional story.

- How could the Twelve and the Seven preach Paul's gospel?
- Do Jesus and the Twelve actually preach Paul's antinomian gospel or do the gospels and Acts overlay Paul's beliefs onto Jesus and his earthly followers? After all, Paul states that "I did not receive it from any man, nor was I taught it; rather, I received it by revelation from Jesus Christ" (Galatians 1:11–12). By Paul's own words he receives his gospel from the Risen Christ.
- Is Stephen a literary stand-in for James, the brother of Jesus?
- In Acts the young Saul gives approval for Stephen's stoning and then persecutes the church (Acts 8:1–3). Josephus writes that Saul persecutes the poorer priest after the stoning of James, the brother of Jesus (*Antiquities* 20.200–214). Why should we believe Acts' chronicling of the 35 CE persecution of Stephen over Josephus's account of the 62 CE persecution of James?
- How can the young Saul of Tarsus have wielded such power in Jerusalem?
- The traditional Paul claims to be a Pharisee, yet the young Saul acts like a thug, employed by the ruling Sadducees. Also, since Paul is from Tarsus, how does he obtain such powers from the authorities?
- What connections does Paul's nephew have in Jerusalem?
- This is an extension of the previous question. How can Paul's young nephew from Tarsus have gained information concerning the Jews' plot to kill him? Also, what is the nephew doing in Jerusalem?
- When does Paul first visit Jerusalem?
- In Acts 9:20–30 Saul goes to Jerusalem shortly after his conversion. But according to Paul his first trip to Jerusalem occurs three years after his conversion (Galatians 1:18). Which account is true—Acts or Galatians?
- Does Paul travel to Jerusalem with famine-relief money?
- In Acts 11:27–30 Saul goes to Jerusalem with famine-relief money. However, Paul does not mention this visit in his own account in Galatians. Since the famine occurs around 44–48 CE (*Antiquities* 20.101), is it possible that Paul's letter to the Galatians predates the famine? After all, Paul's argument with Peter at Antioch (in 44 CE)

is identical to the argument between Ananias and Eleazar in the King Izates conversion of 44 CE. If Paul's letter can be dated to 44 CE or shortly thereafter, the entire Acts chronology is discredited.

- Does Saul really get his new name "Paul" from the proconsul Sergius Paulus?

- In Acts 13:4–13 Saul becomes Paul after meeting Sergius Paulus. Does this name change occur because of this meeting or is the name *Paul,* meaning "small," pejoratively attached to him by the Jews who oppose his teachings?

- Does the Jerusalem Church welcome Paul at the council or does Paul sneak into town quietly and meet only with the leaders (Acts 15:4 as opposed to Galatians 2:1–5)?

- In reconstructing the historical Saul we must understand the dynamics of the time. By Paul's own admission he is not welcomed by the Jews and has to sneak around. This strongly suggests that Paul's gospel is not popular among the Jews.

- Does James endorse Paul's gospel to the Gentiles or does Paul withhold information from him?

- In Acts 15 James supports Paul's gospel to the Gentiles. However, in Galatians 2:1–13 James opposes Paul's gospel, even after the Council of Jerusalem.

- Do Barnabas and Paul become estranged over a disagreement concerning John Mark (Acts 15:36–41) or does Barnabas side with Peter over Paul in the argument at Antioch (Galatians 2:11–13)?

- From Paul's account Barnabas is led astray by James and Peter. In fact, Barnabas simply follows orders from the leaders of the Jesus Movement, forever shunning Paul's antinomian gospel.

- Is the story of Paul's last days in Jerusalem true or is it patterned after the life of Saul, the cousin of Agrippa I? (As we will soon see, Josephus records the activities of Saul—Agrippa I's cousin— in Jerusalem. Coincidentally, Acts uses these same events in its depiction of Paul's time in Jerusalem, leading one to believe that the Saul whose life is chronicled by Josephus is actually the Paul of Acts.)

- Does the shipwreck (Acts 27) actually happen to Paul or is this story borrowed from the life of Josephus? (On his trip to Rome, Josephus experiences a life-threatening shipwreck. Is it possible that Paul also experiences the same thing? It seems unlikely, as Josephus's Saul travels to Achaia (Greece) to meet Nero, not to Rome. If Paul travels to Achaia and not to Rome, then he cannot have been shipwrecked near Malta, which is south of Rome.)
- How can Paul have been bitten by a poisonous snake on Malta if there are no poisonous snakes there? (This may seem like a minor point, but it adds to the fictional elements included in Acts' story of Paul.)
- Does Paul actually meet Nero in Rome or does he (as Saul) meet Nero in Achaia (modern-day Greece)? (According to Josephus, Saul (Paul) meets Nero in Achaia. If Saul/Paul never travels to Rome, as claimed by Acts, then the legend about his death in Rome may also be untrue.)

Using a secondary source document (Acts) to create Paul's time line results in an indefensible story. The Paul whose life story is told in Acts never existed. However, using primary source documents (Paul's letters and Josephus's works), a new, believable story line can be constructed and the above questions satisfactorily answered.

A MORE HISTORICAL PAUL

Important information concerning Paul has been ignored because of the traditional time line. In part one an initial case is made that Judas the Galilean is the actual model for Jesus of Nazareth. Judas is born around 25 BCE, cleanses the Temple in 4 BCE, starts a tax rebellion against Rome in 6 CE, and is crucified sometime between 19 and 21 CE. His second-in-command, John the Baptist, runs the movement until his death in 36 CE and is then replaced by James the Just. So how does Paul fit into this new time line?

According to the traditional time line Paul converts shortly after the death of Jesus, sometime between 31 and 35 CE. However, if "Jesus" actually is crucified in 21 CE, the conversion of Paul could have been as early as 21–25 CE. (Remember, the TF chronicles events occurring around 19 CE, and the *Memoranda* claims that the Messiah dies in 21 CE.) From Paul's letter to the Galatians we know that Paul spends seventeen years in the Jewish Jesus Movement, from his conversion to the Council of Jerusalem. We have also seen that the conflict between Peter and Paul at Antioch is similar to the King Izates conversion of 44 CE, where Eleazar and Ananias preach the same messages as Peter and Paul. A close reading of Galatians and 2 Corinthians shows that after 44 CE Paul no longer has anything to do with the Jerusalem-based Jewish Jesus Movement.

While the book of Acts tries to downplay the rift between Paul and the Jerusalem-based Jewish Jesus Movement, Paul's own letters confirm this conflict. In Galatians 1:6–12 Paul states that his gospel was received by revelation from Jesus Christ and distances himself from the lower form of gospel taught by James and Peter: "I [Paul] did not receive it from any man, nor was I taught it." According to Paul his gospel is superior to the gospel of mere mortals, and those preaching a different gospel than his own will be eternally condemned, thereby condemning the Jerusalem apostles, including James and Peter. This same attitude toward the Jewish Jesus Movement's leaders can also be found in 2 Corinthians 11:4–15, where Paul writes that the "super-apostles" are preaching a "different gospel," and then denigrates these apostles, calling them servants of Satan.

With the help of Josephus a much more sinister picture of Paul emerges.

Acts and Josephus

Several passages in *War* and *Antiquities* cover the same ground as accounts in the book of Acts. If just one similarity in accounts existed, then an argument could be made against my conclusions, based on sheer coincidence. However, as the evidence mounts, a new evaluation of Paul's life and work should be considered.

Paul and the Deaths of Stephen and James

The first mention of Paul in the book of Acts comes immediately after the stoning of Stephen. Interestingly Paul is referred to as Saul in this initial introduction, with Saul being his Jewish name, and Paul, his later adopted name.

> And Saul was there, giving *approval* to his [Stephen's] death. . . . Meanwhile, Saul was still breathing out murderous threats against the Lord's disciples. He went to the high priest and asked him for letters to the synagogues in Damascus, so that if he found any there who belonged to the *Way*, whether men or women, he might take them as prisoners to Jerusalem. (Acts 8:1–3 and 9:1–2) (Emphasis mine)

Although Saul is not physically involved in the murder, he surely approves. This passage suggests that Saul is an authority figure as he gives "approval to his death," an assertion at odds with the traditional time line, which holds that Saul is a very young man at this time. How could such a young man wield so much power, considering he hails from Tarsus, not a power center, like Jerusalem? Saul must have had some highly influential friends! The well-connected Saul then begins to persecute the church or the Way of Righteousness, another designation for the Jewish Jesus Movement.

How do Stephen's stoning and the young Saul's influence compare to the parallel passage in Josephus? Is Josephus's Saul the Saul of Acts? The following account occurs after the stoning of James the Just in 62 CE:

> Costobarus also, and *Saul*, did themselves get together a multitude of wicked wretches, and this because *they were of the royal family;* and so they obtained favor among them, because of their kinship with Agrippa: but still they used violence with the people, and were very ready to plunder those that were weaker than themselves. (*Antiquities* 20.214) (Emphasis mine)

Note the similarities between Josephus's Saul and the biblical Saul/ Paul. First, Saul is introduced after the stoning of Stephen in Acts and after the stoning of James in *Antiquities*. Is this just a coincidence? According to Robert Eisenman, the stoning of Stephen is simply a rewrite of the stoning of James.[1] Eisenman builds his case by using the above passages as well as early Christian writings about James. This explains why the Acts story line ends with Paul in Rome in 62 CE without mentioning the stoning of James, the most influential member of the Jesus Movement, after the deaths of Judas and John the Baptist. Certainly, the story of James is popular, explaining why accounts of his death exist independent of Acts. The author of Acts wants to include a stoning, but not a historical occurrence. Besides the stoning there is one common thread between the two accounts—a character named Saul. In both cases, Saul persecutes those weaker than himself: in Acts Saul persecutes the church, while in *Antiquities* he attacks the lower priesthood, those associated with James. The great difference concerns the timing. In Acts the persecution occurs before Saul joins the Jewish Jesus Movement, around 31–35 CE. In Josephus Saul persecutes the poor priests after the murder of James in 62 CE.

If Saul resides in Jerusalem in 62 CE, then the Acts story must be invented, because Acts places Paul in Rome between 60–62 CE. Perhaps the author of Acts wants to distance Paul far from the scene of the crime. How would it look if the apostle to the Gentiles approves of the murder of James, the leader of the Jewish Jesus Movement? In Acts Saul wields extraordinary power for one so young and, presumably, outside the power structure. However, the passage from Josephus answers this question. Saul is an older man of around sixty at this point, with connections throughout the power structure, and he and his brother are members of the royal family. This connection with Agrippa II certainly persuades many of the "wretches" to follow him. This also explains the power Saul wields with the high priest, as described in Acts.

So the persecution by Saul after the murder of James is used in Acts to portray Saul's hateful beginnings. This is how Saul behaves *before* his conversion to Christianity. Yet Saul hates James and Peter *after* his ouster from the Jesus Movement in 44 CE. His actions in 62 CE are those of a vengeful opponent. James has won the day in 44 CE at Antioch (see Galatians), but Saul claims victory in 62 CE in Jerusalem. This despicable picture of Paul also comes from the Pseudoclementine *Recognitions* 1.70–71, where the Enemy attacks James at the Temple, nearly killing him. This Enemy then receives letters from the high priest and proceeds on to Damascus, hoping to arrest Peter. This second-century story of the Enemy, or Saul, is inserted into the Acts story as well.

Why would the author of Acts include this telling information? Perhaps the episode chronicling the stoning of Stephen in Acts is a composite of two different persecutions by Saul. When Paul is ousted from the Jewish Jesus Movement, he is seething, as is clearly evident from his own letters. The first attack on James, as recorded by the Pseudoclementine *Recognitions,* is not fatal and occurs in the mid-40s. Interestingly, two of Judas the Galilean's sons are also crucified around this time. Could Saul have had a hand in the attack on James and the crucifixions of Simon and James, the sons of Judas the Galilean? The later stoning of James is the second attack, and it too finds a place in the contorted history of Acts.

Why does Acts recast James's stoning as the stoning of Stephen? Why not just ignore the stoning altogether? In Acts Hellenized Christians assume some of the church's responsibilities. Through the years scholars have viewed Stephen and Philip (part of the Seven) as key to the spread of Christianity. Now, if the Stephen story is a recasting of the stoning of James, then the Hellenized Christian group in Jerusalem never existed. In addition, Philip's Pauline-style evangelization of the Eunuch (Acts 8:26–40) is also a rewrite of the conversion of King Izates, where Ananias (a eunuch?) gains access to the king through the king's harem and preaches a superior form of Judaism, in line with Paul's theology (*Antiquities* 20.34–35).

Thus, the two stories spotlighting the Hellenized Christian group are revisionist history. In addition, the Fourth Philosophy would never have tolerated the presence of a Hellenized Christian group in

Jerusalem. So why is this group introduced in Acts? The answer, once again, comes back to Paul. The author of Acts needs to place Paul's ideas within the context of an earlier group. The baptism of the Holy Spirit and the substitution of water baptism for circumcision need to be established so that Paul will not be credited with founding the religion. However, according to Paul's own words, his gospel comes through revelation, not from any man. Thus, Acts' stories about Philip and Stephen are purely fabricated.

Saul's/Paul's Appeal to Agrippa II

The following passage concerning Saul comes from Josephus's *War.* As Josephus notes, around 66 CE Saul is a member of the peace party, a group of influencial men sent to Agrippa II in 66 CE to ask for forces to suppress the insurgents in Jerusalem.

> So seeing that the insurrection was now beyond their control and that the vengeance of Rome would fall upon them first, the most influential citizens determined to establish their own innocence and sent delegations to Florus and Agrippa, the former led by Simon, son of Ananias, the other distinguished by the inclusion of *Saul, Antipas, and Costobar, kinsmen of the king.* They begged both to come to the City [Jerusalem] with large forces and suppress the insurrection before it got beyond control. (*War* 2.418–419) (Emphasis mine)

Saul teams up with his brother Costabar and another relative named Antipas to petition their kinsman, Agrippa II, for an army to help put down the insurrection. This request has nothing to do with spiritual matters, but is simply an attempt to combat the more radical elements of the Fourth Philosophy. How is Saul viewed by the insurgents? As a former member of their movement, Saul would have been viewed as a traitor. This treachery also follows his earlier approval of James's stoning in 62 CE. Surely, Saul's actions are giving him a strong negative reputation. According to Eisenman, Saul is the Liar of the Dead Sea

Scrolls and he certainly could be equated with the Pseudoclementine *Recognition*'s Enemy. I suspect that the life of Saul/Paul is also the foundation for the Traitor story, later ascribed to Judas Iscariot.

The rewrite of Acts 25:13–26:32 also has Paul meeting with Agrippa II. In this account Festus discusses Paul's case with Agrippa, and Agrippa agrees to hear Paul's plea. Instead of the above-mentioned call to arms against the insurgents, Paul's defense before Agrippa recalls his conversion to the Way and his hope for Agrippa's acceptance of his version of Christianity. Again, this is simply false, as we have already proved that Acts' narrative of Saul's conversion is a combination of later persecutions by Saul. And it is safe to say that Paul's Christianity is diametrically opposed to the tenets of the Jesus Movement, once led by James. So, in both accounts, Saul/Paul is trying to convince Agrippa of his own personal viewpoint. The Acts version of events conveniently hides the fact that Paul and Agrippa are kinsmen, a sleight of hand necessary to place Paul above the petty politics of the time and conceal details of his actual biography, as related by Josephus.

Thus, the meeting with Agrippa is turned into a spiritual discussion, setting the stage for Paul's alleged trip to Rome and his appeal to Caesar. According to Acts, Agrippa tells the Roman procurator Festus: "This man is not doing anything that deserves death or imprisonment. . . . [He] could have been set free if he had not appealed to Caesar" (Acts 26:31–32). This concocted statement had two main goals: First, Paul is deemed innocent of any crimes with which the Jews have charged him, and second, this appeal to Caesar gets Paul out of town.

Paul has to be extricated from the scene of the crime. So the author of Acts sends him to Rome. But, as we shall soon establish, this is the mythical Paul, created by the author of the book of Acts, not the actual Paul; the Paul of real history *never went to Rome.*

Saul's/Paul's Escape from Jerusalem

In a third story related by Josephus the ambassadors to Agrippa return to Jerusalem, where they hide from the insurgents, taking cover in the Upper Palace (*War* 2.425–429). They later flee the city around 66 CE.

After the disastrous defeat of Cestius many prominent Jews fled from the City like swimmers from a sinking ship. Costobar with his brother Saul and Philip, son of Jacimus, the commander of King Agrippa's army, slipped out of the City and went over to Cestius. But their companion in the siege of the Palace, Antipas, declined to flee and was put to death by the insurgents. (*War* 2.556–557) (Emphasis mine)

Saul and his brother escape from Jerusalem with their lives while Antipas stays behind and perishes. That Saul is besieged by the Jews should not surprise us. He has been a thorn in the hide of the Fourth Philosophy for over twenty years, since his ouster from the Jewish Jesus Movement. Saul's protector, after he flees the city, is the Roman commander Cestius. So, in Josephus's version of events, Saul escapes from the murderous Jews and finds refuge among the Romans.

In the book of Acts Paul has been mobbed at the Temple and seeks protection from the Jews. In a dramatic speech to the Jews Paul explains his earliest contact with the Way: how he persecuted them with great zeal. He then relates his conversion experience on the road to Damascus, where he receives instruction in the Way from Ananias. Later, after returning to Jerusalem, he is warned in a vision to leave the city and go to the Gentiles, who will listen to him (and God) (Acts 22:1–21). (Note that the three conversion stories in Acts do not accord with Paul's own account in Galatians!) Paul's statement of being sent to the Gentiles enrages the Jews to the point of murder. Conveniently, Paul's ally in his escape from the Jews is the Roman commander, who has just learned of Paul's Roman citizenship, a revelation that saves Paul from the mob and sends him into the protective arms of the Roman procurator, Felix (58–60 CE).

Saul/Paul escapes into Roman protection. Josephus has Saul fleeing from the Jewish Jesus Movement into the Upper Palace, while Acts has Paul escaping from the Jews at the Temple. Acts always puts a spiritual spin on Paul's actions; the Jewish Jesus Movement became the Jews, while the place of refuge is transformed from the unspiritual Upper Palace to the Holy Temple.

One thing is clear: The Acts account never happened. Consider these two points: First, Paul supposedly goes to the Temple to assure James of his adherence to the Jewish covenant. But, as already noted, Paul was ousted from the Jesus Movement in 44 CE, has been party to James's stoning in 62 CE, and has vehemently opposed the everlasting covenant with the Jews (see Galatians). If this occurs in 58 CE, James would have had nothing to do with Paul. Second, according to Paul's own letters, the Temple no longer has any spiritual meaning for him or his followers. If Paul really does return to the Temple, then at best, he is being extremely hypocritical. Placing Paul at the Temple is absurd, for adherents of the Jewish Jesus Movement believe him to be a liar and the enemy of the Law. The only safe place for Paul in Jerusalem would have been the Upper Palace of King Agrippa.

As with the other stories the writer of Acts carefully places Paul in an earlier time frame. The 58 CE arrest is four years before the stoning of James and eight years before the start of the Jewish war. To further reinforce its fictitious time line, Acts has people confusing Paul with the Egyptian, a wonder worker who leads a failed revolt at the Mount of Olives around 58 CE (*Antiquities* 20.169–172 and Acts 21:38). The Acts time line cannot be correct, since Saul/Paul escapes from the Jews around 66 CE, many years after the death of James and the activities of the Egyptian.

Saul's/Paul's Interview with Caesar

The fourth and last mention of Saul by Josephus occurs in 66–67 CE, when Saul is sent as an emissary to Caesar to shift blame from himself and his cronies to the Roman procurator Florus.

> However, Cestius sent Saul and his friends, *at their own desire,* to Achaia, to Nero, to inform him of the great distress they were in; and to lay the blame of their kindling the war upon Florus, as hoping to alleviate his own danger, by provoking his indignation against Florus. (*War* 2.558) (Emphasis mine)

In this final passage about Saul the following should be noted. Saul asks to see Nero in order to shift the blame from Cestius and himself to Florus. This request is similar to Paul's appeal to Caesar in Acts 26:32. In both stories Saul/Paul wants to present his case to Caesar. In Acts, Paul is blamed for causing a disruption in Jerusalem because of his misunderstood antinomian gospel. According to the Roman procurator, Festus, and Agrippa II, Paul is an innocent man. According to Josephus, Saul also proclaims to Nero Cestius's and his own innocence concerning the outbreak of the Jewish war. The location of the meeting should also be of great interest. In *War*, Saul travels to Greece to meet Nero in 67 CE, while Acts sends Paul to Rome in 60 CE, no doubt to suffer with the martyrs of the Great Fire. Unfortunately for the traditional Christian story, Paul never travels to Rome and is never imprisoned there.

Who reigns as Caesar in 66–67 CE? The ruler of the world is none other than the madman Nero. Saul/Paul appeals to Nero in both scenarios, in 66–67 CE in Achaia and in 60–62 CE in Rome, per *War* and Acts, respectively. Nero, who blames the Christians for the Great Fire, is the Caesar Saul asks to meet, not to chastise Nero for the slaughter, but rather to shift blame from himself to another. Saul could bargain with the devil. After all, he has always sided with the powerful. His letter to the Romans states:

> Everyone must submit himself to the governing authorities, for there is no authority except that which God has established. The authorities that exist have been established by God. Consequently, he who rebels against the authority is rebelling against what God has instituted, and those who do so will bring judgment on themselves. . . . This is also why you pay taxes, for the authorities are God's servants, who give their full time to governing. (Romans 13:1–7)

The apostle Paul writes that all government is established by God and the authorities are God's servants. If written around 40 CE or shortly thereafter, then this good-citizen philosophy would have coincided with the regime of Caligula, an equal to Nero in sadistic behavior.

As noted earlier Acts places Paul in Rome in 60–62 CE to remove him from the scene of the crime, the stoning of James the Just. This trip to Rome is also necessary to help concoct an early death for the apostle, a few years before Josephus's history of Saul. Not even the most ardent supporter of Paul (then and now) could have approved of his meeting with Nero in 66–67 CE, after the Great Fire of Rome. So a nice ending is written for Paul. Along with Peter, Paul conveniently suffers martyrdom in Rome around 64 CE. Although Peter may very well have been executed in Rome, Paul definitely is not. (For a further analysis of this legend, see chapter 7, "Foundation Legends.")

From the above four accounts concerning Saul/Paul in Josephus, we get a much revised image of the great apostle to the Gentiles. This Saul/Paul sides with the authorities, hell-bent on destroying the Fourth Philosophy and the Jewish Jesus Movement. The book of Acts completely misrepresents the facts concerning Paul, putting his later life in the 58–62 CE time frame in order to distance him from the history of Josephus's Saul. Yet the real Saul/Paul works with the ruling authorities at the time of James's murder. He also rubs elbows with Agrippa II and Nero, always working against the Jewish Jesus Movement.

Now that is a very different Paul than we are used to. Looking closely at Josephus's Saul we can see the real Paul emerge, one who is at extreme odds with Jesus's first followers—his original disciples and his family members. He gets along with Roman imperial authorities in a way they never could, being insurrectionists, political activists, and rebels.

IS PAUL A HERODIAN?

We have already established that the Fourth Philosophy is a reactionary movement patterned after the Maccabees, with Herod the Great as its chief antagonist. Herod introduces foreign practices among the Jews, just as Antiochus Epiphanes did some 150 years earlier. That Judas the

Galilean opposes Herod is an understatement. The disciples of Judas are willing to fight to the death to bring an end to Herod's Hellenizing practices. This fervor continues from the time of Matthias (who dies in 4 BCE), through the death of John the Baptist to the murder of James, the brother of Judas the Galilean. Thus, if Paul has any connection to the Herodians, his credibility must be called into question. In fact, if Paul is a Herodian, then our picture of Jesus is grossly distorted, because much of the Jesus of the New Testament emanates from Paul's life and teachings.

First, we will examine Paul's own writings for insights. In Romans 16:11 Paul writes, "Greet those who belong to the household of Aristobulus. Greet Herodion the kinsman of me." According to William Barclay both Aristobulus and Herodian are connected to the family of Herod.[2] Also the Greek word for *kinsman* is different than the word for *brother*. Most likely a *kinsman* would be a flesh-and-blood relative, while a *brother* could very well denote a spiritual relationship. Aristobulus and Herodian may have been related by blood ties, but this by itself still leaves doubt. Paul also greets "Lucius and Jason and Sosipater the kinsman of me" (Romans 16:21), suggesting that Paul has ties in Rome to several Herodian relatives. In Paul's other letters, no other Herodian clues are present. So the case against Paul, based on his own letters, is meager at best, but a possible tie to the Herodians exists.

The book of Acts, although historically flawed, may still illuminate Paul's background. Saul/Paul is first mentioned in Acts 8:1, where he gives approval for Stephen's stoning and to the general persecution of Christians. "But Saul began to destroy the Church. Going from house to house, he dragged off men and women and put them in prison" (Acts 8:3). Saul intends to widen his search beyond Jerusalem so "he went to the high priest and asked him for letters to the synagogues in Damascus, so that if he found any there who belonged to the Way, he might take them as prisoners to Jerusalem" (Acts 9:2). As it was perfectly lawful to be a messianic Jew, this persecution is purely political in nature.

Our focus should be on Saul's influence at such a young age. Even though employed as a lowly thug, Saul has unusual influence with the high priest. Note that the parallel passage in *Antiquities* 20.214 directly states that Saul is a member of the royal family. This explains Saul's pull with the high priesthood. In general, those who persecute "Jesus" and his disciples are the Sadducees, high priests, and Herodians. Pharisees have a better feel for the people's pulse, and association with Rome and its policies is unpopular. If Paul were a real Pharisee, as he claims, he never would have associated with the high priest in this persecution.

In Damascus Paul escapes the governor by being lowered in a basket from a window in the wall (2 Corinthians 11:32–33). This scene is obviously altered in Acts 9:23–25, where Paul is lowered from the wall to escape the Jews. Certainly, Paul's letter should be trusted more than the sanitized Acts. And, if so, the enemy of Paul is King Aretas, the same king who opposes Antipas (Herod the Tetrarch) because Herod jilts his daughter and also murders John the Baptist, a vocal critic of Herod's personal life (*Antiquities* 18.109–119). This hatred of Saul/Paul may have had more to do with his Herodian background than with his preaching. In my opinion the escape from Damascus occurs near the end of Paul's career with the Jesus Movement (late 30s). If Paul vocally supports John the Baptist, then Aretas may not have arrested him. But by this time Paul is becoming more and more aligned with his old pals, the Herodians.

In the Church at Antioch Acts mentions Manaen, a member of the court of Herod the Tetrarch (Antipas) (Acts 13:1). Saul is included with him and a few others as leaders of this particular church, again placing Saul right next to a Herodian. Maybe Aretas's mistrust of Saul is indeed well deserved!

Being a member of Herod's family has considerable advantages, including Roman citizenship conferred at birth. Now in Acts 17:3 Paul and Silas both claim Roman citizenship. If Paul were a Pharisee, a Hebrew of Hebrews, and a member of the tribe of Benjamin, then he never would have had Roman citizenship. Paul compares himself to the Jerusalem apostles: "I was advancing in Judaism beyond many Jews of my own age and was extremely zealous for the traditions of my fathers" (Galatians 1:14). Here Paul uses the term *zealous* for the Law, placing himself in an equal or superior position vis-à-vis Peter and James. If true, then his Roman citizenship cannot be believed. It appears as if Paul's Roman citizenship came from his birthright as a member of the royal family.

When added to Josephus's accounts concerning Saul, this additional information supports Saul's membership in the royal family. That family background made Saul a prized convert to the opposition Jesus Movement. Even so, James and Peter must have been wary of his Herodian connections, which may explain why Barnabas travels with Paul, to serve as James's eyes and ears. And, eventually, word of Paul's antinomian gospel reaches James.

So who is Paul, really? Paul is a Herodian. His Herodian ties also explain his influence over the high priests and his friendly attitude toward government and Roman taxation.

IS PAUL A PHARISEE?

This statement appears in Philippians 3:4–6 as a response to those from the circumcision:

> If anyone else thinks he has reasons to put confidence in the flesh, I have more: circumcised on the eighth day, of the people of Israel, of the tribe of Benjamin, a Hebrew of Hebrews; *in regard to the Law, a Pharisee;* as for zeal, persecuting the church; as for legalistic righteousness, faultless. (Emphasis mine)

Before going forward we should first consider the source of this information. Eisenman writes: "No defender of the integrity of the early Church and its doctrines would have had the slightest interest in forging or, for that matter, even preserving [Paul's letters]."[3]

I agree with Eisenman that no one would have invented the story of Paul. His letters raise questions concerning the truthfulness of the gospels and Acts. For example, Paul's pillar apostles are James, Peter, and John. Paul's James and John are the brothers of the Lord (Galatians

1:19; 2:7–10; 2:12; 1 Corinthians 9:5). The gospels present James, Peter, and John as being the core apostles with Jesus. However, the gospels' James and John are the sons of Zebedee, not the brothers of Jesus. Why would a later writer make this incredible blunder, changing the sons of Zebedee into the brothers of Jesus? Considering that the gospels minimized the role of Jesus's family throughout, it is fair to say that the gospel writers turned the brothers of Jesus into the sons of Zebedee. Thus, this one example illustrates that Paul's information is closer to the truth than the gospel accounts.

Most scholars accept Romans, 1 and 2 Corinthians, Galatians, and Philippians as Paul's own letters. I question the letter to the Philippians, since Paul is never arrested and sent to Rome to meet Caesar. Now Philippians opens up in 1:12–14 with Paul writing about his imprisonment. This cannot be the Rome imprisonment because that never occurs. Perhaps this was added later or perhaps the whole letter is a forgery. Such a possibility makes Paul's claim of being a Pharisee a bit questionable.

Let us assume that the letter to the Philippians comes from Paul. If authentic, then three possible alternatives exist concerning his claim of being a Pharisee: he may have been a Pharisee, he may have lied about being a Pharisee, or he was exaggerating his own credentials. The second and third scenarios are similar in that, in either case, Paul is not a Pharisee. The first scenario can only be supported by the above passage in Philippians and possibly another in Galatians 1:13–14. In the Galatians passage Paul claims that he is "extremely zealous for the traditions of my fathers." It appears as if Paul associates himself with the most zealous of the Pharisees, or with the Fourth Philosophy. Recall that Josephus claims that Judas the Galilean and Sadduc/John the Baptist are both Pharisees (*Antiquities* 18.4; 23). Pharisees follow the written and oral Law. The phrase "traditions of my fathers" may refer to this oral Law. How interesting that Paul claims association with the Fourth Philosophy before he actually becomes part of it. The answer is quite simple: Paul is telling his converts that he once lived like the pillar apostles or the circumcision group. However, that precedes his mystical encounter with the Lord. After meeting the Risen Christ, Paul realizes that the Law is dead, and only faith in Jesus Christ can win a person salvation (Galatians 1:15–17; Philippians 3:7–11).

So is it possible that Paul lives as a Pharisee before his conversion to a Pharisaic movement? By Paul's own admission he persecutes the church (Galatians 1:13). If Paul is a Pharisee, then how can he have acted the part of persecutor? According to Acts 9:1–2 and the Pseudoclementine *Recognitions* 1.70–71, Paul is also employed by the high priest, a member of the Sadducees. A zealous Pharisee would never stoop to such a low. By persecuting the church he rules out the possibility of his being a Pharisee. Even in Acts the Pharisees often side with the Jesus Movement. As such the Saul in Acts and in the Pseudoclementine *Recognitions* only reinforces the point that Paul could not have been a Pharisee!

An unnamed Jew in *Antiquities* 18.81–85 (around 20 CE) is driven from Israel "by an accusation laid against him for transgressing their laws." This may be the true picture of the young Saul. This unnamed Jew later goes to Rome, where he "professed to instruct men in the wisdom of the laws of Moses" (*Antiquities* 18.81–84), using his religious knowledge to swindle unsuspecting Jewish converts. Obviously, the unnamed Jew could not have been a zealous Pharisee, as he was accused of transgressing the laws of Moses. However, that same man claims to know the laws of Moses when speaking to the uneducated Jewish converts. This pattern of braggadocio perfectly reflects Paul's character.

So it appears likely that Paul is not a Pharisee. But what about Paul's writing style? Many have claimed that Paul's Pharisaic roots emerge through his letters. Hyam Maccoby, in his book *The Mythmaker,* examines this theory, focusing on three points: the argument of light and heavy, Paul's alleged use of Pharisaic argument, and Paul's use or nonuse of the Hebrew scriptures.

The light and heavy argument can be illustrated as follows: "If offending a father (a relatively light thing) is punished by banishment for seven days, offending God (a relatively heavy thing) should all the more receive such a punishment."[4] Note that offending God does not get fourteen days or any other set term. The argument simply states that if a light offense gets seven days, a heavy offense should merit at least seven days. According to Maccoby Paul uses this form of argument often and usually does not get it right. Maccoby gives four examples of this light and heavy argument from Paul's writings and finds only one to be properly stated (Romans 5:10, 5:17, 11:15, and 11:24). To Maccoby this imprecision on Paul's part proves that he is *not* a trained Pharisee.

Maccoby's next argument concerns Paul's interpretation of scriptural passages. Many scholars argue that Paul uses midrash or biblical exegesis to support his positions. Maccoby uses the passage from Galatians 3:13 to show that Paul does not understand the Pharisaic exegesis of that verse. The verse is as follows: "Christ redeemed us from the curse of the Law by becoming a curse for us, for it is written: 'Cursed is everyone who is hanged on a tree.'" Paul claims that everyone who is hanged on a tree is cursed. Thus, Jesus, by being crucified, becomes a curse for us. But this is not part of the Pharisaic tradition. Maccoby writes:

> The idea that anyone hanged on a gibbet is under a curse was entirely alien to Pharisee thought . . . Many highly respected members of the Pharisee movement were crucified by the Romans, just like Jesus, and, far from being regarded as under a curse because of the manner of their death, they were regarded as martyrs. . . . The Pharisees never thought that God was either stupid or unjust, and he would have to be both to put a curse on an innocent victim.[5]

Who then is cursed in the above passage? The curse is upon those allowing the victim to hang upon the gibbet, desecrating the body made in the image of God. This is the Pharisaic interpretation, which is antithetical to Paul's version.

Maccoby's third argument centers on Paul's nonuse of the Hebrew scriptures. Paul exclusively uses the Greek translation, which sometimes differs from the Hebrew. Maccoby claims that a trained Pharisee could not play so loosely with the word of God.

In short, Maccoby believes that nothing in Paul's letters proves that he has a Pharisaic background. On the contrary Maccoby's analysis proves that Paul is not a Pharisee. This brings me to the third alternative: résumé padding. Paul is not a Pharisee, but his Gentile followers know nothing about the Pharisees or their teachings. Paul can simply state that he is the most learned man in Israel and his gullible disciples will take the bait. From the arguments stated above Paul is certainly not a Pharisee before his conversion to the Fourth Philosophy. But could Paul have become a Pharisee after being converted?

In Galatians 1:15–18 Paul writes that he does not visit Jerusalem for three years after his conversion. Very likely the Herodian Saul undergoes an initiation taking up to three years to complete. In these three years Saul would have been taught much about the Pharisaic teachings. This is evident from Maccoby's own presentation of the light and heavy argument. According to Maccoby Paul only properly states the argument in one of four cases. This may prove that Paul is not a Pharisee, but it may also prove that Paul is somewhat versed in the methods of Pharisaic argument. After all he does get one right out of four. And this dovetails with Eisenman's conclusions about Paul's use of the Dead Sea Scroll materials. Although Paul does not interpret the Scrolls as do the Zealots, he is very aware of the language used in the Scrolls.

Paul does exaggerate his credentials, and he purposely misleads his followers. Paul never has the religious prowess of a Peter or a James, yet claims that he was once more zealous in the observance of the Law than either of those men. This is an out-and-out lie. He then places this lie before his conversion to the Jesus Movement. Thus, Paul paints a pretty picture of himself: a reformed ex-Pharisee who now serves the Risen Christ. In actuality Paul is a Herodian who converts to the Fourth Philosophy and studies with the Pharisees and Zealots. He later devises his own worldview of Judaism, where he, Paul, is the representative of the Risen Christ, and where James and Peter still hold on to the Law and circumcision, discredited by his new gospel of faith.

4 ➤ James the Just and Paul the Liar

I s Paul really the Herodian, known as Saul? Josephus, Acts, and Paul's letters all point in that direction. To support this claim let's compare the letter attributed to James to Paul's four legitimate letters (Romans, 1 and 2 Corinthians, and Galatians). The letter attributed to James may not have been written by James the Just, but it certainly represents his religion and views on the Law, teachings that are certainly the antithesis of Paul's.

Remember, Paul tries to kill James in the 40s and also persecutes the poor priests soon after James's death. This strongly suggests that Paul has no positive feelings for James. Paul converts to the Jesus Movement in the early 20s under the leadership of John the Baptist, who preaches repentance and forgiveness. While James may have reluctantly accepted Paul within the movement, surely no bond of trust is ever formed between them. After John's execution (36 CE) James becomes the leader by default, with Peter at his side. James's guidance of the Jesus Movement may have been more confrontational than John's leadership. Under James's influence Agrippa I is excluded from the Temple and later assassinated. At this approximate time (43–44 CE) James sends out messengers confronting Paul for his antinomian gospel.

Are James and Paul preaching the same gospel, as claimed by the church and its cadre of "scholars," or are the Jewish Jesus Movement and the Gentile Christ Movement two distinct religions?

RICH AND POOR

The letter of James has one consistent theme relating to the scripture: "Love your neighbor as yourself." The only way to love your neighbor is to consider your neighbor's needs: if he's hungry, then feed him. However, according to James, the rich exploit the poor and will be judged for their wickedness. The rich certainly do not love their neighbors. Their treatment of the poor is soundly condemned, with the promise of God's wrathful judgment. Note the following passages:

> Listen, my dear brothers: Has not God chosen those who are poor in the eyes of the world to be rich in faith and to inherit the kingdom he promised those who love him? But you have insulted the poor. Is it not the rich who are exploiting you? Are they not the ones who are dragging you into court? Are they not the ones who are slandering the name of him to whom you belong? (James 2:3–7)

> Now listen, you rich people, weep and wail because of the misery that is coming upon you. Your wealth has rotted, and moths have eaten your clothes. Your gold and silver are corroded. Their corrosion will testify against you and eat your flesh like fire. You have hoarded wealth in the last days. Look! The wages you failed to pay the workmen who mowed your fields are crying out against you. The cries of the harvesters have reached the ears of the Lord Almighty. You have lived on earth in luxury and self-indulgence. You have fattened yourselves in the day of slaughter. (James 5:1–5)

James disapproves of hoarding wealth, claiming that this wealth belongs to those actually doing the work, namely the poor. His analysis of the situation is little different than that of Karl Marx. James condemns the rich, claiming that their hoarded money is nothing more than an idol.

James's attitude is consistent with that of Jesus, who says: "Blessed are you who are poor, for yours is the kingdom of God. . . . But woe to you who are rich, for you have already received your comfort" (Luke

6:20–24). But perhaps the most telling parable from Jesus about the rich is the Rich Ruler passage (Luke 18:18–25). In this parable the rich man claims that he has kept all the commandments since childhood. Even so, Jesus insists that he lacks one thing essential for salvation: "Sell everything and give to the poor, and you will have treasure in heaven. Then come, follow me." The rich man goes away sad because he cannot part with his great wealth. In essence Jesus believes that hoarding wealth while others starve negates the commands of God, especially the most important law to "love your neighbor as yourself."

This insistence on equality is central to Judas the Galilean's Fourth Philosophy. During the war with Rome the Sicarii burn down the Records Office, freeing the poor from their debts to the rich (*War* 2.426–427). As explained earlier James leads the Sicarii Movement, and this act is consistent with James's teachings on the rich and the poor.

The teachings of Judas the Galilean (Jesus) and James concerning the rich and poor are remarkably similar. But how does Paul treat the rich in his dealings throughout the Roman Empire? In Josephus's account of the unnamed Jew who swindles the Jewish convert in Rome, the unnamed Jew (Saul) certainly courts the wealthy (*Antiquities* 18.81–84). In his dealings with his churches Paul encourages his wealthier patrons to give to those in need (2 Corinthians 8:1–15). Although this appears similar in nature to Jesus's plea, Paul asks his rich followers to voluntarily share with those in need. So, in Paul's churches, wealth is not discouraged. (By contrast Jesus demands that the rich man give up all his money.) In fact, if one were wealthy, then one could help out more people. Unfortunately, we do not know if the contributions of the rich ever made it to those in need. Paul may have simply absconded with the money.

In the words of Jesus the rich have to give all their possessions to the poor before becoming followers. To Paul one only has to have faith in the blood of Christ to become a follower. In James 2:3–7 the rich are also taking the poor to court in order to steal the little the poor own. In 1 Corinthians 6:1–11 Paul scolds his disciples for taking each other to court. Paul is not proud of this behavior, but it illustrates the lax qualifications needed for entry into the Christ Movement. In fact, people of all walks of life enter into his new covenant with God. Paul assumes that the Holy Spirit will cleanse them and lead them to holy living. This did not work then and it does not work today. Wicked people often remain wicked people. Such people would have needed to repent (change) before following Jesus and John the Baptist.

FAITH AND DEEDS

Paul uses the example of Abraham to illustrate his ideal of faith. "Abram believed the Lord, and he credited it to him as righteousness" (Genesis 15:6). This passage underpins Paul's gospel, that anyone having faith in the blood of Christ would be considered righteous and forgiven before God.

James also references Genesis 15:6 in his letter. According to James's interpretation, *faith accompanied by works* sets Abraham apart.

> You foolish man, do you want evidence that faith without deeds is useless? Was not our ancestor Abraham considered righteous for what he did when he offered his son Isaac on the altar? You see that his faith and his actions were working together, and his faith was made complete by what he did. And the scripture was fulfilled that says, "Abraham believed God, and it was credited to him as righteousness," and he was called God's friend. You see that a person is justified by what he does and not by faith alone. (James 2:20–24)

Let us apply some logic to the example of Abraham. If Abraham had refused to offer Isaac on the altar, would Abraham have been considered righteous by God? Abraham could have said, "I believe in you God, but I refuse to follow your commands. Try me again next week!" No, Abraham goes against his own better judgment and prepares to sacrifice his son. That is faith. An utterance from our lips does not prove faith; only our actions do. If we cheat and steal, our actions show that we worship money, even though we may go to church twice a week and proclaim our faith in Jesus.

James writes: "Faith by itself, if it is not accompanied by action, is dead" (2:17), and "Show me your faith without deeds, and I will show you my faith by what I do. You believe that there is one God. Good! Even the demons believe that—and shudder"(James 2:18–19). In short faith is not really faith without good works. In essence James is telling Paul's disciples that their faith is absolutely worthless unless it's accompanied by action. And the first action in faith is circumcision, the seal in the everlasting covenant between God and man.

In Galatians certain followers of James teach that observing the law of God is necessary for salvation (Galatians 2:12; 3:1–4). This also is the case in the King Izates conversion, as related by Josephus (*Antiquities* 20.34–48). Afraid of losing his followers Paul writes: "Did you receive the Spirit by observing the law, or by believing what you heard?" Here Paul directly opposes James's theology of faith made relevant by actions.

Remember, James states that even the demons believe. He does not teach the simple faith espoused by Paul. Paul writes "that if you confess with your mouth, 'Jesus is Lord,' and believe in your heart that God raised him from the dead, you will be saved. For it is with your heart that you believe and are justified, and it is with your mouth that you confess and are saved" (Romans 10:9). Paul substitutes believing in the resurrection for obeying the Law. James certainly believes in the resurrection, yet he also knows that God requires us to obey His laws. According to James you cannot substitute belief for following the Law. To James belief is brought to life by following the Law.

Paul differentiates between his Gentiles and the Jews, between faith and works:

> What then shall we say? That the Gentiles, who did not pursue righteousness, have obtained it, a righteousness that is by faith; but Israel, who pursued a law of righteousness, has not attained it. Why not? *Because they pursued it not by faith but as if it were by works.* (Romans 9:30–32) (Emphasis mine)

This Pauline theology has been accepted over the past nineteen hundred years by the Gentile Church, from which emerged all forms of Christianity today—Orthodox, Catholic, Anglican, Reformation Protestant, and Evangelical. But this is not the original teaching of Jesus or by the Jewish Jesus Movement, as represented by James and Peter. Certainly, Paul does not preach his new gospel in the early years of his ministry. This evolving gospel, made possible by revelations from the Risen Christ, makes Paul view the Gentiles differently. He plans to reach them by offering a distinctive message, a mix of the Jesus story and the prevalent mystery religions of the day. In that way his Gentile followers really do not need to change dramatically. If Paul had followed the ways of Jesus, James, and Peter, he would have preached the Law and circumcision to his followers. This would have slowed the growth of his new religion among the Gentiles. In his desire to reach and convert as many Gentiles as possible, Paul abandons the original message of Jesus and creates his own hybrid religion. In the end, due to the Jewish war with Rome, Paul's version triumphs.

TAMING THE TONGUE

Could James have had Paul in mind when writing about the tongue?

> . . . the tongue is a small part of the body, but it makes great boasts. Consider what a great forest is set on fire by a small spark. The tongue also is a fire, a world of evil among the parts of the body. . . . Out of the same mouth come praise and cursing. My brothers, this should not be. (James 3:5–6, 10)

First, James emphasizes that the tongue makes great boasts. This observation can be applied to everyone, but no one more than Paul. The following comes from Paul's letters to his congregations. Note that the bragging comes mostly from 2 Corinthians and Galatians, the two letters written after Paul's expulsion from the Jesus Movement. That is why Paul spends so much time boasting about his qualifications. He wants his disciples to compare his real (or invented) activities with those of mere mortal men.

> Are we beginning to commend ourselves again? Or do we need, like some people, letters of recommendation to you or from you? (2 Corinthians 3:1)

> Rather, as servants of God we commend ourselves in every way: in great endurance; in troubles, hardships, and distresses; in beatings, imprisonments, and riots; in hard work, sleepless nights, and hunger; in purity, understanding, patience, and kindness; . . . genuine, yet regarded as imposters. (2 Corinthians 6:4–10)
> I must go on boasting. Although there is nothing to be gained, I will go on to visions and revelations from the Lord. . . . To keep me from becoming conceited because of these surpassingly great revelations, there was given me a thorn in my flesh, a messenger of Satan, to torment me. (2 Corinthians 12:1–10)

> I was advancing in Judaism beyond many Jews of my own age and was extremely zealous for the traditions of my fathers. But when God, who set me apart from birth and called me by His grace, was pleased to reveal his Son in me so that I might preach him among the Gentiles, I did not consult any man, nor did I go up to Jerusalem to see those who were apostles before I was, but I went immediately into Arabia and later returned to Damascus. (Galatians 1:14–16)

By boasting Paul defends his own ministry in several ways. First, Paul explains why he lacks letters of recommendation from the pillars (2 Corinthians 3:1). He simply states that physical letters are unnecessary, and that his letters are his followers, filled with the Holy Spirit. This bait and switch works well, as most people enjoy being flattered.

In the second passage Paul recounts (or invents) the great number of sacrifices he has made for the faith. He has endured all sorts of trials and tribulations as a servant of God. Surely this hard work counts for something. When reading this one is in awe. Could any man have worked as hard as Paul? But then we must question why Paul recounts these hardships. He states: "[We are] genuine, yet regarded as imposters" (2 Corinthians 6:8). Who regards Paul and his fellow teachers as imposters? This has to be those nasty followers of James.

Perhaps the greatest boast is Paul's claim of revelations from God. Paul is the ultimate name dropper. This boast is not verifiable by anyone, as the Lord only speaks to Paul. How convenient for Paul! Paul himself states that any man would become conceited by these great revelations. Only the thorn in his flesh keeps Paul grounded in this world. Those listening to this claim would either be greatly impressed or incredibly concerned. Does James approve of Paul's claims? James is the brother of Judas (Jesus), and he knows that Paul's claims concerning the Risen Christ are not true. How could Jesus have preached one message all his years on Earth and a different message to Paul after the resurrection? We should ask the same question today.

The last passage goes even further than the claim of revelations from the Risen Christ. Paul writes that God has set him apart from birth, revealing his Son in him, making him part of the cosmic plan for salvation. What a boast! Certainly, James has Paul in mind when writing about the evils of boasting.

WISDOM

James's view of wisdom is much different than the one held by Paul. James ties wisdom to actions.

> Who is wise and understanding among you? Let him show it by his good life, by deeds done in the humility that comes from wisdom. But if you harbor bitter envy and selfish ambition in your hearts, do not boast about it or deny the truth. Such "wisdom" does not come down from heaven but is earthly, unspiritual, of the devil. (James 3:13–15)

To James life and religion are intricately intertwined. You cannot separate the two. Therefore, wisdom is shown through living a good life with deeds illustrating the person's humility. On the other hand Paul's wisdom from God is simply the crucifixion of Christ Jesus.* This spin on wisdom takes all human activity out of the equation.

> When I came to you, brothers, I did not come with eloquence or superior wisdom as I proclaimed to you the testimony about God. For I resolved to know nothing while I was with you except Jesus Christ and him crucified. . . . we speak of God's secret wisdom, a wisdom that has been hidden and that God destined for our glory before time began . . . but God has revealed it to us by His Spirit. (1 Corinthians 1:18; 2:1–10)

Apart from Christ Jesus crucified, nothing exists but worldly wisdom. To Paul, one cannot know the wisdom of God except through the Spirit of God, made possible by the resurrection of Christ Jesus. This wisdom comes from God through the actions of another (Christ Jesus), not through good deeds and humility. James would never have considered the crucifixion of his brother, Jesus, as necessary to show mercy and kindness to others. The death of Jesus is not a prerequisite to the wisdom propounded by James. But to Paul the death of Christ Jesus constitutes a wisdom hidden from the world since the creation.

James believes that God is totally revealed through the everlasting covenant between God and Abraham. With this everlasting covenant we have a responsibility to our fellow people, to love our neighbor as ourself. This is the wisdom expressed by James. But Paul claims that the everlasting covenant is negated by something that God has hidden from the Jews: Christ Jesus crucified. This wisdom can only be accessed through faith in the blood of Christ. James holds on to the Jewish concept of wisdom, while Paul wanders into his own pagan-influenced version of wisdom.

---

*Paul uses the terms *Christ Jesus*, *Jesus Christ*, and *Jesus* interchangeably.

THE LAW

We know from the letters of Paul and selected passages from Acts that James zealously supports the Law. In Galatians the circumcision group has certain ties to James. In the remainder of that letter Paul denounces the Law in contrast to his new religion of faith (Galatians 3–5:12). In fact, Paul calls on the Jews representing James to "go the whole way and emasculate themselves" (Galatians 5:12). This hatred for James and his steadfast observance of the Law help define James. He is zealous in support of the Law. This fact slips out in Acts 21:20, where James and the elders describe the Jerusalem followers: "You see, brother, how many thousands of Jews have believed, and all of them are zealous for the law."

If the believing Jews are zealous for the Law, then it follows that James and the apostles are preaching the law of Moses. Many scholars have assumed that the leaders James and Peter were moving toward Paul's position (see Acts 11–15), and were just humoring their own dim-witted disciples. Nothing could be further from the truth. James and his believing followers are all obsessed with the Law. Therefore, when reading the letter of James, we must be mindful of this steadfast observance of the Law.

James writes this concerning the Law:

Anyone who speaks against his brother or judges him speaks against the Law and judges it. When you judge the Law, you are not keeping it, but sitting in judgment on it. There is only one Lawgiver and Judge, the one who is able to save and destroy. But you—who are you to judge your neighbor? (James 4:11–12)

Again, James ties his interpretation of the law of Moses to his relationships with others, with his neighbor. In essence treat others with respect and let God be the Judge. But God's judgment is tempered by mercy, for James writes that the Lawgiver and Judge can both save and destroy. This Judge can save without the human sacrifice of Jesus. God has always had the power to save. After all is not God all-powerful?

Paul sincerely believes that the law of Moses is dead. The following passages help frame Paul's view of the Law:

> I found that the very commandment that was intended to bring life actually brought death. (Romans 7:10)

> For what the Law was powerless to do in that it was weakened by the sinful nature, God did by sending his own Son in the likeness of sinful man to be a sin offering. And so he condemned sin in sinful man, in order that the righteous requirements of the Law might be fully met in us, who do not live according to the sinful nature but according to the Spirit. (Romans 8:3–4)

In the first passage Paul states that the commandments of God actually bring death and not life. This revelation would have sent the Jews howling in disgust. To Paul following the Law perfectly is impossible; therefore the Law can only bring death and despair. But does God ever expect perfection from the Jews? If God created us, He would have known our limitations. God does not desire perfection, but effort. A passage in Deuteronomy clarifies the Hebrew scriptures' position concerning the Law.

> The Lord your God will circumcise your hearts and the hearts of your descendants, so that you may love him with all your heart and with all your soul, and will live. . . . Now what I am commanding you today is *not too difficult for you or beyond your reach*. . . . No, the word is very near you; it is in your mouth and in your heart so you may obey it. (Deuteronomy 30:6–14) (Emphasis mine)

The Law is to be followed by the present and all future generations. And, unlike Paul's position, the Law is not too difficult to follow. This is important because Paul's theology rests on the inability of humanity to follow the Law perfectly. But if God has given a law that we cannot possibly observe, then God must be sadistic and illogical. James rejects this reasoning.

Paul's response to humanity's imperfection is a sin offering in the form of Christ Jesus (Romans 8:3). Through this sacrifice God makes it possible for us to fulfill the righteous requirements of the Law. But Paul never really explains how this sacrifice nullifies an everlasting covenant. A human sacrifice is abhorrent to God. That God presents Jesus as a sin offering smacks of paganism, and the Jews cannot accept this. Paul does not care, for God's sin offering is targeted at his Gentile audience.

THE LIAR, THE ENEMY, AND THE TRAITOR

Knowing that James thoroughly discredits Paul's gospel, is the Dead Sea Scroll moniker, the Liar, a reference to Paul? Robert Eisenman makes just that assertion in his book *James the Brother of Jesus*. Paul wants to supplant the Jews as God's chosen people. How do the Jews respond to this "gospel"? Leaders of the Jewish Jesus Movement hound Paul and his congregations, calling Paul a liar and the enemy.

The later church tries deflecting such criticism from its main apostle, Paul. The book of Acts makes Paul into a hero and diminishes the roles of Peter and James. However, telltale passages in Paul's letters suggest that he is indeed branded as the Liar.

I speak the truth in Christ—I am not lying, my conscience confirms it in the Holy Spirit. (Romans 9:1)

We are treated as imposters, and yet are true. (2 Corinthians 6:8)

The God and Father of the Lord Jesus, who is to be praised forever, knows that I am not lying. (2 Corinthians 11:31)

I assure you before God that what I am writing you is no lie. (Galatians 1:20)

Obviously the charge of lying to the Gentiles is put forth more than once. Note that the denials are directed to the Romans, the Corinthians, and to those in Galatia. In fact, the charge of lying follows Paul wherever he goes. This may be one reason that Paul develops such an overwhelming hatred of the Fourth Philosophy and is active against them from 44 CE to the beginning of the Jewish war (66–67 CE).

Paul's defense against the lying charge is simple: he simply denies lying and swears by the name of God or by the Holy Spirit. How can you not believe Paul if he claims that the Holy Spirit confirms his message? After all Paul has direct revelations from God. This method of hiding behind God works well for Paul. And Paul's argument is strengthened by his supposed ties to the Risen Christ. Like members of any cult Paul's Gentile followers would have believed almost anything their charismatic teacher asserted.

The Liar label certainly fits Paul, but what about the Enemy? A liar may refer to someone still active in the movement, but an enemy opposes it. Such is the case with Paul, who, while still in the Jewish Jesus Movement, is beset with charges of lying to his followers. This comes to a head in the Antioch argument with Peter, where Paul is ousted from the movement. At this point Paul becomes the enemy.

This *enemy* terminology appears in the letter of James and in Paul's second letter to the Corinthians.

> You adulterous people, don't you know that *friendship with the world is hatred toward God?* Anyone who chooses to be a friend of the world becomes an *enemy of God.* (James 4:4) (Emphasis mine)

> I beg you that when I come I may not have to be as bold as I expect to be toward some people who think that *we live by the standards of this world.* . . . For if someone comes to you and preaches a Jesus other than the Jesus we preached, or if you received a different spirit from the one you received, or a different gospel from the one you accepted, you put up with it easily enough. But I do not think I am in the least inferior to those "super-apostles." (2 Corinthians 10:2; 11:4–5) (Emphasis mine)

James adamantly insists that living by the world's standards is equivalent to being an enemy of God. This is consistent with the words of Jesus: "No one can serve two masters. Either he will hate the one and love the other, or he will be devoted to the one and despise the other. You cannot serve both God and Money" (Matthew 6:24). By the time of the Antioch argument, James is well aware that Paul preaches against the Law, that he denigrates circumcision, and that he allows his disciples to eat food sacrificed to idols. To James anyone preaching against the Law is a friend of the world and an enemy of God.

Paul asserts that his gospel is God-given, breaking down the barriers between the God of the Jews and his Gentile disciples. Therefore, "living by the standards of this world" has no meaning for Paul. In fact, his gospel blurs the line between God and this world. With only the "Spirit" to guide them, his disciples have little chance to live a godly life. In 1 Corinthians 5:1 Paul admonishes his disciples: "It is actually reported that there is sexual immorality among you, and of a kind that does not occur even among pagans: A man has his father's wife." In response to this immoral action Paul asks that his church not associate with this type of individual. In a sense Paul is setting down his own law as the "Spirit" is unable to guide these poor souls. His "Spirit" theology is often used by his followers to cover up their own sins. This same mind-set is used today in Christian churches. If I sin, then God will forgive me because I am saved through the blood of Christ. Maybe Paul does not realize the implications of his new gospel, but when he sees the results, he does try to impose some sort of moral discipline. To the Romans he writes: "What then? Shall we sin because we are not under law but under grace? By no means!"

Paul becomes the enemy of the Jewish Jesus Movement after the Antioch argument with Peter, around 44 CE. Paul, then, is left with a Gentile following but no overarching Jewish Jesus Movement forcing him to play second fiddle to the pillar apostles. Initially, Paul still continues to gather contributions for those in Jerusalem. The title the "Enemy" may have been cast in stone by Paul's dealings with James and Peter after the fallout at Antioch.

The Pseudoclementine *Recognitions,* a second-century document, describes Paul as being the Enemy of the church around the mid-40s. The story may have been a distant memory handed down as an assault on James at the Temple in Jerusalem. This probably occurs when Paul brings the money he's raised to Jerusalem after the Antioch incident. (This money never goes to James, but rather to Paul's own coffers. Josephus tells us that Saul is very influential in 60s Jerusalem, and influence at that time is gained primarily through wealth and family connections.) In Jerusalem, Paul encounters James.

> Much blood is shed; there is a confused flight, in the midst of which that enemy attacked James, and threw him headlong from the top of the steps; and supposing him to be dead, he cared not to inflict further violence upon him. . . . Then after three days one of the brethren came to us from Gamaliel, . . . bringing to us secret tidings that the enemy had received a commission from Caiaphas, the chief priest, that he should arrest all who believed in Jesus, and should go to Damascus with his letters, and that there also, employing the help of the unbelievers, he should make havoc among the faithful; and that he was hastening to Damascus chiefly on this account, because he believed that Peter had fled thither. (Pseudoclementine *Recognitions* 1.70–71)

A marginal note in one of the Pseudoclementine *Recognitions* manuscripts associates the enemy with Paul.[1] This enemy receives a commission from the high priest to go to Damascus to persecute the church. A similar account from the book of Acts is attributed to Paul *before his conversion* (Acts 9:1–2). In the Pseudoclementine *Recognitions* Paul's (the Enemy's) actions occur *after his expulsion* from the movement. So is it possible that Paul attacks and almost kills James shortly after James has pulled the plug on Paul's ministry? From the differences between Paul and James noted above, such a possibility should not be discounted.

But we must go one step further. Paul is not only the Liar and the Enemy, but the Traitor as well. The term *traitor* has always been assigned to Judas Iscariot, but I propose that Paul, the apostle to the Gentiles, is the original traitor.

First, a traitor is someone who switches allegiances. This is certainly true of Paul. When Paul first converts he spends three years studying with the Fourth Philosophy. In Galatians 1:18 Paul states that he goes up to Jerusalem three years after his conversion. The Essenes have a three-year probation period for new recruits, and Judas the Galilean copies many of the same practices. This training would have grounded Paul in the Zealot philosophy. In his letters it is quite apparent that Paul understands the intricacies of the Fourth Philosophy even as he turns the scriptures on its head. He uses the same Genesis passage as James to justify his assertion that faith supersedes Torah observance. This takes knowledge and guts, to say the least. That Paul stays within the Jesus Movement for at least seventeen years is testament that he once followed the original gospel of Judas (Jesus), John the Baptist, James, and Peter.

Second, Paul denigrates the Jewish religion by twisting the Hebrew scriptures to suit his own desires. He somehow takes the Abraham story and makes it a promise to the Gentiles. This, however, would have angered the leadership of the Jesus Movement. Should we be surprised that the Jews all turn their backs on Paul at Antioch? If they had known Paul's entire gospel, they would have stoned him as well.

Third, soon after the split at Antioch, James and Simon, the sons of Judas the Galilean, are crucified. Could Paul have been behind this decision by the Roman procurator, Tiberius Alexander, a kinsman of Philo who knew Agrippa I, a cousin of Saul? Paul, no doubt, has access to Alexander. In addition, the Pseudoclementine *Recognitions* also have Saul attacking James, almost killing him and chasing Peter as far as Damascus. It seems as though Saul/Paul wants to even the score with the Fourth Philosophy.

Fourth, Saul is part of the larger ruling class that has a hand in the stoning of James in 62 CE. This is hidden in Acts as Saul approves of the stoning of Stephen, before his conversion. In reality Saul approves of the stoning of his longtime nemesis, James the Just.

Fifth, Saul tries to persuade Agrippa II to send forces to Jerusalem to defeat the Zealot and Sicarii forces. Saul/Paul would have been the object of the most sincere loathing by this time. No one could match

Paul's résumé when it comes to the traitor label. He earns this badge of dishonor with his every word and action. To the Fourth Philosophy he is the ultimate traitor.

The Epistle of James is addressed to a Gentile audience to combat the unlawful teachings of Paul and his disciples. James's representatives reach Corinth, Antioch, and King Izates' kingdom. In each case Paul's gospel is undermined. Depending on Paul's strength in these areas his gospel has a tough row to hoe. In Antioch Paul states that all the Jews, including Barnabas, have deserted him. In the case of King Izates the king accepts the representative of James over Paul's disciple. In Corinth Paul may have fared better. At least he is still trying; 2 Corinthians is a testament to his tenacity.

One thing must not be overlooked in this comparison of James and Paul: the two are opposed in everything. This is not just a difference of opinion but one gospel against another. James and Peter support the same gospel that Judas (Jesus) champions. Paul's gospel shifts the chosen people from the Jews to the Gentiles and is completely alien to anything taught by Jesus. Paul is rightly called the Liar, the Enemy, and the Traitor, for his gospel and his later actions are hell-bent on destroying the movement of Judas (Jesus).

5 ► Paul's Family Ties

Throughout this book I have been emphasizing the radically different time line that emerges using the Judas the Galilean hypothesis. Not only does the beginning of the Jesus Movement shift back a generation, so does the history of Paul. In the traditional time line Paul converts around 35 CE, visits Jerusalem for the second time around 52 CE, and finally sails to Rome between 60 and 62 CE. Using this traditional time line any connection between Paul and Agrippa I would be nearly impossible to establish, since Agrippa I rules as king of Israel from 37 to 44 CE.

Under my revised time line Paul joins the Jewish Jesus Movement around 21–25 CE, visits Jerusalem for the second time around 38–42 CE, and is ousted from the movement in 44 CE. This revised time line overlaps the kingship of Agrippa I, making it possible to ferret out some connection between the two individuals. In the book of Acts Paul converses with Agrippa II, the son of Agrippa I, also known as Agrippa the Great. Could Paul have known the father as well? If so, then the actual ministry of Paul may have been aligned with Agrippa I and opposed to the Fourth Philosophy; that is, opposed to James and Peter.

ALL IN THE FAMILY[1]

Several important branches stem from Herod the Great's dynasty, the most important being those of Agrippa I and Paul (again, known as

Saul in Josephus's *Antiquities*). Remember that Agrippa I is a friend and advisor to both Caligula and Claudius and wields great power in Judea during his reign. The table below illustrates the close ties between Agrippa's family and Paul's family. To fully appreciate Paul's motives in preaching his new antinomian gospel, we must first understand Paul's possible relationship to Agrippa I. After all Agrippa I is a powerful force, seen as a Messiah figure by many Jews of his time.

AGRIPPA I'S LINE	PAUL'S LINE
Antipater	Antipater (great-grandfather)
Herod the Great	Salome (sister of Herod the Great)
Aristobulus (marries Bernice)	Antipater (brother of Bernice)
Agrippa I (37–44 CE)	Paul
Agrippa II (49–93 CE)	

In *Antiquities* 20.214 Paul, a kinsman of the royal family, persecutes the poor priests after the stoning of James. From Josephus we know that Paul is related to Agrippa. This is further confirmed by another story from Josephus, where Paul petitions Agrippa II for an army to crush the rebellion in Jerusalem (*War* 2.418–419). Once again Josephus calls Paul a relative of the king.

So how exactly are Agrippa and Paul related? From Josephus, the following can be gleaned. Both Agrippa I and Paul have a great-grandfather, Antipater, in common. Agrippa I is a grandson of Herod the Great, while Paul's grandmother is Salome, the sister of Herod the Great. This would make them distant cousins of a sort, but it does not prove that the two branches of the family were close.

But there is more to this family connection. Agrippa's father, Aristobulus, marries Paul's Aunt Bernice. This slightly incestuous relationship produces several children, including Agrippa, who becomes very important in the story of Israel. So there are two different familial connections between Agrippa and Paul—one through a great-grandfather and one through marriage. This enhances the possibility of close relations between the family of Agrippa and the family of Paul, but in no way positively puts the two men together. It is just a starting point.

Agrippa I marries Cypros, a cousin descended from Herod the Great's brother, Phasaelus. Niece and cousin marriages are common among the Herodians, suggesting that the entire family have somewhat close ties. Perhaps this also preserves assets within the family. (No need to grasp the intricacies of the family ties here. Just keep in mind that Agrippa I and Paul are related.)

DIFFERING PATHS

Agrippa I (10 BCE–44 CE) and Paul (5–1 BCE–67+ CE)

Would Agrippa and Paul have known each other as children? The answer is no. Agrippa is born around 10 BCE and is shipped to Rome shortly after Herod the Great executes his father, Aristobulus, in 6 BCE. Paul, on the other hand, is probably born between 5 and 1 BCE, based on his own account and that of Josephus. Paul and Agrippa never met as children, then, but their families were closely connected, which may well have linked the two later in life.

At a very young age Agrippa I becomes close friends with Claudius, a future Caesar. He also befriends Antonia, Claudius's mother, and eventually becomes close with Caligula, Claudius's nephew. So even though Agrippa's life begins in the land of Judea, his friends are the power elites of the Roman Empire.

Agrippa spends money freely as a youth. When his mother, Bernice, dies he quickly runs through his inheritance. A constant search for new funds shapes Agrippa's life. He becomes very good at asking for help and borrows money from Antonia and from Alexander, the governor of the Jews at Alexandria. This Alexander is the brother of Philo and the father of Tiberius Alexander, the procurator of Judea when Judas the Galilean's sons, Simon and James, are crucified. No man could have done more to arouse the anger of the Fourth Philosophy. Agrippa I also draws on the help of his sister's husband, Herod Antipas, the tetrarch, responsible for the death of John the Baptist.

Through Tiberius Agrippa I becomes a great friend to Caligula. Upon the death of Tiberius Caligula becomes emperor and gives Agrippa the tetrarchy of Philip and the tetrarchy of Lysanius (*Antiquities* 18.237). He is later given the tetrarchy of Herod Antipas after he suggests that Antipas is a threat to Caligula. In short Agrippa becomes a very powerful man in a very short period. Agrippa aligns himself with the powers of Rome, so it should not be surprising that his views and those of the Fourth Philosophy are diametrically opposed.

While Agrippa I rubs elbows with the rich and powerful, Paul operates under the radar. Nothing is known of Paul's very early life. Around the age of twenty he is driven from Judea for transgressing the Law. Paul only visits Jerusalem twice after his conversion and he never goes to Rome, having good reason to stay away from these two cities. In Galatians 1:13–17 Paul claims that he converts to the Church of God, and after three years, he travels to Jerusalem to meet with Peter. This three-year stint after the conversion may have been Paul's initiation into the Jewish Jesus Movement. Paul learns the Law from the most zealous of Zealots, but only *after* his conversion. Note that in Galatians 1:13–17 Paul states that he is zealous for the Law *before* his conversion, even though he had been run out of town for transgressing the Law just a few years before his conversion. In fact, Paul is simply distancing himself from the pillar apostles, those Zealots opposed to his gospel of grace. If Paul is telling the truth, he would acknowledge that he was trained to follow the Law, and that the original Jewish Jesus Movement is all about the Law. But Paul would never acknowledge this truth.

From the years 21 to 37 CE Paul is a member of the Jewish Jesus Movement, following the Law and the guidance of John the Baptist and James for most of this time. Not until his seventeenth year in the movement does he come once again to Jerusalem, to present his gospel to the Gentiles, sometime between 38 and 40 CE. While Agrippa I returns to Jerusalem in 37 CE as a king, appointed by Caligula, his cousin Paul also heads back to his roots in Jerusalem. Is this a coincidence or is Paul drawn back in order to meet this new king? From Paul's own words we learn that he met privately with the leaders (the pillars). Could he also have met with his own family? He does not say this, but we must not rule out the possibility.

THE MAKING OF A MESSIAH

Messiah simply means "anointed one" or "king." In this sense many Messiahs can be found in Israel's past. But the expectations of a Great Messiah from God percolate throughout first-century Judea. According to Numbers 24:17: "A Star will come out of Jacob; a scepter will rise out of Israel." This is the Star Prophecy (disguised in Matthew's gospel as the Star of Bethlehem), promising that a world leader will arise in Israel.

The prophesied Jewish messiah would be a political figure, a king, a ruler over Israel in the lineage of David. He would be an important person who would assist God in bringing about the messianic kingdom, a time in human history when God would destroy evil and reward the righteous, those holding steadfast to his laws (the Torah). It would be an era of peace with everyone coming to worship the one God. Others envisage it as a time when the righteous dead would be brought back to life (that is, resurrected) and the exiles would return from around the globe. The Messiah would be the true "king of the Jews." Every would-be messiah covets that title—Judas the Galilean, Simon of Perea, Herod the Great, and "Jesus"—but only Agrippa I is accorded that recognition and honor by Rome.

Few view Agrippa as the Great Messiah, but his entreaty to Caligula on behalf of the Jews, when Caligula wants a statue of himself placed in the Temple, offers food for thought. Standing up to Caligula may have cast Agrippa as the promised Messiah in the eyes of Philo, the Alexandrian representative who actually witnessed Agrippa's efforts to forestall Caligula's plans to erect a statue in the Jerusalem Temple.[2]

According to Josephus (*Antiquities* 18.289–309) Agrippa I provides Caligula with a supper surpassing all others in extravagance and expense. This impresses Caligula so much that he offers to grant any wish of Agrippa's, assuming that Agrippa wants more power, more land to govern. Agrippa's wish that Caligula refrain from putting his statue in the Temple catches Caligula off guard. It bothers Caligula, but he agrees to Agrippa's wish since his promise has been made publicly. So with a great meal and ingenuity, Agrippa I might have saved the Temple. Unfortunately, a letter arrives from Petronius, the commander in Judea, informing Caligula that the Jews will revolt if he places the statue in the Temple. The thought that any subject would revolt against his government drives Caligula wild. He writes back to Petronius, demanding that he take his own life as an example to those who disobey the Roman authorities. Thus, Caligula determines to make the statue a reality in the Temple of Jerusalem. Agrippa I is defeated for the moment, but luck or good planning later saves the day for Agrippa and the Jews.

While the Jews in Jerusalem prepare for war with Rome, due to the impending defilement of the Temple, Agrippa I is active in Rome. In 41 CE the emperor Caligula is assassinated soon after writing to Petronius. Luckily for Petronius the news of Caligula's death arrives before Caligula's letter demanding the commander's own death. Although Agrippa is never implicated in the assassination plot, he nevertheless exploits the situation. No one benefits more from Caligula's death than Agrippa I.

According to Josephus Caligula is slain by Cherea and others (*Antiquities* 19.114). Great confusion ensues as the crowds question whether Caligula is dead or just wounded, affording time for Agrippa and Claudius to leave the scene. Is Agrippa responsible for the confusion? Although Caligula is clearly dead a report claims "that although *Gaius [Caligula] had been wounded indeed, yet was not he dead, but alive still and under the physician's hands*" (*Antiquities* 19.134). Is this report from Agrippa?

Josephus subsequently writes* that it is Agrippa who is responsible for the misleading report and that he later rushes to the support of Claudius, urging him to take the reins of power (*Antiquities* 19.237–238). Agrippa I is everywhere, in total command. The assassination not

---

*Why does Josephus omit Agrippa's role in his initial account of the assassination? Maybe Josephus is uncomfortable writing about the assassination of a Caesar by a Jewish king. This would have cast the Jews in a damning light.

only saves the Temple of Jerusalem and staves off inevitable war with the Jews, but it places a malleable Claudius on the throne. This long-time friend of Agrippa would prove beneficial to Agrippa's future plans.

As a reward for masterminding his ascension, Claudius makes Agrippa's territory equal to that of his grandfather, Herod the Great. Not only does Agrippa return to Jerusalem with more land to control, but he has also helped save the Jewish nation from war with Rome. Without Agrippa's influence and shrewd action, the statue of Caligula would have polluted the Temple. And now Agrippa is the main coun-selor of the Roman emperor. Certainly, to a great number of Jews, Agrippa is beginning to look like the promised Messiah.

PAUL'S REVELATIONS

Most people assume that Paul's message has always been centered on grace and the blood of Christ. However, by his own words, Paul does not seek a conference with James until seventeen years have elapsed since his conversion (Galatians 1:18–2:2). In most of these seventeen years Paul is a loyal worker, obeying the dictates of the Jewish pillars, not at all influential within the Jewish Jesus Movement. This all changes with his wild revelations.

These revelations come late within the seventeen-year period. If Paul converts in 21–22 CE, then the Council of Jerusalem takes place around 38–39 CE. Therefore, the revelations begin around 37–38 CE, a short time before the Council convenes. This date corresponds with the awarding of titles and land to his cousin, Agrippa. Before the rev-elations Paul must have been somewhat despondent over his life within the Jewish Jesus Movement. He is a competitive man, as his letters show. While his cousin Agrippa rubs elbows with the Roman emperor, he is stuck preaching the Law to Jewish converts as well as God-fearing Gentiles. This may have been a noble profession, but it pales in com-parison to his cousin's accomplishments. The question is this: Do Paul's revelations have anything to do with Agrippa's rise to power?

The Fourth Philosophy states that "God [was] to be their only

Ruler and Lord" (*Antiquities* 18.23) with no distinction between the spiritual and earthly realms. The book of Revelation also follows this early pattern. The enemy is Rome and the church will be saved by God through the power of the returning Messiah, Jesus. Adherents of the early Jesus Movement never envision their resurrected Messiah working hand in hand with the earthly powers of the day. On the contrary the resurrected Messiah will return to obliterate the earthly powers.

This concept of good versus evil is inconvenient for Paul. On the one hand Paul preaches the resurrected Messiah. On the other hand Paul's own cousin, Agrippa, is now king of Israel and possesses great influence over Claudius, the Roman emperor. How can Paul follow these two different paths?

Paul simply splits the spiritual from the earthly. Christ Jesus becomes a personal savior god, much like the savior gods worshipped throughout the Roman Empire. Paul's Christ Jesus could wash away sins, making it possible for the convert to enter paradise, far from the troubles of this world. Through the Spirit, Christ Jesus could also help in the present world, but Christ Jesus is not returning to Earth to lead a government. There could be no greater repudiation of the Fourth Philosophy than Paul's glowing tribute to the ruling authorities in Romans 13:1–7. By Paul's own words the authorities are established by God, to be obeyed as one would obey God. Let us ask a few questions of Paul's radical pro-government philosophy. Does God institute the authorities who crucified Jesus? Is Jesus punished by God's servant for being a wrongdoer? Romans, a tribute to the ruling elites, is written in the early 40s, just after Claudius becomes emperor. Caligula has recently been assassinated, in 41 CE. Is Caligula one of God's servants? Is it not Caligula who planned to place a statue of himself in the Temple? Does God sanction this? Though Claudius is a capable emperor the following emperor is Nero, who tortures the early Jewish "Christians" in 64 CE. Is Nero's reign sanctioned by God?

Paul's support of the Roman authorities could not have been condoned by the followers of Jesus (Judas the Galilean), James, and Peter. At this point Paul seeks the favor of Agrippa over James. An expulsion of Jesus's Jewish followers from Rome occurs during the early days of Claudius's reign, when King Agrippa advises him. Only Agrippa can distinguish one group of Jews from another. Certainly, Claudius cannot independently pinpoint which groups of Jews are the most incendiary. Agrippa simply suggests that Claudius ban the practices of the Fourth Philosophy. Interestingly, Paul urges his own disciples to steer clear of the Fourth Philosophy, antigovernment fanatics. Paul calls on his disciples to be good citizens, good followers of Claudius, and a perfect template for Agrippa. Paul is anxious to show Agrippa that he can control this other messianic movement.

In short Paul's tribute to the ruling authorities is meant primarily for Agrippa, for Paul wants to work with his cousin. In a sense Paul envisions himself as the prophet behind the king. In the Jesus Movement Paul is insignificant, but with Agrippa he can wield enormous power. The shift of power to Agrippa in 37 CE coincides with Paul's revelations from God. While these revelations have nothing to do with God and are diametrically opposed to the teachings of the historical Jesus, they serve as a way for Paul to shift his own allegiance from the earthly Jesus to the earthly Agrippa. Christ Jesus is now simply a spiritual force in individual salvation.

This is quite a different read of Paul than the one reflected in the sanitized book of Acts, but it makes sense in terms of Paul's motivation and accounts for his success as well as his protection by Roman authorities.

By now the careful reader is aware that not only do we have a mythologized Jesus overlaying the actual Jesus of history, we also have a mythologized Paul overlaying the real Paul of history. This poses problems for the researcher trying to ferret out the truth about first-century history.

TWO MESSIAHS IN JERUSALEM

Increased power, earned by his close association with Claudius, places Agrippa I in a position to vie for the love and approval of the Jews.

Not since the days of Herod the Great have the Jewish people had such close relations with the greatest power on Earth, Rome. This pleases the upper class, the wealthy of society, but the Fourth Philosophy views Agrippa as a threat to its own claim of Jesus (Judas the Galilean) as the promised Messiah, resurrected from the dead and soon to return in power and glory. But Agrippa's followers can claim that the Messiah already resides on Earth, in the body of Agrippa I. This power struggle focuses on two Messiahs—one governing and one still awaiting the fulfillment of God's final plan.

Up until now Agrippa I has had little concern for the people of Israel, but by 37 CE he has built a formidable résumé.

How then does Agrippa deal with the Fourth Philosophy? After a few years in Jerusalem, Agrippa becomes well aware of his greatest opposition party. In Rome, Agrippa persuades Claudius to expel the Jewish followers of Judas the Galilean. Suetonius writes: "The Jews he [Claudius] expelled from Rome, since they were constantly in rebellion, at the instigation of Chrestus [Judas the Galilean]."[3] Around this time Claudius also publishes an edict proclaiming that the Jews should be treated as other Roman citizens and be allowed to observe their religious customs as long as they exhibit friendship toward Rome (*Antiquities* 19.278–291). This edict applies to the majority of Jews but not those Jews calling for war against Rome. Note that Claudius expels the troublemakers who are members of the Fourth Philosophy and bitterly opposed to both Claudius and his advisor, Agrippa. So the earliest recorded action by Agrippa against the Fourth Philosophy occurs very early in Claudius's reign, around 41–42 CE.

The next recorded conflict between the two Messiah movements appears in Josephus and is also included in the book of Acts as a rewrite of history, dated at 43 CE. A certain preacher named Simon insists that Agrippa be banned from the Temple, since Agrippa is not a native Jew. Agrippa sends for Simon and tries to persuade him to stop preaching this incendiary message (*Antiquities* 19.332–334).

This passage also illustrates Josephus's admiration for Agrippa I and his disdain for Simon and the Fourth Philosophy. Even though

Josephus is a young boy when this event occurs, he adds details that make Agrippa seem magnanimous. Although no one records the conversation between Agrippa and Simon, Josephus writes that Agrippa speaks with "a low and gentle voice."

In Acts' rewrite of history (Acts 10), at the request of an angel, Cornelius (a stand-in for Agrippa I) sends his soldier to Joppa to bring Simon Peter to Caesarea. At this same time Simon Peter experiences his own visions, instructing him to accept Gentiles into the Jesus Movement. This inclusionary message is antithetical to that of the historical Simon, who preaches that Agrippa should be banned from the Temple because he is not a native Jew. After all, Agrippa spends his early life in Augustus's court beside the likes of Claudius, and during the reign of Tiberius he befriends Caligula. This alone is reason to ban him from the Temple. So this divide between Simon and Agrippa is both religious and political, since adherents of the Fourth Philosophy do not distinguish between religion and politics. For them God is the only Ruler. How can they ever accept Agrippa's authority? Agrippa knows Simon's attitude and commands him to stop his preaching. Like Jesus before Pilate, Simon remains quiet before Agrippa. The rewriting of the passage from an exclusionary story to an inclusionary one is important. Certainly, the meeting between Simon and Agrippa has been part of the Fourth Philosophy's tradition, a clash between the good Messiah's representative (Simon) and the evil Messiah (Agrippa).

Simon goes back to Jerusalem and begins preaching against Agrippa again. This can be deduced by the next event described in Acts 12. According to this passage, Agrippa arrests James and Simon Peter. James is beheaded and Simon Peter languishes in prison for a preordained guilty verdict to be carried out after Passover; that is, after the crowds leave Jerusalem. Snippets of truth emerge from this passage. From Josephus we know that the sons of Judas the Galilean, James and Simon, are crucified under the procurator, Tiberius Alexander, around 46 CE (*Antiquities* 20.102). These are the real James and Simon, arrested shortly before Agrippa's death. They later suffer crucifixion as a warning to the Fourth Philosophy. Earlier, during the governorship of Fadus (44–46 CE), Theudas is beheaded (*Antiquities* 20.97–99). The book of Acts combines these two accounts by Josephus, taking the sons of Judas the Galilean, James and Simon, and changing them into James, the son of Zebedee, and Simon Peter. In addition, James, the son of Zebedee, is beheaded consistent with Theudas's story.

This account is further bolstered by the Slavonic Josephus.

> At this time [during the reigns of Fadus and Tiberius Alexander] there appeared many servants of the previously described wonder-worker [Jesus], telling the people about their master, that he was [still] alive although he had died. And [they said], "He will free you from servitude." . . . But the grateful governors seeing the subversion of the people, planned with the scribes to take them and destroy them. (SJ *War* 2.220, from additional passages)

The Slavonic Josephus corresponds to the account of Theudas and the sons of Judas the Galilean (*Antiquities* 20.97–102), stating that these servants were followers of the wonder worker, directly tying the sons of Judas the Galilean to Jesus. The persecution by the governors is designed to silence the Jesus Movement, but it just creates more martyrs.

So even though Acts 12 rewrites history, facts emerge about Agrippa. Agrippa opposes the Jesus Movement and vigorously persecutes it, acting as a king protecting his throne, not wanting the Fourth Philosophy to thrive.

While Agrippa persecutes the Fourth Philosophy, he pursues alliances with other kings in the region. According to Robert Graves, Agrippa has close relations with the following kings: the king of Chalcis, the king of Iturea, the king of Adiabene, the king of Osroene, the king of Lesser Armenia, the king of Pontus and Cilicia, the king of Commagene, and the prospective king of Parthia.[4] These alliances are intolerable to the emperor Claudius, as Israel has always been the crossroads to Egypt. This confederation of kings may have eventually threatened Rome.

The New Judaism of Agrippa I

The above-mentioned king of Adiabene is named Izates, and his account ties Agrippa to Paul. Izates's tale, discussed in chapter 2, plays out near the time of Agrippa's death, around 43–44 CE. Two preachers attempt to sway Izates to their viewpoint concerning circumcision and the Jewish law. The agent of Agrippa is named Ananias, preaching a message consistent with that of Paul. He tells Izates "that he might worship God without being circumcised, even though he did resolve to follow the Jewish law entirely; which worship of God was of a superior nature to circumcision" (*Antiquities* 20.41). Like Paul Ananias preaches a different kind of Judaism, one downplaying the importance of circumcision. This kind of new Judaism appeals to the Gentile community. But why teach such a new Judaism?

Political considerations shape Ananias's new Judaism. Surely, Izates's subjects would be outraged if he converted to a different religion (*Antiquities* 20.42). This shows the genius of Agrippa. He wants to court the kings of the surrounding areas by spreading a new kind of Judaism through his representative Ananias, aimed at binding the rulers together. Again, this gospel differs little from the one Paul peddles. This question must be raised: Is Paul also spreading the gospel of Agrippa? His argument with Peter, as outlined in Galatians, is no different than the argument between Ananias and Eleazar in the King Izates episode.

Also note that the other preacher in the Izates story is named Eleazar, sent from Galilee. His message, consistent with the Fourth Philosophy, persuades King Izates to undergo circumcision and become a full Jew (*Antiquities* 20.43–47). As it turns out Izates's subjects do not revolt against him but accept his decision to embrace another religion. Eleazar is sent from Galilee around 44 CE to combat the preaching of Ananias. This same thing happens at Antioch. While Peter stays with Paul at Antioch, "certain men came from James . . . those who belonged to the circumcision group" (Galatians 2:12). The circumcision group insists that the Gentiles become full Jews by undergoing circumcision.

The Fourth Philosophy is fighting back against Agrippa and his agents (Ananias and Paul) at this time. Also, at the same time, King

Agrippa is poisoned and dies a painful death, as recorded in Acts 12:19–23 and in *Antiquities* 19.343–52.

Several important points in the Acts account must be highlighted. First, the author of Acts supplies some data supporting the idea that Agrippa actively pursues alliances with other kings. In addition, the people of Tyre and Sidon sue for peace because Agrippa controls their food supply. This very well may have happened. Another point concerns the death of Agrippa. According to Acts, Agrippa dies because he fails to immediately give praise to God after he has been compared to a god. Of course, historically, this is absolute folly. People are not struck down because they do not credit God with this or that accomplishment. The fact of Agrippa's death should not be questioned, but we need to come up with a logical alternative to replace the supernatural explanation.

Before exploring the alternative to the supernatural, we must also examine Josephus's take on Agrippa's death. According to Josephus Agrippa wears a garment made of silver that shines brilliantly in the sunlight. Flatterers cry out that he looks like a god. Agrippa does not contradict these flatteries, but immediately looks up and sees an owl, an omen of death. Agrippa becomes ill but lives with "the pain in his belly for five days" before his death (*Antiquities* 19.343–350). The cause of death is not retribution from God. Rather, the pain in Agrippa's belly is due to poison. (If Agrippa died of natural causes, such as appendicitis, then his death was certainly convenient.) Undoubtedly, Agrippa is assassinated. Who has a motive to kill Agrippa? There are two clear possibilities: the Jewish Jesus Movement and the agents of Claudius.

No group had a greater motive to assassinate Agrippa than the followers of the Way of Judas the Galilean. Agrippa advises Claudius to persecute the followers of "Christ" and imprisons two sons of Judas the Galilean. But can the Jewish Jesus Movement, once guided by John the Baptist, commit murder? Yes, since Agrippa represents a real threat. He styles himself as an alternative Messiah, the polar opposite to Judas the Galilean (Jesus). Such a strike against the Herodians and Romans is indeed bold, but possibly the Jesus Movement's best alternative.

Agrippa's death is not viewed as murder but as a gift from God.

In the Golden Eagle Temple Cleansing (4 BCE), Matthias and Judas take advantage of Herod the Great's supposed death and instigate an uprising against the government. Likewise, James the Just and the Fourth Philosophy benefit from Agrippa's death. Shortly after the poisoning Acts 12:24 states that "the word of God continued to increase and spread." If adherents of the Fourth Philosophy did not commit the murder, they nevertheless exploited the power vacuum left by his death.

The only other suspects would be the agents of Claudius. Agrippa's strategy of aligning himself with other kings in the region is a worrisome development for Rome. Before relating the death of Agrippa, Josephus mentions that Marcus, the president of Syria, has concerns that Agrippa's alliances with other kings are not in the interests of Rome (*Antiquities* 19.341–342).

Would Claudius have ordered the assassination of Agrippa I? Their friendship from an early age would have made such an act difficult. However, poisonings were commonplace among the Caesars. Claudius's grandmother, Livia, made a living out of poisoning her real and perceived enemies. Claudius's brother, Germanicus, was also poisoned by Piso while stationed in the East (*Antiquities* 18.54). So the act of poisoning is not unknown to Claudius. Perhaps the deed was carried out by an underling wishing to protect the Empire, knowing full well that Claudius could never order the death of such a close friend and advisor. Marcus may have viewed Agrippa's behavior as dangerous to the empire and could have acted on these notions.

Whether assassinated by the Fourth Philosophy or by Rome, the death of Agrippa must have emboldened the Fourth Philosophy. After his death, Theudas goes out to the Jordan and promises to divide it as Moses parted the Red Sea (*Antiquities* 20.97–98). This messianic act is crushed by Fadus. The messianic fervor must have continued as the next procurator, Tiberius Alexander, orders the crucifixions of Simon and James, the sons of Judas the Galilean (*Antiquities* 20.102). Arrested during the last year of Agrippa's life, they now suffer crucifixion, a warning to dampen the fires of revolution, similar to Herod Antipas's beheading of John the Baptist (*Antiquities* 18.116–119).

The death of Agrippa also causes James the Just to rethink his policy regarding Gentiles. James never fully understands Paul's gospel and fails to recognize how popular Paul's approach is becoming. Agrippa's agents are converting Gentiles to a new Judaism, one thriving without the Law and circumcision. James immediately dispatches envoys to address the situation. In the cases of Paul and Peter in Antioch and the King Izates conversion, representatives of James (circumcision group) reestablish the Law's importance to Gentile converts, ending Paul's participation in the Jesus Movement. His double-agent cover has been blown. No longer can he preach the virtues of both a supernatural Messiah (Christ Jesus) and an earthly Messiah (Agrippa).

At this point, Paul turns against the Fourth Philosophy. His letters to the Galatians and Corinthians point to a severed relationship between himself and the pillars, those super-apostles whom he compares to the servants of Satan (2 Corinthians 11:1–15). Other literature paints Paul as an enemy of the early church in the 40s. The Pseudoclementine *Recognitions* 1.70–71 accuses Paul of trying to kill James and chasing after Peter with the same intent.

QUESTIONABLE FAMILY TIES—PAUL'S SISTER AND NEPHEW

In the story of Paul's arrest in Jerusalem the book of Acts introduces the son of Paul's sister (Acts 23:12–22). This unnamed nephew is privy to information concerning the activities of forty men, in collaboration with the chief priests and elders, who wish to assassinate Paul. Armed with knowledge of the plot, the nephew goes into the Roman barracks and warns Paul. Paul then directs his nephew to inform the Roman commander of this plot. The Romans find the nephew's story credible, and save Paul from the Jews.

Many scholars view the familial details in the Acts account as proof of its veracity. After all, the introduction of a sister and a nephew at this stage of the narrative seems out of place in a completely fabricated story. Why introduce new characters into the story, especially characters related to Paul? Why not just say that the Romans received anonymous information about the plot? Surely, these familial details make the story more authentic.

However, if viewed critically, this episode raises some interesting questions. First, Paul never mentions a sister or a nephew in any of his letters. In his letters and in Acts his only possible familial connections are to the Herodians.[5] This does not rule out a sister or a nephew; it only means that they too would be Herodians.

Second, if Paul hails from Tarsus,* then what kind of connections could he possibly have had in Jerusalem? This same question could also be asked of his sister and nephew. In addition, according to his own writings, Paul only visits Jerusalem twice after his conversion, covering a seventeen-year stretch. Both visits last a short time (Galatians 1:13–2:10).† Paul is an infrequent visitor to Jerusalem, which makes the appearance of his sister and nephew in Jerusalem even more suspect, if they also come from Tarsus. Perhaps Paul writes to his sister, telling her of his Jerusalem plans. But, according to Acts, even the Holy Spirit cannot decide if Paul should visit Jerusalem.‡ With so much indecision, would Paul have arranged for his sister to be in Jerusalem? After all how could a supposedly unconnected woman and her son help him? And would any message have been delivered to her in time?

Third, the dating of the Acts story must be questioned. Supposedly, forty men want to assassinate Paul for his teachings concerning the Law

---

*In Acts 9:11 the Lord commands Ananias to ask for a man from Tarsus named Saul. Saul is then sent back to Tarsus by the Apostles (Acts 9:30) and later brought back to Antioch by Barnabas (Acts 11:25–26).

†Acts 11:27–30 also has Paul visiting Jerusalem during the famine (44–48 CE). If this really happens before the Council of Jerusalem, then why does Paul fail to mention it in Galatians? Paul may have gone to Jerusalem with money, but that occurs after his split from the Fourth Philosophy at Antioch, consistent with the 44 CE King Izates story (*Antiquities* 20.34–48).

‡In Acts 20:22–24 the Holy Spirit compels Paul to travel to Jerusalem. In Acts 21:4 the disciples at Tyre are urged by the Spirit to dissuade Paul from his journey. And finally, in Acts 21:10–15, the Holy Spirit reveals to the prophet Agabus that Paul will suffer in Jerusalem because of the Jews.

and circumcision. These forty would have been members of the Sicarii movement or followers of Judas the Galilean. The author of Acts has these forty men working together with the chief priests in 58 CE. At that time these two groups were mortal enemies (*Antiquities* 20.200–214). Cooperation in this time frame is inconceivable. Could there have been any time when cooperation was possible? After the Temple cleansing by Menahem (66 CE), the Zealot factions control the Temple and would have appointed their own priests to minister at the Temple. So, in 66 CE, the Sicarii and the chief priests may have been in total agreement concerning the fate of Paul.

Identities of Paul's Sister and Nephew

Working on the assumption that Paul of Tarsus is Saul, the cousin of Agrippa I, we can easily identify the sister and nephew. Saul's sister's name is Cypros, the daughter of Antipater and Cypros. She is married to Alexas Selcias, the son of Alexas, a Temple treasurer (*Antiquities* 18.138). This answers the question raised above: How could the sister and nephew have connections with the Romans and have knowledge of happenings around the Temple? Even though Saul may have steered clear of Jerusalem prior to 44 CE, he no doubt spent time there with his Herodian family after being ousted from the Jewish Jesus Movement at Antioch. His sister, who was married to the Temple treasurer, no doubt lived in Jerusalem. Saul and his brother, Costobar, must have been privy to her connections while in Jerusalem.

Paul's nephew is named Julius Archelaus. Josephus notes that Archelaus is married to Agrippa I's daughter, Mariamme (*Antiquities* 19.354–355). He, therefore, had connections through Agrippa's own family as well as being Temple treasurer. Later, Josephus claims him among his own friends in Rome.[6]

Paul's connections to the Romans and the royal family in Jerusalem help explain how his sister and nephew could have been of any use to him while he was in Jerusalem. This added piece to the Paul puzzle may cement Paul's true identity as Saul, cousin of Agrippa I.

PAUL'S ESCAPE FROM JERUSALEM

After the defeat of Cestius, the Jewish collaborators with Rome fear for their lives. Paul, Costobar, and Antipas appeal to Agrippa II to send forces to quell the uprising (*War* 2.418–421). They remain in Jerusalem after the defeat of Cestius, but something compels Paul and Costobar to run from the city while Antipas remains behind (*War* 2.556–558). Is it possible that Saul learns of the plot against him from his nephew? If so, then that would explain his actions. Perhaps Antipas either does not receive the information about the plot or he does not think his own life will be in danger. Why else would he have stayed in Jerusalem? Antipas makes the wrong decision, and he is slain for his traitorous collaboration with the Romans (*War* 4.140–146). A group of ten men are dispatched with the assignment to slay Antipas and other traitors. Could this be the source of the Acts account, where forty men take an oath to kill Paul (Acts 23:13)?

6 ➤ Paul's Motivation

PAUL AND JERUSALEM

What is Paul's motivation throughout his ministry? Is he motivated by greed, by a thirst for notoriety, by fear of damnation, or by the love of Christ? Or do all these elements combine in his complex nature? A few passages from Josephus and from Paul's letters will help pinpoint the overriding motivation behind the extraordinary career of the apostle to the Gentiles.

The first passage, written by Josephus, can be dated at around 20 CE, placed shortly after the *Testimonium Flavianum*. This passage points to Paul's first attempt at fund-raising by means of religion.

> There was a man who was a Jew, but had been driven away from his own country by an accusation laid against him for *transgressing their laws,* and by the fear he was under of punishment for the same; but in all respects *a wicked man:*—he then living in Rome, *professed to instruct men in the wisdom of the laws of Moses. He procured also three other men, entirely of the same character with himself, to be his partners.* These men persuaded Fulvia, a woman of great dignity, and one who had embraced the Jewish religion, *to send purple and gold to the Temple at Jerusalem;* and, when they had gotten them, they employed them for their own uses, and *spent the money themselves;* on which account it was that they at first required it of

her. Whereupon Tiberius, who had been informed of the thing by
Saturninus, the husband of Fulvia, who desired inquiry might be
made about it, ordered all the Jews to be banished out of Rome; at
which time the consuls listed four thousand men out of them, and
sent them to the island Sardinia; but punished a greater number of
them, who were unwilling to become soldiers on account of keeping the laws of their forefathers. Thus were these Jews banished out
of the city by the wickedness of four men. (*Antiquities* 18.81–85)
(Emphasis mine)

Although Josephus does not mention Saul by name, striking similarities exist between the unnamed Jew and Saul.* First, the scoundrel
transgresses the law of Moses and is forced to flee his native land. He
then settles in Rome, where he instructs naive Jewish converts in the
wisdom of the law of Moses. So we know that the con artist would
have burned bridges in both Jerusalem and Rome. According to Paul
he only travels to Jerusalem in private and never once visits Rome,
perhaps due to his infamy there (Galatians 1:18–2:5 and Romans 1:8–
10; 15:23–33).

Second, like Paul, the unnamed Jew instructs men in the wisdom of
Moses. This Jew has earlier been expelled from Israel for transgressing
the law of Moses, but now teaches a version of that Law to unsuspecting
Jewish converts. (Note that Paul teaches his followers a different gospel,
one condemned by James and Peter.)

Third, the unnamed Jew works with three other men to deceive
their willing victims. This modus operandi is used by Paul, who works
with others to spread the gospel of Christ Jesus. Paul often employs the
good cop/bad cop strategy. He acts tender and loving, while his sub-
ordinates warn his disciples that he harbors wrath over their behavior.
He easily adapts his approach to each situation. In addition, after the
stoning of James the Just, Josephus writes that Saul gets "together a

---

*Saul's name may have been removed from Josephus's manuscript by later Christians. The
passage in question comes shortly after the TF, which was altered to read like a confession of faith about Jesus of Nazareth.

multitude of wicked wretches" to do his bidding (*Antiquities* 20.214). In short, the unnamed Jew and Paul both use others to do their dirty work.

Fourth, the unnamed Jew uses the Temple and Jerusalem to raise money. In his teachings he misrepresents his standing with the Jerusalem authorities. Even though he is driven out of Israel, he now pries money from gullible Jewish converts who want to support their religion. Paul invokes Jerusalem and the Temple in his fund-raising appeals to his followers.

Fifth, the money never makes it to Jerusalem or to the Temple, but remains with the unnamed Jew. In the case of Saul Josephus writes of his wealth and association with the political elites. How does Saul come by his wealth? From his unsuspecting converts and disciples?

PAUL AND FUND-RAISING

Four authentic Pauline letters will now be examined to determine if Paul used appeals to Jerusalem and the Temple to raise cash.

> But now that there is no more place for me to work in these regions, and since I have been longing for many years to see you, I plan to do so when I go to Spain. I hope to visit you while passing through and to have you assist me on my journey there, after I have enjoyed your company for a while. Now, however, I am on my way to Jerusalem in the service of the saints there. *For Macedonia and Achaia were pleased to make a contribution for the poor among the saints in Jerusalem.* They were pleased to do it, and indeed they owe it to them. *For if the Gentiles have shared in the Jew's spiritual blessings, they owe it to the Jews to share with them their material blessings.* So after I have completed this task and have made sure that they have received this fruit, I will go to Spain and visit you on the way. I know that when I come to you, I will come in the full measure of the blessings of Christ. (Romans 15:23–29) (Emphasis mine)

Paul makes an amazing sales pitch to the Romans. First, he butters them up, writing that he longs to see them and that they could help him on his journey by just comforting him. He then mentions the generous spirit of the saints in Macedonia and Achaia to spur their giving. Surely, the saints in Rome are as generous as the saints in other parts of the empire.

Having greased the pole Paul then uses guilt to his advantage. He writes that the Jews share their spiritual blessings with the Gentiles, urging the Gentiles to repay this debt by supplying material blessings. In short, if the Jews give you eternal glory, you should pay them for it. You owe them!

Like the unnamed Jew Paul invokes Jerusalem, the city of the Jews, and the spiritual destination for all material blessings, in his fund-raising appeal. This approach is also used with the churches in Corinth and Galatia.

> Now about the collection for God's people: *Do what I told the Galatian churches to do. On the first day of every week*, each one of you should *set aside a sum of money in keeping with his income*, saving it up, so that when I come no collections will have to be made. Then, when I arrive, I will give letters of introduction to the men you approve and send them with *your gift to Jerusalem*. If it seems advisable for me to go also, they will accompany me. After I go through Macedonia, I will come to you—for I will be going through Macedonia. Perhaps I will stay with you a while, or even spend the winter, so that *you can help me on my journey*, wherever I go. (1 Corinthians 16:1–6) (Emphasis mine)

Paul's instructions to the Corinthians mimic those given to the Galatian churches. They are to set aside money on the first day of every week, saving it up for the saints in Jerusalem. The richer you are, the more money you are expected to give. Over the course of a year, each person's savings would have been quite significant. Paul is collecting this substantial sum from every person in every church, making Paul a very rich man.

And at the end of his plea, Paul notes that the Corinthians can help him on his journey, similar to the promise he gives to the Roman churches. This again encourages the Corinthians to set aside a larger sum of money. Who wants to appear cheap in front of the great apostle?

In his second letter to the Corinthians Paul changes his plans regarding a visit to them. Instead he promises to send Titus and others to collect the money (2 Corinthians 2:1–4; 8:16–9:5). He writes, "So I thought it necessary to urge the brothers to visit you in advance and finish the arrangements for the generous gift you had promised." Like the unnamed Jew Paul uses his partners in this extraordinary sting operation. He then goes on in his letter to spur even greater giving.

> And now, brothers, *we want you to know about the grace that God has given to the Macedonian churches.* Out of the most severe trial, their overflowing joy and their extreme poverty welled up in rich generosity. For I testify that *they gave as much as they were able, and even beyond their ability.* Entirely on their own, they urgently pleaded with us for the privilege of sharing in this service to the saints. And they did not do as we expected, but they gave themselves first to the Lord and then to us in keeping with God's will. So we urged Titus, since he had earlier made a beginning, to bring also to completion this act of grace on your part. But just as you excel in everything—in faith, in speech, in knowledge, in complete earnestness and in your love for us—*see that you also excel in this grace of giving.*
>
> I am not commanding you, but *I want to test the sincerity of your love by comparing it with the earnestness of others.* For you know the grace of our Lord Jesus Christ, that though he was rich, yet for your sakes he became poor, so that you through his poverty might become rich.
>
> . . . There is no need for me to write you about this service to the saints. For I know your eagerness to help, and *I have been boasting about it to the Macedonians, telling them that since last year you in Achaia were ready to give; and your enthusiasm has stirred most of them to action.*

. . . Remember this: whoever sows sparingly will also reap sparingly, and whoever sows generously will also reap generously. Each man should give what he has decided in his heart to give, not reluctantly or under compulsion, *for God loves a cheerful giver.* (2 Corinthians 8:1–9; 9:1–2, 6–7) (Emphasis mine)

In this rather long exhortation concerning the virtues of giving, Paul uses competition to his advantage. He compares the Corinthians to the Macedonians and the Macedonians to the Corinthians, challenging each group to match or exceed the giving of the other. Paul calls on the competitive spirit in each one to create a greater willingness to give.

No one enjoys being robbed. But the church in Corinth is being robbed, just as the churches in Rome, Macedonia, and Galatia are. And yet, Paul convinces them that they should be cheerful in their loss, "for God loves a cheerful giver."

Do the monies, no doubt vast, ever make it to the saints in Jerusalem? In Galatians Paul describes his conflict with Peter at Antioch (44 CE), then vehemently denounces the Jews and the law of Moses. Could Paul have been reconciled to the Jerusalem leadership after this? Most likely, the collected monies remained with Paul and his partners. In 62 CE, Paul condones the murder of James and persecutes the poor priests in Jerusalem. He has aligned himself with the rich because he too is rich. The contributions of the Romans, Corinthians, Macedonians, and Galatians make Paul a rich man.

In addition, no evidence exists that the collected monies ever make it to Jerusalem. If they had, Paul would have trumpeted this achievement. His silence on the matter supports my assertion that Paul pockets the cash.

FINANCIAL EXPLOITATION USING THE JESUS MOVEMENT

A great irony exists here: Paul's Christ Movement uses the Jerusalem-based Jewish Jesus Movement in its collection campaign. Keep in mind that the unnamed Jew cites Jerusalem as an object of his fund-raising campaign and Paul also teaches his disciples to remember the poor saints in Jerusalem. In Galatians Paul defends his ministry and his collection policy, recalling his meeting with James at the Council of Jerusalem. In that meeting Paul claims that the Jewish apostles want him to always remember the poor, the very thing that he is practicing (Galatians 2:9–10). Does James approve of Paul's antinomian message as long as money is raised for Jerusalem? Of course not. James and Peter are deceived by Paul into believing that Paul is preaching Judaism to the Gentiles. Paul omits the details of his gospel, that Judaism is a forerunner to faith in Christ Jesus.

Using the poor saints in Jerusalem as a collection strategy ends when the Jerusalem leadership becomes aware of Paul's true teachings. James sends out emissaries from Galilee to confront Paul and his network. Eleazar challenges the teachings of Ananias in the King Izates conversion while Peter challenges Paul at Antioch (*Antiquities* 20.34–48; Galatians 2:11–13). Thus, after 44 CE, the Jewish Jesus Movement can no longer be used in extracting money from the Gentiles. In Galatians Paul puts a remarkable spin on the confrontation, stating that the Jews had been deceived by that hypocrite Peter and that only he (Paul) upholds the new covenant of Christ Jesus. This attempt to restore his reputation among the Gentiles is necessary to keep the funds flowing.

Nothing is known about Paul from his 44 CE confrontation with Peter to his 62 CE persecution of the poor priests in Jerusalem. Obviously, his ministry can no longer depend on the Jewish Jesus Movement for legitimacy. How then can Paul raise money? He still had the old standby: Jerusalem. As long as he can convince his followers of his desire to convert those Jews, he can still use Jerusalem as a fund-raising tool.

But even Jerusalem cannot last forever. After 70 CE the Christ Movement can no longer do fund-raising based on the premise that monies will be going to Jerusalem and the Temple, since both have been destroyed in the Jewish war. The pitch has to change. The post–70 CE message involves fund-raising for a movement built on the invented Jesus of Nazareth, which we will explore further in part three.

SIMON THE MAGICIAN

Concerning money, we must address Simon the magician, or Simon Magus. In the book of Acts Simon the magician is mentioned twice— once given the name Simon the Great, in his meeting with Philip, and once named Elymas the sorcerer, in the story of Paul at Cyprus (Acts 8:9–25 and 13:4–12). Both stories are fictional, but based on a true individual, called Simon the magician by Josephus (*Antiquities* 20.141–144).

The real Simon the magician is a close friend of the Roman governor, Felix (52–60 CE). He is a Jew, by birth a Cypriot. His claim to fame concerns the marriage of Felix to Drusilla, the daughter of Agrippa I. Simon convinces Drusilla to dissolve her marriage to Azizus, king of Emesa in Syria, in order to marry Felix. Josephus informs us that Drusilla "was prevailed upon to transgress the laws of her forefathers, and to marry Felix" (*Antiquities* 20.143). This episode may seem unimportant to us today, but it would have enraged the Fourth Philosophy (Zealots and Sicarii) against the ruling order, the Herodians.

John the Baptist is arrested and beheaded because of his vocal stance against Herod Antipas's marriage to Herodias. Drusilla and Felix's marriage is politically explosive as well. One of the Jewish Jesus Movement's quarrels with the Herodians, the ruling party aligned with Rome, involves the rulers' breaching of Jewish law. That is why the story is rewritten in Acts, disguising its true political ramifications.

Simon the magician is instrumental in the episode involving Drusilla and Felix's marriage. But does this Simon have any connection to Paul? Drusilla is the daughter of Agrippa I and the sister of Agrippa II, Bernice, and Mariamme. It is possible that Paul knew Simon the magician, as Paul lived in Jerusalem by 62 CE and probably long before that. If Paul talked with Simon, surely he would have spoken of his great ministry among the Gentiles. Is Simon intrigued by the prospect of riches that Paul's ministry promises? Does Simon travel to and preach in Paul's old Christ Jesus congregations? This is purely speculative, but Simon may have made his fortune among the Gentile flock.

In the Acts story Simon the Great tries to purchase the power of God with money. In fact, the term *simony,* meaning the buying or selling of a church office, comes from this episode. Is Simon's association with Paul a key element to understanding Simon's thirst for power and money? Or are all of Paul's unsavory actions projected onto Simon, thus clearing Paul's name?

The Pseudoclementine *Recognitions* may shed light on the above speculations. In this second-century document,[1] the enemy attacks James and later receives letters from the high priest to go to Damascus to arrest the faithful. A marginal note in one manuscript states that the enemy is Saul. Note that the above account is incorporated into the Acts account of Saul, before he enters the Jewish Jesus Movement.

> Meanwhile, Saul [Paul] was still breathing murderous threats against the Lord's disciples. *He went to the high priests and asked him for letters to the synagogues in Damascus, so that if he found any there who belonged to the Way,* whether men or women, he might take them as prisoners to Jerusalem. (Acts 9:1–2) (Emphasis mine)

In the Pseudoclementine *Recognitions* the enemy Saul [Paul] attacks James but does not kill him. This would have been in the 40s, after James has ousted Paul from the Jewish Jesus Movement. In Acts the same event is shifted to Paul's preconversion state, thus preserving the illusion of Paul's unending faithfulness to the Way.

The Pseudoclementine *Recognitions* conflates Saul [Paul] with Simon the magician, both presented as enemies of the Way of Righteousness. Are both men working against James and Peter or is Simon used to cover Paul's tracks?

Simon the magician's true story may never be known. He either makes great sums in the Christ Movement or his name is used as a way to shield the real villain in the story, Paul. Either way Paul is the focal point of Gentile collections. He is the great evangelist of his time.

PAUL'S DILEMMA

As noted above the destruction of Jerusalem by the Roman army has a monumental impact on the money-gathering efforts of the Christ Movement. With Jerusalem and the Temple intact, Paul and his minions have guaranteed success in any area of the Roman Empire inhabited by Jews. Jerusalem and the Temple are recognizable symbols of God's covenant with the Jewish people. Even the Gentile God-fearers understand the importance of the city and the Temple of God. Paul, to his credit, realizes the power of these symbols in his efforts to raise funds.

In his authentic letters Paul writes about the Jews' relationship with God. They are the natural children of God, who forfeit their birthright by rejecting his gospel of grace. He is careful not to fully denigrate the Jews, in order to keep the goal of his own gospel alive—the inclusion of Gentiles into the covenant with God. Jerusalem and the Temple are physical representations of this covenant, while his gospel focuses on the spiritual association with the Holy City. Thus, even though Paul's Gentile followers would never visit the city, they would nonetheless support it with their hard-earned money.

After the Jewish war with Rome (66–73 CE), nothing is left to support. The Romans thoroughly destroy Jerusalem, razing the great Temple and killing most of the Jewish resistance. Paul and the Christ Movement can no longer use the Temple and Jerusalem as representations of God's grace. These symbols have been fully discredited.

What are Paul's alternatives now?* He could have fully disassociated his Christ Movement from the rebellious Jews. After all his Christ Jesus has little in common with the actual Jewish Messiah. Christ Jesus could have become another pagan redeemer, with no Jewish roots.

Instead of removing all the Jewish trappings from Christ Jesus, Paul chooses to infuse his redeemer god with a Jewish background. The

---

*In official Church history Paul suffers martyrdom in Rome around 64 CE. However, according to my theory and Josephus's history, Paul meets with Nero in 67 CE and probably survives well beyond 70 CE.

rationale for this might be that he wants to give his new religion an ancient pedigree, back through Jesus and Judaism to Abraham, ignoring the whole history from Moses onward, the time of Torah that Paul dismisses. In reality this new Jewish Messiah is a Gentile dressed up as a Jew. Paul's Jesus of Nazareth opposes all other Jews to establish his own covenant with God through faith. The Gentiles are recipients of this act.

Thus, when Jesus predicts that Jerusalem will fall, the catastrophe is simply the fulfillment of prophecy. The destruction of Jerusalem and the Temple are ordained by God. The new cult of Jesus of Nazareth no longer needs Jerusalem and the Temple.

A new collection strategy emerges, one that has nothing to do with the Jews in Jerusalem. Now, followers can support the spiritual church. The hubs of this collection effort are the great cities: Antioch, Alexandria, Rome, and Athens. The tentacles of the early church have been formed. Money will flow from poor to rich, all in the name of God.

PART THREE

The Creation of Jesus of Nazareth

❖

PAUL'S HAND IN THE GOSPELS

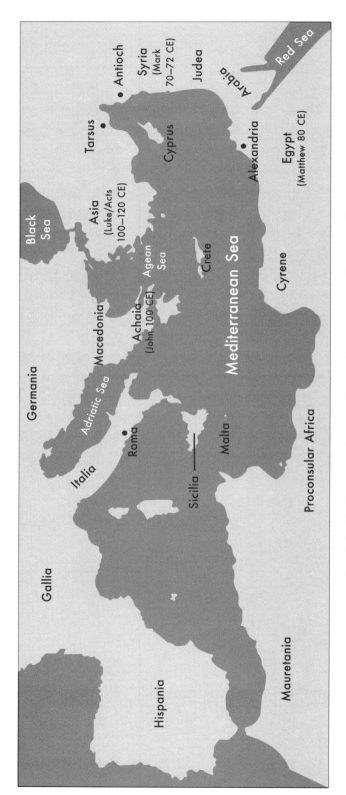

Map of the Mediterranean showing where and when the gospels originated.

THE JESUS OF NAZARETH we find in the New Testament, in the canonical gospels, is not the Jesus of history, but rather a composite. That is, it is a portrait created by the Pauline Gentile Christ Movement to suit its needs after the Jewish Jesus Movement and Judaism wane due to the disastrous Jewish war with Rome in the 60s. A new Messiah figure is needed, worthy of Roman admiration and devotion.

In response Jesus of Nazareth is created. First, "foundation legends" help bridge the gap between the end of Acts in the early 60s and the reality of the emerging Church in the 90s and later on. These foundation legends provide answers to troubling questions concerning the continuity of teachings from Jesus of Nazareth to Paul.

Second, the four gospels of the New Testament are created, based on a story line provided by the author of Mark. As I will show they reflect the theology of Paul as well as his experiences, a fact rarely discussed by scholars and never spelled out in detail. But the astute reader of the New Testament suspects that the gospel Jesus is not the Jesus of history, the person who preaches in Galilee and meets his tragic end in Jerusalem. The gospel Jesus is an invented figure, a fiction, one suited for the Christ Movement and its successors near the end of the first century. It is a remarkable creation for it has stood the test of time.

7 ► Foundation Legends

The early Christian Church story has been buttressed by several "foundation legends," not included in the New Testament but circulated in Christian communities from the early second century. The legends have a twofold purpose: First and foremost, church history has to be consistent and uniform in nature. And second, the period from the end of Acts (approximately 60–62 CE) to the early church historians (early to late second century) has to be accounted for in an appropriate manner.

Two distinct "Christian" movements exist by the fourth decade of the first century: the Jewish Jesus Movement and the Pauline Christ Movement. However, most Christians today have not even considered such a split. The traditional viewpoint states that the church began after Jesus's resurrection and that the apostles, including Peter, Paul, and James, all worked together in a common cause. Any differences between these leaders have been minimized in order to present a unified front.

The fact that Christians today fail to recognize any split is a testament to the foundation legends' success. Would Christians today believe in the traditional Christian unified world if these legends had not been invented?

THE MARTYRDOM OF PETER AND PAUL

When Paul travels to Achaia to meet Nero in 67 CE, he is not in chains but goes of his own volition, in order to lay blame for the Jewish war on

Florus (*War* 2.556–558). Paul enjoys good health at this time, and nothing points to his untimely demise. If Paul still lives and travels freely, then why does the later church insist that he and Peter undergo persecution and martyrdom together? The answer is obvious: The church wants to gloss over any disagreements between the earlier Jewish Jesus Movement and Paul's Christ Movement.

The first mention of Peter's and Paul's martyrdom comes from Clement of Rome (30–97 CE). He does not supply a concrete date for the martyrdom but does concoct this falsehood about Paul, claiming that Paul "taught righteousness to the world."[1] Clement characterizes Paul as righteous, even though that attribute hardly describes Paul, but clearly describes Peter and James the Just. Righteousness, after all, means dedication to the Torah. Compare this to the Ebionite claim, rejecting "the Apostle Paul as an apostate from the Law."[2] If Paul were an apostate from the Law, and his own letters prove that, then no one in the Jewish Jesus Movement could have considered his teaching as a sign of "righteousness."

Eusebius cements the martyrdom legend of Peter and Paul, tying their deaths to the persecution after the Great Fire of Rome in 64 CE. He writes: "It is recorded that in his [Nero's] reign Paul was beheaded in Rome itself, and that Peter likewise was crucified, and the record is confirmed by the fact that the cemeteries there are still called by the names of Peter and Paul, and equally so by a churchman named Gaius, who was living while Zephyrinus was Bishop of Rome [199–217 CE]."[3] He then quotes Bishop Dionysius of Corinth who claims that both Peter and Paul were martyred at the same time.[4]

By the early fifth century the legend has become so entrenched that Augustine writes: "Both apostles share the same feast day, for these two were one; and even though they suffered on different days, they were as one. Peter went first, and Paul followed."[5] Augustine differs from Eusebius, who claims that both were martyred at the same time. However, the important point is that Peter and Paul are viewed as one, one with the same teachings and visions of God. Nothing could have been further from the truth.

The martyrdom legend can be traced to the misinformation contained in the book of Acts. In Acts the argument between Peter and Paul at Antioch is amicably resolved, but if that is true, then why do the Ebionites consider Paul an apostate from the Law? In addition Paul supposedly goes to meet Caesar in Rome in 60–62 CE. In reality Paul meets Nero in 67 CE at Achaia (modern-day Greece). The martyrdom legend simply builds on the faulty history of Acts.

The agenda underlying the legend is clear: Make the apostles agree in all things and present a uniform history of the early church. This legend also brings the working lives of Peter and Paul together. If they are willing to die together, they also are willing to work together. Noted scholars, like the late Hyam Maccoby (*The Mythmaker*) and more recently, Barrie Wilson (*How Jesus Became Christian*), argue that Paul and James represent totally different gospels. (As James's representative Peter also follows strict Torah observance.) Much of the evidence that Peter and Paul have distinctly different worldviews comes from Paul's own letters and from the book of Acts. So, in a sense, the unity of Peter and Paul in life is as much a foundation legend as their unity in death.

THE AUTHOR OF THE GOSPEL OF MARK

Who wrote the Gospel of Mark? According to the New Testament a Mark is mentioned as Paul's fellow worker (Acts 13:13; 15:37–38) and as Peter's son (1 Peter 5:13). However, both documents come from the second century.[6] From these suspect sources the bishop of Hieropolis, Papias (130 CE), claims that Mark is Peter's secretary and wrote the gospel utilizing Peter's own memories.[7] Thus, Peter becomes the source for this legend of Jesus of Nazareth's life.

That the Gospel of Mark originates with Peter is paramount to traditional Christian history. Peter is Jesus's preeminent disciple and must have spent countless hours listening to and questioning the Messiah. If the Gospel of Mark originates with Peter, then its authenticity cannot be questioned.

On the other hand, if the Gospel of Mark is composed by someone in Paul's Christ Movement, then Mark can be rightly questioned. After all Paul never meets "Jesus" in the flesh but only converses with the Risen Christ. If the Gospel of Mark comes from Paul, then Jesus of Nazareth is derived from the Risen Christ tradition and not historically accurate. Keep this in mind as we investigate the Gospel of Mark in more detail in the following chapter.

THE FLIGHT OF JERUSALEM CHRISTIANS TO PELLA

Christian tradition claims that adherents of the Jerusalem Church left the city before it was destroyed in 70 CE by Titus and settled in the Gentile town of Pella. This tradition is first recorded in the fourth century by Eusebius and a century later by Epiphanius. The reason for the escape to Pella is clear: The Jerusalem Church needs to be intact for the later church to make the case of continuity between the earliest Jewish disciples and the later Christ Movement, founded for Gentiles by Paul. The passage by Eusebius is reproduced below:

> Furthermore, the members of the Jerusalem church, by means of an *oracle given by revelation* to acceptable persons there, *were ordered to leave the city before the war began* and settle in a town in Peraea called Pella. To Pella those who believed in Christ migrated from Jerusalem; and as if holy men had utterly abandoned the royal metropolis of the Jews and the entire Jewish land, the judgment of God at last overtook them for their abominable crimes against Christ and His apostles, completely blotting out that wicked generation from among men.[8] (Emphasis mine)

What was the Jewish Jesus Movement's attitude concerning the Law, circumcision, and Jerusalem? Would they have left Jerusalem or have defended it? Paul describes emissaries sent by James as the party of the circumcision (Galatians 2:11–13), insisting that all Jews and Gentiles undergo circumcision as a requirement of the Jewish Jesus Movement. Remember that Eleazar is sent from Galilee in 44 CE to confront the teachings of Ananias in the King Izates conversion. This Eleazar insists on circumcision and adherence to the Torah (*Antiquities* 20.34–48). Those sent to combat the teachings of Paul and Ananias are strict followers of the law of Moses, having great respect for the Temple and for Jerusalem.

In addition, according to Acts 21:20, the Jewish disciples supposedly tell Paul: "You see, brother, how many thousands of Jews have believed, and all of them are zealous for the Law." Now whether or not this event actually occurred is secondary. The primary point concerns the Jewish believers' zeal for the Law, and their rabid attachment to the Temple and to Jerusalem. Those zealous Jews would never have abandoned the Temple and Jerusalem, no matter what the danger.

Before the war with Rome the Jewish Jesus Movement is very attached to Jerusalem and the Temple. What about the Jewish disciples who survive the war? Little is known about this group, called the Ebionites. Although they survive the war they are later characterized as heretics by the Gentile Church. According to Irenaeus the Ebionites use only the Gospel of Matthew, reject Paul as an apostate from the Law, and worship Jerusalem, "as if it were the abode of God."[9] This reverence for Jerusalem suggests they would have given their lives to save the city.[10]

Before and after the war there is no indication that the Jewish disciples abandoned Jerusalem. To remove the Jewish Jesus Movement from Jerusalem, Eusebius claims a revelatory oracle conveniently warns the Jewish disciples to abandon the city. Moving a group based on oracles or dreams is used frequently in the birth narrative of Matthew. The wise men are warned in a dream to avoid Herod the Great and Joseph is led to Egypt by another dream (Matthew 2:12–15). Do these dreams really occur or are they merely literary devices to further the plot line? According to S. G. F. Brandon, the Pella flight is a second-century "foundation legend probably designed to justify the claims of the church later established in Aelia Capitolina, to be a lineal descendent of the original Church of Jerusalem."[11] Note that Aelia Capitolina is established by Hadrian in 130 CE on the site of Jerusalem. Like Pella

Aelia Capitolina is a Gentile city. Hadrian vows to rebuild Jerusalem from its wreckage of 70 CE as a gift to the Jewish people. He changes his mind and builds Aelia Capitolina for his legionnaires instead. He also bans Jews from entering the city and outlaws circumcision, both of which outrage the Jews and help lead to the second Jewish revolt, led by Bar Kochba, from 132 to 136 CE.

Could adherents of the Jerusalem-based Jewish Jesus Movement have functioned within the destroyed city from 70 to 130 CE? Even if they had they would have been evicted from the city, since all Jews were banned from Jerusalem in 130 CE. Also, followers of the first-century Messiah either were so decimated as to be inconsequential or joined forces with the new Messiah figure, Bar Kochba. My contention is that the first-century Jewish Jesus Movement was largely destroyed during the first Jewish war and had an insignificant presence in Jerusalem from 70 to 130 CE.

Eusebius states that the Jerusalem Church is ordered to leave the city before the war begins. From Josephus's account it would have been nearly impossible to leave once the war began. The founder of the later Rabbinical Movement, the religious movement that replaced the decimated Pharisees, Sadducees, Essenes, and Zealots, escapes from Jerusalem in a coffin, not something all the adherents of a movement could do. Understanding this Eusebius claims that the flight to Pella occurs before the war begins. But not only does Eusebius get the Jewish Jesus Movement out of harm's way, he also cites the continuity of the Jerusalem leadership after the death of James (62 CE), stating that Symeon, son of Clopas, occupies the Jerusalem See from 62 to 106 CE.[12] This Symeon supposedly suffers martyrdom at the age of 120.[13] After him at least fifteen other Jews supposedly hold the office in Jerusalem.

According to Eusebius the Jewish Jesus Movement abandons the city before the war but the leadership returns to the city after the devastation, a remarkable assertion on three counts. First and foremost, after 70 CE and the destruction of Jerusalem, the influence of the Jewish Jesus Movement has ended. Brandon reasons that if the Jewish Jesus Movement had survived, its power and prestige would have been recognized in all the records. But because it is not cited in the records he contends that the power shifts to Rome, Antioch, and Alexandria after 70 CE.[14]

Second, Eusebius points to the long list of Jewish leaders coming after James the Just. But that brings up an important question: How could the Jewish Jesus Movement be wholly Gentile with a Gentile bishop by 130 CE if the Jewish leadership is still intact long after the war?[15] Hadrian builds the new city of Aelia Capitolina in 130 CE and bans the Jews from it. Without a doubt Hadrian does not import a Pauline Gentile Christian Church into the city. From the Roman historians of that era (Tacitus, Suetonius, and Pliny), the Romans do not distinguish the Gentile Christian Church from the Jewish Jesus Movement. As such any group with supposed ties to the Jews would have been suspect. Most likely the Gentile Church gradually infiltrates Aelia Capitolina, just as they do other great metropolitan cities of the time.

Third, Eusebius claims that the Jewish Jesus Movement returns to the city after the war. In essence Symeon, a cousin of Jesus and James, is a major player in Jerusalem. However, Eusebius also writes that Vespasian orders "that no member of the royal house should be left among the Jews, all descendants of David should be ferreted out."[16] and similar persecution continued under Domitian.[17] No evidence survives confirming the success of Vespasian's and Domitian's persecutions, but somehow Symeon survives these persecutions, even though he's a leader of the Jewish Jesus Movement . If Symeon does lead the postwar Jewish Jesus Movement, it is as a guerrilla leader, not as one open to easy capture. In light of this evidence it only makes sense that Symeon is part of the Pella flight foundation legend. The Jerusalem disciples do not leave for Pella but are mostly slaughtered in the war with Rome. Those surviving the war coalesce as the Ebionites, later deemed heretics by the Pauline Gentile Church.

Without the Pella flight foundation legend a sobering fact remains: The Jewish Jesus Movement is mostly destroyed by the Romans in 70 CE. But the time line concerning these events has been altered. There are three reasons for that alteration. First, the fictional Acts story gets Paul out of Jerusalem before the stoning of James. Paul cannot be blamed for James's death in Jerusalem if he is in Rome at the time. Second, by placing Paul in Rome, he can be cast as a martyr for the Christian Church. He can be persecuted by Nero after the Great Fire of Rome in 64 CE. However, according to Josephus, Paul meets Nero in Achaia (Greece), not in Rome. Third, the altered time line keeps Paul out of the Jewish war. If he is away from Jerusalem by 60 CE, he cannot have played a role in the uprising in the city. However, the historical Paul is a major player—on the side of the Romans.

In regard to the Pella question we will focus on Paul's escape from Jerusalem after the defeat of Cestius and the corresponding rewrite in the book of Acts. In Acts Paul is sent to the Temple by James to perform a purification rite, to disprove the claim that he preaches against the Law and Moses (Acts 21:20–25). At the Temple Jews from Asia convince the crowd that Paul has been preaching a message against the Jewish people. The Jews seize Paul, but he is immediately rescued by the Roman guard (Acts 21:27–36). Those who attack Paul have to be somewhat familiar with him; thus, the Jews mentioned in Acts must be part of the Jewish Jesus Movement.

The account in Acts chronicles events occurring around 58–60 CE, long before the Jewish war. However, Acts is a rewrite of Paul's escape from the insurgents in 66 CE, after the defeat of Cestius. If Paul and insurgents of the Jewish Jesus Movement are still in Jerusalem after the defeat of Cestius, then the flight to Pella never occurs. If members of the Jewish Jesus Movement overcome Cestius's forces, they would have fought against any Roman army, trusting that God was behind their efforts. As Josephus writes: "This reverse of Cestius proved disastrous to our whole nation: for those who were bent on war were thereby still more elated and, having once defeated the Romans, hoped to continue victorious to the end."[18] The Jewish Jesus Movement tastes victory, so they would never have abandoned Jerusalem or the Temple.

Paul's story presents indirect evidence that the Pella flight is a foundation legend. Can we find any direct evidence disproving the legend?

According to Sulpicius Severus, an early fifth-century church historian, Titus orders the destruction of the Temple as a way to wipe out the religions of both the Jews and the Christians. This raises two interesting points. First, it attributes the decision to destroy the Temple to Titus. Josephus is much kinder to his patron, Titus, not associating him with the Temple's destruction. Certainly, Josephus tries to put a positive spin on the events. With this in mind the passage by Severus appears more reasonable. The second point has a bearing on our discussion of the flight to Pella. Severus states that Titus tears down the Temple to obliterate the religions of the Jews and Christians. This suggests that Titus believes that the Christians are attached to the Temple in such a way that its destruction would cripple their religion. It also strongly suggests that the Jewish Jesus Movement defends the Temple in 70 CE. If that is true, then the flight to Pella is certainly a "foundation legend," not historical fact.

The passage by Severus states:

> It is reported that Titus had first deliberated, in a council called up for the purpose, whether he should destroy a Temple of such workmanship. For it seemed improper to some that a sacred shrine, famous beyond everything mortal, should be destroyed, a shrine which could serve as a witness to Roman moderation, but if torn down would provide continual evidence of their cruelty. But, on the other hand, others, *even Titus himself, argued the Temple had to be torn down above all things, so the religion of the Jews and Christians could be swept away even more completely.* For these religions, although hostile to each other, nevertheless arose from the very same authors. The Christians appeared from among the Jews, so with the foundation torn away, the offspring will easily pass away. And so by the will of God, once everyone's mind was inspired to the task, the Temple was destroyed.[19] (Emphasis mine)

Is this passage from Sulpicius Severus taken from Tacitus's lost portion of *The Annals and the Histories?* If so, then Tacitus believes that

Titus is attacking Christians by destroying the Temple. But another possibility exists. Tacitus might have confused Christians with Zealots. This is the opinion of Edward Gibbon, who argues that Nero punishes the followers of Judas the Galilean after the Great Fire in 64 CE. In his thinking the Christians would have flown under the radar at this point in history and the real troublemakers are the Zealots. Tacitus must have simply confused the two sets of Galileans.[20] If Gibbon's argument is correct, then Tacitus does not mean to indict the group known as Christians. So Nero punishes the Zealots in 64 CE and Titus destroys the Temple of the Jews and Zealots in 70 CE. I agree with Gibbon, with one qualification: I think the Christians *were* the Zealots. Interestingly, Josephus never mentions Christians but refers to Judas the Galilean's followers as Zealots, Sicarii, or the Fourth Philosophy. Tacitus never mentions any of these terms but instead uses the term *Christian*. Both are speaking about the same group using different terms.

After the death of James the Jewish Jesus Movement lacks cohesion, fragmented behind various leaders who use their own tactics against Rome.[21] The Jerusalem disciples fight and die at the Temple; another branch is led by Eleazar, a grandson of Judas the Galilean, who resists the Roman siege at Masada until 73 CE; while yet another group escapes to Alexandria and fails in an attempt to rally the Alexandrian Jews to go to war with Rome. Surely, other pockets of the Jesus Movement survive, but the glory and strength of the movement dissipate. This surviving remnant becomes known as the Ebionites, Jews no longer belonging to either the Jewish religion or the new Gentile Church. In time little trace is left of them.

The flight to Pella, the martyrdom of Peter and Paul, and the supposed authorship of Mark's gospel by Peter's secretary all point to the Jewish apostles' influence on the Jesus of Nazareth story. This Jewish authority is important to the post–70 CE Pauline Gentile Church. Without this authority it could be claimed by opponents that Jesus of Nazareth is simply an invention of the later Gentile Church. Therefore, they are compelled to root their Gentile movement in something more ancient than Paul's vision on the road to Damascus. With these three foundation legends, the Gentile Church can proudly proclaim the authenticity of their Lord and savior, solidifying their claims for a historical "Jesus of Nazareth." But without them we may legitimately question the very existence of this Jesus. So did Jesus of Nazareth really exist or was he an invention of the post-70 CE Gentile Church? Were the teachings of this Jesus really connected to the teachings of Peter and James or were they simply refashioned from the teachings of later Pauline disciples? These questions will be answered in the next chapter on the Gospel of Mark.

8 ► The Gospel of Mark

Modern scholars generally acknowledge that the four canonical gospels were written in light of the success of Paul's Christ Movement, after the Jewish Jesus Movement had been devastated by the war with Rome (66–73 CE). But few have attempted to show how the gospels were shaped by Paul's distinctive Gentile theology. In the following chapters I will detail how the figure of Jesus of Nazareth reflects Paul's perspective as well as events and experiences in his life. The canonical authors intend to render Jesus of Nazareth and his teachings amenable to a Roman audience—Gentiles primarily, some composed of devotees of Mithras and others drawn from followers of Dionysus—who know little and care even less about Jewish culture, life, and values. As such the gospels are not transcripts and not history; they are polemical documents designed to attract prospective converts to the movement in ways they would understand and in terms they would find appealing.

Knowing the time lines and relationships existing within the Herodian family, we can better understand how and why the gospels are created. In the traditional story line Paul is martyred in Rome around 64 CE. If that is true, Paul (who is dead) could have had little or no *direct influence* on the creation of the gospel story, which is a post–70 CE production. However, in Josephus's writings, Paul appeals to Nero in 67 CE and probably lives many years beyond that. At least Paul should be a possible candidate for the creator of the Gospel of Mark. And if Paul were involved in the composition of Mark, then we can conjecture that the greatest foundation legend—the life and death of Jesus of Nazareth—is built on the framework of Paul's own Christ cult.

Even if Paul did not directly compose the Gospel of Mark, the following analysis illustrates that someone with a Pauline bent is behind the narrative, fashioning Jesus of Nazareth after the likeness of the master, Paul. Either way the message of Paul comes through in the story of Jesus of Nazareth.

PROBLEMS WITH THE COMPOSITION OF MARK

The Gospel of Mark is an anonymous document by a religious genius, the first person ever to pen a narrative about Jesus of Nazareth, not just a collection of sayings. It is a tour de force, the creation of a whole new genre of literature, a gospel that other anonymous writers eventually use and build on.

But it is not history.

And, as we shall see, it is malleable. Matthew and Luke feel no compunction about modifying what Mark wrote. In *Who Wrote the New Testament?* Burton Mack makes this point concerning the authorship of Mark: "We do not usually think of mythmaking as the achievement of a moment or the work of a single writer no matter how brilliant. But in Mark's case we have an obvious fiction, masterfully composed by someone who had to be doing his work at a desk as any author would."[1] Could one mind have created Jesus of Nazareth, as depicted in Mark? Mack continues, "Mark insisted that Jesus and his program displaced earlier forms of Judaism."[2] This provides an important clue: What man wanted to displace earlier forms of Judaism with a revised version?

This new Judaism springs forth in Mark's miracle accounts. According to Wolfgang Roth, author of *Hebrew Gospel,* Elijah performs eight miracles and Elisha doubles that with sixteen. Jesus, on the other hand, blows away his Hebrew scripture competition with twenty-four miracles, a progression that clearly positions Jesus of Nazareth above these other wonder workers. Jesus is a super-healer, his superiority superseding traditional Judaism as represented by Moses and the prophets. Again, who envisioned such a super figure?

Who could have rewritten the history of the Jewish Messiah Movement, turning that Messiah into the anti-Jewish-leaning, pro-Gentile Jesus of Nazareth? Certainly, the person who crafted the story line of Mark (used liberally in Matthew and Luke) has no qualms about changing history. This person also has great imagination. Could Paul have had anything to do with this rewrite of history? And, if so, why would he invent this new gospel?

Paul's assessment of himself after his conversion to the Jewish Jesus Movement is quite grandiose. He envisions himself as the most important apostle, a prophet guided directly by the Risen Christ, claiming that God has set him apart from his birth and that God has revealed his Son to him (Galatians 1:11–17). Consider the ramifications of this thinking. Paul believes he has a direct pipeline to the Risen Christ and that others can witness that Son through Paul. In some ways Paul himself is the Messiah or Christ to the Gentiles. Might Jesus of Nazareth have been created using the framework of Judas the Galilean's history and yet modeled after the life and beliefs of Paul? The following discussion supports such a thesis.

PAUL'S INVOLVEMENT WITH THE GOSPEL OF MARK

Before 70 CE leaders of the Jewish Jesus Movement control the message concerning their Messiah. In 44 CE, at Antioch, Paul is ousted from the Jesus Movement for unacceptable teachings, such as the efficacy of faith over the Law. Paul's antinomian stance is wholly rejected by James and Peter and would have been forever lost to history if the Jewish Jesus Movement had survived the Jewish war with Rome. This war devastated the original messianic community, leaving behind a weak and insignificant remnant, the Ebionites. After the war, post–70 CE, Paul takes advantage of the power vacuum and sets out to create his own version of the Jewish Messiah, borrowing some attributes from the historical Messiah but largely based on his own gospel. Paul's Jewish Messiah becomes the Messiah of the Gentiles, just as he, Paul, has been the apostle to the Gentiles. The following are issues that confront the writer of Mark and how he resolves them.

Paying Taxes to Caesar

Perhaps the most quoted and misunderstood passage about Jesus's ministry concerns the paying of taxes to Caesar (Mark 12:13–17). Does Jesus support Roman taxation? Traditionally, the Church has held that Jesus accepts the taxation when he says, "Give to Caesar what is Caesar's." But could a popular Jewish Messiah have supported paying tribute to an occupying power? S. G. F. Brandon states the following:

> If Jesus claimed to be the Messiah, and had been recognized as such by his followers, as Mark relates, then, on Mark's showing, Jesus must have had a very different conception of Messiahship from that which was then current. Thus, instead of leading his people against the hated Romans, he is represented as endorsing their rule in Judaea: for he recognizes the duty of the Jews to pay tribute to Caesar. This issue . . . was the basic test of Jewish patriotism: for *payment of this tribute was tantamount to denying Yahweh's absolute sovereignty over Israel—it was the issue on which the Zealots, the nationalist action party, were prepared to die.*[3] (Emphasis mine)

Crowds would not have welcomed Jesus into Jerusalem with such fervor if he supported the status quo. And why do the officials try to trap Jesus if he holds the same position as they do vis-à-vis the payment of Roman tribute? Obviously, Jesus does not support the payment of taxes to Caesar. Brandon correctly observes that the payment of taxes to Caesar is the most important issue of the day, an issue that fuels the Zealots' popularity and one for which they are willing to die. Like the Zealots Jesus does not carry coinage with Caesar's portrait, asking for someone to bring him a coin. Also note that Luke's gospel claims that the chief charge against Jesus is his opposition to Roman taxation (Luke 23:1–2). And Jesus dies for this teaching.

So what exactly does Jesus mean by "Give to Caesar what is Caesar's and give to God what is God's"? Brandon believes that the things of God are the resources of the Holy Land, and these resources belong to the Jewish people, not to the Romans. Thus, this thinking is in line with Zealot teachings.[4]

If Jesus opposes Roman tribute and dies for his views, then who supports the Roman government? Paul writes this to the Romans:

> *The authorities that exist have been established by God. Consequently, he who rebels against the authority is rebelling against what God has instituted,* and those who do so will bring judgment on themselves. For rulers hold no terror for those who do right, but for those who do wrong. Do you want to be free from fear of the one in authority? Then do what is right and he will commend you. For he is God's servant to do you good. But if you do wrong, be afraid, for he does not bear the sword for nothing. He is God's servant, an angel of wrath to bring punishment on the wrongdoer. Therefore, it is necessary to submit to the authorities, not only because of possible punishment but also because of conscience. *This is also why you pay taxes, for the authorities are God's servants, who give their full time to governing.* (Romans 13:1–6) (Emphasis mine)

Paul writes this epistle during the reign of Caligula and later meets with Nero.* Even these bloodthirsty tyrants cannot shake Paul's faith in the Roman government. In fact, according to Paul, "authorities were established by God." In short Paul's stance concerning Roman taxation is diametrically opposed to that of the Jewish Messiah. Brandon puts forth the logical explanation for the Roman tribute question, but

---

*Romans is written after Paul's vision of the Risen Christ, sometime after the appointment of his cousin, Agrippa I, as king of Israel (37 CE) but before Paul's conflict with Peter at Antioch (44 CE). Caligula reigns from 37 to 41 CE. Paul meets with Nero in Achaia in 67 CE, according to *War* 2.557–58.

the church has interpreted Jesus's saying in light of Paul's theology for nearly two millennia.

What else in Mark's tribute passage relates to Paul? Supposedly, the authorities say to Jesus: "You aren't swayed by men, because you pay no attention to who they are; but you teach the way of God in accordance with the truth." Paul says this about himself: "As for those who seemed to be important—whatever they were makes no difference to me; God does not judge by external appearance—those men added nothing to my message" (Galatians 2:6). Paul and his Jesus follow God without being swayed by others' opinions.

Sadly, Christians today believe that a Jewish Messiah actually endorsed an occupying nation's tribute system. When the masses invite Jesus into Jerusalem, they are hoping and praying for deliverance from Rome. Why else would they have been so excited about his ministry? Unlike Mark's presentation the Jewish Messiah is clearly anti-Roman and would have given his life to defeat Rome and its tax merchants, the Herodians.

Food Restrictions and the Law

"Don't you see that nothing that enters a man from the outside can make him 'unclean'? For it doesn't go into his heart but into his stomach, and then out of his body." *[By saying this, Jesus declares all foods "clean."]* He went on: "What comes out of a man is what makes him 'unclean.' For from within, out of men's hearts, come evil thoughts, sexual immorality, theft, murder, greed, malice, deceit, lewdness, envy, slander, arrogance and folly. All these evils come from inside and make a man 'unclean.'" (Mark 7:18–23) (Emphasis mine)

Jesus says nothing that would have offended his own disciples. Note that John baptizes those whose souls are "thoroughly purified beforehand by righteousness" (*Antiquities* 18.117). The washing of hands is acceptable to Jesus as long as the soul is washed as well. Jesus condemns the hypocrites who wash their hands but harbor evil within their souls.

Mark interprets this entire exchange as a way to dismiss the food purity laws, despite the fact that this whole exchange centers on obeying the laws of God, not dismissing them. Jesus does not declare all foods clean. That is a purely Pauline concept. Paul insists that only the weak follow any purity laws and that those with superior knowledge are not required to follow such laws, unless by their actions they would hurt the weaker brother (Romans 14:1–4). Paul even says it is permissible to eat food dedicated to idols as food does not bring one closer to God (1 Corinthians 8:1–13). Thus, a commentary originating from the Jewish Messiah figure is interpreted through a Pauline lens in the Gospel of Mark.

The Pauline stance on the dietary laws is not endorsed by any Jewish group within Israel. Any messianic candidate with this Pauline agenda would have been rejected by the leaders and the people.

Jesus and Paul Are Commissioned by God and Then Sent into the Desert

> I received it [gospel] by *revelation from Jesus Christ.* . . . But when God, who set me apart from birth and called me by his grace, was pleased to reveal his Son in me so that I might preach him among the Gentiles, I did not consult any man, nor did I go up to Jerusalem to see those who were apostles before I was, but *I went immediately into Arabia* and later returned to Damascus. (Galatians 1:12, 15–17) (Emphasis mine)

Paul claims that he receives his gospel from the Risen Christ at his conversion, that God was revealing his Son through him, even proclaiming himself the embodiment of the Messiah, the Son of God. After this commission by God to spread the gospel, Paul goes immediately to Arabia. This sojourn into the desert is a deliberate attempt to equate himself with Moses. In fact, not only can believers see the Son through Paul, but they could also experience the new gospel of grace, which now replaces the Torah, given to Moses in the desert.

In Mark's gospel Jesus receives the Spirit after being baptized by

John. At once, Jesus is led out into the desert (Galatians 1:11–17; Mark 1:9–13), where he spends forty days, the same number of days that Moses spent with God before receiving the Ten Commandments. In this episode, based on Paul's experience, Jesus of Nazareth becomes the new Moses, with faith now replacing the Torah of God.

The Baptisms of John the Baptist and Jesus

According to Josephus John's baptism is not for the forgiveness of sins but for the purification of the body, "supposing still that the soul was thoroughly purified before by righteousness" (*Antiquities* 18.116–119). So John's baptism requires an active response from the convert— repentance and righteousness.

In contrast to John's baptism Jesus is to baptize with the Holy Spirit (Mark 1:8). In the same way Paul belittles the importance of water baptism (1 Corinthians 1:13–17), claiming that the Spirit is received by faith, not by following the Law (Galatians 3:5). In short, in the gospel as taught by both Jesus and Paul the Spirit comes through faith, while John requires personal commitment through righteousness. This shift away from the law of Moses in favor of faith is perfectly consistent with Paul's theology.

Nazorean into Nazareth

The term *Nazorean* probably refers to those following a specific course of action against Rome. In Acts 24:5 Paul is accused of being a member of the Nazarene sect, which "stirred up riots among the Jews all over the world." In essence the Nazarene sect is another name for the Fourth Philosophy of Judas the Galilean, which Paul joined in the 20s. After 44 CE Paul works against the Nazarene sect. To distance the teacher Jesus from any revolutionary sect, Mark simply states that Jesus is from Nazareth, a town never mentioned in Josephus or in the Hebrew scriptures (Mark 1:9). So Jesus the Nazorean—a political statement— morphs into Jesus from Nazareth—a geographical one.

This fraud is continued by the authors of Matthew and Luke, but with different stories. Matthew writes that Jesus is born in Bethlehem, his family escaping to and returning from Egypt and finally settling in Nazareth. Luke has Mary and Joseph living in Nazareth before Jesus's birth and going to Bethlehem because of the census.

John the Baptist Dies before Jesus and Paul

According to Mark Jesus's ministry begins *after* John's imprisonment by Herod Antipas (Mark 1:14), with John's beheading shortly thereafter (Mark 6:14). However, Josephus writes that John the Baptist dies around 36 CE (*Antiquities* 18.116–119), a date also supported by the Slavonic Josephus (SJ *War* 2.168, from additional passages). If John dies around 36 CE, then Jesus must have been crucified *before* John's execution, not after. Most scholars date Jesus's death to 30–33 CE, *before John's death*. I date the Messiah Judas the Galilean's death to 19–21 CE, also before the death of John.

What important figure begins his ministry after the death of John? Paul's visions of the Risen Christ probably begin about the time of his cousin Agrippa I's reign, around 37 CE, right after the death of John the Baptist. So Paul is the only person to preach after the death of John the Baptist, the historical Jewish Messiah having been crucified years before the death of John.

The Family's Reaction to Jesus or to Paul

A most puzzling passage in Mark concerns Jesus's family's reaction to his ministry. "When his family heard about this, they went to take charge of him, for they said, 'He is out of his mind'" (Mark 3:20–21). Could the Messiah figure have been viewed so negatively by his family? Judas the Galilean's family's struggle against the Herodians stretches back to 37 BCE. They are very familiar with the consequences of an antiestablishment ministry. And in the Slavonic Josephus Jesus's mother and brothers are highlighted as being an important part of the ministry (SJ *War* 1.650, from additional passages). So this passage attributed to the Jewish Messiah cannot be taken seriously.

What preacher's family must have been beside themselves with anger and disgust? Certainly, Paul's family would have considered him mad!

He deserts the ruling dynasty (the Herodians) and joins a revolutionary group (the Jewish Jesus Movement) intent on overthrowing the existing order, which includes his own family. Of course, the negative family reaction occurs in the few early years during which Paul acts as a loyal member of the revolutionary Jewish Jesus Movement. Reconciliation with his family begins after Paul's Risen Christ revelations, when the pro-Roman message of obeying the government becomes the center-piece of his distinctive nonrevolutionary gospel.

James and John: Brothers of Jesus

In Galatians Paul refers to the church pillars as James, Peter, and John (Galatians 2:9). In 1 Corinthians Paul emphasizes Peter and the broth-ers of the Lord over all the other apostles (1 Corinthians 9:5). These church pillars are Paul's main competition for the hearts and souls of his Gentile congregations. Paul's letters show his pent-up hatred for James and Peter:

> For such men [who preach a different gospel than Paul] are false apostles, deceitful workmen, masquerading as apostles of Christ. And no wonder, for Satan himself masquerades as an angel of light. It is not surprising, then, if his servants masquerade as servants of righteousness. Their end will be what their actions deserve. (2 Corinthians 10:13–15)

Is this venomous passage directed at the Jewish pillars? After all, Peter and James do lead the movement called the Way of Righteousness (aka the Jewish Jesus Movement). According to Paul they are servants of Satan, masquerading as servants of righteousness.*

The Gospel of Mark introduces two sets of brothers as the first and most important followers of Jesus: Peter and his brother Andrew, and James and John, the sons of Zebedee (Mark 1:14–20). Note that Peter,

*Some Christian commentators claim that Paul is referring to other local preachers who challenge his gospel. However, after reading Romans, 1 and 2 Corinthians, and Gala-tians, I conclude that his true enemy is James's Jewish Jesus Movement.

James, and John become Jesus's inner circle, while Andrew is never heard from again. If the Jewish Messiah (Judas the Galilean) does have an inner circle, it would have consisted of Peter and his brothers James and John, those reputed to be the pillars. Why does Mark change Jesus's brothers into the sons of Zebedee, unrelated disciples? Perhaps Mark's goal is to totally distance Jesus of Nazareth from the pillars' teachings, to distance Jesus from the Law and circumcision.

John the Baptist and Herod Antipas

Josephus writes:

> Now, when [many] others came in crowds about him, for they were greatly moved [or pleased] by hearing his words, Herod, who feared lest the *great influence John had over the people might put it into his power and inclination to raise a rebellion (for they seemed ready to do anything he should advise), thought it best, by putting him to death,* to prevent any mischief he might cause, and not bring himself into difficulties, by sparing a man who might make him repent of it when it should be too late. (*Antiquities* 18.118) (Emphasis mine)

In 36 CE John has great influence over the people, so much so that he is capable of sparking a rebellion. Herod knows he must act, so he cuts off the head of the beast. The murder of John is both religious and political. John's criticism of Herod's marriage could have incited a large-scale rebellion and that could not be allowed.

The Gospel of Mark simply states, "Herod feared John and protected him, knowing him to be a righteous and Holy man. When Herod heard John, he was greatly puzzled; yet he liked to listen to him" (Mark 6:19–20). According to Mark Herod has only the highest respect for John. In fact, Herod protects John. The question should be asked: Who threatens John, necessitating Herod's protection? Is the threat from his wife, Herodias?

Mark's account of Herod's relationship to John is diametrically opposed to Josephus's version. In Mark Herod likes and protects John against the evil designs of his wife, Herodias. The political ramifications of John's power over the crowds are not mentioned; John is alone, with no support other than Herod's own protection. But this is untrue. John is immensely popular with the opposition crowds. It is Herod himself, not his wife, who wishes John dead, so he can forestall a rebellion against his rule.

Only a Herodian supporter could have written this account of John's death, placing the blame on Herod's wife for purely selfish motives. The real guilty party, Herod Antipas, is exonerated. We are encouraged to believe that Herod even likes John.

Jesus Is a Friend of Both Tax Collectors and Sinners

Mark introduces the reader to Jesus's preferred audience:

> When the teachers of the law who were Pharisees saw him eating with the "sinners" and tax collectors, they asked his disciples: "Why does he eat with *tax collectors and 'sinners'*?" On hearing this, Jesus said to them, "It is not the healthy who need a doctor, but the sick. *I have not come to call the righteous, but sinners.*" (Mark 2:13–17) (Emphasis mine)

First, the thought that Jesus does not call the righteous is absurd. His movement is known as the Way of Righteousness. John baptizes those whose souls have been "thoroughly purified beforehand by righteousness" (*Antiquities* 18.117). A sinner can only become righteous by repentance and starting a new life, based on the Torah's commands. As such tax collectors and "sinners" cannot remain tax collectors and "sinners" if they wish to follow the Jewish Messiah.

The tax collectors and "sinners" are part of Paul's own ministry of forgiveness through faith. Note that the Herodians are the Roman tax collectors and that many of the Herodian women are considered prostitutes, for they have unlawful affairs.* The author of Matthew states

---

*Herodias is the unlawful wife of Herod Antipas. Drusilla is persuaded by Simon the magician to forsake her husband and marry the Roman governor, Felix. And Bernice is rumored to be having an incestuous relationship with her brother, Agrippa II, before becoming the mistress of Titus, who destroys of the Temple and becomes a Caesar.

that the tax collectors and prostitutes are entering the kingdom of heaven ahead of the teachers of the Law (Matthew 21:31–32). In short, the extremely negative labels of *tax collectors, prostitutes,* and *sinners* are removed and even glorified, for they supposedly follow Jesus. This is a complete reversal. These Herodian stand-ins are Paul's disciples. In 1 Corinthians even Paul is shocked by his followers' sinful behaviors, where one "believer" is sleeping with his father's wife (1 Corinthians 5:1–5). This behavior would have been anathema to Judas the Galilean/Jesus.

In the book of Acts Paul meets with Agrippa II and Bernice. Paul is quite friendly with these Herodians and allegedly preaches his gospel to them. From Josephus we know that Agrippa II and his sister, Bernice, are having an incestuous affair. In reality Paul is rubbing elbows with the most sinful elements of Jewish society. Such a meeting would not have occurred between these Herodians and Jesus (Judas the Galilean). Like John the Baptist's condemnation of Herod Antipas, Jesus would have condemned the actions of Agrippa II and Bernice.

Peter Is Married and Jesus (Paul) Is Celibate

Mark claims that Peter is married (Mark 1:29–31). Jesus visits the home of Peter and finds Peter's mother-in-law in bed with a fever. What can we possibly learn from this episode? Peter is married and Jesus is not? Of course, the unmarried and celibate Jesus has the power to cure not only Peter's mother-in-law but everyone else, too.

Not surprisingly Paul also writes about Peter's wife and his own celibacy. In 1 Corinthians Paul defends his much more spartan lifestyle by contrasting his work with that of the other apostles, primarily Peter and the Lord's brothers:

> This is my defense to those who sit in judgment on me. Don't we have the right to food and drink? Don't we have the right to take a believing wife along with us, as do the other apostles and the Lord's brothers and Cephas [Peter]? Or is it only I and Barnabas who must work for a living? (1 Corinthians 9:3–5).

Paul defends himself from criticism by arguing that his celibacy permits him to work harder for God, pitting himself against Peter and the Lord's own brothers. Perhaps the gospel picture of Jesus's celibacy is not factual, but instead is based on the biography of Paul.

In reality only one Jewish group at the time practices celibacy—the Essenes. Jesus and his disciples are not Essenes, since Peter, the Lord's brothers, and all the Jewish apostles have wives. Without a doubt Jesus also has a wife, as procreation was an important aspect of Judaism. After all anyone not following the very first commandment in the Torah—"Be fruitful and multiply"—has not fulfilled that part of the covenant with God. Celibacy is not the norm and certainly not considered more religious in any sense.

Judas the Galilean, the most celebrated first-century Jewish teacher and Messiah, is married and had numerous sons. These sons become important members of his movement and die for the cause. The supposed celibacy of "Jesus" effectively writes these sons out of the gospel story. And the wife of the gospel Jesus also becomes a nonentity. Is Jesus married to Mary Magdalene? Most likely, yes.

Only Paul considers celibacy a badge of honor. And only Paul is celibate, not the Jewish Messiah. So who could possibly gain by presenting Jesus as celibate? Surely, Paul is patterning his Jesus of Nazareth after his own life and ministry.

Reconciliation through Faith

The Gospel of Mark consistently stresses the importance of faith. Those healed by Jesus receive the blessing through faith and not by any effort of their own.* Again, this picture of Jesus does not accord with Josephus's account of John's teachings, where the people prepare themselves for baptism by practicing righteousness. This change from personal responsibility to faith in Jesus comes from Paul and not from Jesus or his brother, James.

---

*In Mark 5:25–34 Jesus says, "Daughter, your faith has healed you." And Mark 6:56 states, "They begged him to let them touch even the edge of his cloak, and all who touched him were healed."

Paul writes that "No one will be declared righteous in his sight by observing the law" and that a new "righteousness from God comes through faith in Jesus Christ to all who believe" (Romans 3:20–22). Knowing the positions of James and Paul, the Jesus of Mark's gospel is based on Paul's theology and not on the historical teachings of the Jewish Messiah.

Miracles of Jesus and Paul

The Gospel of Mark includes three miracles performed by Jesus that correspond to miracles allegedly performed by Paul in the book of Acts. Jesus heals a woman who is bleeding as she touches his cloak and he also heals a boy with an evil spirit (Mark 5:25–34 and 9:14–32). In Acts "God did extraordinary miracles through Paul. Handkerchiefs and aprons that had touched him were taken to the sick, and their illnesses were cured and the evil spirits left them" (Acts 19:11–12). Jesus also raises the daughter of Jairus from the dead (Mark 5:35–43), matched by Paul, when he raises Eutychus from the dead at Troas (Acts 20:7–12).

Is the Jewish Messiah really a miracle worker? According to Josephus leaders of the opposition party (Zealots and Sicarii) promise great miracles for the people. For example, Theudas leads a group out into the desert and promises to part the Jordan River as Moses parted the Red Sea. If the people believe this, then why not believe in lesser miracles? The Jewish Messiah may well have been a healer or at least perceived as a healer. In addition, the Slavonic Josephus refers to its Messiah as the wonder worker, instead of the name *Jesus*.

More importantly Jesus of Nazareth performs miracles through the power of God's Holy Spirit working through faith. This Holy Spirit and the power of faith can do anything. Paul brags about things that no one else can even contemplate. According to Paul he has been whisked up to heaven, a feat beyond that performed by any mere wonder worker. On the other hand Jesus cannot perform any miracles in his hometown because of the people's lack of faith (Mark 6:5). Thus, Jesus of Nazareth and his miracles are tied to faith, just as Paul preaches.

Jesus Predicts His Own Death and Resurrection

The Messiah (Jesus) regularly tells his dim-witted disciples that he is going to suffer and die (Mark 8:31–33; 9:11–13, 30–32; 10:32–34; 14:8, 25, 28, 62). The first account is as follows:

> He then began to teach them that the Son of Man must suffer many things and be rejected by the elders, chief priests and teachers of the law, and that *he must be killed and after three days rise again.* He spoke plainly about this, and Peter took him aside and began to rebuke him. *But when Jesus turned and looked at his disciples, he rebuked Peter. "Out of my sight, Satan!" he said. "You do not have in mind the things of God, but the things of men."* (Mark 8:31–33) (Emphasis mine)

In Galatians Paul claims that Christ gives himself up for our sins and is raised from the dead (1:1–4). Certainly, the words placed into the mouth of Jesus come from Paul's philosophy. It appears unlikely that a Jewish Messiah would have foretold his death in such a manner. In essence Jesus would have been promising the kingdom of heaven concurrent with his prediction of defeat at the hands of Rome. The coming kingdom of heaven is paramount to Jesus's message. Only with victory over Rome can this kingdom be realized. Jesus does not foresee his own death, as he trusts God completely. Through the power of God Jesus believes his kingdom of heaven will be realized. When Jesus hangs on the cross, he shows his utter despair over God's inaction by exclaiming, "My God, my God, why have you forsaken me?" (Mark 15:34).

In addition, Mark singles out Peter for his opposition to Jesus. Jesus states that Peter does not follow the things of God, but, rather, the things of men. Paul writes, "If I were still trying to please men, I would not be a servant of Christ" (Galatians 1:10). Also, Mark makes it clear that Jesus rebukes Peter in front of the disciples. At Antioch Paul also rebukes Peter "in front of them all" (Galatians 2:14). And finally, Jesus calls Peter Satan. Likewise, Paul calls the Jewish Jesus Movement leadership disciples of Satan (2 Corinthians 11:13–15). Thus, it can be asserted that Jesus's prediction, as reported in the Gospel of Mark, of his death and resurrection and his rebuke of Peter really come from Paul, the man who invents his gospel based on the death and resurrection of Christ and who also suffers opposition from Peter.

Jesus and Paul on the Fall of Jerusalem

Jesus's words concerning the fall of Jerusalem and the Temple, as recorded by Mark, are as follows:

> When you see "the abomination that causes desolation" standing where it does not belong—let the reader understand—then let those who are in Judea flee to the mountains. Let no one on the roof of his house go down or enter the house to take anything out. Let no one in the field go back and get his cloak. How dreadful it will be in those days for pregnant women and nursing mothers! Pray that this will not take place in winter, because those will be days of distress unequaled from the beginning, when God created the world, until now—and never to be equaled again. If the Lord had not cut short those days, no one would survive. But for the sake of the elect, whom he has chosen, he has shortened them. (Mark 13:14–20)

According to S. G. F. Brandon this passage is of Zealot origin and can only have referred to two events: the proposed statue of Caligula in 40 CE and the eventual destruction of the Temple in 70 CE by Titus. The passage originally pertained to the earlier event (Caligula) but was adapted to the later event (Titus) by the phrase "let the reader understand." Brandon notes that the reference to winter alludes to Petronius's forces in the winter of 40 CE and the shortening of days refers to the assassination of Caligula.[5] In short, this passage, referring to events in 40 CE, instructs members of the Zealots to withdraw to their strongholds in the mountains.

If this prophecy is not actually uttered by the Jewish Messiah, then its inclusion in Mark's gospel shows that the gospel was written after the destruction of Jerusalem in 70 CE. The author of Mark must have known about the earlier threat to the Temple in 40 CE and then applied this passage to the actual destruction in 70 CE by the phrase "let the reader understand." Paul would have been a member of the Jewish Jesus Movement in 40 CE and would have known about Caligula's threat to the Temple. Paul also would have been in Jerusalem up to 67 CE and would surely have heard of Titus's eventual destruction of Jerusalem and the Temple in 70 CE. If anyone shaped this passage concerning the destruction of the Temple, it was more likely Paul than Jesus.

Even in the gospels and Acts evidence exists supporting Jesus's love of the Temple. He cleanses the Temple as an act of purification, stating: "My house will be called a house of prayer for all nations" (Mark 11:17). Why would he do this, if he knew that the Temple was going to be destroyed? In addition, the early disciples met and prayed regularly at the Temple (Acts 3:1). Again, why would these disciples attend the Temple if they knew it would soon be destroyed? The real disciples of Jesus have a great love for the Temple, never dreaming of its ultimate destruction. They still believe that, with the power of God, they will triumph over Rome.

Peter Disowns Jesus (Paul)

Mark deliberately points out that Peter emphatically supports Jesus before eventually disowning him three times (Mark 14:27–31, 66–72). In fact, Peter does not realize how cowardly his actions are until the cock crows, reminding him of Jesus's prophecy. Considering what is known about the Zealots, Peter would not have denied knowing the Messiah. According to Josephus the followers of Judas the Galilean were not cowardly and underwent all types of torture before calling any person Lord (*Antiquities* 18.23–25).

What can be made of Peter's denial of Jesus? There are two possible explanations. First, Jesus may have instructed his disciples to distance themselves from him so that they might fight another day. After all, how would their capture and crucifixion benefit the movement?

However, such a solution does not accord with the Zealot practice of never denying God and his Law.

The second possibility concerns Paul and his argument with Peter at Antioch (44 CE).

> When Peter came to Antioch, I opposed him to his face, because he was in the wrong. *Before certain men came from James, he used to eat with the Gentiles.* But when they arrived, he began to draw back and *separate himself from the Gentiles because he was afraid of those who belonged to the circumcision group.* The other Jews joined him in his hypocrisy, so that by their hypocrisy even Barnabas was led astray. (Galatians 2:11–13) (Emphasis mine)

Note that Peter supports Paul, just as Peter supports Jesus. But when the circumcision group arrives, Peter withdraws his support for Paul just as Peter disowns Jesus because of his fears. Could this story of Peter's denial have been written or inspired by Paul?

The Last Supper

Most people assume that Jesus and the Twelve celebrated the Last Supper before the arrest in the Garden of Gethsemane. At that Last Supper Jesus predicts Peter's denial and Judas Iscariot's betrayal. In addition, Jesus institutes a new covenant where disciples share his body and blood.

> While they were eating, Jesus took bread, gave thanks and broke it, and gave it to his disciples, saying, "Take it; *this is my body.*" Then he took the cup, gave thanks and offered it to them, and they drank from it. "*This is the blood of the covenant,* which is poured out for many," he said to them. "I tell you the truth, I will not drink again of the fruit of the vine until that day when I drink it anew in the kingdom of God." (Mark 14:22–25) (Emphasis mine)

Does a Jewish Messiah predict his own death and then transubstantiate his own flesh and blood to create a new covenant? What would become of the old covenant? What would become of the purity laws and circumcision? This whole episode, and the speech put into Jesus's mouth, seems utterly invented. Jesus marches triumphantly into Jerusalem with the support of the crowds and cleanses the Temple, an act of rebellion against the Herodians and Rome. Now, Jesus is telling his disciples that the campaign against Rome has been a front; the real mission is his death and their participation in that death. That is why they are to drink of his blood and eat of his body. This is a radical shift. The message is changed totally, from universal world transformation into something akin to cannibalism.

Such a Last Supper is not instituted by the Jewish Messiah but is invented by Paul. Paul states that he has received instructions from the Lord. Since he has never met the Jewish Messiah in person, Paul is referencing the Risen Christ. His revelations concerning the Last Supper are as follows:

> *Is not the cup of thanksgiving for which we give thanks a participation in the blood of Christ? And is not the bread that we break a participation in the body of Christ?* Because there is one loaf, we, who are many, are one body, for we all partake of the one loaf. . . . *For I received from the Lord What I also pass onto you:* The Lord Jesus on the night he was betrayed [*handed over* per the Greek text], took bread, and when he had given thanks, he broke it and said, "This is my body, which is for you; do this in remembrance of me." In the same way, after supper he took the cup, saying, "*This cup is the new covenant in my blood;* do this, whenever you drink it, in remembrance of me." For whenever you eat this bread and drink this cup, you proclaim the Lord's death until he comes. (1 Corinthians 10:16–17; 11:23–26) (Emphasis mine)

Even though the inspiration for his Last Supper interpretation comes from the Risen Christ, Paul places these revelatory words into the mouth of the Jewish Messiah. Paul claims that his revelation begins with the earthly Jesus, even though he receives it through the Risen Christ. The following elements of the Last Supper are in both Mark and 1 Corinthians:

- Jesus offers the bread and wine to his disciples, comparing this food to his own body and blood.
- The blood is the new covenant, a doctrine originating with Paul but refuted by James and Peter.
- The idea that the believer can participate in the body and blood of Christ is a clear nod to the mystery religions of the time.

In short Paul's interpretation of a meal (his revelation from the Risen Christ) is incorporated into the teachings of Jesus of Nazareth.

The real Jewish Messiah celebrates a meal with his closest disciples. They break bread, drink wine, and pray to God. But the Jewish Messiah does not introduce elements that clearly go against Jewish sensibilities. Eating the body and blood of a person is not permissible at any place or any time. The real Jesus does not endorse the mystery religions of the time.

The *Didache* (IX), written by early Christians, addresses the Last Supper. In it the bread and wine are not the body and blood of Jesus. Apparently these early "Christians" had not yet been sold on Paul's (and Mark's) interpretation.

The Charges against Jesus and Paul

Who chronicles the trial of Jesus before Pilate? With no eyewitnesses or transcripts, any information concerning the trial must be viewed with a measure of skepticism. From Mark's account the chief priests accuse Jesus out of envy and Pilate simply wants to please the crowds. Matthew adds that Pilate and his wife believe Jesus to be innocent and that the Jewish people want Jesus crucified. Luke has Pilate send Jesus to Herod Antipas, while the Gospel of John has Pilate working on Jesus's behalf, even asking Jesus, "What is truth?" In short each version of Jesus's trial emphasizes each gospel writer's own agenda.

In the synoptic gospels two traditions exist concerning the charges against Jesus. In Mark and Matthew the false testimony concerning the Temple is played out in front of the Sanhedrin. In Mark Jesus supposedly says, "I will destroy this manmade temple and in three days will build another, not made by man" (Mark 14:58). In Matthew Jesus claims, "I am able to destroy the Temple of God and rebuild it in three days" (Matthew 26:61). However, in Luke the charges before Pilate and Herod are quite different and probably closer to the truth. According to Luke the whole assembly accuses Jesus before Pilate, saying, "We have found this man subverting our nation. He opposes payment of taxes to Caesar and claims to be Christ, a king" (Luke 23:1–2). In essence Jesus's mission is political as well as religious. He claims to be the promised Messiah, who will overthrow Rome's rule and its Herodian puppets. After reviewing the case Pilate supposedly states: "You have brought me this man as one who was inciting the people to rebellion. I have examined him in your presence and have found no basis for your charges against him" (Luke 23:13–14). Instead of focusing on rebuilding the Temple in three days, Luke reveals the true charges against Jesus: claims of kingship (Messiah), refusal to pay taxes to Rome, and inciting rebellion. Even though Luke presents the actual charges against Jesus, he excuses Pilate and places the blame for Jesus's crucifixion squarely on the Jews.

Would the Jewish Messiah have claimed his intention to destroy the Temple and rebuild it in three days? Even in the gospels Jesus has great respect for the Temple built by Herod the Great. While cleansing the Temple Jesus quotes Isaiah 56:7, "My house will be called a house of prayer for all nations." Note that Judas the Galilean and Matthias cleansed the Temple of the polluting Golden Eagle. So no evidence exists that any Jewish Messiah would seek to destroy the Temple of God.

On the other hand Paul preaches a brand of Judaism that disdains the Law. In fact, Paul states that "a man is not justified by observing the law, but by faith in Christ Jesus" (Galatians 2:16). Paul, not Jesus, is accused of destroying the Temple (that is, by undermining the Law and circumcision) and wants to replace the Law with faith in Jesus. Thus, Mark's statement, "I will destroy this manmade Temple and in three days will build another, not made by man," relates to Paul and his teachings. In Acts the charge of desecrating the Temple is brought against Paul (Acts 24:5–8). And finally, the Ebionites claim that Paul is an apostate from the Law, a charge demonstrably and wholly true.[6]

Theologically, the destruction of the Temple points toward Paul, but what about historically? The dating of Mark has been placed at post–70 CE because of Mark 13:2, where Jesus supposedly says, "Do you see all these great buildings? . . . Not one stone here will be left on another; every one will be thrown down." In the first century the Temple is in danger twice, during the reign of Caligula (40 CE) and during the war with Rome (70 CE). Certainly, Jesus does not foresee the Temple's destruction in his lifetime, and his disciples die in Jerusalem in 70 CE. Therefore, no messianic disciple would have envisioned this great calamity or would have lived to write about it.

Paul understands that the Romans would level Jerusalem, so perhaps the warning in Mark 13 is one foreseen by him and not by Jesus. Paul may have taken the Zealot warning in the Caligula affair and applied it to the actual destruction of the Temple in 70 CE.

Judas Iscariot

Is a follower of the Jewish Messiah actually guilty of betrayal? Such a betrayal would have been against the Messiah, the law of Moses, and the Jewish nation.

Mark introduces Judas Iscariot to the world. In naming the Twelve Judas is listed last, as the one who betrays Jesus (Mark 3:19). As his motive Judas is promised money, but the infamous thirty pieces of silver is not mentioned (Mark 14:10). At the Last Supper Jesus predicts that one of the Twelve will betray him (Mark 14:17–21). And finally, in the Garden of Gethsemane, Judas betrays Jesus with a kiss (Mark 14:43–46). Mark writes nothing else concerning Judas Iscariot.

Does Judas Iscariot actually betray Jesus? While still in the Jewish Jesus Movement Paul writes that Jesus is handed over but does not overtly accuse one of the Twelve of betrayal (1 Corinthians 11:23). In fact, in the same letter, Paul states that the postcrucifixion Jesus appears to the Twelve, not the Eleven, as noted by Mark.* The Gospel of Peter also claims that the Twelve, not the Eleven, mourn for Jesus.[7] And finally, the Slavonic Josephus claims that the chief priests hand the wonder worker over to Pilate with a bribe of thirty talents, not mentioning Judas Iscariot at all (SJ *War* 2.174, from additional passages). In three different sources, then, Judas Iscariot is not cited, and Paul's letter to the Corinthians is the earliest account and surely the most accurate.

Is Paul the betrayer? He preaches an antinomian message, claiming that the new covenant with God comes through faith in Christ Jesus. He also, literally, betrays the Messiah's disciples. After Paul's ouster from the Jewish Jesus Movement at Antioch in 44 CE, movement leaders are arrested and put to death, including Theudas and the sons of Judas the Galilean (*Antiquities* 20.97–102). And later, Paul persecutes the poorer priests after the stoning of James the Just (*Antiquities* 20.200–214). Certainly, Paul had earned the title of traitor.[8]

The author of Mark turns the *traitor* label against the Jews; in particular the Sicarii, followers of Judas the Galilean. The name *Judas* represents the Jews, while *Iscariot* is simply a garbling of *Sicarios*. Thus, instead of Paul betraying Judas the Galilean's movement, the Jews betray Jesus of Nazareth, the stand-in for Paul. This simple sleight of hand saves Paul's reputation and forever damns the fictional character, Judas Iscariot.

Mark's account of Judas Iscariot might also shed light on the dating of his gospel. Mark is written after 70 CE, since the destruction of the Temple is recorded. But how far after 70 CE? If Judas Iscariot represents the Jewish resistance movement, then it follows that Mark must have been written *before 73 CE,* the year the Sicarii commit mass suicide at Masada. Otherwise, Mark would have included the suicide of Judas Iscariot, similar to the later Gospel of Matthew and the Acts of the Apostles (Matthew 27:1–10; Acts 1:15–22).

---

*This is found in both 1 Corinthians 15:3–5 and Mark 16:14. The passage in Mark is not in the earliest of manuscripts but the number Eleven has to be put forth as Judas is no longer among the apostles.

Barabbas

The Barabbas story originates in 4 BCE, at the prisoner release of Archelaus. Archelaus succeeds Herod the Great, eager to consolidate his power. Initially, he grants the crowd's wishes, including lower taxes and a prisoner release (*Antiquities* 17.205). In reality the Jewish crowd cries out for the release of Judas Barabbas, the son of Matthias and leader of the early Fourth Philosophy.

The Barabbas story is retained by Mark, but its history and meaning are distorted. In Mark two separate individuals are judged by the Jews: Jesus of Nazareth and Barabbas. Remember Jesus of Nazareth is a stand-in for Paul. As such the Jewish crowd prefers the rebellious Barabbas over Paul's Jesus of Nazareth. In short the Jews choose the Law over Paul's new gospel of grace. The Jews reject Jesus of Nazareth just as they rejected Paul at Antioch (Galatians 2:11–14).

Who Understands Jesus?

Who really understands Jesus's message? Does Peter understand Jesus when Jesus foretells his death? After all, Jesus says to Peter, "Out of my way Satan! . . . You do not have in mind the things of God, but the things of men" (Mark 8:33). Peter understands the typical concept of Messiah. Surely the Messiah will triumph over the Romans and set Israel free. But Jesus of Nazareth is not the typical Messiah. Only someone who actually speaks to the Risen Christ can understand the things of God. And that person is Paul.

Burton Mack writes that the disciples "are negative examples, letting the reader see that one could be a better disciple of Jesus by *following* the story in Mark's time than the disciples who *followed* Jesus in Jesus' time."[9] In short why follow the actual disciples of Jesus, since they constantly appear confused about his true ministry? Mark wants his readers to follow his Jesus of Nazareth, not the real Jewish Messiah. Paul shares this view. In Galatians Paul claims that his revelatory gospel is superior to all other gospels, including the one preached by Peter and James (Galatians 1:6–12).

It must be emphasized that Mark's Jesus of Nazareth is not the

Messiah of history. Rather, Mark's Messiah is a strange amalgam of Paul's new gospel and the actual Messiah of history. However, what remains of the historical Messiah is stripped of all nationalistic goals and political ambitions and shaped into a pro-Roman figure, acceptable to a Gentile audience. Is it any wonder that Peter cannot understand this Jesus?

Jesus Christ, the Son of God

In Mark's introductory statement he refers to his subject as "Jesus Christ, the Son of God" (Mark 1:1). The pairing of Jesus and Christ is consistent with Paul's language in his letters.[10] In addition, unlike the Jewish Jesus Movement, Mark claims that "Jesus Christ" is the Son of God, clearly a title associated with Paul's Christ Movement. In Romans Paul states: "Christ Jesus . . . who as to his human nature was a descendant of David, and who through the Spirit of holiness was declared with power to be the Son of God by his resurrection from the dead" (Romans 1:1–4). Paul's conception of Christ Jesus as the Son of God is placed into the Gospel of Mark to underscore his own teachings on the subject.

Irenaeus claims that the Ebionites believe "that Jesus was not born of a virgin but was the son of Joseph and Mary, like other men, but superior to all others in justice, prudence and wisdom."[11] These Ebionites are the remnants of the Jewish Jesus Movement, their views irreconcilable with the claim of Mark, that Jesus Christ is the Son of God.

The Parable of the Tenants

The parable of the tenants does not originate with the Jewish Messiah. The son in the story is beaten and killed by the Jews, which is evidence that the parable was written after Jesus's death and only for polemical purposes by Pauline Christians. It is nothing less than an allegory of first-century history: the Jews replaced by the Gentiles.

A man planted a vineyard. He put a wall around it, dug a pit for the winepress and built a watchtower. Then he rented the vineyard to some farmers and went away on a journey. At harvest time he sent a servant to the tenants to collect from them some of the fruit of the vineyard. But they seized him, beat him and sent him away empty-handed. Then he sent another servant to them; they struck this man on the head and treated him shamefully. He sent still another, and that one they killed. He sent many others; some of them they beat, others they killed. He had one left to send, a son, whom he loved. He sent him last of all, saying, "They will respect my son." But the tenants said to one another, "This is the heir. *Come let's kill him, and the inheritance will be ours.*" So they took him and killed him, and threw him out of the vineyard. What will the owner of the vineyard do? *He will come and kill those tenants and give the vineyard to others.* (Mark 12:1–12) (Emphasis mine)

The man, the servants, and the son represent God, the prophets, and Jesus, respectively. The tenants are the Jews and those receiving the vineyard from the tenants are the Gentiles. We are to believe that the Jewish Messiah, hailed by the Jews, claims that God will replace them and give their inheritance to the Gentiles. Once again this is the theology of Paul, not that of the Jewish Messiah.

Paul writes about this concept of transferring the inheritance from the Jews to the Gentiles. His most amazing scriptural distortion concerns the covenants represented by Sarah and Hagar (Galatians 4:21–31). First, he associates the Jews with Hagar and the Gentiles with Sarah, a complete reversal of the Genesis story. If Paul had honestly reported the story, he would have also included God's promise to Hagar concerning Ishmael, where God says, "Lift the boy up and take him by the hand, for I will make him into a great nation" (Genesis 21:17–18). In the Genesis story both Isaac and Ishmael are promised inheritances. Isaac becomes the father of the Jewish people while Ishmael becomes the father of the Arabs. Second, Paul then states that Hagar represents Mount Sinai, the mount where Moses receives the Ten Commandments (Exodus 19 and 20). To Paul the Jews are slaves (Hagar) to the law of Moses, while his people were free (Sarah) from its regulations.

This same type of reversal of fortune can be found in Romans. Paul writes: " . . . it is not the natural children who are God's children, but it is the children of the promise who are regarded as Abraham's offspring" (Romans 9:8).

Therefore, the parable of the tenants is a Pauline production, transferring the inheritance from the Jews to the Gentiles. This is a very attractive message for the Gentiles (Mark's audience), knowing that they are the chosen people of God through faith.

Salvation for the Jews First, and Then for the Gentiles

Even though Paul is the apostle to the Gentiles, his early writings show that salvation will be offered first to the Jews and then to the Gentiles. He writes: "I am not ashamed of the gospel, because it is the power of God for the salvation of everyone who believes: first for the Jew, then for the Gentile" (Romans 1:16). Of course, he also argues that the Jews have hardened their hearts against God and their insistence on following the Torah will not save them.

While Paul develops his own gospel of faith, he is still part of the Jewish Jesus Movement, associated with Peter and James and their devotion to the Law. Paul cannot claim that the Law is null and void, but he does dance around this position. He states that the Law has a purpose, but that the followers of the Law could be Gentiles through faith. He writes: "A man is not a Jew if he is one outwardly, nor is circumcision merely outward and physical. No, a man is a Jew if he is one inwardly; and circumcision is circumcision of the heart, by the Spirit, not by the written code" (Romans 2:28–29). This circumcision of the heart is not new. Deuteronomy emphasizes the importance of this inward circumcision of the heart while not abolishing the actual physical circumcision or the Law in general (Deuteronomy 6:4–9; 10:16; 11:22).

Even in the book of Acts Paul goes to the Jews first and, when rebuffed, turns to the Gentiles. In his final statement Paul supposedly says to the Jews, "I want you to know that God's salvation has been sent to the Gentiles, and they will listen!" (Acts 28:28).

This same approach is given to Jesus of Nazareth. Jesus travels to

Tyre, where a Greek woman, born in Syrian Phoenicia, asks him to heal her daughter. The conversation should remind us of the apostle Paul.

> "First let the children [the Jews] eat all they want," he told her, for it is not right to take the children's bread and toss it to the dogs."
>
> "Yes, Lord," she replied, "but even the dogs under the table eat the children's crumbs."
>
> Then he told her, "For such a reply, you may go; the demon has left your daughter." (Mark 7:27–29)

Jesus of Nazareth, like Paul, goes first to the Jews in order to save them but, invariably, real faith comes from the Gentiles. The children's (the Jewish people's) bread is given to the dogs (the Gentiles), because the Gentiles listen and believe.

Does Jesus refer to the Gentiles as "dogs," a pejorative term? Even if he does so, the passage illustrates the importance of faith. Even the lowliest of creatures (the Gentiles) could be reconciled with God through faith. This surely assures Paul's Gentile communities that faith can secure salvation.

Jesus, the Synagogues, and the Gentiles

Mark's Jesus of Nazareth spends much time outside of Galilee and Judea and in lands populated by Gentiles. According to Burton Mack the confrontations with the Pharisees at the synagogues actually reflect the Diaspora situation, not the environs of Galilee.[12] Again, this describes Paul's activities, not those of the Jewish Messiah.

The Spirit Is Willing, but the Flesh Is Weak

After Jesus prays in the Garden of Gethsemane, he returns to find Peter and the others sleeping. "Simon," he says to Peter, "Are you asleep? Could you not keep watch for one hour? Watch and pray so that you will not fall into temptation. The spirit is willing, but the body is weak" (Mark 14:37–38). What a strange statement for the Jewish Messiah to make! After all the Messiah and John the Baptist have preached righteousness to their disciples. This righteousness concerns controlling the flesh. On the other hand Paul preaches that the flesh is uncontrollable; only the spirit guides one in the ways of God.

Paul writes: "I know that nothing good lives in me, that is, in my sinful nature [the flesh]. For I have the desire to do what is good, but I cannot carry it out. . . . Those who live according to the sinful nature [the flesh] have their minds set on what that nature desires; but those who live in accordance with the Spirit have their minds set on what the Spirit desires" (Romans 7:18–8:8). To Paul following the Law can never produce goodness or control the sinful nature of the flesh. However, in practice, his "Spirit-led" disciples are unable to control their sinful nature. In fact, Paul chastises some in his Corinthian congregation who live a life worse than the pagans (1 Corinthians 5:1). Maybe the Spirit is as weak as the flesh.

The Crucifixion

> They crucified two robbers with him, one on his right and one on his left. *Those who passed by hurled insults at him,* shaking their heads and saying, "So! You who are going to *destroy the temple and build it in three days,* come down from the cross and save yourself!"
>
> In the same way, the *chief priests and the teachers of the law mocked him among themselves.* "He saved others," they said, "but he can't save himself! Let this Christ, this King of Israel, come down now from the cross, that we may see and believe." *Those crucified with him also heaped insults on him.* (Mark 15:27–32) (Emphasis mine)

Mark writes that the Jewish people, the teachers of the Law, and even those crucified with Jesus mock him because of his call to destroy the Temple and raise it in three days. Clearly, this comes from Paul's theology. The Jewish Messiah cleanses the temple and defends it against those wishing to use it for political and monetary gain.

In addition, those crucified with Jesus supposedly hurl insults at him. Mark calls these men robbers. According to Brandon Josephus uses the term *robber* to describe the Zealots.[13] Mark actually claims that the captured Zealots hurl insults at Jesus. This seems beyond belief. Why would Zealots, intent on overthrowing Roman rule, hurl insults at a Messiah figure who professes the same goals as they do? The answer is simple: They would not have insulted the Jewish Messiah figure. On the other hand Jesus of Nazareth, as depicted by Mark, is a stand-in for Paul and his teachings. The Zealots, as well as all other devout Jews, reject Paul and his gospel. The later Ebionites call Paul an apostate from the Law. Mark knows that all Jews despise Paul and simply transfers this hatred to Jesus of Nazareth.

The Resurrection of the Dead

The four philosophies in first-century Israel have different beliefs concerning the resurrection of the dead. The Sadducees believe that the soul dies with the body while the Pharisees, Essenes, and Zealots believe in a resurrection of the body, with rewards and punishments handed out according to one's righteousness (*Antiquities* 18:14–23). With this in mind we will examine a passage in Mark detailing Jesus's view on the subject.

> Then the Sadducees, who say there is no resurrection, came to him with a question. "Teacher," they said, "Moses wrote for us that if a man's brother dies and leaves a wife but no children, the man must marry the widow and have children for the brother. Now there were seven brothers. The first one married and died without leaving any children. The second one married the widow, but he also died, leaving no child. It was the same with the third. In fact, none of the seven left any children. Last of all, the woman died too. *At the resurrection, whose wife will she be, since the seven were married to her?*"
>
> Jesus replied, "Are you not in error because you do not know the Scriptures or the power of God? *When the dead rise, they will neither marry nor be given in marriage; they will be like the angels*

in heaven. Now about the dead rising—have you not read in the book of Moses, in the account of the bush, how God said to him, 'I am the God of Abraham, the God of Isaac, and the God of Jacob'? He is not the God of the dead, but of the living. You are badly mistaken!" (Mark 12:18–27) (Emphasis mine)

The passage affirms that the Sadducees do not believe in the resurrection. Their question would have been posed to a Pharisee or a Zealot, who believes in the bodily resurrection. Since Jesus is asked this question, it follows that he is a Pharisee or a Zealot. His reply is acceptable until he states that the dead will "be like the angels in heaven." This belief is unlike that of the Pharisees, Zealots, or Essenes. Where does such a belief come from?

Paul deals with the resurrection issue in his first letter to the Corinthians (1 Corinthians 15:12–57). He first addresses those who claim that there is no resurrection of the dead, corresponding to the Sadducees in Mark's story. Paul then confronts those who believe in the resurrection of the physical body, a group whose views correspond to the Pharisaic beliefs.

Paul then states: "So will it be with the resurrection of the dead. The body that is sown is perishable, it is raised imperishable; it is sown in dishonor, it is raised in glory; it is sown in weakness, it is raised in power; it is sown a natural body, it is raised a spiritual body. . . . I declare to you, brothers, that flesh and blood cannot inherit the kingdom of God, nor does the perishable inherit the imperishable" (1 Corinthians 15:42–50).

Mark's Jesus of Nazareth echoes the beliefs of Paul, in opposition to all other Jewish groups. All Jews, except the Sadducees, believe in the resurrection of the body and that rewards and punishment will be distributed depending on the righteousness of one's life. They do not believe that the body is sown in dishonor. Perhaps the core of Mark's passage goes back to the time of the Jewish Messiah, but the Pauline beliefs are added to make Jesus think and act like Paul.

Abba Father

The redundant phrase *"Abba,* Father" (meaning "Father, Father") is found only in Mark and in Paul's writings. The three instances of this phrase are as follows:

> They went to a place called Gethsemane, and Jesus said to his disciples, "Sit here while I pray." He took Peter, James and John along with him, and he began to be deeply distressed and troubled. "My soul is overwhelmed with sorrow to the point of death," he said to them. "Stay here and keep watch." Going a little further, he fell to the ground and prayed that if possible the hour might pass from him. *"Abba,* Father," he said, "everything is possible for you. Take this cup from me. Yet not what I will, but what you will." (Mark 14:32–36)

> But when the time had fully come, God sent His Son, born of a woman, born under law, to redeem those under the law, that we might receive the full rights as sons. Because you are sons, God sent the Spirit of His Son into our hearts, the Spirit who calls out, *"Abba,* Father." So you are no longer a slave, but a son; and since you are a son, God has made you also an heir. (Galatians 4:4–7)

> For you did not receive a spirit that makes you a slave again to fear, but you received the Spirit of sonship. And by him we cry, *"Abba,* Father." The Spirit himself testifies with our spirit that we are God's children. Now if we are children, then we are heirs—heirs of God and co-heirs with Christ, if indeed we share in his sufferings in order that we may also share in his glory. (Romans 8:15–17)

In Mark we are to believe that Jesus knows what is going to happen and willingly goes to his death for the sins of all humankind. In his time of distress he calls out *"Abba,* Father," claiming God as his father. Paul simply states that his Gentile disciples could also cry out *"Abba,* Father," claiming God as their father through Christ's Spirit.

Which came first—the chicken or the egg? Many scholars believe that Paul simply repeats a phrase being used throughout the early church. However, we know that Paul's letters predate Mark by at least a generation and that Mark's Jesus of Nazareth is a stand-in for Paul. As such it can be argued that the scene at Gethsemane is crafted to include Paul's own language of *"Abba,* Father." In addition, Matthew and Luke both remove *Abba* from their gospels. Perhaps the tradition of *"Abba,* Father" is not known in those parts of the world where Paul does not personally preach.

Absence of the Law

Did the Jewish Messiah live and die without commenting on the Jewish Law given by Moses? In Mark Jesus of Nazareth never mentions the Law. In fact, the Law is not referenced at all. By contrast the Law is part of the other gospels, being mentioned eight times by Matthew, ten times by Luke and a surprising twelve times by John.* We are supposed to accept the view that a Jewish Messiah teaches without reference to the central theme of Judaism and the Hebrew Bible. This is incredible! The absence of the Law in Mark is quite astounding, unless Mark is written by Paul or a disciple of Paul's theology.

Paul states: "Before this faith came, we were held prisoners by the Law, locked up until faith should be revealed. So the Law was put in charge to lead us to Christ that we might be justified by faith. Now that faith has come, we are no longer under the supervision of the Law" (Galatians 3:23–25). This same attitude toward faith and the Law finds expression in Mark's gospel. While the Law is never mentioned, Jesus of Nazareth repeatedly comments on the faith of the disciples and even the Gentiles.

Mark uses faith over Law or, rather, faith over actions. When men lower a paralytic through the roof, Jesus does not say, "Your actions have cured you." No, he supposedly sees their faith and then cures the man (Mark 2:1–12). Mark's Jesus heals people based on faith, not because of their adherence to the Law or for their righteousness before

---

*These mentions can be found in Matthew 5:17, 5:18, 7:12, 11:13, 12:5, 22:36, 22:40, and 23:23; in Luke 2:22, 2:23, 2:24, 2:27, 2:39, 5:17, 10:26, 16:16, 16:17, and 24:44; and in John 1:17, 1:45, 7:19, 7:23, 7:49, 7:51, 8:5, 8:17, 10:34, 12:34, 15:25, and 19:7.

God. This, of course, is at odds with the picture of John the Baptist as portrayed by Josephus. As noted earlier John preaches a baptism "for the purification of the body; supposing still that the soul was thoroughly purified beforehand by righteousness" (*Antiquities* 18.117). Mark's faith-driven Jesus is not a re-creation of a historical Jewish Messiah but rather a new invention, based on the teachings of Paul, an apostate from the Law.

The Noun Gospel

In his undisputed letters (Romans, 1 and 2 Corinthians, and Galatians), Paul uses the noun transliterated as *evangglion,* meaning "gospel" thirty-one times. A representative sample is as follows:

> This will take place on the day when God will judge men's secrets through Jesus Christ, as my *gospel* declares. (Romans 2:16)

> I want you to know, brothers, that the *gospel* I preached is not something that man made up. I did not receive it from any man, nor was I taught it; rather, I received it by revelation from Jesus Christ. (Galatians 1:11–12)

Paul's gospel comes from a direct revelation from Jesus Christ, bypassing all other men, including Peter and James. The usage of the term *gospel* is extensive in Paul's writings. This noun *gospel* is also used by the author of Mark eight times and by Matthew four times, but zero times by Luke or John.* In fact, Mark begins his gospel as follows: "The beginning of the *gospel* about Jesus Christ, the Son of God" (Mark 1:1). This passage clearly reflects Paul's views and is just one more example of why Mark could have been written by the Herodian, Paul.

Note that a gospel (good news) does not promise actual history. A gospel is polemical, a story designed to persuade others to adopt one's

---

*These mentions can be found in Mark 1:1, 1:14, 1:15, 8:35, 10:29, 13:10, 14:9, and 16:15 (this last usage in 16:15 is not in the earliest manuscripts); and in Matthew 4:23, 9:35, 24:24, and 26:13.

point of view. And both Paul's gospel and ultimately the Gospel of Mark are written to persuade Gentiles that they are God's new chosen people.

The Eleventh Commandment

Before Ronald Reagan issued his eleventh commandment to the Republican Party—Thou shall not attack a fellow Republican—Jesus supposedly issued his own eleventh commandment. When recalling the commandments to a rich young man, Jesus says, "You know the commandments: 'Do not murder, do not commit adultery. Do not steal, do not give false testimony, *do not defraud,* honor your father and mother'" (Mark 10:19). In creating the commandment not to defraud, Mark may have simply combined two commandments: Thou shall not steal and thou shall not covet thy neighbor's possessions (Exodus 2:2–17). However, among the gospels, the word *defraud* is peculiar to Mark. Matthew removes *defraud* and replaces it with his own eleventh commandment: "Love thy neighbor as thyself" (Matthew 19:19). Luke removes both eleventh commandments from his account (Luke 18:20).

To defraud means to deprive someone of something through deceit or fraud. Where did the word *defraud* originate? Only Paul uses the term, and it is in connection with lawsuits among believers. He writes:

> In fact, to have lawsuits at all with one another is already a defeat for you. Why not rather be wronged? *Why not rather be defrauded?* But you yourselves wrong and *defraud*—and believers at that. (1 Corinthians 6:7–8) (Emphasis mine)

It seems picky, but Mark uses the same word as Paul used when correcting his congregation at Corinth. In fact, Mark may have had this particular event at Corinth in mind when he composed the eleventh commandment. Regardless, the term *defraud* does connect the Gospel of Mark to the letters of Paul.

LANGUAGE OF THE DEAD SEA SCROLLS

As noted in chapter 2 Robert Eisenman's book, *The New Testament Code,* details the many times that Paul and Mark use the language of the Dead Sea Scrolls. This is significant, since the author of Mark must have had a working knowledge of the Scrolls. Who had a working knowledge of the Scrolls? Surely members of the Fourth Philosophy and the Jewish Jesus Movement had such knowledge. Thus, it follows that the author of Mark came from the Jewish Jesus Movement or from a group associated with it.

However, the Gospel of Mark is pro-Pauline, and this fact precludes it from being written by anyone from the Jewish Jesus Movement. The Ebionites, who label Paul as an apostate from the Law, would never have participated in the composition of Mark. The author of Mark, therefore, is undoubtedly part of Paul's Christ Movement.

But members of the Christ Movement have little knowledge of the historical Messiah. Paul minimizes the historical Jesus's significance compared to his own revelatory Christ Jesus. Clearly, Paul knew the history of the historical Messiah, but most of his disciples did not.

Which member of Paul's Christ Movement has knowledge of the historical Jesus and is also well versed in the Dead Sea Scroll language? The obvious answer is Paul himself. His letters contain Dead Sea Scroll language and he spent enough time with the Jerusalem leadership and Barnabas to know everything about the historical Jesus. Only Paul fits the bill concerning the above three criteria. No one else would have had access to his letters at this time. So the foundation legend concerning Mark, Peter's secretary, is fraudulent. Anyone associated with Peter or James is not a member of Paul's Christ Movement and therefore could not have written the Gospel of Mark.

The Gospel of Mark is the earliest written gospel concerning Jesus of Nazareth, penned sometime between 70 and 73 CE. Although it is the earliest gospel, Mark presents a Messiah who has little in common with the actual Jewish Messiah. That is why scholars have had no success locating Jesus of Nazareth in the writings of Josephus. Josephus could not have written anything about this fictional character! After all, in Josephus's time, no Jewish Messiah figure preached faith over works or belief over Torah. No Jewish Messiah championed the Gentiles over the Jews or the Romans over the nationalists. And no Jewish Messiah promised a spiritual resurrection over an earthly kingdom of God.

In actuality Jesus of Nazareth is a very successfully crafted stand-in for the apostle Paul. The war with Rome had obliterated the Jewish Messiah Movement. Paul takes advantage of this power vacuum to refashion the Messiah, his Christ Jesus, using his own life as a template. For example, the Messiah's family does not really think that he is crazy, but would have been proud of his actions against Rome. On the other hand Paul's Herodian family would have been scandalized by his adoption of an opposition party's platform.

In addition, with no one left to counter his fiction, Paul creates Jesus of Nazareth, a savior god espousing Paul's own views, not those of the defeated Jewish Jesus Movement. For example, no Messiah figure, as reported by Josephus, advocates paying taxes to Caesar. On the other hand Paul does support paying taxes to Caesar. Clearly this teaching comes from Paul and not the original Jewish Messiah.

So Paul uses his own life and his own teachings in the creation of Jesus of Nazareth. This does not mean that elements from the life of the real Messiah are not employed to some extent. As we have already noted, the real Messiah, Judas the Galilean, is crucified during the reign of Pontius Pilate, and the real Messiah is popular among the people and a threat to the ruling elites. Paul creates his Jesus of Nazareth by overlaying the life of the real Messiah with his own and by replacing most of the Messiah's teachings with his own peculiar brand of Judaism.

Why does Paul do this? My own sense is that Paul creates this savior as a fund-raising strategy. Has there ever been a better fund-raising tool than Jesus of Nazareth? And the funds did not have to be sent to Jerusalem anymore. These funds could be sent wherever Paul specified.

9 ► The Gospel of Matthew

As we have seen, the Gospel of Mark was probably written by either Paul or one of his enthusiastic supporters. Mark's Jesus of Nazareth is a thinly disguised Paul.

It's no wonder some people sense continuity between Jesus and Paul; this occurs when someone writes back into history, revising the historical figure to accommodate the author's own thinking and experiences. It is a reverse process to make Jesus conform to Paul, not vice versa. This represents a radically different way of viewing the gospels.

The second gospel to have been written is the one we call Matthew. It is important to recognize that we do not know who Matthew was as the name Matthew was attached to this gospel in the second century. As such, this gospel was not penned by the apostle Matthew.

Here's our question: Is the Jesus we find in Matthew the same as the Jesus we find in Mark? Or does Matthew give us a glimpse of a real historical Jewish Messiah?

Moreover, why another gospel anyway? Why the need for an update?

MATTHEW'S USE OF MARK

We must examine the data concerning Matthew's relationship to Mark. According to William Barclay, Mark consists of 661 verses while the longer Matthew has 1,068 verses. Of these 1,068 verses 561 are copied from Mark, or approximately 52.4 percent of Matthew comes from Mark. And Matthew not only follows the substance of Mark but reproduces his actual wording 51 percent of the time.[1] So, whatever we find in Matthew, at least the basis of his story is the Pauline Jesus of Nazareth.

Is Matthew the most Jewish of the gospels, written by a Jewish Christian? Barclay writes: "First and foremost, Matthew is the Gospel which was written for the Jews. It was written by a Jew in order to convince the Jews."[2] Before accepting this pronouncement the Ebionites must be consulted, those Jewish Christians labeled heretics by the early church fathers.

> Those who are called Ebionites . . . *use only the Gospel according to Matthew; they reject the Apostle Paul, calling him an apostate from the law.* The prophetic writings they strive to expound with especial exactness; they are circumcised, and preserve in the customs according to the Law. And in the Jewish mode of life, even to the extent of worshipping Jerusalem, as if it were the abode of God.[3] (Emphasis mine)

According to Irenaeus, cited above, the Ebionites use only the Gospel of Matthew, rejecting Paul as an apostate from the Law. But do these Ebionites use our Matthew, considering that over half of it comes from Mark, a pro-Pauline document?

Surely, there is an earlier Gospel of Matthew that does not have Mark's slanted story line. This earlier Matthew is pro-Jewish and acceptable to the Ebionites. In addition, Irenaeus associates the Ebionites with Cerinthus, who teaches that Jesus is the actual son of Mary and Joseph, not born of a virgin. Thus, the Ebionites do not believe in Matthew's Hellenistic virgin-birth mythology.

Our current Matthew consists of Mark's material (52.4 percent) and independent material from the M source (47.6 percent).[4] The M material can be broken down into three components.

Certain teachings in Matthew are also included in Luke, and this source has been named Q by scholars. I suggest that all Q materials derive from M, so I designate this as MQ. (See chapter 10 for a full discussion of the Q question.)

A second component of M consists of passages unique to Matthew, but whose themes have been copied by Luke. An example would be the genealogies of Jesus: Matthew traces his ancestry back to Abraham (very Jewish), while Luke traces his ancestry back to Adam (very Gentile). I designate this section of M as ML.

And finally, all passages unique to Matthew are simply designated as M.

Thus, the sources for Matthew are as follows:

Mark	52.4 percent
MQ	22.8 percent
ML	5.3 percent
M	19.5 percent

EXAMINING THE M MATERIAL

Was the independent M material written by a Jewish Christian or incorporated into the text by someone with anti-Jewish leanings? We will examine passages associated with the fulfillment of prophecy, the exclusivity of the Jews and the pro-Torah elements in the Sermon on the Mount. To help in this task we will utilize the Slavonic Josephus, which includes materials consistent with M.

Fulfillment of Prophecy
The Messiah comes in fulfillment of Hebrew scripture prophecies. The Jewish Jesus Movement has several generations to develop this line of argument concerning their Messiah. According to Barclay the phrase "This was to fulfill what the Lord had spoken by the prophets" occurs sixteen times in Matthew.[5] Whether properly interpreted or not, the Old Testament scriptures are being utilized in these New Testament scriptures. In some cases these scriptures support the story line supplied

by Mark. In Mark, Jesus lives in Nazareth, a claim disassociating Jesus from the revolutionary Nazarene sect.* Matthew takes Mark's bogus claim and gives it a Hebrew scripture flavor. "He went and lived in a town called Nazareth. So was fulfilled what was said through the prophets: 'He will be called a Nazarene'" (Matthew 2:23).

However, no prophet ever says: "He will be called a Nazarene." And presumably whoever wrote Matthew could count on his readers not knowing this or bothering to check. Regardless of accuracy this appeal to scripture connects Jesus to the promised Messiah. The use of Hebrew scripture prophecies is generally a tool of the Jewish Jesus Movement, but one also used by the pro-Pauline forces to further their agenda.

I will list seventeen references to fulfilling prophecy. A determination will be made as to whether the prophecy comes from the Jewish Jesus Movement or from Paul's Jesus of Nazareth Movement, created from his own Christ cult.

PROPHECIES ABOUT THE HISTORICAL JESUS
1. Matthew 2:16–18; Jeremiah 31:15—"Herod kills the infants around Bethlehem."
This prophecy concerning Herod probably originated with the early Jewish Jesus Movement. Note that the Slavonic Josephus also incorporates the Star of Bethlehem story and the story of Herod's slaughter of the innocents. This stark contrast between the bloodthirsty Herod and the innocents is good propaganda for the opposition party.

2. Matthew 3:1–3; Isaiah 40:3—"Prepare the way for the Lord."
The prophecy from Isaiah concerning John the Baptist goes back to the Jewish Jesus Movement. From John comes the emphasis on baptism and righteousness before God. This passage suggests that John is simply a messenger preparing the way for the Messiah. Surely, the Jewish

---

*In Acts 24:5 this is the charge against Paul: "We have found this man to be a troublemaker, stirring up riots among the Jews all over the world. He is a member of the Nazarene sect and even tried to desecrate the Temple." The term *Nazarene* or *Nazorean* has a negative connotation in the post–70 CE world.

Messiah outshines John, and, consequently, John is given a secondary role in the movement's history. Matthew merely incorporates this existing prophecy into his gospel.

This prophecy is also used by the Dead Sea Scroll community. These materials are in the possession of the Fourth Philosophy at Masada.

3. Matthew 8:14–17; Isaiah 53:4—"He took up our infirmities and carried our diseases."

This prophecy from Isaiah 53:4 describes the role that miracles play in Jesus's ministry. It probably originated in the early Jewish Jesus Movement and is incorporated into Matthew to illustrate Jesus's power over sickness and death.

4. Matthew 11:10; Malachi 3:1—"I will send my messenger ahead of you, who will prepare your way before you."

Like the second passage referred to above, this passage from the prophet Malachi supports John's role as a messenger who prepares the way for adherents to recognize and follow the Messiah. This, too, would have been part of the Jewish Jesus Movement's propaganda. When one reads the full passage in Malachi, it makes sense in the context of strict Torah observance, for that is what the passage goes on to say. It is simply incorporated by Matthew in order to further his claims for Jesus.

Even though this passage is used by the Jewish Jesus Movement, it is nonetheless an example of where a snippet of information may be taken out of context. In the gospels John's role is to reveal Jesus as the Jewish Messiah. That may be true, but John is also sent to prepare the way for his people, to return them to God's covenant, to point them to their Law. Matthew conveniently forgets to emphasize the return to the Law, the underlying reason for the movement. Deemphasizing the Law is simply a theological exercise, arguably intellectually dishonest and morally deceitful.

5. Matthew 21:5; Zechariah 9:9—"Say to the Daughter of Zion, 'See, your king comes to you, gentle and riding on a donkey, on a colt, the foal of a donkey.'"

The story of Jesus riding into Jerusalem on a colt is included in Mark's gospel, but Mark does not include this prophecy. Surely, this scene is central to the Jewish Jesus Movement. That Jesus picks the donkey to ride into Jerusalem clearly portrays a Messiah figure who understands staging. This would have been incorporated into the Jesus of Nazareth figure.

6. Matthew 26:31; Zechariah 13:7—"I will strike the shepherd, and the sheep of the flock will be scattered."

This prophecy is used by the Jewish Jesus Movement to help explain the failure of the Messiah. After all he has been captured and put to death. Why would anyone want to follow a failed Messiah? The Messiah's followers search the scriptures and find a passage that helps explain the failure. This is just good marketing by the Jewish Jesus Movement.

PROPHECIES ABOUT THE HISTORICAL JESUS THROUGH A PAULINE LENS

7. Matthew 2:3–6; Micah 5:2–"But you, Bethlehem, in the Land of Judah, are by no means least among the rulers of Judah; for out of you will come a ruler who will be the shepherd of my people."

The Star of Bethlehem passage claims that the Messiah will be born in Bethlehem, similar to the claim made by the Slavonic Josephus's Star of Bethlehem story (SJ *War* 1.400, from additional passages). However, the two Star of Bethlehem stories do differ significantly. For instance, the Slavonic Josephus version places the birth at 25 BCE, twenty years before Matthew does. Both stories are probably based on a very early common source.

The dating to the last years of Herod the Great may be due to Pauline influences. In Mark's narrative Jesus of Nazareth ministers to his followers after the death of John the Baptist. Since John is executed around 36 CE, the author of Matthew has to place Jesus's birth at the end of Herod's reign, making Jesus around forty-plus years of age. If Matthew had accepted the Slavonic Josephus dating, then Jesus would have been sixty-plus years old, too elderly for a Messiah figure. Thus, an original Jewish Messiah prophecy is slightly twisted to accord with Pauline goals.

8. Matthew 4:12–17; Isaiah 9:1–2—"Jesus begins his ministry in Galilee of the Gentiles."

When reading that Jesus preaches first in Galilee of the Gentiles, it appears that Jesus has the same attitude as Paul concerning the Gentiles. But, according to Barclay, the phrase "Galilee of the Gentiles" comes from the fact that Galilee is surrounded by Gentiles and their influence, on the north and east by Syria, to the west by the Phoenicians, and to the south by Samaria.[6] In fact, first-century Galilee is a hot spot for revolutionaries or messianic movements. The early Jewish Jesus Movement would have been proud of Galilee and its role in their movement. This prophecy is cleverly incorporated by Matthew to insinuate that Jesus has a message for the Gentiles. So, while it originally comes from the Jewish Jesus Movement, it is used by the Pauline movement to promote its own message to the Gentiles.

This subtle method of incorporating material, not wholly understood by Gentiles, is utilized frequently by Matthew, illustrating that the gospels are not biographies or true history but rather theologically—and politically—motivated tracts.

9. Matthew 27:9–10; Zechariah 11:12–13; and Jeremiah 32:6–9—"They took the thirty silver coins, the price set on him by the people of Israel, and they used them to buy the potter's field, as the Lord commanded me."

This prophecy about Judas Iscariot's thirty pieces of silver is part of the early Jewish Jesus Movement's propaganda. However, since Judas Iscariot is a later invention of Paul, the thirty pieces has to be connected to someone else. In the Slavonic Josephus, the thirty pieces of silver are paid by the chief priests to Pilate as a bribe (?) (SJ *War* 2.174, from additional passages). Therefore, this original passage was hijacked by the Pauline Christ Movement to further its own story line.

PROPHECIES ABOUT PAUL'S JESUS OF NAZARETH

10. Matthew 1:21–23; Isaiah 7:14 (Septuagint)—"The virgin will be with child and will give birth to a son, and they will call him Immanuel—which means, "God with us."

First of all this prophecy supports the virgin birth of Jesus, through the Holy Spirit. Remember, the Ebionites, the last vestiges of the Jewish Jesus Movement, believe that Jesus is the son of Joseph and Mary, not born of a virgin.[7] Second, the Star of Bethlehem story, as related by the Slavonic Josephus, mentions the fatherless nature of the Messiah but does not associate the Holy Spirit with the father (SJ *War* 1.400, from additional passages). This notion of being fatherless might have given the author of Matthew some ideas about Jesus's spiritual father. Third, the term *virgin* has two different interpretations, depending on whether one reads the Hebrew or Greek versions of the Old Testament. In the Hebrew the word translated as *virgin* means "young woman." In the Greek the word for *virgin* means "a woman who has not had sex." Matthew uses the Greek text (the Septuagint), a text adopted by Greek-speaking Gentile Christians. The original Jewish Jesus Movement would have used the Hebrew text. In short this passage is wholly Pauline in nature.

11. Matthew 2:15; Hosea 11:1—"Out of Egypt I called my son."

Matthew has a problem. He has to transfer the baby Jesus from Bethlehem to Nazareth, since Mark claims that Jesus comes from Nazareth. Matthew uses a number of dreams and warnings to move the baby to Egypt and then from Egypt to Nazareth. The dream sequences make it easy to move the baby Jesus through a variety of locations up to Nazareth, but cannot be accepted as true history. Perhaps Matthew would have scrapped the Egypt trip if Jesus did not need to eventually end up in Nazareth.

Brandon also conjectures that the use of Egypt in the story

might supply a hint as to Matthew's origin, possibly Alexandria.[8] If the Gospel of Mark is produced in Rome or Syria, its success might have emboldened the author to explore other markets, an important one being Alexandria. Again, this passage is Pauline in nature as it places Jesus in Nazareth, a geographical transposition of Jesus the Nazarene.

12. Matthew 2:23; No Hebrew Scripture Reference—"He will be called a Nazarene."

Once again Matthew uses prophecy to support the Nazareth claim. Interestingly, as noted earlier, the prophets never utter the name *Nazareth*. In fact, Nazareth is never cited in the Hebrew scriptures. When Matthew says, "So was fulfilled what was said by the prophets," a problem emerges. Matthew implies multiple references to Nazareth and none can be found in scripture. Surely, Matthew knows that his audience is primarily Gentile and will accept this Jewish-sounding prophecy. This is definitely Pauline in nature.

13. Matthew 12:15–21; Isaiah 42:1–4—"In his name the nations will put their hope."

Isaiah's passage originally refers to Cyrus, king of the Persians. Perhaps the Jewish Jesus Movement envisions their Messiah as a world conqueror, but surely Matthew's gospel includes this because it focuses on Jesus's role in the community of nations, those outside the Jewish religion. This dovetails perfectly with the Pauline notion that Christ Jesus is for all believers.

14. Matthew 13:11–15; Isaiah 6:9–10—"You will be ever hearing but never understanding."

According to Mark and Matthew the Jews cannot grasp the teachings of Jesus. Matthew even states that Jesus purposely speaks in parables to confound the people (Matthew 13:11). Would the Messiah have acted this way? The poor people are his supporters; they deserve better! No doubt, this prophecy comes from the Pauline camp, as Paul himself writes that the Jews do not understand his true gospel. He writes: "God gave them [Israel] a spirit of stupor, eyes so that they could not see and ears so that they could not hear to this very day" (Romans 11:8). If this prophecy were used by the Jewish Jesus Movement, it would have been directed at the power structure, at the Sadducees and Herodians, not the everyday people. Therefore, this passage is included in Matthew's text to support the Pauline view that the Jews do not understand Jesus's message.

15. Matthew 13:34–35; Psalm 78:2—"I will open my mouth in parables, I will utter things hidden since the creation of the world."

Again, the utterance of parables is used as a way to confound the crowds. Immediately following his preaching to the crowd, the disciples come to him and ask, "Explain to us the parable of the weeds of the field" (Matthew 13:36). A good teacher uses stories and parables to help people grasp his meaning. Instead, Jesus's parables are meant to confuse, not to elucidate. This cannot be true! The Jewish Messiah would have used parables to further his teachings, not obscure them. This episode is purely Pauline in nature.

16. Matthew 15:8–9; Isaiah 29:13—"These people honor me with their lips, but their hearts are far from me. They worship me in vain; their teachings are but rules taught by men."

This section of Matthew is taken from Mark 7, but Matthew removes one section. In Mark, Jesus supposedly declares all food clean. As explained in the previous chapter, it would have been inconsistent to support the Law against traditions then overturn that same Law. Matthew keeps Mark's passage but removes this obvious contradiction. Regardless, the passage is still pro-Pauline in nature.

17. Matthew 22:44; Psalm 110:1—"The Lord said to my Lord: 'Sit at my right hand until I put your enemies under your feet.'"

In its original context this saying would have applied to the king (Lord) and to God (Lord), the king being the person who would sit at God's right hand, metaphorically speaking, subduing all enemies. It is a political claim on behalf of the human ruler of Israel.

But, in this passage, Jesus claims that the Christ or Messiah is not the son (or a descendant) of David, but much more. In Paul's gospel Christ Jesus is the son of God. While the Jews believe that the Messiah will be the son of David, this prophecy supports the Pauline position.

The Jewish Messiah of history does not reject nationalism. That is a Pauline concept, layered onto the Jesus of Nazareth character. Remember, Paul wants his disciples to obey the Roman government (Romans 13:1–7). In the gospels we are to believe that the crowds welcome Jesus into Jerusalem as Messiah, even though this Messiah is pro-Roman, in that he accepts Roman taxation and has no thoughts of overturning the political realities. If the Messiah had been pro-Roman, then he would have had no popular support among the people. As such this prophecy is Pauline in nature.

The seventeen prophecies concerning Jesus are thought to be proof positive that Matthew has strong Jewish roots. However, upon close examination, Matthew uses many of the prophecies to support a Pauline position unacceptable to any Jewish Messiah or his followers. Of the seventeen prophecies, eight are purely Pauline (10 through 17, pages 174–76), three are twisted to further the Pauline claims (7 through 9, pages 172–74), and six are from the Jewish Jesus Movement and simply grafted onto Jesus of Nazareth (1 through 6, pages 170–72). Thus, the author of Matthew is part of the Pauline movement, a man with sufficient knowledge of the Jewish scriptures to help craft a supposedly Jewish context for this fictional Jesus of Nazareth. We should not forget that Paul uses the scriptures in his arguments, often distorting them to meet his desired goals. Perhaps Paul instructs his disciples to merge his creation, Jesus of Nazareth, with teachings about the real Messiah.

The Jews Are the Messiah's Main or Only Interest

Jesus sends the Twelve out with the following instructions: "Do not go among the Gentiles or enter any town of the Samaritans. Go rather to the lost sheep of Israel. As you go, preach this message: 'The kingdom of heaven is near'" (Matthew 10:5–7). This is a messianic claim that only concerns the Jewish people. Why should the apostles preach the message of the Jewish Messiah to Gentiles? Is not the Jewish Messiah's message anti-Roman? So how does the Gospel of Matthew counteract this pro-Jewish agenda? On the whole Matthew tries to bring Jesus to the Gentile world by first incorporating the pro-Jewish agenda and then by slowly moving away from this exclusive Jewish message. Such statements as "This gospel of the kingdom will be preached in the whole world as a testimony to all nations" (Matthew 24:14) and "go and make disciples of all nations" (Matthew 28:19) certainly diverts our attention away from the Jews and onto the Gentiles, the new chosen people of God.

Statements within the Sermon on the Mount Are Pro-Torah

Matthew combines the pro-Torah statements into one sermon while the statements are interspersed throughout Luke's gospel. As such the Sermon is a significant part of the MQ data. The strongest statement in the Sermon concerns the Law.

> Do not think that I have come to abolish the Law or the Prophets; *I have not come to abolish them but to fulfill them.* I tell you the truth, until heaven and earth disappear, not the smallest letter, not the least stroke of a pen, will by any means disappear from the Law *until everything is accomplished.* Anyone who breaks one of the least of these commandments and teaches others to do the same will be called least in the kingdom of heaven, but whoever practices and teaches these commands will be called great in the kingdom of heaven. For I tell you that *unless your righteousness surpasses that of the Pharisees and the teachers of the Law, you will certainly not enter the kingdom of heaven.* (Matthew 5:17–20) (Emphasis mine)

This passage illustrates the importance of the Torah to Jesus. It also emphasizes righteousness, a concept not wholly endorsed by Pauline thinking, but rather consistent with the teachings of John the Baptist. Jesus says that a person needs a certain righteousness to enter the kingdom of heaven, a view diametrically opposed to Paul's theology. On the other hand this most Jewish of passages has two curious qualifiers. First, Jesus states: "I have not come to abolish them [the Law and the prophets] but to fulfill them." Second, he adds that nothing would disappear from the Law "until everything is accomplished." What exactly is Matthew trying to convey with these qualifying statements about the Law?

To understand Matthew's intent, we must look to Paul's writings for context. Paul writes: "Christ is the end of the Law so that there may be righteousness for everyone who believes" (Romans 10:4). To Paul righteousness is earned by faith and not by actions. He also writes: "Before this faith came, we were held prisoners by the Law, locked up until faith should be revealed. So the Law was put in charge to lead us to Christ that we might be justified by faith. Now that faith has come, we are no longer under the supervision of the Law" (Galatians 3:23–25). In Paul's theology the Law is necessary to lead us to Christ and to faith in his death and resurrection. With faith the Law becomes obsolete to the believer.

In Matthew, Jesus supposedly says that he has come to fulfill the Law and that this Law will be enforced until everything had been accomplished. In short Jesus of Nazareth's death and resurrection will make the Law obsolete. With the resurrection everything had been accomplished! This clearly is from Paul's playbook. Can any real Jewish Messiah have claimed an end to the law of Moses and still be acceptable to the people? Not likely. So even this most Jewish passage concerning the Law is twisted in accordance with Pauline theology.

What does the Messiah mean by saying "until everything was accomplished"? Essentially the messianic age will transcend the Law. Do the Messiah's death and resurrection usher in this new age? The answer is no, at least according to the book of Revelation.

The bulk of Revelation is a Jewish document, anticipating a time when the Messiah will return and defeat the worldly powers. At that time, when the messianic age is introduced, the Law will be supplanted by the new heaven and Earth. This hope in the avenging Messiah is in place throughout the lifetimes of James and Peter and well beyond. That is why James and Peter meticulously follow the Law. They know that the Messiah has not yet returned and that the Law is still in effect. If James and Peter know this simple fact, then why do modern-day Christians ignore their example? The answer is clear: Modern-day Christians follow the teachings of Paul and not the teachings of the Jewish Messiah.

In the Sermon on the Mount other elements appear to be part of the Pauline approach to living. Recall Paul's assertion that the governing authorities (Caligula and Nero) have been established by God to "do you good" (Romans 13:1–7). This same sentiment is included in Jesus's speech on "an eye for an eye." Jesus supposedly says, "If someone forces you to go one mile, go with him two miles" and "do not resist an evil person" (Matthew 5:38–42). This is a radical position with little support from Old Testament writings.

First of all it is important for good people to stand up against evil. Surely, a Jewish Messiah does not encourage his followers to accept evil. And a Jewish Messiah would not have condoned the Roman occupation of Jewish lands. When Jesus of Nazareth says, "If someone forces you to go one mile, go with him two miles," he is condoning the Roman occupation. The Romans could force the Jewish citizens to do their bidding. Is the Jewish Messiah telling his followers to gladly accept this forced labor? Such a teaching does not come from a Jewish Messiah but is consistent with Paul and his relationship with the Herodians and the Roman power structure.

When Jesus gives his opinion of John the Baptist, he states that John is the Elijah who proclaims the Messiah. In fact, this admission may have also included Zealots in the mix. "From the days of John the Baptist until now, the kingdom of the heavens is forcibly entered, and violent men seize it" (Matthew 11:12).[9] This passage has mostly been ignored by scholars, as it suggests that violent men have and are entering the kingdom of heaven. This surely suggests that the Zealots are part of the Jewish Jesus Movement. This may be the most authentic portion of Matthew's gospel. However, a few verses later, a quite astonishing statement is then made by Jesus:

> For John came neither eating or drinking, and they say, "He has a demon." The Son of Man came eating and drinking, and they say, "Here is a glutton and a drunkard, *a friend of tax collectors and 'sinners.'*" But wisdom is proved right by her actions. (Matthew 11:18–19) (Emphasis mine)

Jesus is called a friend of tax collectors and sinners, and this immediately after the association of violent men with the kingdom of heaven. Matthew has to once more connect Jesus to Paul, as one being a friend to tax collectors (the Herodians) and sinners (the prostitutes of the Herodian line). This charge would have been justly leveled against Paul, but not against a Jewish Messiah, who favors righteous living.

THE M SOURCE AND THE SLAVONIC JOSEPHUS (SJ)

Many stories present only in the Gospel of Matthew are derived from a source called "M." Most Christians are not aware that another document shares these same stories, albeit with different details. The Slavonic Josephus has information concerning the following stories: the Star of Bethlehem, the brothers and mother of the Messiah, John the Baptist, Pilate's wife, the Barabbas prisoner release, the thirty pieces of silver, the torn veil at the Temple, the tomb's guard, and the ultimate responsibly for the Messiah's death. Each of these stories will be compared to Matthew in order to ascertain which source, if either, contains credible information.

The Star of Bethlehem
Both Matthew and the Slavonic Josephus have lengthy accounts of the Star of Bethlehem. The similarities between accounts include the

birth of a child who would be king, the visiting Magi or astrologers, an unusual celestial event, the hopeful intervention by Herod the Great, and the slaughter of the innocents at Bethlehem.

However, although important similarities exist, a number of discrepancies also cast doubt on the reliability of at least one of the accounts. These differences are examined below.

The Dating of Herod the Great

Perhaps the most important difference between the two accounts is the dating. According to Matthew the star appears near the end of Herod the Great's life, or around 4 BCE. Matthew follows the story line of Mark, in which John the Baptist is executed before the death of Jesus. John dies around 35–36 CE (*Antiquities* 18.116–119), so the birth of Jesus at approximately 6 BCE would have made him around forty years of age at John's death and a bit older at the time of his own crucifixion. Since Mark provides no information concerning Jesus's age, considering him to have been forty at the time of his crucifixion must have appeared reasonable to Matthew. In addition the positioning of Jesus's birth at 6–4 BCE coincides with the Golden Eagle Temple Cleansing in 4 BCE, which pits Jewish insurgents against King Herod. Herod successfully kills many of these rebels, just as he supposedly slaughters the innocents at Bethlehem.

The account in the Slavonic Josephus also covers the period of Herod the Great's reign, but is positioned in the text at approximately 25 BCE. This earlier date for the Messiah's birth is unacceptable to Matthew, since it would have made Jesus sixty years old at the time of John's death. So, for now, we must just note the differences in the dating of the Messiah's birth.

The Fatherless Infant

In both accounts the infant is fatherless. Matthew uses this to proclaim the virgin birth of Jesus. Most Christians today believe in Matthew's story of the Holy Spirit fathering Jesus. However, the Slavonic Josephus just mentions that the child is fatherless, not even suggesting a supernatural birth. Maybe the father was killed or died right after conception. By contrast the Ebionites hold that Jesus is not born of a virgin, being the son of Mary and Joseph.[10] This interpretation of the Messiah's parentage conforms to the laws of human nature and is preferable to the miraculous virgin-birth account.

The Giving of Gold

In Matthew's gospel the three wise men offer gifts of gold, incense, and myrrh. However, in the Slavonic Josephus, Herod offers a gold gift to anyone turning in a fatherless infant. Herod uses his wealth in an effort to kill the newborn Messiah figure.

The Messiah's Brothers and Mother

Matthew follows Mark's lead and marginalizes the family of Jesus, consistent with Paul's agenda to downplay the Messiah's original disciples and family members. Unlike the Twelve, Jesus's family does not play any part in his ministry.

However, by way of contrast, the Slavonic Josephus tells a different story. In this account the Messiah's brothers and mother are compared to the Maccabees and their fight against Antiochus Epiphanes (SJ *War* 1.650, from additional passages). Familial relationships help decode the mystery of Jesus. While the gospels downplay all family common sense and historical data (from Josephus) suggest that family is very important in Jesus's ministry.

The family also shows devotion to the Law of Moses. The Messiah and his followers are promised a great reward for their adherence to the Torah, even in the face of torture. This zeal for the Law is that of the Fourth Philosophy, not the ministry of Jesus of Nazareth.

The Ministry of John the Baptist

John the Baptist is an important figure in the early Jewish Jesus Movement. Paul, hypothetically the author of Mark, certainly knew all the details of John's life and ministry. In fact, John and Paul's ministries overlap. Paul even writes about water baptism (1 Corinthians 1:10–17).

Matthew follows Mark's description of John the Baptist but does add one other element—John's attitude toward the Sadducees and the Pharisees. John calls them a "brood of vipers" and demands that they "produce fruit in keeping with repentance" (Matthew 3:7–10). This same fervor against the ruling authorities is also present in the Slavonic Josephus where John says, "It is you who should cease from your foul deeds and adhere to the Lord your God" (SJ *War* 2.110, from additional passages). In both accounts John is a critic of the status quo and the existing leadership, a tradition originating from the M source.

If the Slavonic Josephus and Matthew both had access to this M source, then what were their differences?

The Dating of John the Baptist

Matthew does not date the beginning of John's ministry, but it has always been assumed that his ministry started only a year or so before John's death. Matthew's hazy time line is due to his reliance on Mark, who also fails to place John's ministry into a tight time line. However, the SJ does date John's entrance onto the world stage. Supposedly John is examined by Archelaus and his experts in the Law. Archelaus rules after Herod the Great, from 4 BCE to 7 CE. In addition, this text is placed into *War* right before the mention of Judas the Galilean and the census, around 6 CE. So, in this tradition, John begins baptizing in 6 CE, a generation earlier than Mark and Matthew claim he does.

The Reason for John's Ministry

Mark, Matthew, and the Slavonic Josephus all agree that John's form of baptism is for repentance and the forgiveness of sins, and that a king or Messiah will come to the fore. However, the SJ gives John's message a revolutionary spin, emphasizing this life, rather than the afterlife. John "came to the Jews and called them to freedom, saying, 'God has sent me to show you the lawful way, by which you will be rid of [your] many rulers. But there will be no mortal ruling [over you], only the Most High, who hath sent me.'" (SJ *War* 2.110, from additional passages). Note that John emphasizes the law of Moses and promises freedom from Rome. This politically charged rhetoric is absent from both Mark and Matthew.

Pilate's Wife

Matthew adds a curious incident involving Pilate's wife to the account of Jesus's trial. In his telling Pilate's wife warns Pilate to have nothing to do with the innocent Jesus, because she has had a dream concerning him (Matthew 27:19). Consistent with his earlier stories about Jesus's birth, Matthew uses a dream to further his plotline. Not only does Pilate believe in Jesus's innocence, now a dream from God has warned him to have nothing to do with the prisoner. This incident focuses more blame on the Jews and less on the Roman government. This same type of argument appears in the Slavonic Josephus, but instead of receiving information in a dream, Pilate's wife has been healed by Jesus. This makes Pilate sympathetic to Jesus.

The SJ passage was probably reworked by later Christians, since the passage about the wonder worker (Jesus) begins with revolutionary overtones. "And many souls were aroused, thinking that by him the Jewish tribes would free themselves from the hands of the Romans. . . . They bade him enter the city, kill the Roman troops and Pilate, and reign over them" (SJ *War* 2.174, from additional passages). Had Pilate known of the people's sentiment—and he probably did—he would not have been swayed by any dream or healing concerning his wife. As such this episode concerning Pilate's wife is just propaganda.

The Barabbas Prisoner Release

Matthew follows Mark's story of Barabbas, the revolutionary chosen by the people over Jesus of Nazareth. In fact, in some early manuscripts, the man being released is called Jesus Barabbas. Since the name *Barabbas* means "son of the father," the release of Jesus, the son of the father, should raise some questions. Is this Barabbas the real Messiah figure? Is that why the crowd prefers him over Mark's Jesus of Nazareth?

A prisoner release also occurs in the SJ. But in this account the wonder worker, or Jesus, is the one being released (SJ *War* 2.174, from additional passages). This tradition most likely originated with the M source. In Josephus a prisoner release occurs at the beginning of Archelaus's rule, right after the Golden Eagle Temple Cleansing. Interestingly Mark calls Barabbas an insurrectionist, while Matthew labels him as notorious. Hyam Maccoby writes that the Greek word for *notorious* could better be translated as *distinguished,* a term of praise, not derision. And this Barabbas is probably popular with the people, a Zealot leader along the lines of Judas the Galilean or John the Baptist.[11]

Is the Barabbas episode, chronicled in Matthew, simply a garbling of the 4 BCE Golden Eagle Temple Cleansing? During the Barabbas episode the crowds want to free the insurrectionist, a young man named Judas, who later leads a tax revolt against Rome.

The Thirty Pieces of Silver
In Mark, Judas agrees to betray Jesus for the promise of money (Mark 14:10–11). In Matthew this money becomes thirty silver coins (Matthew 26:14–16). After Jesus's arrest Judas Iscariot is filled with remorse, throws the thirty pieces of silver back at the high priests, and says, "I have sinned, for I have betrayed innocent blood" (Matthew 27:1–10). Thus, the thirty pieces of silver are always associated with Judas Iscariot's betrayal.

The SJ also mentions a payment of thirty talents for the wonder worker's arrest. Instead of the high priests paying Judas Iscariot, the money is used as a bribe. "And they [high priests] gave thirty talents to Pilate that they should kill him [the wonder worker]. And he took [it] and gave them liberty to carry out their wishes themselves" (SJ *War* 2.174, from additional passages). This rings true as procurators love bribes and often enrich themselves at the expense of the people.

The Torn Temple Veil
The veil that covered the Holy of Holies* is torn when Titus destroys the Temple in 70 CE. Mark and Matthew both claim this is brought about

---

*This veil separated the most holy part of the Temple from the less holy. Only once a year on the Day of Atonement was the Heigh Priest allowed to enter the Holy of Holies, the area behind the veil, to make sacrifice.

by Jesus's death (Mark 15:38; Matthew 27:51). Curiously this belief also appears in the SJ, with one difference. In Mark and Matthew the veil is torn at the exact time of Jesus's death. In the Slavonic Josephus version the veil is torn in 70 CE, having occurred because the Jews put the wonder worker to death many years before. Since the veil is not torn until 70 CE, this is a very late story, probably originating right after the destruction of the Temple.

The Guard at the Tomb

In both Mark and Matthew, Joseph of Arimathea cares for Jesus's dead body. After preparing the body he has a large rock rolled in front of the tomb, which is "cut out of the rock" (Mark 15:42–47; Matthew 27:57–61).* Mark does not mention any guards at the tomb but Matthew writes that the chief priests are given authority by Pilate to make the tomb secure and to post guards. Nowhere is the number of guards revealed. Are a couple of guards present or do hundreds surround the tomb? If the chief priests are truly concerned about the disciples stealing the body, a very sizable force would have been in place.

This issue is also raised by the SJ: "They said that after his killing and burial he was not found in the tomb. For some claimed that he had risen, but others that he was stolen away by his friends. . . . And others said that it could not be possible to steal him away; for they posted guards around his tomb; one thousand Romans and one thousand Jews." Surely, the one thousand figure is an exaggeration, but the idea corresponds to the passage in Matthew.

Do the chief priests really believe that Jesus predicted his resurrection in three days? As noted before the idea that the Jewish Messiah openly predicts his death and subsequent resurrection is absurd. Jesus enters Jerusalem as Messiah and cleanses the Temple as his first act. He does not then preach his own demise and resurrection in three days. If

---

*The image of Jesus being buried in a tomb "cut out of the rock" may have intentionally been used by Mark to associate the new religion of Jesus with the religion of Mithra.

the Messiah does not claim this, then the chief priests had no reason to guard the tomb.

Where does this legend of the guard originate? Mark apparently knows nothing about it, since his gospel does not mention the guard. But the M source, that source for Matthew and the SJ, does make reference to the guard. Why would the M source invent such a story? The answer is quite simple. Hostile Jewish groups argue that this false Jewish Messiah is not raised from the dead and that his body has been stolen by the disciples to make it seem as though he has risen. In response the early Jewish Jesus Movement claims that such a thing is impossible, since the tomb is sealed and has guards in place. Who could prove otherwise?

Who Really Kills Jesus?

In Matthew, Pontius Pilate washes his hands over the fate of Jesus, placing the blame for his death squarely on the Jews. Pilate knows that Jesus is innocent, but he cannot convince the Jews. "When Pilate saw that he was getting nowhere, but instead an uproar was starting, he took water and washed his hands in front of the crowd. 'I am innocent of this man's blood,' he said. 'It is your responsibility'" (Matthew 27:24). And so, according to Matthew, the Jews are solely responsible for Jesus's death.

This kindly treatment of Pilate is not reproduced in the SJ. In this source Pilate gives the priests permission to execute Jesus themselves, following a sizable bribe. "And they [chief priests] gave thirty talents to Pilate that they should kill him. And he took [it] and gave them liberty to carry out their wishes themselves" (SJ *War* 2.174, from additional passages). Although the chief priests are responsible for Jesus's death, Pilate also plays a role in the crucifixion. Without him and the power of Rome, no crucifixion could have occurred. And this crucifixion takes place because Pilate had been well paid.

Josephus writes that some procurators receive bribes to look the other way or even to work with unsavory groups. Pilate may very well have lined his own pockets over the "Jesus" ordeal. Without the insistence of the chief priests, would Pilate have intervened? Probably, considering that his own rule would have been threatened by an insurgent king. No doubt Pilate closely monitors events through the chief priests. He also could have extorted money from the priests, only offering assistance after receiving the large bribe.

The M source is used by Matthew and the author of the "Christianized" verses in the SJ. However, Matthew adapts many of these events with Mark's story line in mind. That so many differences exist between Matthew and the SJ is quite extraordinary, since both draw from the same source. Which is the more accurate? In my opinion the SJ tells a more probable story, reflecting the political struggles of the time. Do the people long for their Messiah to overthrow the Romans and to set up a new kingdom? Of course, they do! The people are not interested in the later Christian interpretation of Jesus, a man destined to die for the sins of the world.

TO THE GENTILES

Although most scholars claim that Matthew was written by a Jew for a Jewish community, I think Matthew is aimed at the Gentile community. After all, if any literature was produced post–70 CE, the audience had to be mostly Gentile. From the details listed above even the most supposedly Jewish elements are simply an extension of Mark's gospel. And that gospel promotes the Pauline theology of faith over works.

Another clue pointing to a Gentile audience is the vilification of the Pharisees. (Judas the Galilean and John the Baptist are both Pharisees and even the gospel Jesus has some positive exchanges with the Pharisees.) This treatment only makes sense if Matthew were written a decade or more after the destruction of Jerusalem and the priesthood in 70 CE. After the destruction of the priesthood, the Pharisees, aka the rabbis, are in the process of restructuring Judaism. Pitting the Pauline Jesus against them only makes sense in this particular context. Thus, the vilification of the Pharisees is a post–70 CE venture, not one that occurred during the lifetime of the historical Messiah.

To further support my claim a few more passages should be examined relating to the death and resurrection of Jesus, the main concern of the Pauline gospel. First, consistent with Mark, Matthew also presents the Roman guard as the one who recognizes Jesus as the Son of God. The Jews watching the crucifixion say, "Leave him alone. Let's see if Elijah comes to save him." However, the Roman centurion and his guards exclaim, "Surely he was the Son of God!" (Matthew 27:49–54; Mark 15:36–39). The Jews have no mercy for Jesus while the Gentiles recognize him as the Son of God. This certainly is intended for Gentile consumption.

Second, Pilate washes his hands of responsibility for Jesus's death. The Jews greedily accept that responsibility, saying, "Let his blood be on us and on our children!" (Matthew 27:25). Not only do the Jews want the responsibility for Jesus's death, but they want it hung around their children's necks for all eternity. Could there ever be a more anti-Jewish scenario? Matthew wants to vilify the Jews and their children. This could not have been produced for a Jewish audience.

Third, the Great Commission is meant for the Gentiles. The Risen Christ tells the Eleven apostles, who now worship him, to "go and make disciples of all nations, baptizing them in the name of the Father and of the Son and of the Holy Spirit, and teaching them to obey everything I have commanded you" (Matthew 28:16–20). We are to believe that the Jews now worship Jesus and are instructed to preach Paul's Holy Spirit baptism to all nations. As the Messiah does not Jesus have any concern for Israel? Matthew's audience does not care about Israel, so why should Jesus?

These three passages are directed at a Gentile audience. All the attempts to use Hebrew scripture simply place Jesus in an untenable position. He is born a Jew and has to live among Jews, as the scriptures predict. But by his death the gospels also declare that Jesus can reach his true audience, the Gentiles.

WHO? WHY? WHERE? AND WHEN?

Who wrote the Gospel of Matthew? Many scholars point to Matthew's many Old Testament references to assert that Matthew is a knowledgeable Jew. If he is a Jew using the Jewish scriptures, then it might also be assumed that his audience is also Jewish. At first glance this appears very reasonable.

However, it cannot be ignored that the author of Matthew uses 606 of Mark's 661 verses, or approximately 90 percent of Mark's gospel.[12] This utter reliance on Mark should help answer many questions, including the identity of Matthew's author. In the prior chapter I listed the similarities between Mark's Jesus of Nazareth and the person and teachings of Paul. If Matthew uses Mark as a guide, then he must have also embraced this vision of Jesus of Nazareth, invented by the author of Mark. That being said it can be argued that Matthew is a close follower of Paul, with knowledge of Jewish scripture equal to that of Paul.

Paul frequently references Jewish scripture in his letters. He writes of Adam, Abraham, Sarah, Hagar, Isaac, Ishmael, Moses, and David and quotes the Psalms and the prophets. His interpretation of scripture can be debated, but he surely is not shy about using it to his advantage. This liberal use of Jewish scripture and some very unusual interpretations can also be attributed to the author of Matthew. Using the Hebrew scriptures' Greek translation, Matthew turns Isaiah's young woman into a virgin, inventing the miracle birth of Jesus. This smacks of Paul's methodology.

If Mark already exists, why does the author of Matthew write another version of Jesus of Nazareth? The answer points directly at the Jews, but not in a positive way. Matthew is not interested in converting the Jews but in challenging their teachings about the Jewish Messiah.

Up until 70 CE the teachings of and about the pre- and post-resurrected Jewish Messiah are known throughout Judea and in every part of the Roman Empire where Jews reside. Certainly Jews in Rome and Alexandria have heard about the Jewish Messiah. In 64 CE, after the Great Fire of Rome, Jewish followers of this Messiah, known as Christians to Tacitus, are tortured and put to death by Nero. In 70 CE followers of a Jewish Messiah are also put to death in Alexandria, as the Jews there are afraid of extermination if they side with the revolutionaries. This fear of the messianic Jews is well founded. Jerusalem has just been leveled by Titus and the number of crucifixions is beyond count.

Josephus writes of the Sicarii who escape to Alexandria in 70 CE:

> . . . for when all sorts of torments and vexations of their bodies that could be devised were made use of them, they could not get any one of them to comply so far as to confess or seem to confess, that Caesar was their lord; but they preserved their own opinion, in spite of all the distress they were brought to, as if they received those torments and the fire itself with bodies insensible of pain, and with a soul that in a manner rejoiced under them. But what was most of all astonishing to the beholders, was the courage of the children; for not one of these children was so far overcome by these torments as to name Caesar for their lord. (*War* 7.418–419)

Note that the Sicarii's punishment is similar to the "Christian" torments in Rome, as described by Tacitus. These Christians also die because they refuse to confess that Caesar is their lord.

Matthew writes his gospel after these persecutions. The Jews in Alexandria cannot forget the persecutions and deaths of the revolutionaries. Their only defense against this contagion is to attack. The Jews, no doubt, question the legitimacy of the crucified Jewish Messiah. The fact that this Messiah has undergone crucifixion would have been enough to discredit him in the eyes of most. But the resurrection is another matter. How can they prove that this Messiah has not been resurrected?

This is Matthew's response to the Jews' argument concerning the resurrection:

> While the women were on their way, some of the guards went into the city and reported to the chief priests everything that had happened. When the chief priests had met with the elders and devised a plan, they gave the soldiers a large sum of money, telling them,

"You are to say, 'His disciples came during the night and stole him away while we were asleep.' If this report gets to the governor, we will satisfy him and keep you out of trouble." So the soldiers took the money and did as they were instructed. *And this story has been widely circulated among the Jews to this very day.* (Matthew 27:11–15) (Emphasis mine)

The Jews simply put forth the argument that the resurrection is a hoax, perpetrated by the followers of the crucified Messiah figure. Certainly, to most rational Jews and even to the Gentiles, this is an acceptable explanation for the resurrection.

To combat the Jews who refuse to embrace the crucified Jesus as the Messiah, Matthew incorporates their own scriptures in his retelling of the Jesus of Nazareth story. This strategy is aimed at proving that the life, death, and resurrection are all foretold by the Jewish scriptures. This undercuts Jewish authority, making it seem as if the Jews are the bad guys and only Jesus and his disciples can be trusted with God's scriptures.

Why would Matthew go to all this trouble if he already had Mark's gospel? The answer is money. A vast market awaits those promoting Jesus of Nazareth. When Jesus speaks to his disciples on the mountain in Galilee, he supposedly says, "Go and make disciples of all nations" (Matthew 28:19). To bring this new gospel to all nations, the Pauline movement has to once and for all deal with the Jewish question. The author of Matthew makes it seem that the Jewish scriptures support Jesus of Nazareth and that the Jews were opponents of Jesus during his lifetime and opponents still. His Jesus of Nazareth is the fulfillment of the prophecies and the end of the Law, the very argument Paul made decades earlier (Matthew 5:17–20; Galatians 3:15–25).

As noted above Matthew is probably written in or around Alexandria, which has a large Jewish population—the perfect spot for the new scripturally fortified Jesus to fight the Jews. Also, Matthew has this new man-god visit Egypt early in his life. This has a three-fold purpose. First, Jesus can follow in Joseph's and Moses's footsteps.

Joseph goes to Egypt and Moses escapes from the same land. Second, the flight to Egypt is a device to get Joseph and Mary from Jerusalem to Nazareth. And third, Matthew is doing what many entertainers and politicians do. He is appealing to the hometown crowd. Surely the mention of Egypt is a feather in the cap of the Alexandrian disciples.

We have established the scenario that a disciple of Paul, with the Gospel of Mark in hand, travels to Alexandria to write another, more Jewish version of Jesus of Nazareth to help further the spread of this new gospel and to open up a larger market. As usual, follow the money. A larger market means much more money, as the centers of influence begin forming. Money is no longer sent to Jerusalem, since Jerusalem was destroyed by Titus in 70 CE. Money is now sent to support the authors of this new Jesus chronicle and their supporters, often to the large cities of influence. Rome, Antioch, and Alexandria become the centers for this new religion.

This money angle also helps explain why someone would take an existing gospel and "improve" upon it. Presumably Matthew thinks that his new and improved document will supersede Mark, at least in his target market.

The Gospel of Mark is penned between 70 and 73 CE, since Judas Iscariot has not yet committed suicide, as the Sicarii had done at Masada in 73 CE. Matthew includes this mass suicide in his gospel, so the earliest dating can be pegged at 73–75 CE. (Josephus's account of Masada is included in his *War,* finished in 75 CE.) It should also be recognized that the movement of people and ideas is not instantaneous, and that several years probably elapsed between the writing of Mark and Matthew. Perhaps Matthew was written as early as 80 CE; Paul might still have been alive at that time. Alive or not the Gospel of Matthew is a Pauline production. The winners are Paul and his organization; the losers are the Jews, who pay dearly on account of this new religion—then and for the next two thousand years.

10 ► The Gospel of Luke

LUKE'S SOURCES

Most likely the third gospel to be written is the Gospel of Luke. This anonymous writing, like Matthew, relies heavily on Mark and his order of events. All three gospels have Jesus foretelling his own death, with Judas Iscariot as the traitor and Barabbas as the favored choice of the Jewish people. Our question now is this: Why yet another gospel? Why is Luke composed? Doesn't Mark, and then Matthew, get it right?

In what follows I will show that Luke has a different audience in mind than the previous gospel writers, and that this helps shape his material and his portrait of Jesus. Note in passing that these gospel writers feel no compunction about revising the received text. For them, their predecessors are not writing unalterable history. The earlier gospels could be added to, subtracted from, and events could be moved from one time frame to another.

Statistics

Here are some interesting statistics that show how Luke built upon Mark and also Matthew.

Matthew reproduces 561 of Mark's 661 verses, while Luke reproduces 443. In addition, not only the substance of Mark survives, but the very wording, where 51 percent of Mark's wording is reproduced by Matthew and 53 percent by Luke.[1] Obviously Matthew and Luke rely heavily on Mark's gospel, which we have suggested was produced by Paul or by a close disciple of Paul.

I have grouped Luke's gospel into its various sources, based on subject material, not on a verse-by-verse analysis. The percentages may slightly differ from other lists, but these groupings do give an approximate outline of Luke's sources.

Mark	38.2 percent
MQ	19.9 percent
ML	5.9 percent
L	36.0 percent

Luke contains around 231 verses from the Q source, which I have labeled MQ. These verses, mostly sayings, are also included in Matthew, although ordered differently. For example, Matthew's Sermon on the Mount is mostly incorporated throughout Luke, interspersed and not presented as one grand sermon. Does Luke use a separate source for this information (Q) or does he utilize the Gospel of Matthew (MQ)? I suggest he has both Mark and Matthew at his disposal.

An additional sixty-eight verses, or 5.9 percent of the total, come from the ML source. These verses in Luke are different from Matthew, but share common themes. For example, both Luke and Matthew include genealogies for Jesus. Matthew's genealogy goes back to Abraham (very Jewish) while Luke's goes back to Adam (very Gentile). Luke does not copy Matthew's genealogy, but presents his own version. If Luke does not possess Matthew's gospel, would he have included a genealogy for Jesus? Unlikely! As such I suggest that Luke shapes Matthew's ideas to meet the needs of his own audience, not worrying about inconsistencies or what later critics would think.

The first four verses of Luke and the first two verses of Acts may help determine what other sources were used in compiling the L source, that source not found in either Mark or Matthew. In addition, these verses may shed light on the authorship of Luke as well as its date of composition.

Many have undertaken to draw up an account of the things that have been fulfilled among us, just as they were *handed down to us by those who from the first were eyewitnesses and servants of the word.* Therefore, since I myself have *carefully investigated everything from the beginning,* it seemed good also to me to write an orderly account for you, most excellent Theophilus, so that you may know the certainty of the things you have been taught. (Luke 1:1–4) (Emphasis mine)

In my former book, . . . I wrote about all that Jesus began to do and to teach until the day he was taken up to heaven, after giving instructions through the Holy Spirit to the apostles he had chosen. (Acts 1:1–2) (Emphasis mine)

Most scholars believe that the same author wrote both Luke and Acts. Note that in the Acts passage the author writes, "in my former book." If one man wrote both books, then it can be asserted that much of Luke's information came from Josephus's *Antiquities.* The author of Luke and Acts consistently describes events parallel to that of Josephus, more thoroughly discussed in chapter 11, "The Acts of the Apostles."

Also, note that *Antiquities* was written in 93 CE and its distribution probably took several more years. So the absolute earliest writing of Luke and Acts can be estimated at 100 CE, beyond the time of eyewitness accounts.

With no eyewitness accounts where does Luke obtain 36 percent (L source) of his gospel? As I will show he uses Josephus as a source for L, but he also incorporates scenes from the pagan worship of Mithras as well as new information about the actual Jewish Messiah. Thus, actual information about the historical Messiah is available as well as early mythmaking material. In short Luke and Acts are treasure troves of foundation legends interwoven with bits of truth.

To better understand Luke and his additional sources, let's examine the religion of Mithraism, a religion that influenced the thinking of Paul and later Gentile Christianity.

PAUL'S ADAPTATION OF MITHRAISM

J. M. Robertson, a mythicist of the early twentieth century, writes:

> The Mithraic mysteries, then, of the burial and resurrection of the
> Lord, the Mediator, and Savior (buried in a rock tomb and resurrected
> from that tomb), the sacrament of bread and water, the marking on
> the forehead with a mystic mark—*all these were in practice* . . . and
> the representation of his entombment and resurrection, *before the pub-
> lication of the Christian Gospel* of a Lord who was buried in a rock
> tomb, and rose from that tomb on the day of the sun, and before the
> Christian mystery of the Divine communion.[2] (Emphasis mine)

The Jesus of Nazareth Movement (post–70 CE) competes with
Mithraism, a mystery religion popular among the Roman troops stationed throughout the Empire, which predates the post–70 CE Jesus
of Nazareth Movement and curiously preaches a very similar message,
including the burial and resurrection of the Lord. Is this pure coincidence? Or are the beliefs of Mithras incorporated into the person of
Jesus of Nazareth?

Who could have been behind this wholesale theft of ideas? The
answer once again may be Paul. But why would Paul steal ideas from
the Mithraic religion if he had Judaism as his own religion? Paul's audience is Gentile and his cleverly disguised gospel is very attractive to
these Gentiles. One should always follow the money. Paul's gospel to
the Gentiles has to compete with the Jewish gospel put forth by Peter
and James. In addition, Paul also has to contend with other pagan cults.
To make his movement more appealing than these alternative religions,
Paul merges his particular brand of Judaism with the rites of Mithras in
order to create a distinctive religion, with the history of Israel blended
with the attractive salvation properties of Mithras. Does Paul do this
knowingly or is it a subconscious action? Again, follow the money. I
contend that Paul's actions are premeditated, aimed at eliciting funds
from his followers.

So where in the Bible is this reliance on Mithras cited? First, we must look to Paul's letters. Paul's interpretation of the death and resurrection of Christ Jesus is quite different from that of the Jewish Jesus Movement. While Peter and James preach a resurrected Messiah who promises victory over the Roman occupiers, Paul's resurrected Christ has a role in salvation of the soul, consistent with the mystery religions of his day. In addition, James is no fan of his brother's crucifixion, attaching no cosmic significance to it. To him it is a huge tragedy, plain and simple, an untimely death that occurs before the advent of the promised kingdom. Paul, however, glorifies this death as an atoning sacrifice for the sins of the world. Certainly, Paul's Christ Jesus is closer to Mithras than to the actual Jewish Messiah.

Paul also adapts a Jewish meal to become his Lord's Supper. Like the Mithraic rite, the bread and wine become associated with the body and blood of the sacrificed deity, namely Jesus. The lamb of God, slaughtered for the sins of humankind, is patterned after Mithras. So, in Paul's gospel, Christ Jesus and Mithras are virtually interchangeable.

Also, note that Paul is responsible for the writing of Mark, the first of the synoptic gospels. His Jesus of Nazareth supposedly initiates the Lord's Supper (Mark 14:12–26) and also predicts his own crucifixion, in accordance with God's plan (Mark 8:31–32; 10:32–34). One other Mithraic detail occurs in Mark. After his death Jesus is placed in a tomb cut out of rock (Mark 15:46). Since Mithras is identified with rock or a cave, such symbolism's appeal to first-century Gentiles should not be lost on us today.

The Mithraic base is expanded in the Gospel of Matthew, also a later production of Paul's fertile imagination. In Matthew the church is built upon Peter, or rather, built upon a rock (Matthew 16:18). Gentiles in the first and second centuries surely recognized this reference to the rock as a Mithraic endorsement. This certainly helped spread the message, as Mithraism was already well established throughout the Roman Empire.

Mithras is born to a virgin, to the Mother of God. Matthew supplies his own version, where Mary conceives through the Spirit of God, a birth that would save the world from its sins (Matthew 1:18–25). This mythology is supported by the Gospel of Luke, where the child is named the Son of the Most High and where Mary is called the mother of the Lord (Luke 1:32, 43).

The above efforts to associate Jesus with Mithras pale in comparison to Luke's masterstroke in retelling Jesus's birth. Most scholars assume that Luke was unaware of Matthew's gospel, since the birth narratives have little in common. However, I contend that Luke wanted to cement the connection of Jesus with Mithras. Robertson writes:

> It is well known that whereas in the Gospels Jesus is said to have been born in an inn stable, early Christian writers, as Justin Martyr and Origen, explicitly say he was born in a cave. Now, in the Mithras myth, Mithras is both rock-born and born in a cave, and the monuments show the newborn babe adored by shepherds who offer first fruits. And it is remarkable that whereas a cave long was (and I believe is) shown as the birthplace of Jesus at Bethlehem, *Saint Jerome actually complained that in his day* the Pagans celebrated the worship of Tammuz (Adonis) and presumably, thereafter, the festival of the birth of the sun, Christmas Day, at that very cave.[3] (Emphasis mine)

At Christmas, Christians retell the story of Mary and Joseph and the adoration by the lowly shepherds toward the newborn Jesus, a story of Luke based on the myth of Mithras (Luke 2:8–20). Luke actually replaces Matthew's story of Herod the Great and the Three Wise Men, even though Herod the Great is part of the true Messiah's story. This hardly matters for Luke, as he is intent on co-opting Mithras for the Christian membership drive.

The early Christian Church borrows from Mithraism without giving this older religion any credit. In fact, Justin Martyr actually claims that the older religions parody Christian practices, stating that the pagan religions anticipate the sacraments beforehand. Hence, the devil is behind the Mithraic practice of the bread and wine. It never occurs to

Justin Martyr that the Christians pilfered this sacrament from the rites of Mithras. Christian apologists, throughout the ages, refuse to admit that their religion is adapted from older pagan sources.

The significance of Mithraism in the creation of our modern Christian myth is often overlooked. Paul's vision of the Risen Christ originates from his understanding of the Mithraic mythology. Paul consciously adapts Mithraism to his own purposes. His Christ Jesus becomes equal or superior to Mithras and offers a framework for Jesus of Nazareth. This nonhistorical Jesus of Nazareth has been accepted by church leaders and scholars alike, explaining why Jesus of Nazareth cannot be found in Josephus's writings. Jesus of Nazareth and Mithras only exist in the minds of their followers.

JOHN THE BAPTIST

By cleverly incorporating the birth of Mithras into his gospel, Luke paves the way for followers of Mithras to more easily convert to the very similar religion of post–70 CE Christianity. However, co-opting the religion of Mithras is not a singular event. The same process occurs with John the Baptist.

In the second century the Pseudoclementine *Recognitions* author writes this about the followers of John the Baptist: "Yea, some even of the disciples of John, who seemed to be great ones, have separated themselves from the people, and proclaimed their own master as the Christ."[4] This separation does not occur in the second century but arises shortly after John's death.

We have noted that John preaches a baptism of purification, for which the disciple prepares his soul beforehand by practicing righteousness (*Antiquities* 18.117). The reason for John's baptism is completely obscured by the synoptic gospels and Acts, where John preaches a baptism of the Holy Spirit (Acts 2:38) and everyone from the beginning of the church understands baptism in this way. However, in that same document (Acts), some disciples know only the baptism of John and have not encountered the Holy Spirit (Acts 19:1–7). How do these disciples know of Jesus and the baptism of John for repentance, but not the baptism of the Holy Spirit? Obviously, the original Jewish Jesus Movement uses John's baptism of purification, not Paul's baptism of the Holy Spirit.

Paul's Jesus of Nazareth supposedly receives the Holy Spirit at John's baptism. In Mark, John preaches that the promised Messiah will come soon. He then baptizes Jesus, and Jesus experiences the Holy Spirit. Whether John understands the significance of this baptism is debatable (Mark 1:1–13). John's lack of awareness is remedied by Matthew, in which John immediately recognizes Jesus as the promised savior and even says, "I need to be baptized by you, and do you come to me?" (Matthew 3:11–17).

The Gospel of Luke reinforces John's awareness of Jesus's status as the Son of God. In Luke's birth narrative John's mother praises Mary: "Blessed are you among women, and blessed is the child you will bear! But why am I so favored, that the mother of my Lord should come to me? As soon as the sound of your greeting reached my ears, the baby in my womb leaped for joy" (Luke 1:42–44). Not only does Elizabeth know that Mary's child will be the Messiah, but her fetus also knows, for he leaps for joy in her womb. This is utter nonsense, but it does show the development in the John the Baptist story. In Mark, John baptizes Jesus but is not wholly aware of the significance of that act. In the later Gospel of Luke, John, still in utero, recognizes the fetus in Mary's womb as Jesus the Messiah and savior.

To win over adherents of competing religions, such as Mithraism or John's followers, Luke simply incorporates these competing religions into the story of Jesus. How can anyone even consider John to be the Christ when John himself, as a fetus, understands Jesus as the true Christ? Again, the Gospel of Luke co-opts the story of John just as it co-opts the religion of Mithras.

THE TIME LINES IN LUKE

Scholars have universally used Luke's gospel to date Jesus's ministry as well as his age. Luke's dates, as well as other data from Matthew and Josephus, are as follows:

- John is approximately six months older than Jesus (Luke 1:23–45).
- Jesus is born at the census of Cyrenius, in 6 CE (Luke 2:1–7; *Antiquities* 18.1–4).
- John begins baptizing in Tiberius's fifteenth year, around 28–29 CE (Luke 3:1–2).
- Jesus begins his ministry at thirty, making John thirty as well (Luke 3:23).
- Matthew's Jesus is born in the last years of Herod the Great, or around 6 BCE (Matthew 2:1–18).
- Pontius Pilate is governor of Judea from 26 to 37 CE (*Antiquities* 18.26–84), or from 18 to 37 CE. Either way, Pilate is gone by 37 CE.
- Per Josephus, and confirmed by the Slavonic Josephus, John the Baptist is killed by Herod Antipas around 35–36 CE (*Antiquities* 18.116–119) (SJ *War* 2.168, from additional passages).
- Claudius is Caesar from 41 to 54 CE.

With these eight data points, a logical time line for John and Jesus should be possible. Let's examine various scenarios using Luke's data, then Matthew's, then a blend of Luke and Matthew. Note that these various time lines logically fall short, especially in light of important fixed dates, such as the death of John in 36 CE, per Josephus.

Proving the veracity, or lack thereof, of Luke's history is paramount in importance. If Luke cannot be wholly trusted, then the traditional time line for John and Jesus should not be used in the search for the Messiah's true history.

Time Line 1: Luke's Data

Using just Luke's first four data points, we arrive at an interesting time line for both John and Jesus. If John and Jesus are approximately the same age, then both are born in 6 CE at the census. This suggests that John began his ministry at the age of twenty-two, baptizing at the Jordan River in 28 CE. John's ministry must have continued for nearly eight more years, because Jesus's ministry begins at around the age of thirty, or around 36 CE.

John is put to death in 35–36 CE, shortly after baptizing Jesus in the Jordan. Jesus's ministry must have lasted only about a year, since Pilate is gone by 37 CE. Therefore, according to Luke, Jesus must have been crucified in 37 CE. Luke's data is four to seven years later than traditional time lines.

How does this late date for Jesus's crucifixion affect the later church time line as put forth by Paul and the book of Acts? Paul claims that he spends nearly seventeen years in the Jewish Jesus Movement before the Council of Jerusalem (Acts 15; Galatians 1:13–2:1). If Paul joined the movement by 38 CE, just months after the crucifixion of Jesus per Luke's time line, then the Council of Jerusalem takes place seventeen years later, or around 55 CE. This presents a problem, since Acts later claims that the Jews are driven out of Rome by Claudius (Acts 18:1–2). Since Claudius dies in 54 CE Luke's time line cannot be accurate.

Such a time line has never been considered before, but it offers illumination. By faithfully following Luke's data, Jesus's crucifixion comes after the historical death (36 CE) of John the Baptist. However, the remainder of the church time line appears to fall apart with this later date.

Loyal apologists for Luke maintain that his dating for Cyrenius's census is accurate, arguing that the first census of Cyrenius occurs around 6–4 BCE, a date that accords with Matthew's birth narrative. Two problems exist concerning this explanation. First, Josephus never mentions this census under Herod the Great. More importantly Herod the Great is loyal to Rome and quite capable of carrying out any taxation project or census himself. Why would Augustus Caesar send Cyrenius to help Herod? Herod is a master builder, credited with erecting a new Temple and constructing the great city of Caesarea. With these abilities Herod would have been trusted to collect taxes for his overlords. Thus, an earlier census in 6–4 BCE does not fit the historical realities.

Robert Eisenman explains why the census occurred in 6–7 CE, after the removal of Archelaus and was not imposed during the reign of Herod the Great, one of Rome's greatest friends. The census was made "in advance of the imposition of direct Roman rule following the removal of the inept Archelaus."[5]

So why does Luke ascribe Jesus's birth to 6 CE, to the time of the census? Luke is not concerned with historical truth. Matthew places his birth narrative at the time of Herod's last days, around the time of the Golden Eagle Temple Cleansing, a seminal moment to the early Jewish Jesus Movement. Likewise Luke uses the census as his date for Jesus's birth, since the census officially begins the Fourth Philosophy's fight against Rome. In short Matthew and Luke select the two most important dates in Fourth Philosophy history to announce the birth of their savior.

Luke knows exactly what he is doing by placing Jesus's birth date at the census, in 6 CE. The historical time line is unimportant to him. He just wants to co-opt the history of the Fourth Philosophy completely in his gospel. After all who would analyze his history? For the past two thousand years scholars and church historians have accepted Luke's dates as accurate, the very word of God. However, such a conclusion is not borne out by the facts.

Time Line 2: Matthew's Data

A second time line can be constructed using the Gospel of Matthew, which contends that Jesus was born in 6 BCE. The coming of John the Baptist and the deaths of Jesus and John are assumed to have occurred during the governorship of Pilate (26–37 CE) and Herod Antipas (4 BCE–39 CE). This end data for Jesus and John is not confirmed by Matthews's source, Mark.

Without a definite date of death for either John or Jesus, scholars should use Josephus's date for John's death, or 35–36 CE. In addition, Matthew uses Mark's order of death, where John's death precedes Jesus's crucifixion. As such Matthew's date for the crucifixion must have been around 37 CE.

Therefore, if Jesus were born in 6 BCE and died in 37 CE, he must have been approximately forty-two years old at his time of death. This appears reasonable until one piece of Luke's data is added to the mix. Luke states that Jesus was about thirty years old when he started his ministry. Thus, if Jesus had been born in 6 BCE, his ministry should have started around 25 CE, but this date is too early if John's ministry really began in 28–29 CE, as Luke declared.

A reliance on Matthew's data brings up more questions than answers. This uncertainty concerning Jesus's birth and ministry only arises because of Luke's extra data. Without Luke we could readily accept the birth of Jesus in 6 BCE and his death under Pilate in 37 CE, at the ripe old age of forty-two.

Time Line 3: The Mixing of Data from Matthew and Luke

The traditional time line accepted and promoted by Christianity includes the mixing of Matthew's and Luke's data as well as ignoring Josephus's dating of John the Baptist's death (35–36 CE). This mixing of some sources while ignoring others is not good history but was necessary to produce a viable story line.

The traditional birth of Jesus is considered 6 BCE, during Herod the Great's reign, and includes a census at this time, even though common sense and Josephus's history do not support such a census. So the invention of this earlier census of Cyrenius is necessary for the story to proceed.

Matthew has Jesus being born in Bethlehem in 6 BCE and returning to Nazareth after the death of Herod. Luke has Mary and Joseph living in Nazareth and then being forced by the census to register at Bethlehem, where, like Mithras, Jesus is born in a cave, adored by shepherds. Both Matthew and Luke follow Mark's lead in associating Jesus with Nazareth, but they go about it from totally different directions. Again, this discrepancy is somehow harmonized or better yet, ignored.

Tradition accepts Luke's dating for the beginning of John's ministry at 28–29 CE. In fact, this is the most important date for Christian chronology. Everything in Jesus's and John's ministries depends on this date. So if Jesus were born in 6 BCE, he would have been around thirty-four years old at the beginning of his ministry. This is a bit older than reported by Luke, but Christians assume Luke is right and accept Jesus as thirty at the beginning of his ministry.

The traditional time line also assumes that John dies before Jesus, shortly after Jesus's arrival. In fact, this is what the gospels say, ignoring the evidence in Josephus. Thus, Christians believe that John the Baptist dies around 30 CE, even though Josephus and the Slavonic Josephus date his death at 35–36 CE. Jesus does not have to die in 37 CE but could have died anywhere from 30 to 33 CE, depending on the length of his ministry. Some sources claim Jesus preached one year while others believe he preached three years. If Jesus were thirty when he started his ministry and if his ministry lasted three years, then he would have been thirty-three years old at the crucifixion. Put another way: Jesus is born in 6 BCE and dies in 33 CE at the age of thirty-three, an impossibility since this would have made Jesus thirty-eight years old.

This mix of unsupportable and conflicting data cannot be true history. The only reliable date concerns John the Baptist's death in 35–36 CE, from the pen of Josephus, and the traditional story line disregards this.

In short not one date put forth by Matthew or Luke should be trusted.

But Matthew and Luke may present a larger truth. Both gospel writers place Jesus's birth at a very important time in Jewish history. Matthew's birth story coincides with the Golden Eagle Temple Cleansing by Judas and Matthias, the first strike by the Fourth Philosophy against Herod and Rome. Luke's birth scene at the census of Cyrenius also coincides with an important uprising against Rome. In 6 CE Judas the Galilean and John the Baptist oppose Roman taxation and set the stage for further conflicts with Rome.

The birth of Jesus is brilliantly removed from the political arena by the genius of Matthew and Luke. The baby Jesus, the prince of peace, is forever distanced from the patriot Jews opposing foreign occupation by Rome. In fact, we celebrate the birth of Jesus in these time periods, not the fight for freedom. The Christmas story, like it or not, is just a rewrite of history. The real historical Messiah was not born in 6 BCE or 6 CE, but the Jewish Jesus Movement is originally defined by these important dates.

THE PROBLEM OF Q

Although Mark's gospel is the earliest (composed 70–73 CE), Jesus of Nazareth in Mark's gospel mouths Paul's own doctrines, making it no more authentic than the later gospels. Matthew incorporates 90 percent of Mark and adds his own source to the mix, the M Source. This combination is wildly successful, giving Mark's Jesus of Nazareth more history, including a birth narrative and a resurrection scenario.

Luke's gospel is penned after Matthew, with his own material adding to the picture of Jesus. While Matthew is composed around 80 CE, Luke's dependence on Josephus's *Antiquities,* published in 95 CE, dates Luke at or after 100 CE. (See chapter 11 for more on Luke's reliance on Josephus.)

Luke also utilizes Mark for the outline of his gospel. In addition, Luke and Matthew have a number of passages in common, absent from Mark. Scholars have postulated that these shared passages come from a separate source, named Q, derived from *Quelle,* the German word for "source." And, along with Mark and Q, Luke adds his own source, named the L Source.

Why do scholars claim that Matthew and Luke both used a common source Q in addition to Mark? Could it be that the birth narratives in Matthew and Luke are irreconcilable? Those wanting to believe in a logical historical record of Jesus of Nazareth find it hard to believe that Luke could actually have copied material from Matthew, considering all the discrepancies in the various time lines. If Luke really has Matthew as a guide, then why does he change Matthew's story of Herod the Great and the Magi? It makes little sense. That is why scholars have favored the Q source, which explains the similarities between Matthew and Luke, but denies Luke's use of Matthew.

The majority opinion claims that if Luke wrote independently of

Matthew, and if both contained similar material absent from Mark, they both had access to another document. Thus, Q was born, a recent invention to explain the similarities between Matthew and Luke, a product of wishful thinking.

Not all scholars accept the Q theory. After all no copy of Q exists and no mention of it survives in any ancient document. In 1955 Austin Farrer proposed that Luke followed Matthew's gospel, arguing that since the two documents contain common material, identical in the words and phrases used to describe some scenes, the simplest explanation is that one of the two uses the other as a source, rather than both using a third document or Q.[6] This alternative to Q is logical and should not be dismissed without further review. Often the simplest explanation is correct.

Why, then, does Luke write another gospel? First and foremost the Gospel of Luke is a production of the Pauline story line. Paul invented Jesus of Nazareth in Mark to present his own ideas to the Gentiles. This effort is continued by Matthew and then by Luke. Also, note that Luke's companion history of Acts is an effort to forge harmonious relations between the Jews and Gentiles, between Paul and James, with all agreeing with Paul's vision of faith. Luke and Acts are propaganda tools, elevating Paul to preeminent apostle and ensuring that Jesus follows in Paul's footsteps.

Second, Luke's audience differs greatly from Matthew's. If the audiences had been similar, then why compose another gospel? While Matthew incorporates Jewish scripture into his gospel to give Jesus of Nazareth some real history, Luke pursues another strategy. As time passes the importance of Jesus's relationship to the Jews wanes. Luke's Jesus needs to be fused with another popular god, Mithras, whose birth narrative Luke co-opts.

Why would Luke chase after Mithras's supporters?

Follow the money, once again. Mithras is popular with the Roman military all across the empire. Any inroads into Mithras's following promise huge financial rewards. Paul traveled across the Roman Empire earlier in his career as he peddled his Christ Jesus gospel. The spread of Jesus of Nazareth is no different; both Jesus of Nazareth and Christ

Jesus emphasize faith over deeds. But Jesus of Nazareth has one great advantage over Christ Jesus. While Christ Jesus is born of Paul's revelation, Jesus of Nazareth can be passed off as a real person, a God incarnate in history. This Jesus of Nazareth experiences birth, life, and death, just like ordinary people, and can relate to trials and tribulations.

Similar Themes, Different Stories

I have labeled the Q section as MQ, emphasizing Luke's dependence on Matthew. Also identified are passages labeled ML, where themes present in Matthew are also used by Luke. These passages have never been associated with Q because the information contained in Matthew and Luke is so different. However, upon closer investigation, we see that Luke incorporates these M Source materials into his own story. These ML passages are as follows:

1. Matthew 2:1; Luke 1:5—In the Days of King Herod
2. Matthew 1:17; Luke 3:23b–38—Genealogies of Jesus
3. Matthew 1:18–25; Luke 1:26–38—The Virgin Birth of Jesus
4. Matthew 1:21–23; Luke 1:31–33—The Naming of Jesus
5. Matthew 2:1–12; Luke 2:8–20—Worship by the Magi and Shepherds
6. Matthew 2:5–8; Luke 2:4–11—The Naming of Bethlehem
7. Matthew 2:19–23; Luke 1:26; 2:4—To and from Nazareth
8. Matthew 27:1–10; Acts 1:15–20—The Death of Judas Iscariot
9. Matthew 28:16–20; Luke 24:36–49; Acts 2:38—The Great Commission

Luke, like Matthew, references King Herod when introducing the birth of John the Baptist. Since Jesus and John are both born within six months of each other, the assumption can be made that Luke intends the King Herod reference to apply to Jesus as well. But this is where the problem begins. Luke copies Matthew's time line in the beginning of his gospel (nearly word for word), but then wildly changes that time line when mentioning the census of Cyrenius. Critics of Luke insist that he erred concerning the census. However, the evidence suggests that Luke is well aware of Matthew's time line. He simply chooses to introduce different elements into his gospel. After all his audience could not fact-check his gospel, and even if they did notice a discrepancy, all could be harmonized, just as modern-day Christians do.

Points 2 through 7 contain similar themes derived from the birth narratives. Do the birth narratives prove or disprove the existence of Q? Both Matthew and Luke provide genealogies for Jesus, report virgin births, name Jesus, create stories to tie Bethlehem to Nazareth, and have adoring followers. Luke simply steals the plot and pencils in his own peculiar story, tying Jesus to Mithras and co-opting the Jewish census, an event whose history belongs to the Fourth Philosophy. In one daring piece of fictional drama, Luke incorporates true Jewish history and pagan myth into the birth of his Jesus.

What are the odds that Luke and Matthew composed their particular birth narratives if Q really existed? It seems that Luke either borrowed the ideas of Matthew or Matthew borrowed from Luke. Since Matthew is assumed to have predated Luke, it follows that Luke borrowed from Matthew.

A further similarity can be noted concerning discrepancies in Matthew's and Luke's narratives. Unlike Mark both Matthew and Luke mention the death of Judas Iscariot. In Matthew, Judas hangs himself because of his grief over betraying Jesus. In Luke's book of Acts, Judas's body bursts open due to his wickedness and his intestines spill out. The reason for the death is changed from grief to wickedness and the method of death also changes. Since Judas Iscariot is a fictional character, he could not have been included in any Q document. In addition, Judas's death is not included in Mark, so the finger points again to Luke borrowing from Matthew, only now adjusting the story to fit his own particular narrative for the early church.

Finally, both Matthew and Luke have separate versions of the Great Commission, preaching the gospel to all nations. Scholars have omitted this from the Q sayings and it does not appear in Mark. In Matthew the eleven disciples go to Galilee to worship Jesus, even though some doubt his divinity. Jesus says to them, "Therefore, go and make disciples of all nations, baptizing them in the name of the Father and of the Son and of the Holy Spirit" (Matthew 28:19). Luke moves this meeting to Jerusalem but uses the same elements in his story. Luke's Jesus answers his disciples' doubts by showing them the wounds on his hands and feet. He then says, "The Christ will suffer and rise from the dead on the third day, and repentance and forgiveness of sins will be preached to all nations, beginning at Jerusalem" (Luke 24:46–47). Unlike Matthew, Luke's gospel does not associate baptism with the Holy Spirit.

While Luke places the Commission in Jerusalem, in order to segue into his account in Acts, he also includes Matthew's doubters, the Commission to preach to all nations, and the instruction to baptize. In Matthew this baptism is in the name of the Father, the Son, and the Holy Spirit. Luke says that the baptism is for repentance and for the forgiveness of sins. However, in Acts, Luke writes this about baptism, "Repent and be baptized, every one of you, in the name of Jesus Christ so that your sins may be forgiven. And you will receive the gift of the Holy Spirit" (Acts 2:38). Thus, like Matthew's gospel, Luke's Acts of the Apostles includes the Holy Spirit in his baptism.

This evidence illustrates that Luke borrows heavily from Matthew—not only Matthew's stories included in the so-called Q, but also Matthew's general story concerning the birth narratives, Judas Iscariot's death, and the Great Commission. In short this proves that a Q source never existed.

Did Luke Use Mark or Matthew, or Both?

The sources used by Luke are the Gospels of Mark and Matthew as well as his own knowledge of the times, based primarily on Josephus's writings: *War* and *Antiquities*. That Luke knew Matthew's gospel can also be proved from passages supposedly derived from Mark. So, if Luke copied only from Mark, we would expect that these particular passages would be similar or identical to Mark. However, in three cases, Luke follows the accounts as described by Matthew.

The first account concerns Jesus and the Sanhedrin, after the arrest at the Garden of Gethsemane.

All of them condemned him as deserving death. Some began to spit on him, to *blindfold* him, and to strike him, saying to him, "Prophesy!" The guards also took him over and beat him. (Mark 14:64–65) (Emphasis mine)

They answered, "He deserves death." Then they spit in his face and struck him, and some slapped him, saying, "Prophesy to us, you Messiah! *Who is it that struck you?*" (Matthew 26:66–68) (Emphasis mine)

Now the men who were holding Jesus began to mock him and beat him; they also *blindfolded* him and kept asking him, "Prophesy! *Who is it that struck you?*" They kept heaping many other insults on him. (Luke 22:63–65) (Emphasis mine)

In Mark, Jesus is blindfolded and then asked to prophesy. Why he is asked to prophesy cannot be positively determined. Matthew tries to clarify this by adding, "Who is it that struck you?" Obviously, they want the blindfolded Jesus to determine who struck him. Unfortunately Matthew forgets to mention that Jesus is blindfolded. This is corrected by Luke who states that Jesus is blindfolded and is asked to prophesy, "Who is it that struck you?" So Luke uses both Mark and Matthew in developing his own passage about Jesus before the Sanhedrin.

In fact, Luke uses the exact Greek words as Matthew in the question, "Who is it that struck you?" If Luke does not have a copy of Matthew, then how does he perfectly reproduce this question? Supporters of the Q hypothesis must argue for sheer coincidence. How many coincidences will disprove the Q source?

Luke copies Matthew a second time concerning Peter's denial of Jesus.

At that moment the cock crowed for the *second* time. Then Peter remembered that Jesus had said to him, "Before the cock crows

twice, you will deny me three times." *And he broke down and wept.*
(Mark 14:72) (Emphasis mine)

At that moment the cock crowed. Then Peter remembered what Jesus
had said, "Before the cock crows, you will deny me three times." *And
he went out and wept bitterly.* (Matthew 26:75) (Emphasis mine)

At that moment, while he was still speaking, the cock crowed. The
Lord turned and looked at Peter. Then Peter remembered the word
of the Lord, how he had said to him, "Before the cock crows today,
you will deny me three times." *And he went out and wept bitterly.*
(Luke 22:60–62) (Emphasis mine)

In Mark's account Jesus foretells that Peter will deny him three
times before the cock crows twice. In both Matthew and Luke the cock
crows only once. Perhaps Matthew removes the word *twice* because it
makes Peter look bad. This is a minor point and does not necessarily
mean that Luke follows Matthew's account. However, after the denial,
Matthew and Luke both write, "And he went out and wept bitterly."
The exact Greek words are used again. In Mark the phrase is "And he
broke down and wept." The meanings of all three passages are similar,
but Luke obviously copies Matthew and not Mark.

The reliance of Luke on Matthew cannot be denied. Luke uses both
Mark and Matthew and supplies his own information. In the above passage Luke writes that Jesus looks at Peter and that look trips Peter's
memory. This is just good fiction, as Luke has no credible information
that Jesus looks at Peter during the denial.

The third time that Luke uses Matthew over Mark concerns the
temptation of Jesus.

At once the Spirit *sent* him out into the desert, and he was in the
desert forty days, being tempted by Satan. He was with the wild
animals, and angels attended him. (Mark 1:12–13) (Emphasis mine)

Then Jesus was *led by the Spirit into the desert* to be tempted by the
devil. After *fasting* forty days and forty nights, he was hungry. The

tempter came to him and said, "If you are the son of God, tell these stones to become bread." (Matthew 4:1–3) (Emphasis mine)

Jesus, full of the Holy Spirit, returned from the Jordan and was *led by the Spirit in the desert,* where for forty days he was tempted by the devil. *He ate nothing during these days,* and at the end of them he was hungry. The devil said to him, "If you are the Son of God, tell this stone to become bread. (Luke 4:1–3) (Emphasis mine)

In Mark the Spirit drives Jesus into the desert, while Matthew changes that to being led by the Spirit. Luke follows Matthew's lead and has the Spirit lead Jesus into the desert. Also, both Matthew and Luke mention that Jesus is hungry at the end of forty days. Matthew follows the example of Moses and states that Jesus fasts for forty days and nights. Luke's audience cares little about Moses or fasting, so Luke simply states that Jesus is hungry. The detail of being hungry is absent in Mark, but not in Matthew and Luke.

These three episodes clearly illustrate that Luke has access to both Mark and Matthew.

Other Opinions on Q

Scholars argue other points, which, on the surface, may support Q. Some suggest that if Luke has access to Matthew, then the Sermon on the Mount would have been reproduced. However, upon close examination, Luke incorporates most of Matthew's Sermon on the Mount (Matthew 5–7), spreading the passages throughout his gospel. He does remove Matthew passages written solely for Jewish consumption. For example, Luke excludes passages relating to the importance of the Law (Matthew 5:17–20); murder, which was answerable to the Sanhedrin (Matthew 5:23–24); adultery (Matthew 5:27–30); oaths (Matthew 5:33–37); giving to the needy (Matthew 6:1–4); and fasting (Matthew 6:16–18). All else is included. So Luke simply refashions Matthew's information to meet his own needs, removing Jewish references.

Luke does keep one Jewish reference but adjusts it to support his own case to his Gentile audience. In Matthew 5:18, Jesus says "I tell you the truth, until heaven and earth disappear, not the smallest letter, not the least stroke of a pen, will by any means disappear from the Law until everything is accomplished." What does Jesus really mean by saying "until everything has been accomplished"? Luke includes Matthew's language but answers the question regarding "until everything has been accomplished."

> *The Law and the prophets were proclaimed until John. Since that time,* *the good news of the kingdom of God is being preached,* and everyone is forcing his way into it. It is easier for heaven and earth to disappear than for the least stroke of a pen to drop out of the Law. (Luke 16:16–18) (Emphasis mine)

Luke states that the Law ends with John the Baptist and the preaching of the gospel. This could not have been the original meaning, as John the Baptist preaches that the soul had to be cleansed through righteousness. This righteousness comes from following the Law and its implications concerning God and one's fellow man (*Antiquities* 18.117). To a Jewish audience such a notion is absurd, but the Gentile audience, for whom Luke writes, gladly receives such a pronouncement.

The fact that Luke includes this passage on the Law suggests that he is aware of Matthew's presentation. In most cases Luke simply removes Jewish references, but here he clarifies a Jewish passage for his Gentile audience. It would certainly have been a coincidence if Luke and Matthew had copied this passage out of the Q source.

Some scholars, represented by S. G. F. Brandon, support Q based on the different post-resurrection appearances.[7] In Matthew the Risen Lord appears to the disciples in Galilee while Luke places the appearances in Jerusalem, a far distance from Jerusalem.

Brandon is right that the locations being served by Matthew and Luke are quite a distance from one another. However, that distance does not prove that Luke uses Q instead of Matthew. Luke frequently relies on Josephus's *Antiquities,* changing the data to meet his own needs. In the same way Luke locates the postresurrection appearances in Jerusalem instead of Galilee.

Luke has two reasons for locating the postresurrection stories in Jerusalem. First, he wants to downplay the importance of Peter and James by having the first postresurrection appearance occur outside of Jerusalem to two relatively unknown individuals. Certainly this narrative suggests that the Risen Lord has no preference for Peter and James. Second, the apostles have to be in Jerusalem in order to commence his story of the early church. If he followed Matthew's story line, he would have had to somehow get the Eleven back to Jerusalem from Galilee. Instead Luke simply has Jesus appear to the Eleven in Jerusalem. The problem is solved.

Do the disciples compare the different versions of Jesus of Nazareth? Probably not. Those living in the areas around Alexandria read Matthew, while Luke is favored in other locales. If another version of Jesus appears in either area, the people just conflate the stories. Even today Christians combine the birth narratives presented by Matthew and Luke. The Star of Bethlehem is merged with the census of Cyrenius and the adoration by the Magi and the shepherds are both included in the Christmas story.

The history of Q begins as a way to explain similarities between Matthew and Luke without admitting that Luke uses Matthew as a source. This is necessary since Luke radically departs from Matthew's story line. For example, if Luke knows of Matthew's gospel, then he would have reproduced Matthew's birth narrative instead of creating his own. But this perspective assumes that Luke wants to follow Matthew's birth narrative.

I suggest that Luke relies on the Gospels of Mark and Matthew as well as the writings of Josephus. Luke sometimes follows Mark and sometimes follows Matthew. Even when departing from Matthew's detail, as in the case of the genealogies, he replaces material with his own version. Instead of a genealogy of the Jews, his is a genealogy of the human race, including Gentiles in the mix.

The author of Luke is a follower of Paul, the original inventor of Jesus of Nazareth. The Gospels of Mark, Matthew, and Luke all have the same purpose—to spread the word about Jesus of Nazareth. If the gospel writers have the same purpose and are part of the same organization, then it would be absurd to think that the left hand does not know what the right hand is doing. Simply put Luke knows of Matthew and adjusts this source to his own needs.

Thus, the Q source is a modern-day theory that does not account for the invention of Jesus of Nazareth by Paul. When the creation of Jesus of Nazareth is understood, the need for Q ends.

LUKE'S AGENDA
CONCERNING HISTORICAL DATA

A number of passages in Luke are relevant in discerning the true nature of the Jewish Messiah. Although Luke copies Mark and Matthew's Jesus of Nazareth, he does include useful information not included in those earlier gospels. In doing this Luke simply co-opts known information about the Messiah. This strategy helps defend the fictional Jesus of Nazareth against historical traditions known to be associated with the true historical Messiah. Now, all messianic history resides in the composite Jesus of Nazareth. Even today scholars cannot distinguish between the true historical Messiah and the invented Jesus of Nazareth.

Co-opting history to further one's goals is both devious and ingenious. A twist to any event can produce whatever effect is desired. For example, placing an event in the wrong time frame can yield a totally different outcome. In the book of Acts the author places the stoning of James the Just in 35 CE instead of 62 CE, as reported by Josephus. As we have seen this switch in Acts ensures that Paul can be distanced from Josephus's Saul/Paul.

Luke uses the following historical events to obscure the truth or to further the party line of faith over law. By recognizing Luke's agenda actual history may be uncovered.

The Two Swords: Luke 22:36–38

At the Last Supper the disciples ask if two swords will be enough. Jesus answers, "That is enough." What just happened? Why take any swords if Jesus believes he will be a human sacrifice and accepts that role? Or does Jesus really believe that a token resistance will prod God into action?

While Mark and Matthew both state that Jesus goes to the Garden of Gethsemane to pray, Luke changes that to the Mount of Olives. In reality, the Garden of Gethsemane is very close to the Mount of Olives. But why change the story? Again, Luke may have been borrowing. In Zechariah, God promises to deliver Israel from the nations on the Mount of Olives. "The Lord will be king over the whole earth. On that day there will be one Lord, and his name the only name" (Zechariah 14:1–21). Does the real historical Messiah believe in this prophecy? If so, then two swords will be enough, as God will do the rest. This apocalyptic message is included in Luke but downplayed so that we fail to recognize its significance.

If the Jewish Messiah expects the fulfillment of Zechariah's prophecy, then Jesus's words, as expressed in Mark and Matthew, make sense: "My God, my God, why have you forsaken me?" (Matthew 27:46; Mark 15:34). While Luke includes the two swords and the Mount of Olives references, he omits this last questioning plea of Jesus. Luke's strategy entails including important historical data while shaping this data to his own time line and story line, making it difficult to grasp what really happens to the Jewish Messiah and his dreams for a new Israel.

The Charges against Jesus: Luke 23:2

Perhaps Luke's most important contribution to the search for the historical Jesus concerns the charges brought against Jesus. Both Mark and Matthew claim that Jesus will destroy the Temple and rebuild it in three days, a claim acceptable to the Romans as long as tax revenues keep streaming in. However, Luke's account of the charges appears closer to the truth, the real reason why the Romans crucify Jesus.

> Then the whole assembly rose and led him off to Pilate. And they began to accuse him, saying, "We have found this man subverting our nation. *He opposes payment of taxes to Caesar and claims to be Christ, a king.*"

So Pilate asked Jesus, "Are you the king of the Jews?"

"Yes, it is as you say," Jesus replied.

Then Pilate announced to the chief priests and the crowd, "I find no basis for a charge against this man."

But they insisted, *"He stirs up the people all over Judea by his teaching. He started in Galilee and has come all the way here."* (Luke 23:1–5) (Emphasis mine)

Some truth emerges from this passage. First, Jesus begins his ministry or movement in Galilee. Then he comes to Jerusalem, suggesting that his organization is well developed. Jesus truly believes that he is king or Messiah and that all of Israel will soon follow him. This, in and of itself, must have greatly troubled Pilate, who as governor, is responsible to Caesar for controlling Israel. Only a king sanctioned by Rome will be allowed, and until another Herod the Great emerges, Rome is willing to govern the land for itself.

Second, Jesus opposes the payment of taxes to Caesar. This is interesting, considering that Luke introduces Jesus's birth during the census of Cyrenius. During that census, Judas the Galilean rallies the people against the payment of taxes to Rome (*Antiquities* 18.4). Judas, like Jesus, fights against the payment of foreign tribute, likening it to slavery. As Jesus stirs up people all over Galilee and Judea, Judas also exhorts the whole nation to assert their liberty. Thus, the charges against Jesus are identical to those leveled against Judas the Galilean. Either Jesus follows in Judas's footsteps or Luke derives his Jesus story from Judas the Galilean.

Luke does something quite astounding in his story, making the ruthless Pilate sympathetic to Jesus. Even after hearing the charges against Jesus, Pilate finds no basis for his arrest, a clear violation of Roman governing practice. In reality Pilate would have prosecuted Jesus to the fullest extent of the law, the result being crucifixion, the very sentence that is carried out.

Why does Luke mention this charge against Jesus that makes him a potential enemy of Rome? Most likely the story of the Jewish Messiah's stand on foreign taxation is well known, especially by the

Roman government and the military that fight in the Jewish war. Luke co-opts the tax story through the census birth narrative and the charge of opposing taxes to Caesar. Jesus, being only a baby, does not participate in the census tax revolt, and the tax charge at his trial is dismissed by Pilate.

Interview with Herod Antipas: Luke 23:5–12

Unlike Mark and Matthew, Luke introduces Herod Antipas into the trial of Jesus. Luke's take on Herod Antipas is closer to Josephus and Matthew than to Mark. Mark states that Herod "feared John and protected him, knowing him to be a righteous and holy man" and that he "liked to listen to him [John]" (Mark 6:20). In Matthew's account Herod "wanted to kill John, but he was afraid of the people, because they considered him a prophet" (Matthew 14:5). However, Matthew and Mark both blame Herodias for John's ultimate death. In Josephus, Herod knows of John's power over the crowds and has him put to death in order to stop any rebellion (*Antiquities* 18.116–119). Luke's account shows that Herod is not a friend to either John or Jesus.

> But when John rebuked Herod the Tetrarch because of Herodias, his brother's wife, and all the other evil things he had done, Herod added this to them all: He locked John up in prison. (Luke 3:19–20)

> When Herod saw Jesus, he was greatly pleased, because for a long time he had been wanting to see him. From what he had heard about him, he hoped to see him perform some miracles. He plied him with many questions, but Jesus gave no answer. The chief priests and the teachers of the law were standing there, vehemently accusing him. Then *Herod and his soldiers ridiculed and mocked him. Dressing him in an elegant robe, they sent him back to Pilate.* (Luke 23:8–11) (Emphasis mine)

> Then the *governor's soldiers* took Jesus into the Praetorium and gathered the whole company of soldiers around him. They *stripped him and put a scarlet robe on him,* and then wove a crown of thorns and

set it on his head. They put a staff in his right hand and knelt in front of him *and mocked him.* (Matthew 27:27–29) (Emphasis mine)

Two factors account for Luke's inclusion of Herod Antipas in Jesus's trial. First, Herod and his soldiers are responsible for some of the abuse heaped upon Jesus: it is Herod's soldiers, not those of the governor, as reported by Matthew, who place a robe upon Jesus and ridicule and mock him. This may seem insignificant, but the constant shift of blame from the Romans to the Jews (or half-Jews) has biased generations against the Jewish people. This shift of blame is necessary as the Pauline Jesus of Nazareth is being preached to a Roman audience.

Second, Luke once again co-opts the story of Judas the Galilean. After the Golden Eagle Temple Cleansing, Judas and Matthias are arrested and interviewed by Herod the Great, who then sends them to Jericho to answer questions in front of the "principal men among the Jews" (*Antiquities* 17.151–167). In Luke, the chief priests and teachers of the Law assist Herod in the interrogation. Luke borrows this account of Judas the Galilean to embellish the story of Jesus of Nazareth.

Does Pilate send Jesus to Herod Antipas? Probably not. Pilate orders Jesus's execution, a perfectly normal act for a Roman governor.

The Road to Emmaus: Luke 24:13–35

Paul writes to the Corinthians concerning the resurrection.

> For what I received I passed on to you as of first importance: that Christ died for our sins according to the Scriptures, that he was buried, that he was raised on the third day according to the Scriptures, and that *he appeared to Peter, and then to the Twelve.* After that, he appeared to more than five hundred of the brothers at the same time, most of whom are still living, though some have fallen asleep. *Then he appeared to James, then to all the apostles,* and last of all he appeared to me also, as to one abnormally born. (1 Corinthians 15:3–8) (Emphasis mine)

According to Paul, Christ appears first to Peter, then to the Twelve, and later to James. This is significant for two reasons. First, although Paul competes against the pillar apostles, he nevertheless confirms that Peter and James have witnessed the resurrection. He downplays their importance by adding five hundred others to the mix and by comparing his hard work to theirs. Even though he is the last to witness the resurrection, Paul maintains his superiority over the pillars. The last will be first. Second, Paul states that the Twelve witness the resurrection, clearly contradicting the Judas Iscariot story and the gospel claim of the Eleven. So Paul actually relates a somewhat biased view of the resurrection, totally excluding Mary Magdalene and the other women, but at least crediting Peter and James with witnessing Christ's first appearance.

Luke's account concerning the resurrection shifts the first eyewitness accounts from Peter and James to Cleopas and his friend, probably simply stand-ins for Peter and James.

Why would Luke credit two unknown disciples with first witnessing the resurrected Jesus? He simply wants to diminish the importance of the first witnesses. How important could James and Peter be if the Christ appeared to other unnamed disciples as well? This downplaying of Peter and James is continued in Luke's second work, the book of Acts.

The authors of the other three gospels credit Mary Magdalene as the first witness to the empty tomb and the Risen Christ. In his zeal to discredit the family of Jesus and his closest companions, Luke marginalizes Mary Magdalene, placing her with a group of women at a distance from the cross and as a bearer of the good news of the resurrection.

Scattering of the Disciples

When Jesus is arrested, his disciples flee for their lives, hoping to escape crucifixion by the Romans. However, not all flee. In the gospel story Jesus is crucified between two bandits or revolutionaries, most likely his own followers.

What do the synoptic gospels say concerning those who flee? In Mark, "everyone deserted him and fled" (Mark 14:50). Matthew repeats Mark's claim, writing, "All the disciples deserted him and fled" (Matthew 26:56). Curiously, in Luke, the disciples fight for Jesus and their desertion is never mentioned. Instead Jesus rebukes the soldiers and his own disciples for fighting: "Am I leading a rebellion, that you have come with swords and clubs?" (Luke 22:52). This antiviolence stance by Jesus is quite remarkable, considering that he approves the two swords carried by his disciples and certainly is aware that his entry into Jerusalem and the Temple cleansing incident have put his movement on a collision course with Rome. Is Luke overcompensating here, portraying a Jesus totally indifferent to the political aspirations of his own disciples and of the Jewish people?

What do the disciples really do in Luke's tradition? Remember, Acts is the second part of Luke's history of Jesus and the early church. While Matthew writes of Judas Iscariot's death, Luke does not mention it until the first chapter of Acts. Luke also mentions the fleeing of disciples in Acts.

> After him [Theudas], *Judas the Galilean* appeared in the *days of the census* and led a band of people *in revolt. He too was killed, and his followers were scattered.* (Acts 5:37)(Emphasis mine)

Remembering that Luke places the birth of Jesus at the census, in line with the tax revolt of Judas the Galilean, the main charge against Jesus is his refusal to pay taxes to Rome. Finally, the fleeing disciples are associated with Judas the Galilean. Is Luke's Jesus of Nazareth a thinly disguised Judas the Galilean?

Critics argue that the Acts passage claims that Judas is a one-hit wonder and that his movement collapses at his death. But, according to Josephus, "All sorts of misfortunes also sprang from these men [Judas the Galilean and Sadduc/John the Baptist], and the nation was infected with this doctrine to an incredible degree" (*Antiquities* 18:6). In fact, Judas's movement is extremely successful. Thus, if Judas's disciples are really scattered after his death, they later coalesce even stronger. The same can be said of Jesus and his followers.

We must note that if the disciples scatter once Jesus is arrested, then no eyewitness accounts of the trial of Jesus exist. The gospel stories are fabrications, explaining why the details vary considerably, including Luke's insertion of Herod Antipas into the action.

So who wrote the Gospel of Luke? According to tradition, Luke is a coworker of Paul, a view supported by the book of Acts, in which the narration changes in chapter 16 from third person to first person. The passages using first-person plural (*we, us, our,* and *ours*) suggest that Luke is a firsthand eyewitness to Paul's later years.

But what does Luke say about himself? Unlike Mark and Matthew, Luke actually offers some information about himself, claiming that he has carefully investigated all the accounts that have been handed down from the first eyewitnesses (Luke 1:1–4), and mentioning his former book, in which he wrote about Jesus's ministry (Acts 1:1–2).

Luke states that he is not an eyewitness and that others have written about Jesus beforehand. Certainly he has possession of and had read Mark, and most likely the Gospel of Matthew. In addition, he claims to have investigated "everything from the beginning." But what does that mean? Does he talk directly to eyewitnesses or just incorporate stories supposedly handed down by eyewitnesses?

If Luke bases his gospel on Mark, then he has no real eyewitness testimony, as Paul is behind the nonhistorical creation of Mark. And Matthew, too, is based on Mark. So none of the gospels are the product of actual eyewitnesses. Luke is also further removed in time from the actual occurrences in Judea.

What can be confidently stated about the author of Luke? He is connected with the Jesus of Nazareth Movement (Pauline Christianity) that springs from Paul's Christ Movement after the Jewish war had decimated the Jewish Jesus Movement. Scholars place Mark between 70–73 CE and Matthew a few years later at around 80 CE, so, arguably, Luke is penned sometime after 80 CE.

If we step back and look at the geography, we acknowledge that Luke may have been tapping into a new market. Just as a company expands its market through innovative advertising, the Jesus of Nazareth Movement (Pauline Christianity) is infiltrating a new area. This market can be identified based on the two most important messages of Luke's gospel.

First, Luke ties Jesus of Nazareth to the taxation issue. Most likely the original Messiah is still viewed as an antitax, anti-Roman Jewish revolutionary. Luke deliberately places the birth of Jesus of Nazareth at the census of Cyrenius, distancing Jesus from the most revolutionary political statement made by Judas the Galilean, the founder of the Fourth Philosophy. Luke also attaches to Jesus the political charge of refusing to pay Roman taxes. However, at his trial and at the cross, Jesus is declared innocent of those charges. In effect Jesus of Nazareth is crucified based on a false charge. Being innocent of anti-Roman activity would have reassured Luke's audience.

Second, while Mark and Matthew associate Jesus of Nazareth with the cult of Mithras, Luke does them one better by plagiarizing elements of the Mithras birth narrative, a very attractive feature to the followers of Mithras. In addition, Acts claims that Paul comes from Tarsus, even though Saul/Paul was Herodian and has his roots in Jerusalem. Why Tarsus?

> It was in Tarsus that the Mysteries of Mithras had originated, so it would have been unthinkable that Paul would have been unaware of the remarkable similarities [between] . . . Christian doctrine and the teachings of Mithraism. Tarsus was the capital of Cilicia, where, according to Plutarch [46–125 CE], the Mythraic Mysteries were being practiced as early as 67 BCE.[8]

Tarsus is the center of Mithras worship, an ideal place to associate with Jesus of Nazareth's Church. Luke achieves this by claiming that Paul comes from Tarsus. Surely, Paul is aware of Mithraic doctrines and weaves them into his own Christ cult, but as we learn from chapter 6, he is not from Tarsus.

Note that the Roman soldiers are involved in the Mithras cult. Are

Luke's infancy story and his inclusion of Tarsus aimed at this vast market? An inroad into the military market ensures a wider distribution of the Jesus of Nazareth story. Remember, increasing the market increases monetary gain.

Where does Luke write his gospel? According to Brandon and Mack, Luke's work is written around the Aegean Sea, encompassing modern-day Greece and Turkey.[9] Marcion, the bishop of Pontus (northern Turkey), exclusively uses a redacted version of Luke while Tarsus is on the southern border of modern-day Turkey. This area separates the Roman Empire from the Persian Empire and is flooded with Roman troops. In addition, Corinth, Ephesus, Galatia, and Tarsus are influenced by Paul's Christ Movement from the 30s CE. No doubt, Luke's new and improved gospel had many eager followers.

11 ► The Acts of the Apostles

Luke produces a version of Jesus of Nazareth with a Gentile audience in mind. He then concentrates on early church history, covering a time period from 33 to 60 CE, from the resurrection of Jesus to Paul's escape from the Jews. This time period has been used by some scholars and preachers to date the book of Acts to around 60 CE.

In the 1920s Henry Halley logically dated Acts to around 63 CE, as the trial of Paul was omitted.[1] In addition to Halley's concerns about the trial, note that James the Just is martyred in 62 CE, the persecution of Christians in Rome occurs in 64 CE after the Great Fire, and the Jewish war with Rome begins in 66 CE. Remarkably the author of Acts omits some of the most important events in Christian history.

I am a bit more cynical than Halley. I find it fascinating that Acts concludes before these major events. Does the author of Acts really write his history before these major events? I suggest that the author includes what is convenient and decides against recording all the other major events.

In chapter 7 I detailed three different "foundation legends": the martyrdom of Peter and Paul in Rome, the author of the Gospel of Mark, and the flight by the Jewish Jesus Movement from Jerusalem to Pella. The martyrdom legend of Peter and Paul relates to Nero's persecution of Christians in 64 CE and the flight to Pella explains how the Messiah's Jewish followers survived the Jewish war with Rome. Acts does not deal with these issues, but later church officials do. Why does Acts ignore these great events and what was Acts' overall purpose?

I will show that the author of Acts means to ignore all these important events in order to pursue his own agenda, an agenda that glorifies Paul's gospel and Paul himself.

RELIANCE ON JOSEPHUS

Various passages in Acts are connected to Josephus's two histories of the Jewish nation: *The War of the Jews* (75 CE) and *Antiquities of the Jews* (93 CE). In addition, Josephus writes an autobiography, *The Life of Flavius Josephus,* which is published as an appendix to *Antiquities*. Acts fashions itself as church history, adjusting Josephus's stories to fit its own agenda. A list of corresponding passages and dates illustrates my point.

1. Theudas and Judas the Galilean are used as examples of failure in Acts 5:33–39 (35 CE). In *Antiquities* 20.97–102 the deaths of Theudas and the sons of Judas the Galilean are detailed (45–47 CE).
2. The stoning of Stephen is included in Acts 7:54–8:1 (35 CE). Josephus places the stoning of James in 62 CE (*Antiquities* 20.200–214). Saul/Paul plays a part in both accounts.
3. Simon the magician is cast differently by Acts 8:9–25 (35 CE) and by *Antiquities* 20.141–144 (52–60 CE).
4. Philip converts the Eunuch to Christianity and has him baptized (Acts 8:26–40) (35 CE), while Eleazar converts King Izates to Judaism and has him circumcised (*Antiquities* 20.34–48) (44 CE).
5. Saul/Paul persecutes the church after the stoning of Stephen (Acts 9:1–2) (35 CE), and Saul/Paul persecutes the lower priests after the stoning of James the Just (*Antiquities* 20.214) (62 CE).
6. In Paul's conversion story (Acts 9:1–19) (35 CE) Ananias introduces Paul to the faith by the laying on of hands. In *Antiquities* 20.34–48 (44 CE) Ananias is a Pauline teacher in the King Izates conversion story, not a representative of Peter and James.

7. Simon Peter *includes* Gentiles in the Christian religion (Acts 10:1–48) (35–40 CE), and Simon the teacher *excludes* Agrippa I from the Temple because he is not fully Jewish (*Antiquities* 19.332–334) (43 CE).

8. Simon Peter, son of John, and James, son of Zebedee, are imprisoned (Acts 12:1–19) (40–45 CE), while Simon and James, the sons of Judas the Galilean, are imprisoned and later crucified (*Antiquities* 20.100–102) (47 CE).

9. Both versions recount Agrippa I's death (Acts 12:19–25 and *Antiquities* 19.343–352) (44 CE).

10. Another version of Simon the magician is related by the author of Acts (Acts 13:4–12 [45–50 CE]) (*Antiquities* 20.141–144 [52–60 CE]).

11. Another version of Simon and James in prison stars Paul and Silas (Acts 16:16–40 [50 CE]) (*Antiquities* 20.100–102 [47 CE]).

12. Paul pleads his case before Agrippa II (Acts 25:23–26:32) (60 CE), while Saul/Paul leads the Peace Party in an effort to have Agrippa II's army fight against the insurgents (*War* 2.418–419) (66 CE).

13. In Acts 21:27–23:35 (60 CE) Paul is saved by the Romans, while Saul/Paul also flees to the Romans in *War* 2.556–557 (66 CE).

14. Paul appeals to Caesar and then travels to Rome (Acts 26:32) (60 CE). In *War* Saul/Paul is sent to Nero in Achaia by Cestius to plead his innocence and to lay any blame for the war on Florus (*War* 2.558) (67 CE).

15. Both Paul and Josephus travel to Rome to plead their cases before Caesar, with both playing heroic roles in the shipwrecks of their ships. Clearly, Paul's experience is modeled after this story by Josephus (Acts 27 [60 CE]) (*The Life of Flavius Josephus* 14–15 [60 CE]).

These fifteen overlaps between Acts and Josephus strongly suggest that Luke tailored actual historical data to fit his particular agenda for the church. If just one or two similarities existed, an argument could be made in favor of coincidence. However, fifteen parallel passages should not be dismissed lightly. The sheer number and nature of the similarities should shake the reader's preconceived notions concerning church history.

Note that Acts changes the Josephus time line. For example, the stoning of James in 62 CE is presented as the stoning of Stephen in 35 CE. The corresponding attack by Saul/Paul is also changed from 62 CE to 35 CE. The reason for this particular change is clear: Acts wants to transport the evil Saul/Paul to a time before his conversion to the Way of Righteousness. The actual story by Josephus had Saul/Paul persecuting the poor priests long after his conversion to the Way (21–25 CE) and after his ouster from the Jewish Jesus Movement (44 CE).

If Luke authored Acts, then any time line presented in his gospel should be viewed skeptically. For example, Jesus's birth in 6 CE at the census should be questioned as well as John the Baptist's introduction in 28–29 CE. Luke's dating of John the Baptist has been universally accepted by scholars. But was John really introduced to the public in 28–29 CE? In short everything should be questioned concerning the traditional Christian time line.

Some argue that Josephus simply altered data from Acts, not the other way around. This scenario assumes that Josephus had a working copy of Acts long before 93 CE, and that he rewrote the Christian story to fit into his overall Jewish narrative. But why would Josephus have done that? If the church, as described in Acts, had really existed, then Josephus would have included this in his history. It would have made good reading. No, Josephus did not know of Acts' history.

As proof we need look no further than the story of Theudas and the sons of Judas the Galilean, as reported by Josephus. In his narrative Josephus describes Judas the Galilean, the father of those being crucified. The author of Acts incorrectly places Judas the Galilean, and not his sons, after Theudas in Acts 5. If Josephus had copied Acts, he never would have mentioned the sons of Judas the Galilean at this point in his narrative.

Thus, the book of Acts was most certainly written after 93 CE, the publication date of Josephus's *Antiquities*. In addition, much of Acts comes from a limited number of Josephus's passages. Josephus's history of the King Izates conversion, the crucifixions of Judas the Galilean's sons, the confrontation between Agrippa I and Simon, and the stoning of James the Just were all reworked into Acts' history of the early church. The altered Josephus passages are revered by "scholars" who view Acts' time line as history.

THE AGENDA OF ACTS

To the Galatians, Paul writes:

> I am astonished that you are so quickly deserting the one who called you by the grace of Christ and are turning to a different gospel— which is really no gospel at all. Evidently some people are throwing you into confusion and are trying to pervert the gospel of Christ. But even if we or an angel from heaven should preach a gospel other than the one we preached to you, let him be eternally condemned! As we have already said, so now I say again: *If anybody is preaching to you a gospel other than what you accepted, let him be eternally condemned!* . . . I want you to know, brothers, that the gospel I preached is not something that man made up. *I did not receive it from any man, nor was I taught it; rather, I received it by revelation from Jesus Christ.* (Galatians 1:6–9; 1:11–12) (Emphasis mine)

The Galatian Church is accepting a gospel different from Paul's own gospel. Note that Paul's gospel of grace does not originate with the apostles but comes from revelations from the Risen Christ. This should amaze Christians and scholars alike.

Which competing gospel does Paul denounce as being worthy of eternal condemnation? The competing gospel is the original, represented by Peter and James. It emphasizes following the Torah, just as the earthly Messiah has done. The entire letter to the Galatians consists of attacking the Law and circumcision. Do not be confused; Paul's gospel has nothing to do with the earthly Messiah and the message preached by his earliest Jewish disciples.

By the second century the original Jewish Jesus Movement has nearly been extinguished. Its remnant, the Ebionites, call Paul an "apostate from the Law," preaching that he had forsaken the Jews' responsibility to follow God's law and is no longer under the everlasting covenant between God and the Jewish people.[2]

The book of Acts is written in the second century to downplay this negative opinion of Paul. But how is this accomplished? Certainly, Luke cannot simply regurgitate historical facts; such a strategy would have destroyed Paul's legacy. Instead Acts shifts Paul's gospel to the Twelve, headed by Peter.

The Gospels of Mark, Matthew, and Luke all present Jesus of Nazareth as the source of Paul's gospel of grace. From Jesus of Nazareth, with the prodding of the Holy Spirit, the Twelve eventually realize that the Law is unnecessary for salvation.

When Peter preaches to the crowd on Pentecost, he exhorts them to repent, but then promises the gift of the Holy Spirit.

> Repent and be baptized, every one of you, in the name of Jesus Christ so that your *sins may be forgiven*. And you will *receive the gift of the Holy Spirit*. The promise is for you and your children and for all who are far off—for all whom the Lord our God will call. (Acts 2:38–39) (Emphasis mine)

Peter ties baptism in the name of Jesus Christ to the forgiveness of sins and to the gift of the Holy Spirit, an interpretation of baptism far different from that of John the Baptist, who preaches a baptism of cleansing, assuming that the recipients have already cleansed their hearts beforehand (*Antiquities* 18.116–119). Evidently Paul's Holy Spirit baptism now comes from Peter's mouth at the beginning of the church.

This bait and switch can be illustrated by another passage in the book of Acts. Apollos, a native of Alexandria influenced by the Jews, comes to Ephesus with an incorrect understanding of baptism (50 CE, per Acts). He knows the scriptures well and teaches about Jesus accurately but has never heard of the Holy Spirit (Acts 18:24–19:7). How can a disciple of Jesus, twenty years after his death, have never heard of the gift of the Holy Spirit at baptism? Can it be that Peter and James never taught such a thing? In fact, James and Peter teach John's baptism and not Paul's Holy Spirit baptism.

Acts then introduces the Grecian Jews into its history. These Grecian Jews, led by Stephen and Philip, are accepted by the Twelve. They teach Paul's theology and are accused of blaspheming the Law.

> Jews of Cyrene and Alexandria as well as the provinces of Cilicia and Asia . . . began to argue with Stephen, but they could not stand up against his wisdom or the Spirit by which he spoke. Then they secretly persuaded some men to say, "We have heard *Stephen speak words of blasphemy against Moses* and against God."
>
> So they stirred up the people and the elders and the teachers of the law. They seized Stephen and brought him before the Sanhedrin. They produced false witnesses, who testified, *"This fellow never stops speaking against the holy place and against the Law. For we have heard him say that this Jesus of Nazareth will destroy this place and change the customs Moses handed down to us."* (Acts 6:9–15) (Emphasis mine)

Note that the charges against Stephen are similar to those brought against Jesus, and in both trials, the charges are made by false witnesses (Mark 14:55–59). Clearly Acts stresses continuity between Jesus and Stephen in that both preach Paul's gospel. If these fictional characters really spoke against the Law, then the charges against them would have been true. However, Acts portrays them as being within the Jewish religion, not outside it, as was the case with Paul's antinomian gospel.

After Stephen's martyrdom Philip brings Paul's gospel to Samaria. Philip's message concerns baptism, which bestows the gift of the Holy Spirit on the believer. Again, Acts asserts that the Holy Spirit baptism predates Paul, even though Paul claims that his gospel was received through personal revelation through the Risen Christ.

The last attempt to shift Paul's theology onto the Twelve (and Jesus) occurs when Peter is summoned by Cornelius, a centurion in the Italian Cohort (Acts 10:1–48). Up to this point Peter has never eaten anything impure or unclean. However, God tells Peter not to "call anything impure that God has made clean." In one short passage Acts nullifies the law of Moses and destroys the barriers between Jews and Gentiles.

While Peter speaks to Cornelius and his family, "The Holy Spirit came on all who heard the message. The circumcised believers who had come with Peter were astonished that the gift of the Holy Spirit had been poured out even on the Gentiles" (Acts 10:44-45). Why should the Jews be astonished? After all Jesus supposedly teaches his disciples to bring the Word of God to all nations.

In the meantime, as Stephen, Philip, and Peter bring Paul's gospel of faith and the Holy Spirit to the Gentiles, Paul dutifully follows orders. When asked to go home to Tarsus, Paul complies. When recruited from Tarsus, Paul accepts the Jerusalem apostles' orders. The impression is made that Paul has nothing to do with the creation of his own gospel.

Only after years of service does Paul gain any preeminence among the disciples. In Acts 15 Paul is given the task of preaching the gospel to the Gentiles and the rest of Acts raises Paul to the top of the pecking order.

Acts' agenda creates a foundation legend. Paul's gospel becomes the Gospel of Jesus of Nazareth and of Peter. Thus, Paul does not invent his gospel but inherits it from others. Of course, this totally contradicts what Paul himself proclaims: "I did not receive it [the gospel] from any man, nor was I taught it; rather, I received it by revelation from Jesus Christ" (Galatians 1:12).

IS PAUL OF TARSUS INVENTED?

As noted in part two Saul/Paul is a member of the Herodian family. This is the Paul of history, a real flesh-and-blood individual. But preachers and even scholars speak of the exploits of Paul of Tarsus. Did Paul of Tarsus really exist? Did he perform the miracles as outlined in the book of Acts?

I contend that Paul of Tarsus was created by the author of Acts, just as Jesus of Nazareth was created by the author of Mark. In the pre–70 CE (pre–Jewish war) environment, two movements exist: the Jewish Jesus Movement, centered in Jerusalem and Galilee and fiercely loyal to the law of Moses, and the Christ Movement, founded by Paul and preaching faith through the Holy Spirit throughout the Roman Empire. These two movements separate in 44 CE when Paul's true views are exposed to Peter and James.

When the Jewish war ends, the Jewish Jesus Movement is largely destroyed. In its absence Paul, or his disciples, create Jesus of Nazareth to mouth Paul's own views. In doing this the author of Mark makes Jesus of Nazareth the originator of Paul's gospel. This downplays Paul's role in the creation of his own gospel.

Creation of the fictional Paul of Tarsus is necessary to hide the activities of Saul/Paul , the cousin of Agrippa I. It was and still is easier for Pauline Christians to identify with this outsider than with a member of the royal Herodian family. But such a claim needs proof, and this proof must be consistent with Josephus's history.

In Josephus's story of the stoning of James the Just, Saul/Paul hires a group a men to plunder the sparse assets of the lower priests.

> Costobarus also, and *Saulus,* did themselves get together a multitude of wicked wretches, and this because *they were of the royal family;* and so they obtained favor among them, because of their kindred to Agrippa: *but still they used violence with the people,* and were very ready to plunder those that were weaker than themselves. And from that time it principally came to pass, that our city was greatly disordered, and that all things grew worse and worse among us. (*Antiquities* 20.214) (Emphasis mine)

This account by Josephus comes right after the death of James. Saul/Paul is a member of the royal family and uses this fact to influence others to do his bidding. He has only one goal: to obtain wealth and power for himself. Josephus then reports that conditions in Jerusalem deteriorate after Paul's attack. Paul may have unknowingly contributed to the war fever among the Zealots, as he represents everything considered evil by the insurgents.

The story in Josephus's account occurs in 62 CE, eighteen years after Paul's expulsion from the Jewish Jesus Movement by Peter and James. From Josephus one can sense that this Paul is an evil character. Acts uses this episode to introduce its Saul/Paul of Tarsus character. But in Acts these despicable actions came prior to Paul's "conversion" to the Jesus Movement.

> And Saul [Paul] was there, giving approval to his [Stephen's] death. *On that day a great persecution broke out against the church at Jerusalem,* and all except the apostles were scattered throughout Judea and Samaria. Godly men buried Stephen and mourned deeply for him. But *Saul began to destroy the church.* Going from house to house, he dragged off men and women and put them in prison. (Acts 8:1–3) (Emphasis mine)

This is a very important point. Acts simply transfers the deeds of Josephus's Saul (that is, Paul) to the beginning of Paul's career before his "conversion." The evil acts of Paul are thereby attributed to a zealous Jew unfamiliar with the life-changing gospel of Jesus. Since the event described actually occurs in 62 CE, the very beginning of Paul's association with the Jewish Jesus Movement can be categorically described as false.

After his miraculous conversion, where God intervenes directly, the temporarily blinded Saul/Paul is led by the hand into Damascus. In Damascus the Lord speaks to Ananias, ordering him to go and lay hands upon Paul. Paul's eyesight is immediately restored and he undergoes baptism (Acts 9:1–19). Does Ananias impart the gospel to Paul or is that the job of the Holy Spirit? According to Paul his gospel does not come from any man (Galatians 1:11–24). So where does Paul's gospel come from?

Paul never reveals to the Gentiles when he received his gospel. He does claim that he preaches "the faith he once tried to destroy," but that was the message of the Jewish Jesus Movement, not the gospel arising from his own revelations. Only after seventeen years of ministry does Paul go to Jerusalem and present his gospel to James and Peter (Galatians 2:1–2). His revelation or gospel to the Gentiles comes to Paul sometime in those seventeen years, probably around 37 CE, the year that his cousin Agrippa I becomes king of Israel.

The book of Acts conflates the Jewish Jesus Movement and the Christ Movement of Paul in the conversion story. Paul may have converted to the Jesus Movement, but his revelations occur later. Was Paul instructed by Ananias? Scholars believe that Ananias was a member of the Jesus Movement, but, according to Josephus, as we have noticed, the Ananias of the King Izates conversion is a Pauline teacher. In fact, Eleazar, a member of the Jesus Movement, refutes Ananias's teachings, just as Peter and James refute Paul's teachings at Antioch. Paul may have been a loyal member of the Jesus Movement in the beginning, when he was teaching the importance of the Law and not his later message of grace through faith.

Just as Jesus allegedly comes from Nazareth, downplaying his association with the radical Nazorean sect, Paul also is given a bogus birthplace. Acts sends Paul to his hometown of Tarsus to avoid the Jews' attacks. Later, Paul is recruited from Tarsus by Barnabas to begin their extraordinary mission work among the Gentiles at Antioch (Acts 9:29–30; 11:25–26).

Tarsus is chosen for important reasons. It is necessary to hide Paul's true identity and his family connections. Scholars have failed to explain how a young man from Tarsus could have wielded such power in Jerusalem, including the authority to arrest and imprison members of the church. And Paul's relatives also have connections in Jerusalem (see chapter 5, "Paul's Family Ties"). This information, supplied by Acts, seems to contradict the claim that Paul comes from faraway Tarsus. Yet, scholars and preachers have faithfully accepted Tarsus as Paul's hometown.

As we have already discussed Tarsus was home to the greatest cult of its day, the religion of Mithras, with which the author of Luke and

Acts wants to identify his new religion. Placing the Gentile's greatest Christian prophet in Tarsus is a stroke of genius, surely appreciated by those initiated in the rites of Mithras.

The author of Acts also incorporates information from Paul's letters, changing important details to fit the narrative. For example, Paul claims to have gone to Jerusalem in private (Galatians 2:1–2) and asked for the opportunity to visit Rome (Romans 15:23–29). In Acts, Paul is the center of attention at the Council of Jerusalem (Acts 15:1–6) and is sent to Rome to meet Caesar (Acts 28:14–31).

Acts changes Paul's own claims for the following reasons: first, if Paul travels openly to meet with the apostles, then the Jewish apostles surely condone Paul's message; and second, the trip to Rome in Acts gives Paul the perfect alibi concerning the stoning of James. Acts simply rewrites history by sending Paul to Rome *before* the death of James.

The middle of Paul's career in Acts comes primarily from his own letters, albeit with some changes, but the pattern for Paul's last days comes directly from Josephus. In Acts, Paul plans to visit Jerusalem to describe his ministry to the apostles. Before going he issues this warning to his followers: "I am ready not only to be bound, but also to die in Jerusalem for the name of the Lord Jesus" (Acts 21:13). Like Jesus of Nazareth, Paul knows that he will undergo pain and suffering in Jerusalem. And like Jesus, Paul courageously goes anyway.

In Jerusalem, Paul describes his ministry to the Gentiles, to the approval of the majority. However, some Jews are not willing to accept Paul or his message. These Jews drag Paul from the Temple and attempt to kill him. Fortunately for Paul the Roman commander hears of his troubles and comes to the rescue (Acts 21:27–36). Like Jesus, Paul is attacked by the Jews and nearly killed. The Roman commander acts like Pilate in trying to understand Paul's crimes against the Jews.

Paul is brought to trial before the Sanhedrin and then Felix, as innocent as Jesus had been. He languishes in prison for a short while, then once again stands trial before Festus.

When Paul appeared, the Jews who had come down from Jerusalem stood around him, bringing many *serious charges against him, which they could not prove.*

Then Paul made his defense: "I have *done nothing wrong against the law of the Jews* or against the temple or against Caesar." (Acts 25:7–8) (Emphasis mine)

From the passage above we learn that Paul believes the charges against him are false, as he has done nothing to violate the Law. A simple reading of Galatians proves this passage to be wholly invented.

Is the Law, therefore, opposed to the promises of God? Absolutely not! For if a law had been given that could impart life, then righteousness would certainly have come by the law. But the Scripture declares that the whole world is a prisoner of sin, so that what was promised, being given through faith in Jesus Christ, might be given to those who believe. Before this faith came, we were held prisoners by the Law, locked up until faith should be revealed. So the Law was put in charge to lead us to Christ that we might be justified by faith. *Now that faith has come, we are no longer under the supervision of the Law.* (Galatians 3:21–25) (Emphasis mine)

Paul does not accept the Law as the everlasting covenant between the Jews and God. To Paul the Law is temporary and no longer in effect. As such the charges against Paul are not false.

Paul then appeals the charges to Caesar and is given an interview with King Agrippa II. In this interview Paul tries to convert Agrippa to his new faith. We are led to believe that Paul has spiritual matters on his mind. The die is cast: Paul is on his way to Rome to plead his case before Caesar.

Paul's story in Jerusalem is a rewrite of Josephus's account of the life of Saul/Paul, the cousin of Agrippa I. Paul escapes from the Jews and is saved by the Roman commander, Cestius. He also is a member of the Peace Party, petitioning Agrippa II for troops to put down the insurgents. He is then sent to Caesar (Nero) in order to plead his own innocence in starting the war. And, last but not least, Josephus himself is shipwrecked on his way to Rome. All these stories are rewritten and applied to the fictional Paul of Tarsus.

The beginning, the middle, and the end of Paul's ministry, according to Acts, are patently untrue. An individual does exist who wrote letters to his Christ cult, but this is Saul, the cousin of Agrippa I. Paul of Tarsus is just a fictional character, created to mislead people and conceal the truth. This process worked in the creation of Jesus of Nazareth and it certainly worked in reshaping the history behind Saul, now known as Paul of Tarsus.

THE NEW JESUS AND THE NEW PAUL

Jesus of Nazareth is a composite character, with the life and deeds of Judas the Galilean infused with Paul's new gospel. Paul of Tarsus is also a composite character, with the life and deeds of the Herodian Saul and Josephus himself rewritten in order to hide Saul's true identity.

The synoptic gospels succeed in placing Paul's gospel back in time. It is not history but sheer invention, shaping Jesus from the image of Paul. No wonder some see continuity between Jesus and Paul, but they are looking at the relationship from the wrong perspective. In the gospels Jesus of Nazareth supposedly introduces Paul's gospel, that gospel of faith intent on replacing the everlasting covenant between God and the Jewish people. Jesus is killed by these Jews but the message survives through the Twelve, the Seven, and then through Paul of Tarsus. In Acts, Paul is represented as simply following the teaching of Jesus and the Jewish apostles.

In reality the Herodian Saul, a cousin of Agrippa I, joins the Jewish Jesus Movement. In the beginning he teaches the Law, circumcision, and nationalism. However, these parochial teachings do not further his attempt to reach Gentiles.

As we have learned Paul's new "revealed" gospel has nothing to do with the Jewish Messiah, Peter, or James. It is a gospel that appeals to

Gentiles, with no requirements from the law of Moses; a gospel of faith, resembling the cult of Mithras more than the teachings of the original Jewish Jesus Movement. Acts successfully replaces the Jesus Movement, or Way of Righteousness, with the Christ Movement of Paul. Even today, most people assume that the Jewish Messiah, Peter, James, and Paul all preached the same gospel. But they did not. The Messiah's original teachings are overshadowed by the Pauline gospel, leaving a strange mix that has confused and confounded scholars to this very day.

Acts' sloppy history and obvious dependence on Josephus have been widely ignored by scholars. Very few realize that the dates and events in Acts cannot be trusted. In fact, Acts' history is polemical revisionism. In every other historical study the ancient historian would be given more credence than a religious text. But in the study of Christianity Christian history (the gospels and Acts) is accepted as true, even if contradicted by contemporary historians (chiefly, Josephus). As noted in the introduction the scholarly community places greater emphasis on the gospels and Acts than on Josephus and the Roman historians.

12 ► The Gospel of John

The Gospel of John is presumed to have been written later than the synoptic gospels and hence is thought to be less reliable because of its later date, its departure from the synoptic message, and its heavy theologizing.

As such it is generally believed that the synoptic gospels present a more authentic picture of Jesus than the one portrayed in John. Certainly, the Jesus of John's gospel never existed in first-century Israel, but neither did the Jesus of the synoptic gospels. All four gospels present a Jesus who does not correspond to the historical realities of the time. However, each gospel has information that may help unravel the mystery of Jesus.

The Gospel of John follows the basic framework of Mark, so it can be confidently stated that John did not develop independently from Mark, Matthew, and Luke.[1] As already discussed the synoptic gospels came from a Pauline source. The same can be claimed for the Gospel of John.

But why produce another gospel? Remember Jesus of Nazareth is an efficient marketing tool to help raise funds for the Pauline Church. The Gospel of Matthew gives Mark's Jesus of Nazareth a more well-developed history, while Luke co-opts Mithras's legends into his version. What group or religion does John hope to co-opt in his version of Jesus?

DIONYSUS

Dionysus is the Greek god of the vine, the god associated with wine, and one of the few gods who could bring a dead person out of the underworld. Dionysus is also an important god in everyday life, one who represents rebirth.[2] The cult of Dionysus is popular in Greece and Asia Minor, important areas for the Jesus of Nazareth Movement.

John's first miracle or "sign" concerns Jesus and his mother Mary at the wedding banquet at Cana. Here, Jesus supposedly turns water into wine. People cannot turn water into wine and neither did Jesus! This is a story meant for followers of Dionysus, where the wine at the banquet is inferior to the wine produced by Jesus. Thus, Jesus is superior to Dionysus. When the disciples see this miracle they put their faith in Jesus. John hopes that followers of Dionysus will switch their allegiances to Jesus as well.

While this story is intended to reach followers of Dionysus, the wedding banquet story may hide some historical truth. First, Jesus's mother knows he is special and powerful. In Mark, Jesus's mother and brothers think that Jesus is "out of his mind" (Mark 3:20). John's later gospel no longer denigrates Jesus's mother, but still treats the brothers shabbily (John 7:1–5). This is an early attempt to begin deifying Mary as the mother of God.

Second, why are Mary and Jesus even consulted about the wine situation? That is the concern of the wedding party and the banquet manager. Does this story mask the true Cana wedding banquet between "Jesus" and his bride, possibly Mary Magdalene? If so, then it makes sense that "Jesus" and Mary Magdalene are involved in the ordering of more wine.

Dionysus can also resurrect the dead from the underworld. This is exactly what Jesus does in the story of Lazarus. In fact, this was Jesus's greatest miracle, although it is missing from the canonical synoptic gospels. Why? Unlike John the synoptic gospels are not playing to the Dionysus crowd. In the story of Lazarus, John expounds upon death and resurrection.

Jesus said to her [Martha, the sister of Lazarus], "I am the resurrection and the life. He who believes in me will live, even though he dies; and whoever lives and believes in me will never die. Do you believe this?

"Yes, Lord," she told him, "I believe that you are the Christ, the Son of God, who was to come into the world." (John 11:25–27)

Jesus is a real person who can raise the dead and promise resurrection to all who believe in him, extremely attractive concepts to Dionysus's disciples. The power of these teachings cannot be overstated. Even today people believe in the resurrection, ignoring scientific proof that a man cannot be physically raised from the dead, especially after rotting four days in the tomb.

Note that John, like Paul, emphasizes faith or belief in Jesus. The true Jewish Messiah emphasizes faith in God, put into practice by following God's law. Thus, the story of the raising of Lazarus does not stray too far from its Pauline roots.

THE WORD BECOMES FLESH

John presents a picture of Jesus quite different from the one in the synoptic gospels. Mark claims that Jesus of Nazareth is the Son of God. The prologue in John claims that "the Word [logos] was with God, and the Word was God. He was with God in the beginning." (John 1:1–2) To John, Jesus is God and all creation comes through him. This concept of a man-god is foreign to adherents of the Jewish Messiah. The original Jewish followers believe that their Messiah as king will lead them to victory in their struggle against Rome, but now the Jesus of Nazareth Movement has progressed far beyond those provincial boundaries; now Jesus of Nazareth is God.

According to William Barclay, Jesus's story is restated to appeal to the Greek world and its conceptions. The Logos or the "Word" (the principle of reason and order) is familiar to the Greeks.[3] The Logos is responsible for the order of the world, so the application of Logos to

Jesus can be seen as a clever marketing tool. The Greeks now have to contend with a new God, one who creates the world and willingly dies for it as well.

John's assertion of Jesus being with God in creation refutes the Gnostic claims about God. The Gnostics believed that the God of the Old Testament created the world but was an evil force. This evil God did not know the true God and his representative, Jesus. Thus, if the God of the Jews were evil, then logically, the Jews themselves were evil. While John reasserts that Jesus and the God of the Jews are together in creation, his gospel also pictures the Jews as being evil. As such the Gospel of John lacks the consistency in thought that drives the Gnostics to their conclusions about God.

John does stay within the boundaries set forth by the Gospel of Mark. Both God and Jesus are together in purpose, while the Jews are forever conspiring against Jesus. In the synoptic gospels the Jewish leaders are against Jesus, while in John, the Jewish people as a whole oppose Jesus. John even disconnects the Jewish people from God.

> Jesus said to them, "If God were your Father, you would love me, for I came from God and now am here. I have not come of my own; but he sent me. Why is my language not clear to you? Because you are unable to hear what I say. *You belong to your father, the devil, and you want to carry out your father's desire.* He was a murderer from the beginning, not holding to the truth, for there is no truth in him. When he lies, he speaks his native language, for he is a liar and the father of lies. Yet because I tell the truth, you do not believe me! Can any of you prove me guilty of sin? If I am telling the truth, why don't you believe me? He who belongs to God hears what God says. *The reason you do not hear is that you do not belong to God.*" (John 8:42–47) (Emphasis mine)

In a sense the decoupling of the Jewish people from God in John is consistent with Gnosticism. For the Gnostics the Jewish people are evil because their God is evil. To John the Jewish people are evil because they follow the devil and not God. Thus, John protects the God of the Old Testament while placing total blame on the Jewish people for rejecting Christ.

Some in the Gentile Christian community deny that Jesus came in the flesh, a belief known as Docetism. They assert that "Christ's human body was a phantasm, and that his sufferings and death were mere appearance. 'If he suffered he was not God; if he was God he did not suffer.'"[4] Again, this reasoning does make sense. How can God suffer and die? In their minds God could not suffer and die. Therefore, Jesus was not real flesh, but rather a phantasm. To this John writes, "The Word became flesh and lived for a while among us" (John 1:14).

John is not willing to stray too far from Mark's gospel. In Mark, Jesus is the Son of God who suffers and dies. Even though it makes little sense to some, it nevertheless is unchangeable.

Where do these "Christian Gnostics" come from? First, both Gnostics and Docetists consider themselves Christian. They simply disagree on certain points. They cannot accept the death of God, and they also divorce all evil from God. But, as noted above, their logic cannot be disproved by John's emphatic statements.

Second, kernels of Gnostic beliefs can be found in Paul's letters. Paul claims that a good and perfect God is the God of Jews and Gentiles alike (Romans 3:29–30). Most would not dispute this claim, but it is possible to assert that the God of the Jews is not this good God.

Paul also denigrates the Law, saying that the veil of Moses blinds the Jews to the purposes of God. Paul writes: "Even to this day when Moses is read, a veil covers their hearts. But whenever anyone turns to the Lord, the veil is taken away" (2 Corinthians 3:13–18). Clearly, Paul blames the Jews for their stubbornness, not God. However, other teachers may have reasoned this out another way. How could the good God give the Jews a veil to blind them? Surely the veil was given by the God of the Jews, not the good God.

In short some of Paul's teachings could have been misinterpreted. Paul's Christ Movement begins around 37 CE with his revelations from the Risen Christ. Many of Paul's teachings are preserved in Romans, 1 and 2 Corinthians, and Galatians. But around 44 CE the Jewish Jesus Movement cracks down on Paul's ministry and ousts him from the movement. Paul certainly tries to keep his hold on his churches, but we know that he spent most of his time from 62 to 67 CE in Jerusalem. I suggest that after the last great collection of funds, Paul abandoned these churches, as he would have been dogged relentlessly by the followers of James and Peter.

Without Paul a vacuum is created. Certainly Paul's teachings are remembered, but reinterpreted by others with differing agendas. The varying Gnostic sects arise from this vacuum in the anti-Jewish culture in much of the Roman Empire.

So, in a sense, the Gospel of John is a product of Paul's post-70 creation: the Jesus of Nazareth Movement. It is pitted against remnants or mutants of the Christ cult, which were created earlier by Paul. However, the Jesus of Nazareth Movement is now a moneymaking proposition with full authority to crush these last vestiges of the Christ cult, just as it had obliterated the Jewish Jesus Movement after the Jewish war.

DEMONIZATION OF THE JEWS

Christianity's main character, Jesus, works on a different plane than ordinary Jews. Apparently he just happens to be a Jew. The Judaism of his native land is something he has to overcome in order to get his real message across to the nations. Thus, on one hand, Jesus is a Jew, but on the other, he is using Judaism to further his goals and God's.

How do the different gospel writers treat the Jewish people in their descriptions of Jesus? The Pauline gospel of Mark simply ignores the Jewish Law altogether. The Law plays no part in Jesus's life or ultimate mission. In fact, Jesus teaches that the Law has been superseded, as in the case of "clean and unclean" (Mark 7:1–23). Mark does blame the Jewish leadership for Jesus's death, but does not indict the Jewish people.

Matthew takes Mark's lead, strengthening the case against the Jews. While appearing to be more Jewish than Mark, Matthew is ultimately used by later Christians to persecute the Jews. When Matthew's Pilate washes his hands of responsibility for Jesus's death, the Jewish people cry out, "Let his blood be on us and on our children!" (Matthew 27:25). This plea provides justification for various persecutions and even the twentieth-century Holocaust.

Luke adds his own anti-Jewish touches to the mix. When Jesus teaches in his hometown of Nazareth, the people "took him to the brow of the hill on which the town was built, in order to throw him down the cliff" (Luke 4:28–29). What a lovely homecoming for the Son of God!

So the stage is set for the last gospel. John outdoes all the others in his sheer demonization of the Jews, opening his attack by having the Jews question Jesus's Temple cleansing (John 2:18). Jesus then travels through Samaria, where he finds many believers (John 4:1–26, 39–42). The die is cast: Everyone but the Jews has the capacity to believe in Jesus. John expands Luke's denigration of the hometown nonbelievers when he states, "Now Jesus himself had pointed out that a prophet has no honor in his own country" (John 4:44). While Luke has the locals persecute Jesus, John has the whole Jewish nation lining up against him.

Why do the Jews hate Jesus? According to John 8:42–47 the Jewish people are children of the devil and are unable to understand Jesus's words of truth because they follow the words of the devil, who is a liar. The Jews not only embraced these lies but also wish to carry out the devil's murderous plot. Yes, the Jews and their father, the devil, are hell-bent on killing Jesus.

Of course this is utter nonsense. The historical Messiah is wildly popular among the Jewish people. Even according to John, Jesus is welcomed into Jerusalem with great fanfare (John 12:12–19). But John then realizes that the traditional story line gives some credit to the Jews. So he shifts gears and writes about the Greeks welcoming Jesus (John 12:20–22).

Why does John hate the Jews? He is simply pandering to his Gentile audience, using their hatred of the Jews to his advantage. He, too, hates the Jews. He is just like them, and, more importantly, his Jesus is just like them.

One other point arises from this hatred of the Jews. If the Jews' father is the devil, then the God of the Old Testament is not the father of Jesus. This becomes one of the central tenets of Gnosticism, where the God of the Old Testament creates the evil world but is not connected to either Jesus or to his true Father. So, when Jesus prays to God, he is not praying to the God of the Old Testament. It seems logical, but racism often seems logical to its practitioners.

WHAT IS TRUTH?

A memorable line in John occurs when Pilate asks Jesus, "What is truth?" (John 18:38). A similar question must be asked: Does any historical truth emanate from the Gospel of John? Most Christians and many scholars generally believe the historical record of the synoptic gospels while accepting the spiritual truths of John. But the historical record of the synoptic gospels cannot be trusted. Could John have tidbits of information, varying from the synoptic gospels, conveying some truth?

Caiaphas and Annas

In Mark, Jesus is questioned before the Sanhedrin, with an anonymous high priest leading the questioning (Mark 14:10–11, 43, 53–65; 15:1, 11). In Matthew the high priest is named Caiaphas, but nothing else about him is noted (Matthew 26:3–5, 57). According to Josephus, Caiaphas is appointed by the Roman governor, Gratus, as high priest in 18 CE and continues in that capacity under Pilate until 37 CE (*Antiquities* 18:35). Like Mark, Luke fails to mention any high priest by name (Luke 22:1–6, 50, 54, 66; 23:1–4, 13).

In John two high priests are named: Caiaphas and Annas. Each occurrence will be examined below.

> Then one of them, named Caiaphas, who was high priest *that year,* spoke up, "You know nothing at all! You do not realize that it is better for you that one man die for the people than that the whole nation perish." He did not say this on his own, but as high priest

that year he prophesied that Jesus would die for the Jewish nation, and not only for that nation but also for the scattered children of God, to bring them together and make them one. So from that day they plotted to take his life. (John 11:49–53) (Emphasis mine)

John pits Jesus against the religious authorities in Jerusalem, led by Caiaphas, who prophesies that Jesus must die for the nation. This plot to kill Jesus is meant to bring the Jewish people together. This, of course, is the thinking of John, who claims that the Jews are the devil's children, conspiring together to kill Jesus.

If one piece of truth comes from John, it is the claim that Caiaphas is high priest *that year.* During the governorship of Gratus a new high priest was appointed each year with Caiaphas being appointed in 18–19 CE (*Antiquities* 18:34–35). Could Jesus have been arrested in 19 CE? That is exactly what my Judas the Galilean theory posits.

Then the detachment of soldiers with its commander and the Jewish officials arrested Jesus. They bound him and brought him *first to Annas,* who was the *father-in-law of Caiaphas, the high priest that year.* Caiaphas was the one who had advised the Jews that it would be good if one man died for the people.

. . . Meanwhile, the high priest questioned Jesus about his disciples and his teaching. . . . Then Annas sent him, still bound, to Caiaphas the high priest. (John 18:12–14, 19, 24) (Emphasis mine)

If Jesus is brought to Annas first and only transferred to Caiaphas after Annas's interrogation, who is in charge of the investigation—Annas or Caiaphas?

It appears that Annas is the real power behind the scenes, directing Caiaphas to do his bidding. According to Josephus, Annas is high priest from 7–15 CE, responsible for dealing with Judas the Galilean and the Fourth Philosophy (*Antiquities* 18:26, 34). We have seen that Judas's census uprising begins in 6 CE and the movement grows dramatically until 70 CE. In this time frame Annas is the father of five high priests, including the one who puts James the Just to death (*Antiquities* 20.197–203).

So the high priesthood from 7 to 62 CE is dominated by Annas, his sons, and Caiaphas, a son-in-law. This high priesthood is aligned against Jesus and James and is responsible for their deaths, information gleaned from the Gospel of John and Josephus.

The Wedding at Cana

As noted earlier the wedding at Cana illustrates Jesus's great powers. Like the god of wine, Dionysus, Jesus miraculously provides fine wine for the wedding banquet. Is this story just a literary device to further the brand name of Jesus of Nazareth or is a kernel of truth hidden beneath the surface?

Paul mentions that the apostles, other than he and Barnabas, are married (1 Corinthians 9:5–6), a list that includes Peter and James, the Messiah's brother. Since all the Jewish disciples are married it only follows that their Master also married. (Marriage is a cultural imperative in Judaism, based on Genesis 2:18: "It is not good for the man to be alone. I will make a partner for him.")

In the wedding story Jesus and his mother, Mary, take control of the wine situation. That is the job of the banquet manager and those being married. Can it be that this was originally a story about the Messiah's marriage? Is Mary Magdalene the bride? This is mere speculation, but the Jewish Messiah certainly is married with children, a positive example for his followers. The Jewish Messiah does not practice celibacy, as Paul does. Of the Jewish groups only the main faction of Essenes practice celibacy, and "Jesus" and his disciples are definitely not Essenes.

Also note that Jesus's first resurrection appearance is to Mary Magdalene (John 20:10–16). In the synoptic gospels Mary Magdalene finds the empty tomb and sees the angels, but does not see the resurrected Jesus (Mark 16:1–8; Matthew 28:1–10; Luke 24:1–12). John's gospel elevates Mary Magdalene, even more than the synoptic gospels. Could Mary have been Jesus's wife?

The Temple Cleansing

In all four gospels Jesus cleanses the Temple. In the three synoptic gospels this occurs in the last days before his crucifixion. However, in John, the Temple cleansing occurs at the start of his ministry, right after the wedding story.

Four possibilities exist: (1) Jesus cleanses the Temple twice, (2) he cleanses it at the beginning of his ministry, (3) he cleanses it at the end of his ministry, or (4) he does not cleanse it at all. Most scholars believe that Jesus cleanses the Temple after riding into Jerusalem, a messianic claim establishing his rule. The possibility that he also cleanses the Temple at the beginning of his ministry has not been seriously entertained because of Roman rule. If Jesus had cleansed the Temple at the beginning of his ministry, he would have been captured and put to death at that point.

Does John just put one Temple cleansing in the wrong time frame? Not necessarily. In the story of Judas the Galilean, Judas is arrested by Herod the Great and later released by Archelaus, after the Golden Eagle Temple Cleansing. This is at the beginning of Judas's long career. So it is very possible that John recounts this story about the Jewish rebel, Judas the Galilean.

Galilee or Bethlehem?

> Still others asked, "How can the Christ come from Galilee? Does not the Scripture say that the Christ will come from David's family and from Bethlehem, the town where David lived?" Thus the people were divided because of Jesus.
>
> . . . They replied, "Are you from Galilee too? Look into it, and you will find that a prophet does not come out of Galilee." (John 7:41–44, 52)

According to John the authorities cannot believe in Jesus because he comes from Galilee. They insist that the Messiah would come from David's line, from Bethlehem. Why are the authorities misinformed about Jesus's true birthplace, in Bethlehem, and why is this fact withheld by Jesus and his disciples?

In Mark's gospel the birthplace of Jesus of Nazareth is not even considered. In John, Jesus helps create the universe. Only in Matthew and Luke do we find data concerning Bethlehem. Is it possible that Matthew and Luke invented their stories in response to criticisms like the one presented above? Is the Messiah really born in Galilee and not Bethlehem?

The author of John must have been aware that the Jewish leaders do hold Galilee against Jesus. Galilee is a hotbed for revolutionaries, not the desired birthplace of their Messiah. If Jesus were really from Bethlehem, he could have easily defused the Galilean criticism. That he did not may point to the fact that he came from Galilee and not Bethlehem.

John's gospel is the logical ending of Pauline Christianity. Jesus of Nazareth is introduced in the synoptic gospels as the Son of God. John furthers this claim by stating that Jesus is with God and is God. Through Jesus the world is created. With the Gospel of John, Jesus can never be subordinate to any other God; he is greater than the Greek gods and possesses the same spiritual powers as popular mystery religion deities.

While Paul does not create John's ultimate god-man, he does produce the prototype. His Jesus of Nazareth does become flesh, at least in our minds. And his Jesus of Nazareth becomes the hope of Gentiles and the enemy of Jews. Without Paul none of this would have been accomplished, nor would Jesus of Nazareth have captured the imagination of the religious world, from the days of the Roman Empire, through the Dark Ages, to the confusing era in which we now live. But, without Paul, historians might have actually discovered the identity of the true Jewish Messiah. In the next section we will follow this historical Messiah.

The Real Jesus of Nazareth

A cts gives the short, depressing history of Judas the Galilean: "After him [Theudas], Judas the Galilean appeared in the days of the census and led a band of people in revolt. He too was killed, and all his followers were scattered" (Acts 5:37). To this day scholars teach that Judas the Galilean dies in 6 CE, at the census. After all the New Testament, the very word of God, supports this dating.

However, accepting a secondary source that contradicts a primary source is not good scholarship. In Josephus, Theudas is beheaded during the administration of Fadus (44–46 CE) and the *sons* of Judas the Galilean are crucified under Tiberius Alexander (46–48 CE) (*Antiquities* 20.97–102). The author of Acts misreads history (accidentally or purposefully?) and substitutes the death of Judas the Galilean for that of his sons. So this proof of the death of Judas in 6 CE cannot be supported by the primary source, Josephus.

In fact, Josephus states that the movement started with Judas and Sadduc/John the Baptist enjoying incredible success (*Antiquities* 18.9–10), in total opposition to the Acts account, stating that "Judas was killed, and all his followers were scattered" (Acts 5:37). Who is right—Josephus or the author of Acts?

As noted in chapter 11, the book of Acts routinely misrepresents information from Josephus. No doubt Josephus is right about Judas the Galilean. However, the author of Acts may have inadvertently included information tying Judas the Galilean to "Jesus." In Mark and Matthew the apostles scatter after the arrest of Jesus. Luke (the author of Acts) does not scatter the apostles of Jesus, but, rather, the followers of Judas.

Historically speaking Luke's sleight of hand concerning Judas the Galilean is brilliant. No one could ever link Judas to Jesus if Judas died a failure in 6 CE. If Luke had been honest about Judas the Galilean's career, others would also be claiming that Judas the Galilean was the historical Jesus.

FORTY-TWO SIMILARITIES SHARED BY JUDAS THE GALILEAN AND JESUS

The following list draws attention to the fact that the life of the gospel Jesus shares striking similarities with that of Judas the Galilean, as chronicled by Josephus. Scholars and Christians alike may find this list hard to swallow, as it forces a reexamination of their basic belief system. But this list will also madden the mythicists, who claim that a Messiah figure named Jesus never really existed. While I agree that Jesus of Nazareth is fictional, I do believe that this Jesus is a rewrite of a real individual, Judas the Galilean, infused with the theology and life experiences of Paul. Unlike Paul's Jesus of Nazareth, Judas the Galilean is not fictional! If Judas the Galilean lived, then so did his brothers and sons. Combined, they formed the Fourth Philosophy, a movement that scholars and mythicists have overlooked in their search for the real "Jesus."

1. Date of Birth

Jesus is born in 8–4 BCE (Matthew) and in 6 CE at the census of Cyrenius (Luke). Judas is mentioned by Josephus in 4 BCE, relating to the Golden Eagle Temple Cleansing (*Antiquities* 17.149–167), and in 6 CE, regarding the census of Cyrenius (*Antiquities* 18.1–10).

Inconsistencies abound in the birth narratives in Matthew and Luke, relating to the reign of Pilate and the ministry of John the Baptist, and with one another. If Jesus were born in 4 BCE and died thirty-three years later, then he died around 30 CE, during the reign of Pilate but five years *before John the Baptist's death* (*Antiquities* 18.116–119). If Jesus were born in 6 CE and died thirty-three years later, then he died in 39 CE, a few years after John the Baptist but two years *after Pilate left Judea*. Both accounts are historically flawed.

These two birth narratives are strategically placed in an era when Judas the Galilean's ministry flourished. This deception moves the adult Jesus twenty or so years away from Judas the Galilean, thus hiding the Messiah's true identity, a misdirection that has worked brilliantly. Very few scholars have even considered Jesus outside of the 30 CE time frame. This is even more disturbing considering that Jesus's brother, James, is purported to be ninety-six years old in 62 CE by the church historian Epiphanius. Even if James's age has been slightly exaggerated by ten years, his birth date can be estimated at approximately 35–25 BCE. Jesus is the older brother and could not have been born any later than 25 BCE.

Why do Matthew and Luke pick different dates for Jesus's birth, especially when Luke likely knows the Gospel of Matthew? If one solid date existed, then both gospel writers should have easily followed that date. However, if the writers are trying to present an alternate date, then each may have tied the birth date to a different event. Matthew ties his birth date to the Golden Eagle Temple Cleansing, while Luke uses the census of Cyrenius, the two major events in Judas the Galilean's career.

2. The Star of Bethlehem

In Matthew's "Star of Bethlehem" story the Magi are drawn to Jerusalem by a star, near the end of Herod the Great's reign, around 4 BCE. These Magi find the baby Jesus but do not report their findings to Herod. Incensed, Herod orders the slaughter of all the baby boys two years old and younger in the vicinity of Bethlehem.

In the Slavonic Josephus Persian astrologers go to Herod the Great, identifying the star in the sky and explaining its significance. Herod insists they return to him after finding the infant. However, the astrologers are warned by the stars to avoid Herod on the return trip. In

his rage Herod wants to kill all the male children throughout his kingdom, but his advisors convince him that the Messiah will come from
Bethlehem, hoping to confine the slaughter to that small town. An
early Christian inserts this Star of Bethlehem passage in *War*, placing
it in the early years of Herod, between 27 and 22 BCE (SJ *War* 1.400,
from additional passages).

As noted in chapter 9, this Slavonic Josephus passage originates
from the same source as the gospel version. The Slavonic text has
some interesting details missing from Matthew, who writes that the
chief priests and teachers of the Law inform Herod that the infant
will be born in Bethlehem. Herod then sends the Magi to Bethlehem,
ordering them to return when they have located the infant (Matthew
2:3–8). This version does not give Herod much credit, for if he really
knows that the child king is in Bethlehem, he would have slaughtered
every child in Bethlehem before the Magi could even reach the place.
On the other hand the Slavonic Josephus version has Herod learning about the location after waiting for the Persian astrologers to
return. This blunder on Herod's part wastes precious time, allowing
the infant and his parents to escape. Herod's advisors also tell Herod
the meaning of the star, tying it to the promised Star Prophecy, which
foretells a leader coming from Judah (Numbers 24:17). The same
sentiment is included in Matthew 2:6, but his quote from Micah 5:2
promises that a ruler will come from Bethlehem. All in all the two
versions have much in common, the difference being the time frame:
25 BCE versus 4 BCE.

If Jesus were born in 25 BCE, then he was thirty years old at the
time of the census (6 CE), the exact time when John baptizes in the
Jordan and proclaims the coming of the Messiah (SJ *War* 2.110, from
additional passages). This date is also marked by the nationwide tax
revolt, led by Judas the Galilean, the historical Jesus (*Antiquities* 18.4).

3. Genealogy

The genealogy of Jesus can also be compared to information known
about Judas the Galilean. In Matthew 1:15 and Luke 3:24 Mattan

and Matthat are listed as great grandfathers of Jesus. Since the gospels add a few generations to distance Jesus from Judas, one of these great grandfathers may have been Jesus's father. Judas's father may have been Matthias, a name closely resembling Mattan and Matthat.

On Mary's side a similarity exists concerning the town of Sepphoris. In Christian tradition Mary's parents, Joachin and Anna, come from Sepphoris, while Judas is linked to Sepphoris by Josephus, who writes that Judas is the son of Sepphoris, or rather from Sepphoris, and that he also raids the armory at Sepphoris. Certainly Judas is well acquainted with this town.

4. Killing the Enemy

Herod the Great plans to execute Judas after the Golden Eagle Temple Cleansing, ordering his prisoners put to death after his own death, in order to create great sorrow in Israel. Luckily for Judas Herod's advisors renege on the insane plan (*Antiquities* 17.149–167). According to the gospels Herod the Great tries to kill the baby Jesus (Matthew 2). Herod's goal of eliminating Jesus ends with his own death. In both stories an elderly, paranoid Herod tries to kill a perceived threat to his rule. Clearly the infant narrative is not actual history but rather a recasting of Moses's infancy legend.

5. Settling in Galilee because of Archelaus

Joseph returns to Israel after the death of Herod the Great but is afraid to settle in Judea because Archelaus is waging war on the followers of Judas and Matthias. Having been warned about this in a dream, Joseph moves his family to Nazareth, in Galilee (Matthew 2:19–23).

After being released by Archelaus (4 BCE) Judas goes to Sepphoris in Galilee, where he leads an uprising against the son of Herod (*War* 2.56). Sepphoris is in the tetrarchy of Herod Antipas, not under the control of Archelaus. The prudent move to Galilee allows Judas to reorganize his forces without fear of being attacked by Archelaus. The events chronicled in Josephus and the New Testament both occur because Herod the Great has died, leaving the country in turmoil.

6. The Missing Years

The gospels' only mention of Jesus's early life is his teaching at the Temple at the age of twelve (Luke 2:41–52). Otherwise no information is given from 6 CE (census of Cyrenius) to 26 CE (supposed date of Pilate's arrival in Judea). This lack of information mirrors Josephus's *War*, where nothing is chronicled from 6 CE to 26 CE (*War* 2.167–169). Josephus barely expands on this paucity of information in *Antiquities,* where he lists the Roman procurators during this twenty-year stretch, but little else (*Antiquities* 18.26–35).

Perhaps these missing years from Josephus are the result of judicious editing. The actual crucifixion of Judas the Galilean may have been deleted or transformed into the TF (*Antiquities* 18.63–64). Note that Josephus details the deaths of Judas's three sons—James, Simon, and Menahem—and his grandson—Eleazar—referring back to Judas the Galilean in each instance. Would Josephus have omitted the circumstances behind the death of Judas? It is far more likely that the writings of Josephus were edited to remove some interesting details of Judas's life and eventual crucifixion.

7. The Child Prodigy at the Temple

When he is only twelve Jesus spends three days at the Temple, "sitting among the teachers, listening to them and asking them questions. Everyone who hears him is amazed at his understanding and his answers" (Luke 2:41–52). Judas teaches young men at the Temple and is "the most celebrated interpreter of the Jewish laws and . . . well beloved by the people, because of [the] education of their youth" (*Antiquities* 17.149–4 BCE). How many others also teach at the Temple?

Is Judas's early career as a teacher at the Temple made legendary by placing his wisdom and knowledge within the body of a twelve-year-old? Consider this: If Judas had been born around 25 BCE (see number 2), then he would have been just twenty years old at the time of the Golden Eagle Temple Cleansing (4 BCE). His status as one of the finest teachers of the Law, at such a young age, must have been legendary.

This child prodigy legacy is woven into the gospel fabric by Luke in his story of the twelve-year-old Jesus.

8. The Dating of John the Baptist

John the Baptist may be the most important link between Judas the Galilean and Jesus. In Luke 3:1–3 John introduces Jesus to the world in 28–29 CE, the reason why scholars look nowhere else for Jesus.

According to the Slavonic Josephus this same John comes baptizing at the Jordan in 6 CE, right before the mention of Judas the Galilean and during the reign of Archelaus (4 BCE–7 CE) (SJ *War* 2.110, from additional passages). In addition, the Pseudoclementine *Recognitions* acknowledge John right before describing the various Jewish sects,[1] and Josephus describes these same sects right after his introduction of Judas the Galilean (*Antiquities* 18.4–22 and *War* 2.118–166). So the 6 CE time frame for John the Baptist is affirmed by more than one source.

Could this John the Baptist have been baptizing and proclaiming different Messiahs in both 6 CE and 29 CE? The odds of that would be incalculable. The only logical conclusion is that Jesus and Judas the Galilean are one and the same. This explains why the Slavonic Josephus's version of events has been ignored over the years. If John actually comes in 6 CE, then the New Testament chronology is clearly inaccurate.

9. The Second-in-Command: John the Baptist and Sadduc

Both Jesus and Judas the Galilean have a second-in-command, John the Baptist and Sadduc, respectively. This organizational setup is modeled after the Maccabees, where Mattathias leads the movement, with his son Judas Maccabee as his lieutenant. After Mattathias dies Simon takes Judas Maccabee's place and Judas Maccabee is elevated to the leadership role. In the later Fourth Philosophy movement Matthias and Judas work together at the Temple and are responsible for the Golden Eagle Temple Cleansing incident. After Matthias suffers martyrdom his son Judas fills this position with Sadduc (a stand-in for John the Baptist) (*Antiquities* 18.4).

In the gospel accounts Jesus picks Simon Peter as his second-in-command, but in reality Jesus is first paired with John the Baptist.

When Jesus is crucified he is replaced by his brother, James the Just. At this stage, John the Baptist and James share control of the movement. In 35–36 CE after John is beheaded by Herod Antipas, James appoints Peter as John's successor. The gospels minimize the roles of John the Baptist and James. According to these accounts John dies before Jesus, but per Josephus, Jesus dies first. James the Just is barely mentioned by Acts, his leadership role unannounced until Acts 15, at the Council of Jerusalem. By marginalizing John the Baptist and James the Just, the gospels are able to skip a generation, designating Peter as the leading apostle after the death of Jesus.

Dual leadership may have safeguarded the Jewish Jesus Movement. If one leader is captured or killed, then the other can take control. The Jewish Jesus Movement differs from that of Judas Maccabee in that the later movement believes in the resurrection of its leader. Thus, even though John the Baptist and James lead the movement after the death of Jesus, they still await the return of Jesus in power and glory. So, in essence, John and James are merely caretakers.

10. Nazareth and Sepphoris

Jesus and Judas are both called the Galilean. Actually, Jesus is referred to as Jesus of Nazareth, a village allegedly located near Sepphoris in Galilee. Note that Sepphoris is central to Judas the Galilean's ministry. Placing Nazareth close to Sepphoris is more than just coincidence. In *War* 1.648 Judas is said to be the son of Sepphoris or from Sepphoris. And in *War* 2.56, after being harassed by Archelaus, Judas retreats to Sepphoris, where he arms his disciples with weapons from the armory. Judas's history with Sepphoris is no doubt changed to Nazareth to hide these embarrassing revelations. After all both of the above references to Sepphoris are in the context of armed rebellion against Herod the Great and, later, Archelaus.

No references to Nazareth appear in the Hebrew scriptures or in Josephus. In fact, John Crossan and Jonathan L. Reed state that, in addition to Josephus's silence concerning Nazareth, it is never mentioned in either the Mishnah or the Talmud.[2] Jesus's disciples are called

Galileans (Mark 14:70) and a sleight of hand may have changed Jesus the Galilean into Jesus of Nazareth.

Nazareth may be a corruption of *Nazirite,* meaning "one consecrated to God by a vow." Samson and John the Baptist are notable Nazirites. But, more likely, Nazareth depoliticizes the revolutionary Nazorean sect, which, according to Acts 24:5, is inciting riots among the Jews throughout the Empire. Obviously the gospels want to keep their Messiah free of any taint of revolutionary fervor.

Judas the Galilean is mentioned in several passages by Josephus (*War* 2.118 and 2.433 and *Antiquities* 20.102), who states that this Judas hails from Gamala, across the River Jordan (*Antiquities* 18.4). But he is known as the Galilean, as attributed to the above references. At this time Galilee is a hotbed for revolutionaries. Both Jesus and Judas have similar backgrounds, influenced by those struggling for years against Herod the Great and Rome.

11. Zealous for the Law

The disciples of Jesus and Judas are zealous for the Law (Acts 21:20; *Antiquities* 17.149–154). Paul teaches his Gentile followers to disregard the Law, but the Jewish Jesus Movement denounces that teaching and ousts Paul and his followers from the movement (see Galatians).

Some forty years after the death of Judas (19 CE) a splinter group of the Fourth Philosophy, known as Zealots, appears on the scene. As their name suggests these individuals are obsessed with the Law, comparable to the fanatical followers of James the Just (Acts 21:20).

12. Wise Men

Judas and Jesus are both called wise men by Josephus (*Antiquities* 17.152 and 18.63). As the Jesus passage is a late third- or early fourth-century interpolation, the use of the term *wise man* is probably taken from the description of Judas and Matthias. Also note that Josephus does not freely use the term *wise man.* He does, however, use that term when describing himself. If Josephus calls himself a wise man, then this indeed is a great compliment.

13. Pure Communism

Both teachers stress the sharing of wealth, or pure communism (Matthew 6:19–27; Acts 2:42–45; James 5:1–6; *Antiquities* 18.7; *War* 2.427). In fact, sharing is the central message in "Love your neighbor as yourself." How can you love your neighbor if you let that neighbor go hungry or unclothed? When Jesus confronts the rich young ruler, he does not say, "Give 10 percent to the poor," but rather, "Give everything to the poor and then come follow me" (Matthew 19:16–24).

Members of the Fourth Philosophy are known as bandits by Josephus, for they exploit the wealthy, akin to a Robin Hood movement. During the war with Rome the debt records are burned in order to free those enslaved to the wealthy by their debt (*War* 2.426–427). This is truly class warfare! As for the Zealots Josephus shares his contempt for their practices concerning wealth and private property: "The dregs, the scum of the whole country, they have *squandered their own property* and practiced their lunacy upon the towns and villages around, and finally have poured in a stealthy stream into the Holy City . . ." (*War* 4.241). Considering what Jesus advises the rich young ruler, Josephus would have had the same attitude toward Jesus's lunacy!

In Acts 2:42 disciples are urged to share everything, an approach to living in line with the kingdom of God as preached by Jesus. The feeding of the five thousand is simply the sharing of one's food with others and has nothing to do with miraculous hocus-pocus. The letter of James also favors the poor over the rich (James 5:1–6).

14. Fine Teachers of the Law

Both Jesus and Judas are considered fine teachers of the Law (Matthew 5:17–20; Mark 12:28–34; *Antiquities* 17.149; *War* 1.648). As for Judas's abilities Josephus writes: "[Judas and Matthias were] the most celebrated interpreters of the Jewish laws, and well beloved by the people" (*Antiquities* 17.149). The earlier assessment from *War* 1.648 states that "there were two men of learning in the city [Jerusalem], who were thought the most skillful in the laws of their country, and were on that account held in very great esteem all over the nation."

From the gospels we know that Jesus uses parables in relating his message, in line with Pharisaic practices. For Jesus the two greatest commandments are to love God and to love your neighbor. To love God involves obeying God and the Law handed down by God to Moses, while to love your neighbor means sharing your possessions, so that no one is left hungry or homeless. In addition, both Judas and Jesus follow Judas Maccabee in his interpretation of the Sabbath: The Sabbath is made for humanity, not humanity for the Sabbath. Judas Maccabee permits his disciples to defend themselves if they're attacked on the Sabbath. Likewise, Jesus preaches that it is proper to do good on the Sabbath. In fact, when reprimanded by some Pharisees for breaking the Sabbath laws as he flees from Herod, Jesus quotes the Hebrew scripture story of David eating consecrated bread in order to maintain his strength in his flight from the authorities. Jesus has good reason to follow David and Judas Maccabee: He is a marked man. Neither Jesus nor Judas Maccabee would have flouted the Sabbath law without a good reason.

From Josephus, Judas the Galilean is known throughout the nation for his ability in interpreting the Law. We get the same feeling about Jesus when reading the gospels. The Pharisees constantly invite him to dinner in order to discuss key issues of the day. While we are privy to only the negative aspects of those meetings, in reality, most teachers in Israel consider Jesus an important figure and are constantly amazed at his teachings.

15. Movement Centered in Jerusalem and Galilee

Judas the Galilean's movement is centered in Jerusalem and in Galilee. Judas begins his public career in Jerusalem, teaching young men at the Temple. He convinces his students to take part in the Golden Eagle Temple Cleansing and is arrested by Herod the Great and imprisoned (*Antiquities* 17.149–167). Released by Archelaus he flees to Sepphoris in Galilee, where he preaches until his return to Jerusalem. His disciples crown Judas Messiah, and he later leads a tax revolt against Rome (*Antiquities* 17.271–272; 18.1–10).

Jesus is also in Jerusalem at the start of his career, according to

John. Coincidentally John places his Temple cleansing at the start of Jesus's career, consistent with the story of Judas the Galilean (John 2:12–17). Jesus then returns to Galilee, where he is proclaimed Messiah and spends most of his public ministry. When Jesus finally returns to Jerusalem, he is captured and crucified.

Even after Judas's death his movement revolves around Jerusalem and Galilee. In fact, Josephus notes that Eleazar is sent by his leaders in Galilee to teach King Izates true Judaism, which includes circumcision. King Izates has previously been taught by Ananias that he can become a full-fledged Jew without circumcision. The Jewish Jesus Movement practices circumcision. Note that Paul and Peter also have a similar disagreement in Antioch, caused by men sent from James. James may have centered his movement in either Jerusalem or in Galilee. However, since this occurs around the time of Agrippa's assassination, James probably relocates himself to a safer place, no doubt, Galilee.

16. Two Temple Cleansings

Both Jesus and Judas cleanse the Temple in Jerusalem (Matthew 21:12–13 and *Antiquities* 17.149–167). Actually Judas probably purifies the Temple twice. The first cleansing is the Golden Eagle Temple incident, when Matthias and Judas are captured by Herod the Great. The Golden Eagle is a sign of fealty to Rome, and the teachers cannot condone this alliance, considering that God is their only Lord and Ruler (*Antiquities* 18.23). The second cleansing can be deduced by inference. Judas the Galilean's son, Menahem, follows his father's modus operandi and seizes an armory before marching on Jerusalem. Menahem promptly cleanses the Temple after being hailed as Messiah by his disciples (*War* 2.433–444).

Interestingly the Gospel of John places the Temple cleansing at the beginning of Jesus's career (John 2:12–25), while the synoptic gospels have it near the end of his ministry. What are the odds of two different men cleansing the Temple once, not to say twice? Outside of the cleansing in 4 BCE (Judas) and the cleansing by his son in 66 CE (Menahem), Josephus does not record one other Temple cleansing from 4 BCE to 66 CE. This was certainly not an everyday occurrence.

The Slavonic Josephus verifies that the Golden Eagle is in honor of Caesar and is even named "the Golden-winged Eagle" (SJ *War* 1.650, from additional passages). Josephus states that Pilate brings his standards bearing the emblem of the Roman Eagle into Jerusalem in 19 CE, right before the crucifixion of Judas/Jesus (TF). In both the Temple cleansing of 4 BCE and the one in 19 CE, the power of Rome is attacked by the Jewish Messiah.

17. Opposition to Roman Taxation

Judas opposes the Roman tax, and Jesus is crucified for opposing the Roman tax (*Antiquities* 18.4 and Luke 23.2). The ministry of Judas (4 BCE–19 CE) focuses on the tax issue. At the Barabbas-style prisoner release ordered by Archelaus in 4 BCE, the Jewish crowd demands the release of prisoners, the easing of annual tax payments, and the removal of an onerous sales tax (*Antiquities* 17.204–205). Judas then leads a tax revolt at the time of the census (6 CE), but this does not end the extortion by Rome. Tacitus states that Judea is exhausted by its tax burden (16–18 CE) (*Annals,* ii. 42). This struggle against Roman taxation is well documented by both Tacitus and Josephus.

Jesus does not oppose every tax, but his hatred of Roman taxation is beyond doubt. "Give to Caesar what is Caesar's and to God what is God's" is not a pro-tax message. Jesus is saying this: Take your coinage with Caesar's portrait and leave our country, a statement that goes well beyond a "yes" or "no" answer to the tax question. To "Give God what is God's" harkens back to the days of Judas Maccabee and his struggle for Jewish independence. This is why Jesus is crucified by the Romans.

Paul, on the other hand, teaches his disciples to pay their taxes to Rome without hesitation (Romans 13:1–7), an accommodation to Roman taxation totally antithetical to the view of Judas (Jesus). Many people read Paul's view into the interpretation of Jesus's statement: "Give to Caesar what is Caesar's and to God what is God's." But we must remember that Jesus is crucified and that form of death is reserved for insurrectionists and slaves, not a result of supporting Roman taxation.

18. A New Religion or Philosophy

According to Josephus, Judas founds the Fourth Philosophy during his fight with Herod the Great's dynasty and Rome (*Antiquities* 18.1–10). Jesus of Nazareth is credited with the founding of Christianity, a new religion, though that is never mentioned by Josephus—an amazing omission. It is my contention that Josephus is very concerned with the followers of Jesus, but under the moniker of the Fourth Philosophy.

The Fourth Philosophy joins the earlier movements—the Pharisees, the Sadducees, and the Essenes—clinging to Pharisaic beliefs with an extremely nationalistic agenda. Also, Judas's disciples share some practices with the Essenes, though not the practice of celibacy. Thus, the nationalistic movement has drawing power that the other philosophies lack. This may explain why John the Essene is a leader in the war against Rome, no doubt influenced by the Fourth Philosophy. Essenes are known as pacifists, so the mention of a warlike Essene has confounded scholars through the years.

In reading the New Testament one must admit that Jesus is quite often portrayed as friendly with the Pharisees. He does blast those who love themselves more than their fellow Jews, but his overall feeling for the Pharisees is positive. "You are not far from the kingdom of heaven," Jesus says to one Pharisee (Mark 12:34). Like Judas, Jesus is very close to the Pharisees in belief and action.

19. Josephus on the Death of Judas and the Life of Jesus

Josephus details the life but not the death of Judas, while mentioning the death of Jesus but not one word about his life. Josephus invests much effort in recounting the events of Judas's life, even touching on the lives of his sons and his grandson (*Antiquities* 20.102; *War* 2.433–434 and 7.253). Each time Josephus recounts events in the lives of Judas's descendants, the historian specifies their pedigree. This does not occur in just one isolated time period: Simon and James are crucified in 46–48 CE, Menahem stoned in 66 CE, and Eleazar leads the Sicarii at Masada in 73 CE. This legacy of Judas the Galilean runs throughout Josephus's narrative.

Perhaps the death of Judas by crucifixion was removed from Josephus's works by a later Gentile Christian who believed the death might attract too much unwanted attention. Most scholars believe that the passage in Josephus detailing the death of Jesus is a late third- to early fourth-century forgery. The question is this: Was the spurious Jesus passage (TF of *Antiquities* 18.63–64) a replacement for Judas's death by crucifixion? The death of Judas by crucifixion should not be seriously doubted. Judas fights against Rome, actions punishable by crucifixion. In addition, two of Judas's sons, James and Simon, are crucified a generation later (46–48 CE).

20. Zealots and Sicarii

Zealots and Sicarii are part of the following of both Judas the Galilean and Jesus. Josephus asserts that Zealots and Sicarii arose from Judas's Fourth Philosophy. Two of Jesus's apostles are named Simon the Zealot and Judas Iscariot (a garbling of *Sicarios*). Since the Zealots and Sicarii are not introduced until the late 50s and early 60s by Josephus, titles of that sort are not used in Jesus's time (4 BCE–19 CE [the dates of the ministry of Judas the Galilean]). These names are given to the apostles by Gentile Christians, after the disastrous war with Rome. In addition, the moniker "Sons of Thunder," for the sons of Zebedee, denotes a power associated with the Fourth Philosophy, not the mild Christianity of the gospels.

21. Dying for the Cause

Disciples of both Judas and Jesus are willing to die for their respective causes. The Neronian persecution reported by Tacitus and the description of the Fourth Philosophy by Josephus indicate a willingness to die happily for God. (In fact, Edward Gibbon conjectures that Tacitus really is describing the Fourth Philosophy, not the traditional Christians.[3]) Jesus says: "Blessed [are] the ones being persecuted because of righteousness, for theirs is the kingdom of God" (Matthew 5:10). In the same way Judas and Matthias stress the rewards of righteousness if they are to be punished by Herod the Great (*Antiquities* 17.149–167), and the followers of Judas the Galilean gladly accept death for the sake of righteousness (*Antiquities* 18.23–24).

Unlike the Fourth Philosophy Paul's Gentiles are urged to pay taxes to Rome and to follow their rulers. Paul's philosophy of acting like a Gentile to the Gentiles and like a Jew to the Jews is totally contrary to Judas's and Jesus's teachings. Judas (Jesus) is who he claims to be. He never acts a part, as Paul does.

22. Sons and Brothers

Two sons of Judas and two "brothers" of Jesus are named James and Simon. How easy it would have been for an early gospel writer to change children into brothers and a wife into a mother? This would have been done for several reasons. First, by making sons and a wife into brothers and a mother, the gospel writers wipe out a generation, making Jesus a much younger man of about thirty. Second, to follow in Paul's footsteps, one has to be celibate. Although marriage and sex have no negative connotations in Jewish society, the later church finds it difficult to accept the fact that God's Son had sex, resulting in children. Third, it is easier to disassociate Jesus from brothers and a mother. A good father and husband would have been more understanding with his wife and his own children. I have argued throughout this book that the real first-century Messiah had a wife and family.

23. Drinking the Same Cup as Jesus: Crucifixion

Two sons of Judas are put to death by crucifixion. Jesus is the only other individual crucified to be mentioned by name. Also two apostles are to drink the same cup as Jesus, namely crucifixion (Matthew 20:20–23 and *Antiquities* 20.102). It is my contention that these two apostles are the sons of Jesus (Judas the Galilean).

This is significant because crucifixion was a form of punishment exacted by Roman authorities. One was crucified because of political activity, not for religious beliefs. In fact, the Romans allow all types of religions, as long as they support Rome and its tax machine, making Paul's version of Christianity the model Roman religion. Jesus is crucified because he preaches against Roman taxation and is proclaimed king or Messiah. The two sons of Judas the Galilean are also crucified for opposing Roman law.

24. Alternative Names

Many members of the Jewish Jesus Movement have alternative names. Sadduc is a priestly title denoting righteousness, while John the Baptist "commanded the Jews to exercise virtue, both as to righteousness toward one another, and piety toward God" (*Antiquities* 18.117). James is known as the "Just," Judas the Galilean is known as Jesus (*Joshua* means "savior"), Saul is renamed Paul ("small"), and Simon becomes Peter, which means "rock." These alternative names generally describe the character of the individual, and are not known or used by those outside the movement. Thus, Josephus writes of Judas the Galilean, Simon, and Saul, never using the names Jesus, Peter, and Paul.

Alternative names are also used in the Maccabean movement. Judas Maccabee is called just Maccabee or "Hammer." Since the Jewish Jesus Movement is based on the Maccabean movement, the use of alternative names should be expected.

Other alternative names in the Jewish Jesus Movement include the "Sons of Thunder" (James and Simon, the sons of Judas the Galilean). Simon the "Zealot" and James the "Younger" are probably references to these sons of Judas. Remember, the gospel writers are intent on hiding the true identities of Jesus's sons. One other alternative name is Thomas, used for the name Judas, another son of Judas the Galilean. The combination of Judas and Thomas may have yielded Theudas or Thaddeus.

The appellation of "Mary called the Magdalene" deserves special mention. The Aramaic root word *magdala* means "tower." Since the town now assumed to be the hometown of Mary Magdalene—Migdol, located on the shores of the Sea of Galilee—is called Taricheae during her lifetime, it is unlikely that this beloved Mary is ever at home there. Far more likely, according to Margaret Starbird, an independent "Magdalene" researcher, is that this title is given to Mary, the sister of Lazarus, who is credited in John's gospel as the woman who anoints

Jesus, proclaiming him "Messiah" at the banquet in Bethany shortly before his arrest.[4] Starbird believes the honorific "H Magdalhnh" is derived from a prophetic passage, Micah 4:8–11, addressed to the *Magdal-eder,* the "Tower of the Flock."

25. Proclaimed Messiah

Jesus is proclaimed Messiah or king in Galilee, or close by. Before the Transfiguration Jesus and the Twelve are in Caesarea Philippi (Matthew 16:13) and afterward travel to Capernaum (Matthew 17:24). After Jesus is proclaimed king he marches to Jerusalem.

Judas is also proclaimed king in Galilee, probably near Sepphoris, soon after he captures Herod's armory and arms his followers (*Antiquities* 17.271–272; *War* 2.56). He also may have marched on Jerusalem, a speculation deduced by examining the later behavior of his son, Menaham, who proclaims himself king after capturing Herod's armory at Masada in 66 CE and then marches straight to Jerusalem (*War* 2.433). Judas the Galilean's entrance to Jerusalem may have been in 19 CE, so his kingship may have actually lasted twenty-two years, from 4 BCE to 19 CE, far longer than that of the gospel Jesus who proceeds directly to Jerusalem. Remember, however, the gospels telescope the career of Jesus into a few short years, just as Josephus compresses the seventy-five-year movement created by Judas into a few paragraphs (*Antiquities* 18.1–10).

26. The Scattering of Disciples

In Acts 5:37 Judas the Galilean is killed "and all his followers were scattered." This passage is meant to minimize Judas's influence, giving the impression that Judas's movement ends with his death. However, Josephus clearly records that Judas's movement grows and expands over the next fifty to sixty years (*Antiquities* 18.9–10).

There is an amazing convergence between Judas and Jesus concerning the disciples' reaction to his arrest. In Matthew 26:56, after Jesus's arrest, "the disciples deserted him and fled." In Mark 14:50, "Everyone deserted him and fled." These two gospels are in complete agreement concerning the disciples' behavior after the arrest. However, in Luke, the disciples do not flee, but Simon Peter follows at a distance. Why is the account in Luke different from that in the other synoptic gospels? The answer may be in Acts 5:37, that passage distorting the picture of Judas the Galilean. Since a direct correlation between Judas and Jesus can be established. Luke attributes the fleeing disciples to Judas the Galilean and not to Jesus.

27. Annas

After his arrest Jesus is brought first to Annas, the father-in-law of Caiaphas and a former high priest (John 18:12–24). This Annas is appointed high priest in 6 CE by Cyrenius and Coponius, in the days of the census. Judas the Galilean opposes the census and Annas. Certainly Annas would have been much more interested in the death of Judas the Galilean than that of the gospel Jesus. But why would the ex–high priest take a leading role in the arrest of Jesus? Under the governorship of Gratus (15–18 CE) four different high priests are appointed. This musical-chair approach to the high priesthood must have maddened the religious people of the day, including Judas/Jesus. Perhaps this prompted him to enter Jerusalem. In all probability Annas is calling the shots even after his stint as high priest, since, as Josephus reports, this Annas has five sons who are high priests (*Antiquities* 20.198). The existence of this dynasty reveals that Annas is a force in first-century Judea.

The Gospel of John may have inadvertently connected Jesus with Judas's old adversary. The synoptic gospels are careful to avoid mentioning Annas, preferring to have the whole affair tried before Caiaphas and the elders. John's mention of Annas certainly lends credence to my Judas the Galilean hypothesis, in that he functions in a leadership role during the lifetime of Judas. Also, Annas would have been physically stronger in 19 CE than later in 30–33 CE, per the traditional gospel dating. Annas may well have been dead by then.

28. Dreams and the Washing of Hands

In the trial of Matthias after the Golden Eagle Temple Cleansing, the high priest is also named Matthias. This latter Matthias once relinquished his office for a day, a day celebrated by a fast, because of a dream where he had sexual relations with his wife. Pilate washes his hands of responsibility on a single day because of his wife's dream concerning Jesus's innocence (Matthew 27:19–24 and *Antiquities* 17.166). In both cases a dream sequence is used to remove responsibility for a short period. In the case of Pilate this conveniently shifts the blame for Jesus's crucifixion from the Romans to the Jews, even though crucifixion is a Roman punishment. The Jews supposedly say, "Let his blood be on us and on our children" (Matthew 27:25). Unfortunately this curse has been used as an excuse to persecute Jews throughout history.

The scene where Pilate washes his hands and the Jews greedily usurp his sentencing power appears extremely unlikely. According to the gospels the Jews welcome Jesus into Jerusalem as Messiah, just a few days earlier. Were they now willing to have his blood on their heads for all eternity? This is completely illogical. The alternative is radical but at least logical: this dream scene is adapted from the Matthias episode and reworked using the new Pauline thinking, casting Jews—not Romans—as the enemies of Jesus.

29. Questioning by Herod

Herod the Great sends Matthias, Judas, and the rebels to Jericho for questioning concerning the Golden Eagle Temple Cleansing. There Herod hears the reasons for the uprising (*Antiquities* 17.160). Pilate sends Jesus to Herod Antipas for questioning (Luke 23:6–7), an interrogation mentioned only by Luke, who has a tendency to take events from Josephus's works and incorporate them into the fictional story of Jesus and the early church. There are two purifications of the Temple—the Golden Eagle Temple Cleansing and the one recorded in the gospels near the end of Jesus's career. Two trials or interrogations also occur, one before Herod the Great in 4 BCE and the other before Pilate in 19 CE. Luke simply combines these two trials in his gospel.

30. The Barabbas Prisoner Release

Under Herod the Great's son Archelaus (4 BCE) prisoners are released to appease the Jewish mob. One of these prisoners is Judas the Galilean

(*War* 2.4 and *Antiquities* 17.204–205). This same story is repeated at the trial of Jesus. In that account Pilate releases Barabbas to the mob instead of Jesus (Matthew 27:15–26). Note that the Romans do not routinely release political prisoners, but rather, crucify them. On the other hand the release of prisoners by Archelaus rings true as he is dealing with the remnants of the Matthias and Judas following. In Matthew's gospel the crowd wishes for the release of Barabbas—literally, "son of the Father." Which "Father" is meant—Matthias or God?

A critic of my theory insists that Archelaus never released the prisoners, but only promised to release them. For two reasons this scenario does not make sense. First, Archelaus could have quickly appeased the mob by releasing prisoners immediately. He also promises to reduce taxes. Since that could not be accomplished immediately, Archelaus may very well have reneged on that promise. Second, after the prisoner release, Archelaus also grants the mob's request regarding the removal of the high priest, which could also be done immediately. So there should be no doubt that the prisoner release actually occurs.

31. Insurrection in Jerusalem

In the gospel story Barabbas leads an insurrection in Jerusalem (Mark 15:7 and Luke 23:19). Shortly before the prisoner release of 4 BCE, Matthias and Judas lead the Golden Eagle Temple Cleansing, an insurrection in the city, where many of the rebels suffer martyrdom, while others, Judas included, are held for later punishment (*Antiquities* 17.149–167; 17.204–206).

Insurrections in Jerusalem are not commonplace in the time frame noted. From 4 BCE to 50 CE the only ones recorded are the Golden Eagle Temple Cleansing (4 BCE) and the one supposedly led by Barabbas. This should reinforce the statement that Barabbas is really a stand-in for Judas (Jesus). (In some manuscripts Barabbas is referred to as *Jesus Barabbas*.) Both insurrections are aimed at Rome. The Golden Eagle is a symbol of Rome and Barabbas of gospel fame is undoubtedly a member of the Fourth Philosophy. Judas and Barabbas are also very popular with the anti-Roman Jewish crowd.

32. The Prisoner Release at Passover

The trial of Jesus and the release of Barabbas both occur at the Passover feast (Mark 14:12). The release of prisoners in 4 BCE also coincides with Passover (*Antiquities* 17.213). As there were three Jewish pilgrim festivals (Passover [Pesach], Pentecost [Shavuot], and Tabernacles [Sukkot]), the odds of this coincidence can be calculated as three to the second power, or one in nine.[5]

33. Purple Robe and Crown

King Herod the Great dies a week or so before the Passover feast. At his death Herod is clothed in purple, with a crown of gold on his head and a scepter in his right hand (*Antiquities* 17.197). This occurs soon after the Golden Eagle Temple Cleansing and before the prisoner release, an important part of the Judas the Galilean story.

Before his death Jesus is mocked by the Roman soldiers who put a purple robe on him and weave a crown of thorns to be placed upon his head. A staff is used to beat him (Mark 15:16–20).

34. Mockery

Jesus is mocked by the Roman soldiers (Mark 15:16–20). Herod the Great, after the Golden Eagle incident, is afraid that the people will mourn his death in "sport and mockery" only (*Antiquities* 17.177). The gospels and Acts often use information from Josephus or from Paul's Christ Movement to flesh out the story of Jesus and his church. Jesus not only wears the same garb as Herod, but he is treated as poorly by his adversaries.

Points 33 and 34 conflate Herod the Great and Jesus. Giving Jesus attributes belonging to Herod the Great should not surprise us, since Paul, a Herodian, also creates Jesus in his own image, placing his own ideas and actions into the mind of the Messiah.

35. The Sounds of Silence

Many religious scholars have questioned the silence of Jesus before Pilate. To the amazement of Pilate, Jesus makes no reply when charged with a crime (Mark 15:3–5). Unlike Paul who gives speeches everywhere in Acts, Jesus remains silent. Josephus mentions this strategy of silence in connection with Simon, who has been summoned to answer charges by Agrippa I (43 CE).

Silence is a way to protect the Jewish Jesus Movement, whose members under interrogation will not betray their compatriots. The questioning of Jesus is probably more severe than we are led to believe in the gospel accounts. Pilate and his henchmen want information, and they no doubt torture Jesus. He, however, does not betray his friends. The Fourth Philosophy also is famous for steadfast loyalty to God and fellow members. "They do not value dying any kind of death, nor indeed do they heed the deaths of their relations and friends, nor can any such fear make them call any man Lord" (*Antiquities* 18.23–25). In short they would rather die than betray God and their fellow disciples.

36. The Crowd's Preference

In the gospel story the crowd prefers Barabbas over King Jesus (Mark 15:1–15). This is not only an endorsement of Barabbas but also demonstrates an intense hatred for Jesus. We are to believe that the same crowd that welcomes Jesus into Jerusalem as Messiah is now calling for his death.

Josephus describes the crowd as followers of Matthias and Judas, who prefer these teachers over King Herod (*Antiquities* 17.204–206). (Note that the later followers of Judas/Jesus also hate the Herodian Paul). The disciples really love Judas and Matthias, but their hatred of Herod and all he represents is unparalleled. Their hatred of Herod is incorporated in the gospel story where the chief priests and the Jews hate Jesus.

37. Matthias

After the Golden Eagle incident Matthias is burned to death, while Judas eventually gains freedom in a Barabbas-style prisoner release. Once released Judas assumes the leadership role previously held by Matthias. The second-in-command role is then given to John the Baptist.

In Acts, Matthias replaces Judas Iscariot as one of the Twelve. While the Josephus story has Judas replacing Matthias, the Acts version has Matthias replacing a Judas. This Matthias is never mentioned in the gospels and is absent from any subsequent activities recorded by Acts. Matthias is just a name taken from Judas the Galilean's past and playfully included in the Judas Iscariot story.

In fact, James the Just replaces the crucified Jesus. Since Judas Iscariot is an invented character to further lay blame on the Jewish people for the death of the Messiah, he could never actually be replaced because he never existed. On the other hand Jesus is crucified and is the one being replaced. With the death of Jesus, John the Baptist becomes the movement's leader, with James the Just as his second-in-command.

38. The Two Bandits

Jesus is crucified between two "bandits" (*lestes*), Josephus's term for members of the Fourth Philosophy. The term *bandit* does not refer to thieves or highway robbers, but rather to terrorists (freedom fighters) or those fomenting political turmoil.[6] That Jesus is crucified between these two should come as surprise. Jesus is their leader.

John Crossan and Jonathan L. Reed admit that Jesus is an apocalyptic preacher, claiming that he never advocates violence. They conclude that if Jesus were a military threat, then Pilate would have captured a large number of Jesus's disciples with him and crucified them as well.[7] There are two fundamental errors in Crossan and Reed's reasoning. First, adherents of the Jewish Jesus Movement do not advocate or practice violence, as compared to the later Fourth Philosophy, a movement dominated by Zealots and Sicarii. The Jewish Jesus Movement, as preached by Jesus (Judas), would rid Israel of Roman occupation by the power of God, not by armed rebellion or by assassinations. This same philosophy is still in place by the 40s when Theudas calls upon God to part the River Jordan (*Antiquities* 20.97). Second, Crossan and Reed do not recognize that Jesus is placed between two bandits. Obviously Pilate has captured some of Jesus's disciples as they are crucified to his left and to his right.

The treatment of the bandits in the gospels is not consistent. John 19:18 simply states that Jesus is crucified with "two others—one on each side and Jesus in the middle." Mark and Matthew tell a different tale, writing that "those crucified with him [the bandits] also heaped insults on him" (Mark 15:32). In this Mark and Matthew align the bandits with the high priest, against Jesus. But no one does the story better than Luke.

> One of the *criminals* who hung there hurled insults at him. "Aren't you the Christ? Save yourself and us!"
>
> But the other *criminal* rebuked him. "Don't you fear God," he said, "since you are under the same sentence? We are punished justly, for we are getting what our deeds deserve. But this man has done nothing wrong."
>
> Then he said, "Jesus, remember me when you come into your kingdom."
>
> Jesus answered him, "I tell you the truth, today you will be with me in paradise." (Luke 23:39–43) (Emphasis mine)

Three major discrepancies can be noted here. First, Luke calls the two men criminals, not bandits. This changes the two into common criminals and not members of a religious or political movement—the Fourth Philosophy. Second, one of the criminals hurls insults at Jesus, but the other now sides with Jesus, exonerating Jesus of any guilt in his own crucifixion. Third, this second criminal is pardoned by Jesus, a Pauline move. Jesus always preaches a lifelong commitment to God. All of a sudden, he now accepts deathbed conversions. Again, Luke adds this story to make Jesus accept the Pauline notion of being saved by faith, not by works.

39. The Continuing Movements

The movements continue after the deaths of Judas the Galilean and Jesus. Interestingly Acts downplays the movement of Judas the Galilean, claiming Judas is killed "and all his followers were scattered"

(Acts 5:37). In reality the Fourth Philosophy of Judas does not end with Judas's death but grows to a great degree, according to Josephus (*Antiquities* 18.1–10). So the above speech by the Jewish rabbi Gamaliel in Acts, claiming that Judas dies and his followers are scattered, is an attempt by Luke to alter history. Luke does not want people to associate the rebellious Jews with the second-century Gentile Jesus of Nazareth Movement. However, when the story of Acts was written (early second century), the followers of Judas the Galilean had been smashed and scattered.

40. Expansion of the Movements

The movements of Judas and Jesus expand throughout the Roman Empire. The Fourth Philosophy of Judas is responsible for the war against Rome. Although centered in Jerusalem and Galilee, Judas's followers are numbered throughout the Empire. Paul's Gentile churches are scattered among the great cities, but the Jewish Jesus Movement must have had even greater sway and more adherents. While Paul is the lone apostle to the Gentiles, the influence of Peter and others surely reaches a great multitude. In fact, the early Jewish Jesus Movement focuses most of its resources on the "conversion" of the Jewish community to the Way of Righteousness.

Note that Suetonius ties the rebellious, troublemaking Jews to Chrestus or Christ (*Twelve Caesars,* Claudius 25), a passage that definitively connects the Fourth Philosophy to Christ. While this particular disturbance occurs in Rome, certainly all large Jewish congregations of the Diaspora have elements sympathetic to the nationalism of Judas the Galilean (Jesus). Near the end of the *Jewish War* Josephus writes that after the destruction of Masada (73 CE), some Sicarii escape to Alexandria, where they attempt to gain support from the Alexandrian Jews to rebel against the Romans. This attempt only makes sense if some sympathy already exists for their movement. However, they are rebuffed by the majority of Alexandrian Jews, and then caught, tortured, and killed by the authorities (*War* 7.407–419).

41. Genuine Christians

In Pliny the Younger's letter to Trajan, he writes that *genuine* Christians cannot be forced to worship Caesar's image or any of the pagan deities.[8] Josephus writes that the followers of Judas the Galilean "say that God is to be their only Ruler and Lord" and that not even the fear of death can "make them call any man Lord" (*Antiquities* 18:23). Pliny's genuine Christians are indistinguishable from Josephus's Fourth Philosophy.

42. Dead Sea Scroll Language

For years after the 1947 Dead Sea Scrolls discovery, many scholars maintained that the Scrolls belonged exclusively to a religious sect known as the Essenes. However, in recent years, other information has shaken that view.

Dead Sea Scroll materials found at Masada belonged to the Sicarii (members of the Fourth Philosophy). Whether or not the Sicarii wrote the Scrolls is not at issue. The important point is that the Sicarii used the Scrolls and the ideas they contained.

In various works Robert Eisenman maintains that the early Jewish Jesus disciples relied heavily on the Dead Sea Scroll concepts, giving many examples of how Paul and the gospels inverted these very concepts to further their antinomian message.

So the only thing that we know for sure is that the Fourth Philosophy and the Jewish Jesus Movement were both well versed in the Scroll language.

APPENDIX A

The Messianic Time Lines

The traditional gospel time line is an anachronistic nightmare. Perhaps the most damning evidence against this time line is the sequence of events concerning John the Baptist. The New Testament claims that John the Baptist comes onto the scene in 28–29 CE and is executed a few years later, approximately 30–32 CE. From this dating springs the dating of Jesus's birth and the later ministry of Paul. Most scholars reluctantly buy into this time line because they see no alternative. My goal is to supply an alternative, one that is consistent with Josephus and other early writers. For example, both Josephus and the Slavonic Josephus date the death of John the Baptist at 36 CE, several years later than the gospel death of Jesus. In addition, the Slavonic Josephus introduces John in 6 CE, not 28 CE. These alternative dates for John make sense and are clearly more accurate than the gospel dates.

To make it easier to understand the various movements involved in the creation of Christianity as we know it today, time lines will be presented highlighting the major events in each movement. The time lines do overlap. For example, in the heyday of the Jewish Jesus Movement, the Christ Movement of Paul also existed. This overlapping has caused a great deal of confusion among scholars who believe in one uniform movement. Even today many wonder how Jesus could have been a pacifist and still qualify as a threat to Rome, resulting in death by crucifixion.

THE JEWISH JESUS MOVEMENT AND
THE FOURTH PHILOSOPHY

36–25 BCE	Judas is born in Gamala, near Galilee.
25	The Star of Bethlehem is reported by the Slavonic Josephus.
35–24	James the Just, the brother of the Messiah, is born.
25	An assassination attempt on Herod the Great fails.
4	Matthias and Judas lead the Golden Eagle Temple Cleansing. Matthias and Judas base their movement on that of Mattathias and Judas Maccabee.
4	Herod captures Matthias and Judas, putting Matthias to death by fire and imprisoning Judas.
4	Herod the Great dies.
4	Judas is released by Archelaus to the Jewish crowd.
4–3	Judas raids the armory at Sepphoris and arms his followers.
4–2	Judas is proclaimed Messiah in Galilee.
4 BCE–73 CE	The Dead Sea Scrolls are appropriated by the Fourth Philosophy. (Copies have recently been found at the Masada side.)
6 CE	John the Baptist introduces Judas right before the census tax revolt.
6	Judas the Galilean leads a nationwide tax revolt against Rome.
6–9	Coponius is named governor of Judea.
6–15	Annas is named high priest by the Roman governor Coponius.
9–12	Ambivulus replaces Coponius as Roman governor.
12–15	Rufus replaces Ambivulus as Roman governor.
14–37	Upon the death of Augustus, Tiberius becomes Roman emperor.
15–18	Gratus replaces Rufus as Roman governor.
18–37	Caiaphas, son-in-law of Annas, is named high priest by Gratus.
18–37	Pontius Pilate assumes the governorship from Gratus.

THE JEWISH JESUS MOVEMENT AND
THE FOURTH PHILOSOPHY

19	Judas the Galilean (Jesus) is arrested on the Mount of Olives.
19	An unnamed Jew (Paul) swindles Jewish converts in Rome after being thrown out of Judea.
21	Per the Memoranda the Messiah (Judas/Jesus) is crucified under Pilate.
21–36	John the Baptist leads the movement with James as his second-in-command.
21–22	Paul, a Herodian, converts to the Jewish Jesus Movement.
22–25	Paul studies with the Pharisees for three years. Per Maccoby, Paul is aware of but never masters Pharisaic methods. Paul also learns of Dead Sea Scroll concepts during this time.
25	Paul makes his first postconversion trip to Jerusalem.
35–36	John the Baptist is beheaded by Herod Antipas.
36–62	James replaces John the Baptist and Peter becomes his second-in-command.
37–41	Caligula replaces Tiberius as Roman emperor.
37	Agrippa I, a close friend of Caligula, becomes tetrarch.
37	The rise of Agrippa I, Paul's cousin, may have prompted Paul's visions of the Risen Christ.
38–39	The Council of Jerusalem attempts to consolidate power under James.
38–39	Seventeen years after joining the Jewish Jesus Movement, Paul attends the Council of Jerusalem, getting approval for his Gentile mission.
39–44	Unbeknownst to James, Paul preaches his new antinomian gospel.
40–41	Agrippa I tries to persuade Caligula to stop his plans for desecrating the Temple in Jerusalem.
41	Caligula is assassinated after ignoring Agrippa I's pleas. (Is Agrippa I behind the assassination?)

41	Agrippa I helps install Claudius as the next Roman emperor. As a reward Agrippa I is given more land than ruled by Herod the Great.
41	With Agrippa's advice Claudius expels the Jewish Jesus Movement from Rome.
41–44	Agrippa I is seen as a Messiah figure to many Jews.
43	Agrippa I interrogates Simon for excluding him from the Temple.
44	James and Simon, sons of Judas the Galilean, are imprisoned by Agrippa I and Paul is ousted from the Jewish Jesus Movement
44	Agrippa I is assassinated by the Fourth Philosophy or by agents of Claudius.
44–46	After Agrippa I's death Fadus is governor (appointed by Rome).
Sometime between 44–46	Theudas is beheaded after trying to part the waters of the Jordan.
46–48	Tiberius Alexander is governor.
Sometime between 46–48	Two sons of Judas the Galilean (James and Simon) are crucified.
48–52	Cumanus succeeds Tiberius Alexander as governor.
52–60	Felix is governor.
52–60	With the help of Simon the magician Felix persuades Drusilla to divorce her husband and marry him.
60–62	Festus is Roman governor, replacing Felix.
62	James the Just is stoned to death after the removal of Festus and before his replacement, Albinius, arrives.
62	The rich high priests, along with Paul, steal money from the poorer priests.
62–64	Albinius arrives and becomes Roman governor.
64	The Jewish Jesus Movement is persecuted by Nero after the Great Fire at Rome.
64–66	Florus replaces Albinius as Roman governor. His corrupt rule leads to the Jewish war.

THE JEWISH JESUS MOVEMENT AND THE FOURTH PHILOSOPHY

66–70   The Jewish war with Rome—ends in utter defeat for the Jews. The Jewish Jesus Movement is essentially destroyed.

73   The Fourth Philosophy ends with the mass suicide of the Sicarii at Masada, led by Eleazar, the grandson of Judas the Galilean.

73–?   Only the Ebionites survive the destruction of the Jewish nation. They soon fade into history.

THE CHRIST MOVEMENT (PAUL'S GENTILE MISSION)

19 CE   An unnamed Jew (Paul) is thrown out of Judea for his teachings and then swindles Jewish converts in Rome.

21–22   Paul becomes a member of the Jewish Jesus Movement. This shocks his Herodian family.

25   Three years after joining the Jewish Jesus Movement, Paul visits Peter and James in Jerusalem.

37   Paul's cousin Agrippa I is named tetrarch by his close friend Caligula.

37   Frustrated by his own insignificance, Paul concocts his own religion or gospel, based on the Risen Christ.

38–39   Paul introduces his gospel to James at the Council of Jerusalem, omitting the antinomian aspects of his gospel.

39–44   Paul teaches his new gospel of grace and writes Romans and 1 Corinthians.

39–44   Paul's gospel meshes with Agrippa I's goal of converting Gentile kings to Judaism.

39–44   The Jews brand Paul as the Liar, as his gospel becomes known.

44   King Izates converts to Judaism after being proselytized by Ananias (Paul's gospel) and by Eleazar (Jewish Jesus Movement).

44   Paul is ousted from the Jewish Jesus Movement at Antioch. All Jews, including Barnabas, side with Peter.

44   Paul writes Galatians and 2 Corinthians, blasting the Jewish apostles.

44–67	Paul is now branded as the Enemy.
44–48	A famine spreads throughout Israel.
44–48	Paul comes to Jerusalem with famine relief, but keeps the money for himself.
44–48	The Enemy (that is, Paul) attacks James at the Temple.
44–46	Theudas is beheaded.
46–48	James and Simon, the sons of Judas the Galilean, are crucified.
44–62	Nothing is known about these eighteen years in the life of Paul.
62	James the Just is stoned to death, the original Stephen story.
62	After the stoning Paul persecutes the Jewish Jesus Movement.
62	By now Paul is also known as the Traitor.
66–70	The war with Rome ends in utter defeat for the Jews.
66	Menahem, Judas the Galilean's son, cleanses the Temple as a Messiah figure.
66	Menahem is stoned to death by his adversaries.
66	Paul meets with Agrippa II to petition for an army to fight the insurgents.
66	Paul escapes from Jerusalem with the help of his nephew.
67	Paul meets with Nero to focus blame for the war on Florus.
70	The Temple is destroyed by Titus.
70	With the destruction of the Jewish Jesus Movement, Paul's Christ Movement has no obstacles to expanding.
70	With the destruction of Jerusalem and the Temple, Paul needs to change his message to continue his fund-raising efforts.

THE JESUS OF NAZARETH MOVEMENT

70–72 CE	Mark is penned by Paul or a close disciple, overlaying the Christ Movement's gospel onto the Jewish Jesus Movement's Messiah. Thus, the Jewish Messiah becomes more of a savior-god to the Gentiles than a king to the Jews.
70–140	Jerusalem and the Temples are no longer the focus of Paul's fund-raising efforts.

THE JESUS OF NAZARETH MOVEMENT

73	At Masada the Sicarii commit mass suicide.
75	Josephus writes *The Jewish War*.
70–85	The Jewish portion of Revelation is written. In this book the Messiah crushes Rome, an act that never occurs.
80–85	Matthew is written near Alexandria, in order to combat Jewish teachings and to attract new Gentile converts.
93	Josephus writes *Antiquities of the Jews*.
95–120	Acts and Luke are written, based to some extent on Josephus's writings. These writings are meant to attract followers of Mithras (Roman soldiers) in Asia Minor.
110–120	Suetonius, Tacitus, and Pliny write their accounts of the early Christians.
120–140	The more powerful Jesus of Nazareth is introduced by John, targeted at a Greek audience.
130–150	The Pseudoclementine *Recognitions* is penned.

These three time lines include the major events in the development of the Christian religions. Unlike the traditional story of a single Christian movement, championed by the Catholic and Protestant churches and supported by mainstream scholars, my time lines present three distinct movements extant in the first century CE. The Jewish Jesus Movement and the Christ Movement coexist for a short time. However, with the destruction of the Jesus Movement, the Pauline Christ Movement morphs into the Jesus of Nazareth Movement. All that is needed is a story, and Paul supplies that, combining elements from the historical Messiah (Judas the Galilean) with his own gospel, based on revelations from the Risen Christ.

As a result of this curious blending Jesus of Nazareth has become a champion of many viewpoints. Some see the more historical elements of the Jewish Jesus Movement and focus their worship on striving for financial equality, a type of primitive communism. Others see the Risen Christ with his promise of eternal life through identification with his death and resurrection. To these modern-day Christians a righteous life is not the purpose of religion; salvation on the Day of Judgment is their goal.

So who was Jesus, really? Believe it or not Jesus of Nazareth never existed. The mythical Jesus gained life through the pen of Paul, the Herodian who created a new gospel. The real Jewish Messiah was Judas the Galilean, but he was not as marketable to citizens of the Roman Empire as was Paul's new and improved version.

APPENDIX B

John the Baptist

The actual Jesus of history lived in a world of stark choices: either succumb to Roman rule or oppose it. As a Messiah figure the historical Jesus champions the poor against the rich, the law of God against the Hellenizing invaders. This Messiah is worthy of a following, and this Messiah pays the ultimate price: he is crucified by the Roman authorities, not by the Jews. How can we possibly find this elusive Messiah in the sources at our disposal?

John the Baptist is the key to unraveling the riddle of the historical Jesus. According to the gospels John's life and death parallel Jesus's life and death. In fact, the dating of John's ministry is crucial in determining the years in which Jesus preaches the kingdom of heaven, so we must investigate everything written about John in the earliest known documents. We will first lay out the traditional viewpoint concerning John, derived straight from the various gospels. Then, an alternative history will be proposed, based on the gospels and other early writings, such as Josephus's *Antiquities,* the Slavonic Josephus, and the Pseudoclementine *Recognitions.*

THE TRADITIONAL VIEWPOINT

The traditional viewpoint can be summed up quickly. John the Baptist's mission begins around 28 CE and ends shortly afterward. He is executed by Herod Antipas, who views him as a threat to Roman authority. His disciples morph into Jesus's band of followers. End of story. John is the promised forerunner to the Messiah and he knows that Jesus is the Chosen One. Now, we will examine the particulars of John's story.

The angel answers,

> The Holy Spirit will come upon you, and the power of the Most High will overshadow you. So the holy one to be born will be called the Son of God. Even Elizabeth your relative is going to have a child in her old age, and she who was said to be barren is in her sixth month. For nothing is impossible with God. . . . At that time Mary got ready and hurried to a town in the hill country of Judah, where she entered Zechariah's home and greeted Elizabeth. When Elizabeth heard Mary's greeting, the baby [John] leaped in her womb, and Elizabeth was filled with the Holy Spirit. In a loud voice she exclaimed: "Blessed are you among women, and blessed is the child you will bear! But why am I so favored, that the mother of my Lord should come to me? As soon as the sound of your greeting reached my ears, the baby in my womb leaped for joy. Blessed is she who has believed that what the Lord has said to her will be accomplished." . . . Mary stayed with Elizabeth for about three months and then returned home. (Luke 1:35–56)

Luke includes incredible detail concerning the parents of John and the reason for naming the child John. The above passage details the relationship between Mary and Elizabeth as well as their soon-to-be-born sons, Jesus and John. Three major points can be gleaned from the above passage and Luke's earlier recorded history of the family. First, John and Jesus are related to one another; therefore, there is a close relationship between the two families. Second, John is born six months before Jesus, meaning that both started their ministries at the age of thirty (Luke 3:23). Third, both Elizabeth and her fetus are aware that Mary is carrying the Son of God in her womb. If John believes in Jesus as a fetus, then he surely believes in him as an adult!

> In the fifteenth year of the reign of Tiberius Caesar—when Pontius
> Pilate is governor of Judea, Herod, tetrarch of Galilee; his brother
> Philip, tetrarch of Iturea and Traconitis; and Lysanias, tetrarch of
> Abilene—during the high priesthood of Annas and Caiaphas, the
> word of God comes to John son of Zechariah in the desert. He
> travels throughout the country around the Jordan, preaching a bap-
> tism of repentance for the forgiveness of sins. . . . John said to the
> crowds coming out to be baptized by him, "You brood of vipers!
> Who warned you to flee the coming wrath? Produce fruit in keep-
> ing with repentance.". . . The people were waiting expectantly and
> were all wondering in their hearts if John might be the Christ. John
> answered them all, "I baptize you with water. But one more power-
> ful than I will come, the thongs of whose sandals I am not worthy
> to untie. He will baptize you with the Holy Spirit and with fire. His
> winnowing fork is in his hands to clear the threshing floor and to
> gather the wheat into his barn, but he will burn up the chaff with
> unquenchable fire." (Luke 3:1–3:17)

The above passage describes John's preparing the way for the
Messiah, in fulfillment of Isaiah's prophecy (Isaiah 40:3–5). According
to Luke, John's ministry begins in the fifteenth year of Tiberius's reign.
Tiberius comes to power in 14 CE, so John's emergence onto the stage
can be dated to 28–29 CE. The beginning of Jesus's ministry can also
be dated to his own baptism by John, around 29–30 CE (Luke 3:21–
23). Since both Jesus and John are thirty years old, their birth dates
must have been approximately 2–1 BCE. Unfortunately Matthew
places Jesus's birth date at around 9–6 BCE, while Luke claims they
were born in 6 CE. No matter how one figures, these dates do not
accord. Something must be wrong!

But what?

John the Baptist's message of repentance is ideal to usher in the day
of the Messiah. John is simply preparing the people for Jesus's arrival,
but not everyone is thrilled by John's message. Those in power are
threatened by a new Messiah and are reluctant to embrace John's call

for repentance. However, John is not sensitive to their reservations, calling them a "brood of vipers." This straightforward approach eventually earns John a prison sentence. But one thing is certain: Luke's John believes Jesus is the Messiah. This steadfast belief is consistent with the earlier story of Elizabeth and Mary, where John as a fetus leaps in Elizabeth's womb. This story, while fanciful, does supply information that Jesus and John are close while young, and that the baptism of Jesus is not the first meeting between the two preachers.

Luke's and Matthew's versions of John's description of the coming Messiah are unusual, as the Messiah is resurrected, with judgment at hand. "His winnowing fork is in his hands to clear his threshing floor and to gather the wheat [the righteous] into his barn, but he will burn up the chaff [the wicked] with unquenchable fire" (Matthew 3:12 and Luke 3:17). Thus, we must question whether John is ushering in the earthly Messiah or the heavenly (resurrected) Messiah. Most scholars believe John points toward the earthly Messiah, but lets us keep the heavenly Messiah in our thoughts for further analysis.

The Gospel of Mark does not refer to a judgment scene and adds the following colorful description of John:

John wore clothing made of camel's hair, with a leather belt around his waist, and he ate locusts and wild honey. (Mark 1:6)

According to William Barclay, John's mode of dress reminds the people of the great prophets, who live the simple life without life's many luxuries. Elijah wears "a garment of hair and a leather belt around his waist" (2 Kings 1:8). This Spartan attire is either provided to John by Mark or is purposely worn by John to evoke the power of the famous prophet of old. The food mentioned in the passage is either actual locusts and honey or carobs and sap from certain trees.[1] Regardless, the diet is simple, as John relies on God to provide from nature.

John the Baptist is indeed an unconventional character. He introduces the Messiah to the world and is not afraid to criticize those in positions of power. This unwillingness to live comfortably with the world eventually leads John to prison and to his death.

> But when Herod heard this [talk of John being raised from the dead] he said, "John, the man I beheaded has been raised from the dead!"
> For Herod himself had given orders to have John arrested, and he had him bound and put in prison. He did this because of Herodias, his brother Philip's wife, whom he had married. For John had been saying to Herod, "It is not lawful for you to have your brother's wife." So Herodias nursed a grudge against John and wanted to kill him. But she was not able to, because Herod feared John and protected him, knowing him to be a righteous and holy man. When Herod heard John, he was greatly puzzled, yet he liked to listen to him. (Mark 6:16–20)

After learning of Herod's infatuation with John we are told of John's death. Herodias tricks her husband into granting her daughter a wish after she pleases him with a dance. The girl asks for John the Baptist's head on a platter. In this way Mark's gospel deflects blame away from Herod and toward his wife, Herodias.

John is a social critic, and those in power hate social critics. Unlike Paul, who entertains Bernice and Agrippa II, those Herodians accused of an incestuous relationship, John never hesitates to criticize actions he deems inconsistent with the law of Moses. This criticism enrages Herodias, and she eventually gets her way: the death of John the Baptist.

One other passage must be examined. This concerns John's attitude toward Jesus while he languishes in prison.

> When John heard in prison what Christ was doing, he sent his disciples to ask him, "Are you the one who was to come, or should we expect someone else?" (Matthew 11:2–3)

This passage should confuse the reader. Throughout John's story John is sure of his own role in history and certain of Jesus, the Messiah.

So why does John now doubt his role as well as the mission of Jesus? To go one step farther: Why does John even have disciples at this point? If he truly believes in Jesus, then why not become part of the Jewish Jesus Movement? But he does not. John has his own separate movement, one of repentance and water baptism. Why do Jesus and John not work together?

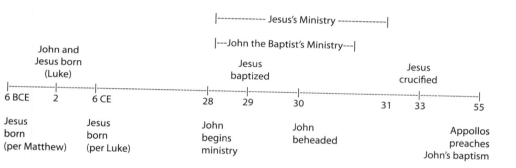

THE TRADITIONAL TIME LINE

|-------------- Jesus's Ministry --------------|

|---John the Baptist's Ministry---|

John and Jesus born (Luke) — Jesus baptized — Jesus crucified

6 BCE   2   6 CE   28   29   30   31   33   55

Jesus born (per Matthew)

Jesus born (per Luke)

John begins ministry

John beheaded

Appollos preaches John's baptism

The Traditional Time Line Cannot Be Correct

The following problems emerge when considering the gospel story of Jesus and John the Baptist.

1. Birth Dates

Since Jesus and John are the same age at the beginning of their respective ministries (thirty years old), and if their missions begin around 28 or 29 CE, their birth dates can be calculated to 2–1 BCE. This is inconsistent with the birth narratives related by Matthew and Luke. Matthew's birth of Jesus is dated between 9 and 6 BCE, while Luke has the birth at 6–7 CE. Either way these cannot be reconciled with the John the Baptist story. In addition, the Gospel of John reports that the Jews say that Jesus is not yet fifty years old (John 8:57). If Jesus preaches into his forties, then that again calls the various birth narratives into question.

2. Mission Dates

If we accept Matthew's dating for Jesus's birth, then Jesus's ministry would have started in 22–25 CE with his crucifixion occurring between 25–28 CE. (These dates assume a birth date of 9–6 BCE, the beginning of Jesus's ministry at the age of thirty, and the duration of that ministry of three years.)

The calculated beginning of Jesus's ministry and his crucifixion both occur before John the Baptist's ministry as recorded by Luke.

Obviously one or both accounts are false.

3. John the Baptist's Movement

If John really believes that Jesus is the Messiah, then why does he continue promoting his own movement? After baptizing Jesus and recognizing the Holy Spirit, we would expect both John and all his disciples to jump onto the Jesus bandwagon. But they do not. In addition, the gospels even note that John has his doubts about Jesus (Matthew 11:3). If true, then the earlier stories about John's certainty might be sheer fantasy. Even today followers of John the Baptist believe that he, not Jesus, is the awaited Messiah.

As evidence that John the Baptist's movement persists, John has disciples into the 50s (Acts 18:24); according to Acts, Apollos teaches about Jesus accurately but knows only the baptism of John. This explanation for Apollos answers the statement posed by Paul in 1 Corinthians 3:6: "I planted the seed, Apollos watered it, but God made it grow." Why is Apollos preaching John's baptism? The baptism of John should have been long since forgotten, since John supposedly dies before Jesus and before the baptism of the Holy Spirit. Why would anyone use John's water baptism at this late date? This cannot be explained by the traditional time line.

4. Josephus's Dating for John the Baptist

According to Luke's gospel John begins baptizing in 28–29 CE, preaches a short while, and is beheaded before Jesus's arrest and crucifixion, so the traditional date for John's death is sometime before 33 CE. However, according to Josephus, John is put to death in 35–36 CE, some years after the supposed crucifixion of Jesus (*Antiquities* 18.116–119). This discrepancy has been overlooked by scholars and church historians because it questions the very gospel story.

Does John outlive Jesus? If he does, then the entire traditional time line must be discarded.

WHAT REALLY HAPPENED

From the traditional story several discrepancies cannot be explained, particularly the dating of events. The main thrust of John the Baptist's story is clear: John announces the coming of the Messiah. But is this proclamation by John before the earthly Jesus comes onto the scene, or is John proclaiming a return of the resurrected Jesus?

From the gospel accounts arguments can be made for both views. In Mark, John appears to be ushering in the coming of the earthly Messiah, but Matthew and Luke invoke imagery of the Messiah at Judgment Day, similar to the scenes in the book of Revelation. Is it possible that John the Baptist preaches his message of repentance before the earthly Jesus and again after the crucifixion, to prepare his audience for the return of a conquering Jesus? I claim that is exactly what happened. If John dies *before* Jesus, as tradition claims, then such a scenario is impossible. But what if John dies *after* Jesus? Then John the Baptist can testify both to the messianic character of Jesus before his death and to the return of Jesus afterward.

Josephus, the Slavonic Josephus, and John the Baptist

Before answering the question concerning John's death we must pinpoint the date of the beginning of John's ministry. In Luke, John's ministry begins in the fifteenth year of Tiberius's reign, or approximately 29 CE. That is why most scholars place Jesus's ministry at 30 CE, even though the birth narratives contradict such a beginning date. The other three gospels are silent on the beginning date of John the Baptist's ministry. Josephus also offers no direct information about the early years of John's ministry. Perhaps Josephus underestimated

John's importance, or mentioned him under a different name, or maybe such information was expunged from his record. After all a charismatic character like John would certainly have made for interesting material for Josephus. So only one source flatly contradicts Luke's dating—the Slavonic Josephus.

The Slavonic Josephus was composed in Russia a thousand years after the events, but many scholars believe that it was not an original Russian document, but rather a translation from Greek or Aramaic. (See appendix D, "The Slavonic Josephus.") Was this work entirely from Josephus himself or was some other early Jewish writer involved in its composition? Essentially this version of Josephus contains the seven books of the *War,* but other "Christian" information is included as well, information that was either part of the original Josephus or from the pen of a first-century disciple. No one will ever know for sure. Either way the following passage about John the Baptist's beginning is fascinating:

> Now at that time a man went about among the Jews in strange garments; for he had put pelts on his body everywhere it was not covered with his own hair; indeed to look at, he was like a wild man. *He came to the Jews and summoned them to freedom,* saying, "God hath sent me, that I may *show you the way of the Law, wherein ye may free yourselves from many holders of power.* And there will be *no mortal ruling over you, only the Highest who hath sent me.*" And when the people heard this, they were joyful. And there went after him all Judea, that lies in the region around Jerusalem. And he did nothing else to them save that he plunged them into the stream of the Jordan and dismissed them, instructing them that they should cease from evil works, and [promising] that there would [then] *be given them a ruler who would set them free.*
>
> . . . And when he had been *brought to Archelaus* and the doctors of the Law had assembled, they asked him who he [was] and where he [had] been until then. And to this he made answer and spoke: "I am pure; [for] the Spirit of God hath led me on, and [I live on] cane and roots and tree-food." But when they threatened to *put him to*

torture if he would not cease from those words and deeds, he nevertheless said: "It is meet for you [rather] to cease from your heinous works and cleave unto the Lord your God." (SJ *War* 2.110, from additional passages) (Emphasis mine)

The similarities between this John and the gospel's John the Baptist include the following. First, this John covers his whole body in pelts and appears as a wild man. This description is not quite as dignified as the one in the gospels, where John dresses like one of the prophets of old. In addition, John's diet of cane, roots, and nuts approximates the locusts and honey of the gospels. Regardless, a picture emerges of an unusual preacher, not at all at home with the comforts of this life. In fact, this John's appearance is so unlike that of others that he must have stood out, in the manner of true prophets.

Also, as in the gospels, John preaches repentance to the crowds gathering around the River Jordan, and baptizes them. The passage goes on to talk about those who disapprove of John, whose response is similar to the gospel rebuke of the vipers. In both versions John promises a ruler who will set them free, an attractive message to the crowd but a dangerous threat to the ruling authorities. In short, this Slavonic Josephus depiction of John has the same charm and power of the gospels.

However, three points distinguish this John from the Baptist of the gospels. First, the John of the Slavonic Josephus has a radical political agenda while the gospel John the Baptist focuses strictly on repentance and baptism. The John of the Slavonic Josephus says: "God hath sent me, that I should show you the way of the Law, wherein ye may free yourselves from many holders of power. And there will be no mortal ruling over you, only the Highest who hath sent me" (SJ *War* 2.110, from additional passages). This political agenda, to oust the Herodians and Romans in favor of God, is identical to that of the Fourth Philosophy. In both *War* and *Antiquities* Josephus writes about Judas the Galilean:

. . . it was that a certain Galilean, whose name was Judas, prevailed with his countrymen to revolt; and said *they were cowards if they would endure to pay a tax to the Romans, and would, after God, sub-mit to mortal men as their lords.* This man was a teacher of a pecu-liar sect of his own, and was not at all like the rest of those their leaders. (*War* 2.118) (Emphasis mine)

. . . yet there was one Judas, a Gaulonite, of a city whose name was Gamala, who *taking with him Sadduc [John the Baptist], a Pharisee,* became zealous to draw them to a revolt, who *both said* that this taxation was no better than an introduction to slavery, and exhorted the nation to assert their liberty. . . . for *Judas and Sadduc, who excited a fourth philosophic sect among us,* and had a great many fol-lowers therein, filled our civil government with tumults at present, and laid the foundation of our future miseries. . . . But of the fourth sect of Jewish philosophy, Judas the Galilean was the author. These men agree in all things with the Pharisaic notions; but they have an inviolable attachment to liberty; and say that *God is to be their only Ruler and Lord.* (*Antiquities* 18.4, 9, 23) (Emphasis mine)

No doubt about it: John of the Slavonic Josephus preaches the same way of thinking as Judas the Galilean. Since Judas is the Fourth Philosophy's leader it follows that John is either a disciple of Judas, or more likely, the Sadduc mentioned by Josephus in the above passage. Although Josephus does not directly mention the coming of John the Baptist, he may have introduced him in the Sadduc reference. According to Robert Eisenman *Sadduc* or *Saddok* is a "term linguistically related both to the word 'Sadducee' in Greek and the 'Zaddik' in Hebrew."[2] The Hebrew word *zaddik* is associated with the idea of righteousness. It should be noted that Josephus does associate John with the idea of righteousness (*Antiquities* 18.117). Either Josephus refers to John as the Sadduc or later Christians change the reference of John to Sadduc. The idea of interpolation should certainly be considered, as the one pas-sage about Jesus in *Antiquities* is surely an interpolation, changing the death of Judas the Galilean into the crucifixion of Jesus (*Antiquities* 18.63–64).

John the Baptist and the Fourth Philosophy

By linking John the Baptist with Judas the Galilean and the Fourth Philosophy, the Slavonic Josephus also helps explain a passage from Matthew. "From the days of John the Baptist until now, the kingdom of heaven has been forcefully advancing, and forceful [violent] men lay hold of it" (Matthew 11:12). It is quite likely that "Jesus" (Judas the Galilean) is referring to the Fourth Philosophy, which he and John champion.

The location of the Slavonic Josephus passage is in SJ *War* 2.110 (in the additional passages). The passage concerning Judas the Galilean cited above is just eight verses later, in *War* 2.118. How interesting that the Slavonic Josephus author introduces John right before Judas the Galilean, just as the gospels introduce John right before Jesus. This reference to John in 6 CE is also supported by the passage itself, where John is brought before Archelaus, shortly before Archelaus is summoned to trial for his atrocities against the Jews and the Samaritans. In his ninth year (6 CE) he is banished to Vienna, a city in Gaul (*War* 2.111). This Archelaus is the son of Herod the Great and rules from 4 BCE to 7 CE. With this mention of Archelaus it is safe to assign a beginning date to John's ministry of 6 CE, right before the tax revolt of Judas the Galilean, ensuring that John the Baptist's Messiah is none other than Judas the Galilean.

In support of the Slavonic Josephus passage the Pseudoclementine *Recognitions* states, "For the people [Israel] was now divided into many parties, ever since the days of John the Baptist."[3] These groups are then denoted as Sadducees, Samaritans, scribes, and Pharisees, and even some of John's disciples. Note that in both *Antiquities* and *War* Josephus writes of the Jewish sects immediately after introducing Judas the Galilean, the Sadduc (John the Baptist), and the Fourth Philosophy. Josephus mentions four philosophies of the Jews: Sadducees, Pharisees, Essenes, and the Fourth Philosophy. Is it just coincidence that the Pseudoclementine *Recognitions* recounts the different Jewish sects right after mentioning John the Baptist? Or is it possible that the *Recognitions*'s placement of John the Baptist comes from a source similar to the Slavonic Josephus?

In addition, one last piece of information connects John to Judas the Galilean. When threatened by torture John does not flinch but keeps on preaching. This, too, is a hallmark of the Fourth Philosophy. "They also do not value dying any kind of death, nor indeed do they heed the deaths of their relations and friends, nor can any such fear make them call any man Lord" (*Antiquities* 18.23). These followers of Judas do not fear torture and death, just as this John refuses to be bullied by the authorities. Such a stance is indeed dangerous, but it plays well with the people.

This is the key to discovering the identity of the historical Jesus. Considering all the other similarities between Judas the Galilean and Jesus of Nazareth (itemized in the conclusion, "The Real Jesus of Nazareth"), the identification of John the Baptist with Sadduc may be the smoking gun. Introducing John the Baptist during the reign of Archelaus moves the Jewish Jesus Movement back to at least 6 CE, to the exact time of Judas the Galilean's tax revolt. Only the most stubborn believer will not recognize that Judas is the Messiah whom John recommends to the people. My contention is that Judas the Galilean and Jesus are two names for the same person. The Slavonic Josephus's version of John simply confirms this.

The next mention of John the Baptist outside the gospel record comes once again from the Slavonic Josephus. Without being asked John interprets a dream by Philip, tetrarch of Trachonitis.

And in those days Philip, while being in his own domain, saw [in] a dream an eagle tear out both his eyes. And he called together all his wise men. And when others were resolving their dreams otherwise, the man we have already described as walking about in animal hair and cleansing people in the streams of the Jordan, *came to Philip suddenly, unsummoned,* and said, "Hear the word of the Lord. The dream you have seen: the eagle is your rapacity, for that bird is violent and rapacious. Such also is the sin; it will pluck out your eyes which are your dominion and your wife." *And when he had spoken thus, Philip passed away by evening and his domain was given*

to Agrippa. And his wife Herodias was taken by Herod, his brother.
Because of her all those who were learned in the Law detested him
but did not dare accuse him to his face. Only the man they call wild,
came to him in fury and said, "Since you, lawless one, have taken
your brother's wife, just as your brother died a merciless death, so
you too will be cut down by heaven's sickle. For divine providence
will not remain silent but will be the death of you through grievous afflictions in other lands, for you are not raising seeds for your
brother but satisfying your carnal lust and committing adultery,
since there are four children of his own."

Hearing this, Herod was enraged and ordered him to be beaten
and thrown out. *He, however, did not cease but wherever he encountered Herod, spoke thus [and] accused him until he was put in a dungeon.* (SJ *War* 2.168, from additional passages) (Emphasis mine)

Four important points must be considered. First, John is a social
critic. While others refuse to comment on Philip's dream John appears
on the scene without invitation to criticize Philip. It is easy to criticize
those in power, but how many do so publicly? This brash act is clearly
dangerous, since Philip has the power to silence John at any time.

Shortly after John's repudiation of Philip's character the tetrarch
dies. This brings us to the second point, which concerns the date of
Philip's death. According to Josephus, Philip dies in the "twentieth
year of the reign of Tiberius," or in 34 CE (*Antiquities* 18.106). This
does not accord with the gospel account. According to Luke 3:1 John
begins his ministry in the "fifteenth year of the reign of Tiberius" or
around 29 CE. While Jesus is still preaching John is imprisoned and
then beheaded, this occurring within the three-year ministry of Jesus
(Matthew 11:1–3 and 14:1–13). Thus, according to the gospels, John is
imprisoned sometime between 29 and 32 CE. Since John is still roam-
ing free at the time of Philip's death in 34 CE, John's freedom cannot
be reconciled with the gospel time line.

Third, when Philip dies, his wife is taken in marriage by his brother,
Herod. This is clearly a mistake made by the Slavonic Josephus's author,

who confuses Philip the Tetrarch with Herod, also known as Philip. Philip the Tetrarch dies childless (*Antiquities* 18.137) while Herod, also known as Philip, is married to Herodias. The mistake proves that the author of the Slavonic Josephus *War* is very careful in matching his new material to the events in *Antiquities,* but the confusion over the Philips may point to a person not totally familiar with Jewish history. The claim that John the Baptist is outraged by Herod Antipas's marriage to Herodias is 100 percent true, but the reason for his outrage is not true. According to the cited passage John is upset because Herod takes his dead brother's wife in marriage, out of lust and not to continue the bloodline of the brother. However, per *Antiquities,* Antipas takes the wife of his stepbrother Herod (Philip) while the stepbrother is still alive (*Antiquities* 18.109–110). This is the act that enrages John and others throughout Jewish society.

The fourth point supports point 2, as John is imprisoned and put to death by Herod Antipas in 35–36 CE. This timing for John's death comes well after the traditional date for the death of Jesus. The Slavonic Josephus's story of Herodias and Herod Antipas correlates with a passage from *Antiquities* 18.109–112, which has John hounding Antipas at every turn. This treatment of Antipas is quite different from that of the Gospel of Mark, where Antipas admires John. Let's list the gospel accounts of Herod Antipas's feelings for John and compare these inclinations to that of Josephus's account.

So *Herodias* nursed a grudge against John and *wanted to kill him.* But she was not able to, because *Herod feared John and protected him, knowing him to be a righteous and holy man.* When Herod heard John, he was greatly puzzled; yet he liked to listen to him. (Mark 6:19–20) (Emphasis mine)

. . . John had been saying to him: "It is not lawful for you to have her [Herodias]." *Herod wanted to kill John, but he was afraid of the people, because they considered him a prophet.* (Matthew 14:4–5) (Emphasis mine)

Now, some of the Jews thought that the destruction of Herod's army came from God, and very justly, as a punishment of what he did against John, that was called the Baptist; for *Herod slew him*, who was a good man, and commanded the Jews to exercise virtue, both as to *righteousness* toward one another, and piety toward God, and so to come to baptism; for that the washing [with water] would be acceptable to him, if they made use of it, not in order to the putting away [or the remission] of some sins [only], but for the purification of the body; supposing still that the soul was thoroughly *purified beforehand by righteousness.* Now when [many] others came in crowds about him, for they were greatly moved [or pleased] by hearing his words, *Herod, who feared lest the great influence John had over the people might put it into his power and inclination to raise a rebellion (for they seemed ready to do anything he should advise), thought it best, by putting him to death,* to prevent any mischief he might cause, and not bring himself into difficulties, by sparing a man who might make him repent of it when it should be too late. Accordingly *he was sent a prisoner, out of Herod's suspicious temper,* to Macherus, the castle I before mentioned, and was there put to death. Now the Jews had an opinion that the destruction of this army was sent as a punishment upon Herod, and a mark of God's displeasure against him. (*Antiquities* 18.116–119) (Emphasis mine)

Mark places the blame for John's death upon Herodias and even states that Herod protects John. No doubt Herodias despises John, since he constantly drags her name through the mud. However, to place the blame solely upon Herodias is too severe. On the other hand Matthew squarely states that Herod wants to kill John, but is constrained by his fear of the people, who consider John a prophet. So the gospel accounts of Herod Antipas are somewhat conflicting.

Josephus paints a much clearer picture of the situation. After describing the Herod and Herodias affair, Josephus writes that Herod slays John because Herod fears the great influence that John has over the people. Herod Antipas arrests John because of John's constant criticisms of his dealings with Herodias, his brother's wife, and later kills John to head off any chance of insurrection.

Herod's desire to defuse a rebellion led by John in 35–36 CE clearly upsets the traditional Christian time line, which holds that John dies before Jesus with his ministry waning. The actual history has John outliving Jesus, with John's power at its zenith.

The gospel account of John the Baptist also turns the Jews against John, similar to their rejection of Jesus. In Matthew 21:31–32 Jesus reportedly says, "Truly I tell you, the tax collectors and the prostitutes are going into the kingdom of God ahead of you. For John came in the Way of Righteousness and you did not believe him, but the tax collectors and the prostitutes believed him." What an incredible rewrite of history! The Josephus passage says that the people are ready to do anything that John wants them to, and that it is Herod (the tax collector) and Herodias (the prostitute) who put John to death. In reality the people believe in John and his message of righteousness—the same Way of Righteousness that Jesus also preaches.

The gospels successfully denigrates the Jews in their actions toward Jesus and John. In the gospel narrative the Jews pressure Pilate into crucifying Jesus, thereby shifting blame for Jesus's death from the Romans to the Jews. In the case of John the gospels state that the tax collectors and prostitutes admire him and will surely attain the kingdom of heaven before any of the religious Jews. Most scholars accept the gospel presentation, because it is in line with Paul's relationship with the Jews and with the Herodian hierarchy. The Jews do hate and hound Paul (see Galatians), and his refuge is with Gentiles who believe in his vision of the Risen Christ. Paul is a Herodian (that is, a tax collector). That explains why the gospel story of Jesus and John has been slanted against the Jews in favor of tax collectors and prostitutes.

John the Baptist's Dating according to Josephus and the Slavonic Josephus

Other revealing clues lurk within the Josephus passage and the various Slavonic Josephus passages cited earlier. First, the dating of John's death can be positively placed at 35–36 CE, five or so years later than the gospel narrative and many years *after* the death of the gospel Jesus. Also, the beginning of John's career is in 6 CE, not 29 CE, as claimed by Luke—an astounding find. Instead of a short two-year ministry John's influence in Judea lasts for thirty years (6–36 CE). Might Jesus's ministry have lasted beyond the three years assigned to him by the gospels? It certainly appears so. My Judas the Galilean hypothesis posits that Judas's career lasts from 4 BCE to 19–21 CE, an amazing 22–24 years. If John is careful enough to avoid arrest for thirty years, then it is entirely possible that Judas the Galilean (Jesus) does as well.

Second, in 35–36 CE, John has a considerable following, willing to revolt at his urging. This poses problems for the gospel story in which John introduces Jesus to the world, is imprisoned shortly thereafter, and is then put to death on the whim of a wicked woman. In reality John's rise to stardom begins in 6 CE and grows over the next thirty years. In 6 CE John introduces Judas the Galilean to the world, because he is a member of Judas's Fourth Philosophy. If John were really related to Jesus, as claimed by Luke, then this familial connection is consistent with the Maccabean movement, where family members work together. Does Judas send his cousin John out to proclaim himself Messiah? How would this preplanning be any different from Jesus's symbolic entry into Jerusalem riding on a donkey? Both events can be found in the Hebrew scriptures, in Isaiah 40:3 and Zechariah 9:9, respectively. To make sure the people understand John's importance, Jesus says, "And if you are willing to accept it, he [John] is the Elijah who was to come" (Matthew 11:14). Jesus also says this, quoting Malachi 3:1: "I will send a messenger ahead of you, who will prepare your way before you" (Luke 7:27). All this talk of John the Baptist is merely a way for Jesus to reinforce his messianic claim. Josephus calls Judas the Galilean a clever rabbi, proved by his use of John the Baptist to support his goals, embedded in scripture.

However, John outlives Judas the Galilean. If Judas suffers crucifixion in 19–21 CE, then John's ministry lasts another fifteen to seventeen years. During these years John's influence grows to a point almost rivaling that of Judas himself. This may explain the gospel description of John's message to the crowds. In John's later years he proclaims the return of the resurrected Jesus, the Jesus who will judge with a winnowing fork (Matthew 3:11–12). Thus, John's baptism may have been used before the introduction of the earthly Jesus (Judas) in 6 CE and after Jesus's crucifixion as well.

Another possibility exists. According to the Pseudoclementine *Recognitions,* some of John's disciples disassociate themselves from the Jewish Jesus Movement and proclaim John as the Messiah.[4] Since Judas the Galilean dies in 19–21 CE and John's ministry lasts until 36 CE, some surely question the validity of Jesus's kingship. This may explain why John has such a large following. A live Messiah is preferable to a dead Messiah. Josephus claims that John is put to death because Herod Antipas is afraid of John's influence over his myriad of disciples. Undoubtedly, this is why the New Testament writers expend so much energy in placing John behind Jesus (and Paul) in importance.

John's popularity in 36 CE may also explain why Apollos knows of John's baptism. Indeed, everyone in this era knows of John's baptism. It also helps date the letters of Paul. If Apollos teaches people about Jesus while using John's baptism, then John's influence is still strong, suggesting that the Apollos incident is fairly close to the date of John's death (post–36 CE), although traditionally, the letters to the Romans, Corinthians, and Galatians are assigned a date of approximately 55 CE. I suggest that these letters were written from the late 30s to the mid-40s, much closer to the time of John's death.

From what has been uncovered concerning John's ministry, a startling claim can be made. John supports Jesus (that is, Judas the Galilean) from 6 CE until the crucifixion (19–21 CE). In fact, John is the second-in-command to Jesus, just as Sadduc is co-teacher with Judas the Galilean, according to Josephus. When Jesus is crucified, John becomes the leader of the movement. It is no coincidence that the apostles preach water baptism after the death of Jesus (Acts 2:38). This is the directive from John the Baptist.

The gospels and Acts remove nearly a generation from the church's history. Jesus's death is recorded at around 33 CE instead of 19–21 CE while John is written out of the story around 32 CE, instead of 36 CE. By removing this generation the gospels eliminate John the Baptist from church leadership. To prove this point let us look at the divisions in the Corinthian Church, as reported by Paul.

My brothers, some from Chloe's household have informed me that there are quarrels among you. What I mean is this: One of you says, "I follow Paul"; another, "I follow *Apollos*"; another, "I follow *Cephas [Peter]*"; still another, "I follow *Christ*." (1 Corinthians 1:11–12) (Emphasis mine)

I date this passage to around 38 CE. Note that Paul has his own following, but the other three factions are disciples of Jesus (represented by Christ), John the Baptist (represented by Apollos), and James (represented by Peter), the first three leaders of the Jewish Jesus Movement. At this early date, the confusion over leadership is causing splits among the disciples, which may explain why James calls the Council of Jerusalem, in order to establish his own authority over the movement. Regardless, John the Baptist is still highly regarded, even after his death.

Finally, Josephus describes John's baptism, which does not remove sins but is simply a purification of the body, "supposing still that the soul was thoroughly purified beforehand by righteousness" (*Antiquities* 18.117). The baptism is a confession before men of an inward change toward God, consistent with Deuteronomy 30, where the circumcision of the heart comes from a willingness to follow God. This is righteousness before God, the same message preached by Judas the Galilean and by Jesus throughout the gospels. Josephus states: "[John] was a good man, and commanded the Jews to exercise virtue, both as to righteousness towards one another, and piety towards God" (*Antiquities* 18.117). The two greatest commandments were: Love your neighbor as yourself and love God with all your heart, soul, and strength. In philosophy John and Jesus (Judas) are inseparable. However, John's philosophy is quite different from that of Paul. In John's view a person can be reconciled with God by righteousness, while Paul insists that a blood sacrifice is necessary: that is, the death of Christ.

REVISED TIME LINE FOR JOHN THE BAPTIST

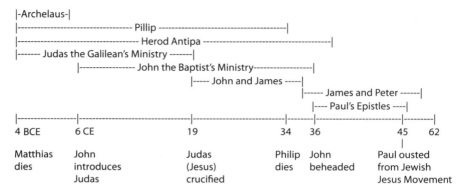

```
|-Archelaus-|
|--------------------------------- Pillip -------------------------------------|
|-------------------------------------- Herod Antipa ------------------------------------|
|------- Judas the Galilean's Ministry -------|
          |----------------- John the Baptist's Ministry-----------------|
                              |----- John and James -----|
                                              |------ James and Peter ------|
                                              |---- Paul's Epistles ----|
|-------------------|--------------------------|-----------------------|----------|----------------|-----------------------------|--------|
 4 BCE       6 CE                      19                34     36                     45       62
                                                                                                |
 Matthias    John                      Judas             Philip  John               Paul ousted
 dies        introduces                (Jesus)           dies    beheaded           from Jewish
             Judas                     crucified                                    Jesus Movement
```

Questions Concerning John Have Been Answered

The revised time line represents all information concerning John the Baptist. Problems associated with the traditional time line have all been resolved.

Jesus's Birth Dates Correspond
to Judas the Galilean's Great Exploits

Josephus first mentions Judas the Galilean in 4 BCE. Judas and his co-teacher Matthias incite a rebellion against Herod the Great, urging their followers to tear down the Golden Eagle, a sign of Herod's fealty to Rome. Matthias and Judas are captured. Matthias is executed while Judas escapes death and is eventually released by Archelaus in a Barabbas-style prisoner release. The dual ministry of Matthias and Judas is repeated a decade later by the Judas and John the Baptist pairing.

A New Birth Date

The traditional dating cannot be reconciled, when considering all the data against it. For example, the birth date of Jesus may have been 9–6 BCE, 2–1 BCE, or 6 CE. The revised time line gives a much more consistent birth date for Judas the Galilean (Jesus) and for John. Both come onto the national scene at the time of the census of Cyrenius, in 6 CE. John has the same philosophy as Judas the Galilean and is strategically used to announce the coming of the Messiah, Judas (Jesus). If both are approximately thirty years old in 6 CE, then they must have been born around 25 BCE, the exact time of the Slavonic Josephus's Star of Bethlehem story (SJ *War* 1.400, from additional passages).

The dating in the New Testament is dependent on the erroneous dating of John the Baptist. The only reason for assigning such a late date for the coming of John the Baptist (28–29 CE) is to place Jesus into a later time frame, closer to 30 CE. By doing this Jesus is separated from historical ties to Judas the Galilean, and John's ministry is cut short, from an amazing thirty years to just a year or two. This late date also helps hide embarrassing revelations about Paul's eventual ouster from the Jewish Jesus Movement in 44 CE.

John the Baptist's Role after the Death of Jesus

Even after Judas (Jesus) dies, John continues preaching his message of repentance. However, now it focuses on the return of the resurrected Jesus. This is unknowingly confirmed by Matthew and Luke, who make the coming Messiah judge good and evil on Judgment Day. Also note that *after* the death of Jesus, the apostles still preach repentance and water baptism (Acts 2:38), proving that John's influence is very strong, even though the gospels contend that he dies years before Jesus.

The Date of John the Baptist's Death

As we have noted John is alive when Philip dies (34 CE) and is put to death by Herod Antipas in 35–36 CE. This is at least five years after John the Baptist's death in the gospel narrative, several years after the gospel crucifixion of Jesus, and fifteen to seventeen years after the actual crucifixion of Jesus (Judas the Galilean).

The historical death of John the Baptist wreaks havoc with the gospel story. In reality John is alive and well many years after Jesus's crucifixion. Thus, many of the gospel passages about John are placed into an earlier time frame (30 CE), in order to overcome the problem of John's great popularity around 35 CE. Therefore, the gospels present John and his followers as being disciples of the precrucifixion Jesus, right up to the time of John's death.

John's Baptism and His Representative Apollos

This later death date of John in 36 CE makes the reference to Apollos and water in 1 Corinthians more relevant. John has a great following until his death and probably for some time beyond his death. Therefore, his form of baptism is probably well known and practiced well into the 40s.

Jesus and John the Baptist, Judas the Galilean and Sadduc

This new time line confirms that *Jesus* (literally meaning, "God saves") is a title for Judas the Galilean and that the name *Sadduc* is a title for John the Baptist. John's introduction right before Judas the Galilean (6 CE) in the Slavonic Josephus confirms this. In addition, John holds the same philosophy as Judas the Galilean. Could John have prepared the way for Judas the Galilean in 6 CE and for another Messiah (Jesus) in 29 CE? Unlikely. Judas and Jesus are one in the same, with John at his side.

THE REAL HISTORY OF
THE JEWISH JESUS MOVEMENT

The following sections show the approximate dates for each leadership pair.

4 BCE and Earlier

Matthias and Judas lead their students in the Golden Eagle Temple Cleansing, an awakening for the movement. I contend that Matthias or the Temple cleansing may have been associated with the Root of Planting, a term taken from the Dead Sea Scrolls. The Fourth Philosophy did not write the Scrolls, but used them to their own advantage. Some Scrolls were found at Masada and the heaviest coin usage at Qumran occurs during the heyday of the Fourth Philosophy, from 4 BCE to 68 CE.[5] With the death of Matthias, Judas heads to Galilee. Matthias is eventually replaced by Sadduc, sometime between 4 BCE and 6 CE.

Josephus pairs Judas the Galilean with Sadduc (John the Baptist) in 6 CE, but that does not preclude their close collaboration before that date. If related, as Luke claims for Jesus and John, then the two preachers surely plan their respective paths. Their coming together in 6 CE is an ingenious way to respond to the new Roman tax. "Jesus" (Judas the Galilean) adopts water baptism while John proclaims Judas as Messiah.

6–19 or 21 CE

This period of the Jewish Jesus Movement brims with excitement, as both Judas (Jesus) and Sadduc (John the Baptist) roam the countryside. They preach the kingdom of heaven on Earth. In 19 CE Judas marches to Jerusalem and is hailed as Messiah by the crowds. However, God's promised kingdom on Earth does not prevail and Judas (Jesus) is crucified.

19 or 21–36 CE

After Judas's (Jesus's) death by crucifixion James became second-in-command to John the Baptist. Acts 1 obscures the election of James by reporting that a Matthias replaces Judas Iscariot. Judas Iscariot is purely an invention of the gospel writers as a way to hide the importance of Judas the Galilean and James. Robert Eisenman proves that the election of James is the real event, not the election of Matthias.[6]

Even though James replaces Judas, the movement is still headed by John the Baptist, despite the gospels' insistence that John dies before Jesus. But history does not match the gospel account, since John survives until 36 CE, many years after the gospel story suggests, and many more years after the actual crucifixion (19–21 CE), as outlined above. Even within the pages of Acts the truth emerges. Peter preaches this strong sermon after the death of Jesus.

> When the people heard this [sermon], they were cut to the heart and said to Peter and the other apostles, "Brothers, what shall we do?"
>
> Peter replied, *"Repent and be baptized, every one of you, in the name of Jesus Christ so that your sins may be forgiven. And you will receive the gift of the Holy Spirit.* The promise is for you and your children and for all who are far off—for all whom the Lord our God will call."
>
> With many other words he warned them; and he pleaded with

them, *"Save yourselves from this corrupt generation."* Those who accepted his message were baptized, and about three thousand were added to their number that day. (Acts 2:37–41) (Emphasis mine)

The above passage combines some truth with some Pauline teachings. Since John leads the movement it only makes sense that the cornerstone practice is water baptism. Acts tries to combine this water baptism with Paul's Holy Spirit baptism, but this is never part of the early Jewish Jesus Movement.

Peter's speech in Acts 2:40 states, "With many other words he warned them; and he pleaded with them, 'Save yourselves from this corrupt generation.'" Could this admonition have been taken from John the Baptist and placed in the mouth of Peter?

In fact, Peter's sermon includes three elements of John's message: water baptism, repentance, and a condemnation of a corrupt society. Acts simply substitutes Peter for John the Baptist, as John has already been killed off in the gospel story. We would expect to hear from the second-in-command after the death of "Jesus." This is John, not Peter.

36–38 CE

This is a time for consolidation of power. When one reads Galatians it appears as if the Council of Jerusalem is called simply to decide Paul's place in the movement. Paul states that he goes to Jerusalem in "response to a revelation" and presents his gospel before the pillar apostles (Galatians 2:2). In Jerusalem Paul claims that he is "given the task of preaching the gospel to the Gentiles, just as Peter had been given the task of preaching the gospel to the Jews" (Galatians 2:7). Perhaps, the most important part of the so-called Council of Jerusalem is to install Peter as the second-in-command. Any dealings with Paul are secondary in nature. Besides, at this point in Paul's relationship with James, Paul still hides the true vision in his own gospel. In 1 Corinthians 9:20 Paul makes it quite clear that he has told the Jews what they want to hear, not his own unique antinomian gospel.

So the Council of Jerusalem is used by James as a way to consolidate power. John the Baptist has just been put to death and his fervent followers still cling to his memory. It is James's task to place all emphasis back on the resurrected Jesus, making himself a caretaker leader until the Messiah's return in power and glory. Interestingly the fourth-century church historian, Epiphanius, states that James rules the church for twenty-four years until his death in 62 CE, making James the leader of the Jewish Jesus Movement from 38 CE until 62 CE.[7] This is generally the period covered by the book of Acts, although Acts' version is a twisted jumble of times and events.

The new strategy during the tenure of James focuses more intently on the return of "Jesus" in power and glory, explaining why the passages about John the Baptist in the gospels appear to talk about the return of the resurrected Jesus—for example Matthew 3:11-12, where Jesus will come to separate the wheat from the chaff. Even John preaches the return of "Jesus," but the nationalistic fervor grows under James's leadership.

Using this more exact time for the Council of Jerusalem at 38–39 CE, we can better calculate Paul's so-called conversion into the Jewish Jesus Movement. If Paul joins seventeen years prior to the Council, then he becomes a member around 21–22 CE. Paul spends several more years in the movement after the Council, until he's thrown out in 44 CE. In all Paul is a member of the Jewish Jesus Movement for twenty-two or twenty-three years.

38–62 CE

The Jewish Jesus Movement is guided by James and Peter. As the years roll by it is more difficult to keep the young disciples under control. After all waiting for the expected return of a dead Messiah is not easy. Many, like Theudas, try to prod God into action, but this simply leads to their own deaths. In time the movement splinters, and when James dies in 62 CE, havoc soon breaks loose.

APPENDIX C

Pontius Pilate

Jesus is crucified under Pontius Pilate. Tacitus writes the following:

> Nero set up as the culprits and punished with the utmost refinement
> of cruelty a class hated for their abominations, who are commonly
> called Christians. Christus, from whom their name is derived, was
> executed at the hands of the procurator Pontius Pilate in the reign
> of Tiberius. (*Annals,* xv.44)

Tacitus writes about the Great Fire of Rome (64 CE) around 120
CE. Surely the legend of the Christ is well known by those who have
investigated the cult. The above passage appears genuine, since a later
Christian apologist would not have denigrated the Christians in such
a manner. Also, note that Pilate is procurator during the reign of
Tiberius, sometime between 14 and 37 CE.

According to *Antiquities* Pontius Pilate becomes procurator of Judea
in 26 CE. As noted earlier the traditional dating for Jesus's crucifixion
is between 30–32 CE. Thus, the traditional crucifixion occurs near the
middle of Pilate's reign. However, the text of Josephus suggests that
Pilate arrives in Judea in 18 CE. The time line of Josephus as detailed
in *Antiquities* 18.26–84 is as follows:

JOSEPHUS'S EARLY FIRST-CENTURY TIME LINE*

6 CE	Joazar—Serves as high priest
6–9 CE	Coponius—Serves as Roman governor
6 CE	Judas the Galilean—Leads tax revolt
6–15 CE	Annas—Appointed high priest by Coponius
9–12 CE	Ambivulus—Serves as Roman governor
12–15 CE	Rufus—Serves as Roman governor
15–26(18) CE	Gratus—Serves as Roman governor
15 CE	Ishmael—Appointed high priest by Gratus
15–16 CE	Eleazar—Appointed high priest by Gratus
16–17 CE	Simon—Appointed high priest by Gratus
18–37 CE	Caiaphas—Appointed high priest by Gratus
26(18)–37 CE	Pilate—Serves as Roman governor
18 CE	City of Tiberius completed
19 CE	Germanicus, famous Roman general and father of Caligula, poisoned (this date is also confirmed by Tacitus)
26(19) CE	Pilate—Roman effigies introduced into Jerusalem and money earmarked for sacred use is diverted to build aqueducts
26(19) CE	The spurious Jesus passage from *Testimonium Flavianum* is placed into Josephus's text, replaces Judas the Galilean's death with the death of Jesus of Nazareth
19 CE	Paulina is swindled out of money by an unnamed Jew (Saul/Paul) in Rome (corroborated by Tacitus)

*Boldface entries indicate events with contradictory dates given in the text. For example, the text describes Gratus serving as Roman governer for three years, yet it also states that he serves eleven years. If he serves eleven years, then Pilate must become governer in 26 CE. But both of Josephus's entries concerning Pilate refer to events in 19 CE. This time line does not work. However, if Gratus serves for three years, then Pilate becomes governer in 18 CE and the flow of events is logically restored.

Note the following points. First, the text of Josephus chronicles only three years for Gratus's reign instead of eleven years, which is crucial to traditional dating of the New Testament. Second, Caiaphas is appointed high priest by Gratus in 18 CE and then serves nineteen consecutive years as high priest. According to John 18:13 Jesus is brought before Caiaphas, "the high priest *that year*." Such wording only makes sense after the merry-go-round of high priests from 15 to 18 CE. In addition, Tiberius likes his procurators to stay in the provinces for extended periods, to cut down on corruption. The high priesthood of Caiaphas would overlap with Pilate's tenure if Pilate arrived in 18 rather than 26 CE. Third, after both mentions of Pilate (traditionally 26 CE), Josephus describes events occurring in 18–19 CE. If Pilate were really procurator from 26–37 CE, then the whole rhythm of the time line is disrupted; if, however, Pilate becomes procurator in 18 CE, then the Josephus chronology flows seamlessly.

Why would anyone change the tenure of Gratus from three to eleven years, thus delaying Pilate's governorship until 26 CE? I contend this was done by a Christian redactor to distance Jesus from Judas the Galilean. Note that the spurious Jesus passage (TF) is located at the precise point where we would expect to see an account of Judas's execution for sedition. Thus, not only is the death of Judas the Galilean replaced with the crucifixion of Jesus, but the beginning of Pilate's career is also a victim of chronological tampering.

One further source supports the earlier time line for Pilate. Eusebius, the fourth-century church historian, writes the following concerning Pilate:

> In *Antiquities* Book XVIII, the same writer [Josephus] informs us that in the twelfth year of Tiberius, who had mounted the imperial throne after the fifty-seven-year reign of Augustus, Judea was entrusted to Pontius Pilate, and that Pilate remained there ten years, almost until Tiberius's death. This clearly proves the forged character of the *Memoranda* so recently published, blackening our savior; at the very start the note of time proves the dishonesty of the forg-

ers. If they are to be believed the crime of the Savior's Passion must be referred to Tiberius's fourth consulship, i.e. the seventh year of his reign, but at that time it is clear that Pilate was not yet in charge of Judea, if we may accept the testimony of Josephus, who explicitly declares, in the passage already quoted, that it was in the twelfth year of his reign that Tiberius appointed Pilate procurator of Judea.[1]

The *Memoranda* contends that the Messiah is crucified in 21 CE, a date very close to the actual text of Josephus, as chronicled above. Note my claim that Pilate came to Judea in 18 CE and that the spurious Jesus passage (TF) fits into the 18–19 CE sequence of events. Perhaps the arrest takes place in 19 CE and the actual crucifixion occurs in 21 CE. Prisoners are often held until the most opportune time to carry out their sentence.

The Slavonic Josephus

To understand the importance of the Slavonic Josephus, thirteen passages will be displayed and analyzed. These passages come from a translation by H. Leeming and K. Leeming, which places the Greek and Slavonic versions of *War* side by side, making Christianized verses easy to identify.[1] After each passage I will reference the spot relative to the Greek version of *War* and the approximate date. A short analysis will follow.

THIRTEEN PASSAGES

Passage 1: The Priests Discuss the Messiah

Immediately the priests started to grieve and complain to one another, saying among themselves in secret [things] they would not dare to say in public because of Herod's friends. For they were saying: "The Law forbids us to have a foreigner [as] king, but we are expecting the Anointed, the Meek one, of David's line. Yet we know that Herod is an Arab, uncircumcised. The Anointed One will be called meek but this [king] has filled our whole land with blood. Under the Anointed the lame were to walk, the blind to see, the poor to prosper, but under this [king] the hale have become lame, those who could see have gone blind, the rich are beggared.

What is this? Or did the prophets lie? They wrote that we shall never lack a prince of Judah until there comes the One to whom it is given back; in him the nations will hope. But is this [King Herod] the hope of nations? We detest his misdeeds; are the nations going to hope in him? . . . But Herod sent [his men] by night and slew them all in secret from the people, so that they should not cause a riot. And he appointed others [in their place]. (SJ *War* 1.369, from additional passages)

The priests are utterly contemptuous of Herod the Great. Inserted into the text of *War* after the discussion of Actium (a navel battle fought between the fleets of Octavian and Anthony in 31 BCE), this episode can be dated to 31–30 BCE. Along with despair concerning Herod the Great, referred to as "an uncircumcised Arab," a hope in the coming of the Messiah is envisioned, an Anointed One who will surely heal the land and be a true light unto the nations. When Herod hears of the priests' grumblings, he puts them to death and replaces them with his own loyal priests.

Passage 2: The Star of Bethlehem

Having so spoken [Herod] sent them [Persians] off to the innkeepers, escorting them with guards who were to keep watch on them, and also appointing other guards who knew the Persian tongue to listen to what they said. When they were closeted with a Persian who was [there] they began to grieve, saying: "Our fathers and our children have been excellent astrologers and, watching the stars, never lied. And we, too, taught by them, have never distorted the message of the stars. What can this be? Deceit or error? The star image appeared to us signifying the birth of [a] king by whom the whole world will be held. And gazing on that [star] we have been making our way for a year and a half to this city; and we have not found the son of [a] king. And the star is now hidden from us. We have indeed been deceived! But we shall send the gifts we had prepared for the infant to the king and ask him to let us return to our fatherland."

And while they were thus speaking, the guards came to the king and told him everything. And he sent for the Persians. But while they were on their way, that remarkable star appeared to them [again]. And they were filled with joy. And they went by night to Herod with boldness. And he said to them [confidentially], away from everybody [else]: "Why do you sadden my heart and distress my soul by not speaking the truth? Why have you come here?"

They told him: "King, we have no double-talk. But we are sons of Persia. Astronomy, which is our science and our craft, our ancestors took over from the Chaldaeans. As we gazed on the stars we have never been wrong. And a star [of] ineffable [beauty] appeared to us, separated from all [the other] stars. For it was not one of the seven planets . . . and gazing on it we have even reached you. And while we were here, the star disappeared right up to the present [moment]. But now, as we were coming to you, it appeared [again]."

And Herod said: "Can you show it to me?"

And they said: "We reckon the whole world sees it." And they stepped out on to an open porch and they showed him the star. And when Herod saw it, he marveled greatly. And he worshipped God for he was a devout man. And he gave them an escort [composed of] his brother and [some] nobles, to go and see the one born. But as they were on their way the star disappeared once more, and they came back again. And the Persians begged him to let them go on their own, [promising] that having sought out [the child], they would come back and tell him. And they swore him an oath, believing that the star would tell them to return by that road. And they followed the star.

And after waiting a year for them, they did not even come to [see] him. And he was furious and summoned the priests [who were his] advisors and asked if any of them understood [the meaning of] that star. And they answered him: "It is written: *A star shall shine forth from Jacob and a man shall arise from Judah.'* And Daniel writes that a priest is to come but we do not know who this is. We reckon that he will be born without a father."

[Then] Herod said: "How can we discover him?" And Levi said: "Send throughout the whole land of Judea [asking] how many male infants have been born since the Persians saw the star right up to the present day, kill them all, and that [child] will also be killed. And your kingdom will be secure for you and your sons and even for your great-grandsons." And immediately he sent forth heralds throughout the whole land that all [of] the male sex born from now and [back] to the third year are to be honored and to receive [a gift of] gold. When inquiring whether any [male infant] had been born without a father they were to pretend that [Herod] would adopt him as his son and make him king. And since they did not discover a single such [infant], he gave orders to kill all 6 myriad and 3000 infants. When all were weeping and wailing at the shedding of blood, the priests came and begged him to release the innocents; but he threatened them all the more, [telling them] to keep silent. And they fell prostrate and lay to the sixth hour at his feet. And the king's rage prevailed. Later, they rose and told him: "Listen to your servants, so that the Most High may favor you. *It is written that the Anointed One is [to be] born in Bethlehem.* Even if you have no mercy on your servants, kill those infants of Bethlehem and let the others go." And he gave the order and they killed all the infants of Bethlehem. (SJ *War* 1.400, from additional passages) (Emphasis mine)

This Star of Bethlehem story corresponds to Matthew's birth narrative (Matthew 2:1–18). Both Persian astrologers and the Magi follow a star or some other celestial event to the child Messiah. In Matthew the birth occurs toward the end of Herod the Great's life, or around 6 BCE, while in the Slavonic Josephus, the search by the astrologers takes place between 27 and 22 BCE.*

The Slavonic Josephus version explains the Star Prophecy's promise that a great ruler will arise from Israel (Numbers 24:17), a belief that

---

*Herod's tenth year in office is 27 BCE and 22 BCE is the fifteenth year of his reign. Both dates can be ascertained by passages in Josephus's *War,* before and after the birth narrative.

leads to the war with Rome. The Jews believe that the star refers to their Messiah, while Josephus attributes the prophecy to General Vespasian, the future Caesar.

When placed side by side with the time line in *Antiquities,* the murder of the innocents corresponds to Herod's murder of the sons of Baba, the last of the Maccabees (*Antiquities* 15.263–266). Perhaps the birth of the Messiah is placed at the time of the last Maccabee. This promised Messiah will resurrect the dynasty and fight Herodian and Roman influence.

Passage 3: The Golden Eagle Temple Cleansing

For at that time Herod had had a golden eagle made over the great temple gate in honor of Caesar, and had named it "the Golden-winged Eagle." *This the two [Matthias and Judas] ordered the people to hack down, saying: "It is a fine thing to die for the Law of our fathers.* For immortal glory will follow; we shall die, and our souls will have eternal joy. Those who die unmanly, who are lovers of their bodies, unwilling to die like men, but ending [their lives] through sickness, inglorious they suffer unending torments in hell."

"*Come, men of Judea, now is the time for men to behave like men, to show what reverence we have for the Law of Moses.* Let not our race be shamed, let us not bring disgrace on our Law-giver. Let us take as the *model for [our] exploits Eleazar first and the seven Maccabee brothers and the mother who made men [of them].* For, when Antiochus had conquered and subjected our land and was ruling over us, he was defeated by these seven youths and [their] old teacher and an old woman. Let us also be worthy of them, let us not prove weaker than a woman. *But even if we are to be tortured for our zeal for God, a greater wreath has been plaited for us.* And if they kill us, our souls as they leave [this] dark abode will return to [our] forefathers, where Abraham and his offspring [dwell]." (SJ *War* 1.650, from additional passages) (Emphasis mine)

This Christianized text is added to the Golden Eagle Temple Cleansing story appearing in both *War* and *Antiquities* (*War* 1.647–655;

Antiquities 17.149–167). The additional data corresponds to the dating of Matthew's birth narrative for Jesus. Certainly, this is a momentous event for the early Jewish Jesus Movement, led by Judas the Galilean. If Judas is born in 25 BCE, per passage 2, then he is twenty years old at the time of the Temple Cleansing in 4 BCE. Matthew erases this history by placing the birth of Jesus in this exact year.

Judas and Matthias are zealous for the Jewish law, urging their disciples to risk death to uphold it. Could this be the same attitude of Jesus, who asks his disciples to carry their cross, knowing full well that many will be crucified under the Roman regime? Judas and Matthias also promise a great reward to those who endure torture in defense of the Law, which may explain why Zealots and Sicarii, members of the Fourth Philosophy, never waver in their faith when tortured. This steadfast devotion can also be observed in Tacitus's Christians, martyred in Rome during the Great Fire.

The first-century struggle against Rome is modeled after the fight led by Judas Maccabee and his brothers against Antiochus Epiphanes. Interestingly the above text places great importance on brothers and a mother, ignoring the father. In the case of Judas Maccabee his father Mattathias dies before his sons cleanse the Temple and overthrow Antiochus. After the Golden Eagle incident, Matthias is burned to death. Is Matthias the father of Judas? This may well be the case. This fatherless situation also dominates the life of the gospel Jesus, where Joseph is absent from Jesus's ministry.

And finally, the aims of Judas and Matthias in 4 BCE are identical to those of Judas the Galilean and John the Baptist in 6 CE.[2] So the Fourth Philosophy does not begin in 6 CE, but at least ten years earlier, in 4 BCE.

Passage 4: The Death of Herod the Great

For God's eye, unseen, had observed his [Herod's] sins. For he had defiled his reign by bloodshed and adultery. *And, because he had made others childless, so too he killed his own children with his own hands.* And because he had not spared his body from his fornication, he was attacked by such a vile disease. (SJ *War* 1.656, from additional passages) (Emphasis mine)

The painful death of Herod in 4 BCE is attributed to his sins, which include killing his own children as well as the innocents at Bethlehem, a judgment also made about the early kings of Israel who violate God's laws. It also hints at the evil nature of the Herodian ruling class, who, along with Rome, are enemies of the Jewish people.

Passage 5: John the Baptist's Introduction

And at that time a certain man was going about Judea, [dressed] in strange garments. He donned the hair of cattle on those parts of his body which were not covered with his own hair. And he was wild in visage. And he came to the Jews and called them to freedom, saying, *"God has sent me to show you the lawful way, by which you will be rid of [your] many rulers. But there will be no mortal ruling [over you], only the Most High, who hath sent me."*

And when they heard this, the people were joyful. And all Judea and the environs of Jerusalem were following him. And he did nothing else for them, except to immerse them in Jordan's stream, and dismiss them, bidding them refrain from their wicked deeds, and *a king would be given to them, saving them and humbling all the unsubmissive,* while he himself would be humbled by no one. Some mocked his voices; others believed them. And when he was brought before *Archelaus* and the experts of the Law were assembled, they asked him who he was and where he had been up until then. In answer, he said, "I am a man. Where the divine spirit leads me, I feed on the roots of reeds and the shoots of trees." When those [men] *threatened him with torture* if he did not cease those words and deeds, he said, "It is you who should cease from your foul deeds and adhere to the Lord, your God."

And arising in fury, Simon, an Essene by origin [and] a scribe, said, "We read the divine scriptures every day, and you who have [just] now come in like a beast from the woods dare to teach us and to lead people astray with your impious words." And he rushed forward to tear his body apart.

But he, reproaching them, said, "I am not revealing to you the mystery which is [here] among you, because you have not wished it. Therefore, there will come [down] on you an unutterable calamity, because of you and the people." Thus he spoke and left for the other side of the Jordan. And as no one dared to prevent him, he was doing just what he had done before. (SJ *War* 2.110, from additional passages) (Emphasis mine)

John the Baptist's introduction is placed during the reign of Archelaus, in 6 CE, inserted into the text just a few verses before the introduction of Judas the Galilean. In addition, John the Baptist's political message is identical to that of Judas—both wanted to oust the mortals (that is, the Roman authorities) who ruled over Israel. Also note that thirty years have passed from the Slavonic Josephus Star of Bethlehem to this introduction of John. This is the number of years that the Gospel of Luke claims Jesus has lived before the time of his baptism by John (Luke 3:23).

The teaming up of John the Baptist and Judas the Galilean corresponds to the account in *Antiquities,* where Judas takes with him a Pharisee, referred to as Sadduc (*Antiquities* 18.4), a connection fully explored in appendix B. In addition, the Slavonic Josephus version makes it clear that John the Baptist is willing to undergo torture for his beliefs, a trait common among members of the Fourth Philosophy.

It can be assumed that Judas sends John out to baptize, to preach repentance, and to question the current power structure (Herodian and Roman rule). The clever rabbi may have used this as a strategy to incite the masses, just as the gospel Jesus uses the donkey to ride into Jerusalem, both wildly popular.

Passage 6: Judas the Galilean

This passage is not an insertion into the text but an alternative version of the Greek text. The Greek text precedes the Slavonic Josephus text here:

Under his [Coponius's] administration it was that a certain Galilean, whose name was Judas, prevailed with his countrymen to revolt; and said *they were cowards if they would endure to pay a tax to the Romans, and would, after God, submit to mortal men as their lords.* This man was a teacher of a peculiar sect of his own, and was not at all like the rest of those their leaders. (*War* 2.118) (Emphasis mine)

During his [Coponius's] time there was a man from Galilee who upbraided the Jews because, although they were the free seed of Abraham, they were now in thrall to the Romans, *paying tribute and having mortal masters,* since they had deprived themselves of their immortal [Lord]. The name of this man was Judas, who had found [a way of] *living apart and unlike others.* (SJ *War* 2.118, from additional passages) (Emphasis mine)

The description of Judas the Galilean is quite similar in the Greek *War* and its Slavonic Josephus version. In both Judas opposes payment of taxes to Rome, calling Rome the people's "mortal masters." This viewpoint matches that of John the Baptist, detailed in passage 5. The Slavonic version adds that the Jews are the "free seed" of Abraham. This wording may have been in Josephus's original version of *War,* written not in Greek but in Chaldaic.[3] The *free seed of Abraham* had meaning to the Jews but not to any Greek reader.

In the Greek version Judas is unlike most of the leaders while the Slavonic Josephus version states that Judas lives apart and is unlike the others. The Slavonic version stresses that Judas not only leads a different sect, but that his sect acts differently from other sects. Once again, stressing actions over faith may have had more appeal to a Jewish audience.

Passage 7: The Last Days of John the Baptist

And in those days Philip, while being in his own domain, saw [in] a dream an eagle tear out both his eyes. And he called together all his wise men. And when others were resolving the dreams otherwise, the man we have already described as walking about in animal hair and cleansing people in the streams of the Jordan, came to Philip suddenly, unsummoned, and said, "Hear the word of the Lord. The dream you have seen: the eagle is your rapacity, for that bird is violent and rapacious. Such also is the sin; it will pluck out your eyes which are your domain and your wife." And when he had spoken thus, *Philip passed away by evening and his domain was given to Agrippa.* And his wife Herodias was taken by Herod, his brother. Because of her all those who were learned in the Law detested him but did not dare accuse him to his face. Only the man they called wild {but we call John, Baptizer of the Lord},* came to him in fury and said, "Since you, lawless one, have taken your brother's wife, just as your brother died a merciless death, so you too will be cut down by heaven's sickle. For divine providence will not remain silent but will be the death of you through grievous afflictions in other lands, for you are not raising seeds for your brother but satisfying your carnal lust and committing adultery, since there are four children of his own."

Hearing this, Herod was enraged and ordered him to be beaten and thrown out. He, however, did not cease but *wherever he encountered Herod, spoke thus [and] accused him until he was put in a dungeon.* And his character was strange and his way of life not that of a human being, for he existed just like a fleshless spirit. His mouth knew not bread nor did he even taste the unleavened bread at Passover, saying that it was in remembrance of God, who had delivered the people from servitude, that it had been given to eat for escape, [since] the journey was urgent. Wine and fermented liquor he would not allow to come near himself. And he detested the eating of all animal [meat]. And he denounced all injustice And for his needs there were tree shoots and {locusts and honey}. (SJ *War* 2.168, from additional passages) (Emphasis mine)

---

*This appears to be a later addition to the Slavonic Josephus version. Perhaps, later scribes placed their own thoughts into the text. The use of curly brackets—{}—in this passage and others indicates possible later tampering by Christians.

John the Baptist is described in two separate stories. The first story about Philip can be dated to 34 CE (*Antiquities* 18.106).* John predicts Philip's demise and Philip immediately dies. This dating is important because if John lives until 34 CE, then the traditional time line cannot be correct.

The Philip confusion starts when the author states that Philip is married to Herodias and has four children. The Philip of the first story is married to Salome, Herodias's daughter, and has no children. Herodias is married to another Herod, known as Philip in the gospels. Herod Antipas steals this Philip's wife, so the connection with the first Philip is simply an error.

Two points can be derived from this second story: First, the death of John the Baptist can be moved to around 35–36 CE, consistent with Josephus's account in *Antiquities* (18.109–119), and second, the Slavonic Josephus author is not Josephus but an early Jewish "Christian" who confuses the facts concerning Philip the Tetrarch and Herod, called Philip.

Passage 8: The Wonder Worker

{At that time there appeared a man, if it is proper to call him a man, whose nature and form were human but whose appearance was more than human and whose deeds were divine. And he worked wonder-ful and powerful miracles. Therefore it is impossible for me to call him a man. Then again, in view of his common nature, they shall not call him an angel [either]. And everything, whatever he did, he did by some unseen power, by word and command. Some said of him, "[Our] first lawgiver has risen from the dead and has been demonstrating many cures and skills." Others thought that he had been sent by God. But he was in much opposed to the Law and did not observe the Sabbath according to the ancestral custom, yet did nothing dirty, [unclean], nor with use of hands but worked every-

---

*According to Josephus, Philip, tetrarch of Trachonitis, dies in the twentieth year of Tiberius's reign, or approximately 34 CE.

thing by word alone.}* And many of the people followed and listened to his teachings. *And many souls were aroused, thinking that by him the Jewish tribes would free themselves from the hands of the Romans.* But it was his habit rather to remain in front of the city on the Mount of Olives; and there he also [freely] gave cures to people. And there 150 servants and a multitude of people joined him, seeing his power [and] how by words he did everything he wished. *They bade him enter the city, kill the Roman troops and Pilate, and reign over these.* {But he did not care [to do so].} Later, when news of this came to the Jewish leaders, they assembled to the chief priests and said, "We are powerless and [too] weak to oppose the Romans, like a slackened bow. Let us go and inform Pilate what we have heard; and we shall be free of anxiety; if at some time he shall hear [of this] from others, we shall be deprived of [our] property, ourselves slaughtered and [our] children exiled."

And they went and informed Pilate. And he sent and killed many of the people and brought in that wonder-worker. After inquiring about him Pilate understood that he was a doer of good, not of evil, [and] not a rebel nor one desirous of kingship; and *he released him. For he had cured his wife who was dying.* And he went to his usual places and performed his usual deeds. And [once] again, as more people gathered around him, he became renowned for his works more than all [others]. Again the lawyers were struck with envy against him. *And they gave thirty talents to Pilate that they should kill him. And he took [it] and gave them liberty to carry out their wishes themselves.* And they sought out a suitable time to kill him. For they had given Pilate thirty talents earlier, that he should give Jesus up to them. And they crucified him against the ancestral law; and they greatly

---

*This part of the passage clearly follows the lone passage (TF) in *Antiquities* 18.63–64, which relates the death of Jesus. In *Antiquities* Jesus is called "a wise man, if it be lawful to call him a man." This is similar to the Slavonic Josephus, where the text states: "It is impossible for me to call him a man." Since most scholars believe that the TF is a late third- or early fourth-century interpolation, it is safe to assume that this part of the Slavonic Josephus is also a later (fourth-century or later) Christian interpolation.

reviled him. (SJ *War* 2.174, from additional passages) (Emphasis mine)

This passage about Jesus, the wonder worker, has several strata. In the earliest stratum, Jesus appeals to the nationalistic goals of the Fourth Philosophy, to kill the Romans and Pilate. The crowds support him with great enthusiasm as he proclaims revolution. And the chief priests are afraid for their livelihoods. They inform Pilate, who metes out Roman justice, killing many of the followers and arresting the wonder worker.

However, like the gospels, the earliest stratum also contains unlikely elements. Pilate is convinced that the wonder worker is good and not evil. He releases Jesus after Jesus cures his wife.* As in the Gospel of Matthew, Pilate is exonerated for Jesus's death and the blame is placed on the Jews. It is even claimed that the Jews—not the Romans—crucify Jesus. In this text Pilate releases Jesus, just as the gospel Pilate releases Barabbas. Now, the release of Jesus or Barabbas by Pilate has been questioned by scholars because it is not a Roman practice, and Pilate is a cruel ruler, not likely to set free dangerous criminals or insurrectionists. However, Archelaus (4 BCE) does free prisoners after the death of Herod the Great, shortly after the Golden Eagle Temple Cleansing led by Judas the Galilean and Matthias. So this release of the wonder worker may have been more historically accurate than the gospel story of Barabbas.

The earliest stratum may also have included the story of the thirty pieces of silver. In the Slavonic Josephus version thirty talents are given to Pilate by the chief priests in order to arrest the wonder worker. There is no mention of the thirty pieces of silver given by the chief priests to Judas Iscariot. Undoubtedly Judas Iscariot is a literary device to shift blame from the Romans to the Jews.[4]

Later strata include the introduction of the wonder worker claimed to be nearly divine. This undeveloped concept of the divine Christ is

---

*In Matthew 27:19 Pilate's wife warns Pilate that Jesus is an innocent man.

not consistent with the claim that the wonder worker is nationalistic, bent on eradicating the Roman occupation. In addition, the wonder worker reputedly flouts the Sabbath and other laws of Moses, completely inconsistent with the character of John the Baptist as described by the Slavonic Josephus *War*.

Passage 9: Are the Teachings from Human Sources or from God?

Again, Claudius sent his officials to those kingdoms, *Cuspius Fadus and Tiberius Alexander,* who kept the nation at peace, allowing nothing to be removed from the pure laws. If anyone departed from the letter of the Law and was denounced to the teachers of the Law, he was then punished and banished or sent to Caesar. *At this time there appeared many servants of the previously described wonder worker, telling the people about their master, that he was [still] alive although he had died. And [they said], "He will free you from servitude."* And many of the people listened to them and paid attention to their instructions, not because of their renown. For the apostles were from the lowly [folk]; for some were sail makers, some were sandal makers, some were manual workers, others fishermen. But they performed wonderful signs, in truth what [ever] they willed. *But the grateful governors seeing the subversion of the people, planned with the scribes to take them and destroy them,* lest a small [thing] be not small when in its fullness it becomes great. But they were ashamed and terrified by the signs and said, "Such great wonders do not happen by magic; if they do not come by God's forethought, they will be soon unmasked." And they gave them authority to go about freely. Later, being pestered by them, they released them, some to Caesar, some to Antioch, others in distant lands, for an investigation of the matter. (SJ *War* 2.220, from additional passages) (Emphasis mine)

This policy concerning the early Jewish Jesus Movement can be dated to 44–48 CE, the dating for Fadus and Tiberius Alexander. The time frame includes the beheading of Theudas and the crucifixions of two of Judas the Galilean's sons, James and Simon (*Antiquities* 20.97–102).

According to this passage the disciples are given a short time to prove whether they are sent by God. This very same sentiment is expressed in Acts 5:36–42, when Gamaliel persuades the Sanhedrin to allow Peter and others to continue their ministry. The difference between the two accounts concerns the dating. The Slavonic Josephus dates this policy from 44–48 CE, during the governorships of Fadus and Tiberius Alexander, while Acts dates it to the mid-30s. Which is the correct dating? According to Josephus, Theudas and the sons of Judas the Galilean are put to death during the time of Fadus and Tiberius Alexander. In Acts, Theudas and Judas the Galilean are mentioned as having been killed before the time of Gamaliel, sometime before 35 CE. In this case the Slavonic Josephus's dating is consistent with *Antiquities,* while Acts presents Gamaliel as referring to future events (Theudas and the sons of Judas) in 35 CE as if they had happened in the past. The account in Acts is simply an anachronistic nightmare.

Also note that the followers of the wonder worker preach a message of freedom from servitude, the same freedom preached by John the Baptist and the wonder worker in the Slavonic Josephus (SJ *War* 2.110 and 2.174, from additional passages). And, of course, Josephus records that Judas the Galilean and Sadduc (John the Baptist) preach the same message of freedom from servitude and from Roman oppression (*Antiquities* 18.4).

Passage 10: An Inscription in the Temple

> And above these inscriptions, a fourth inscription hung, in those letters, declaring Jesus, [a] king who had not reigned, crucified by [the] Jews, because he foretold the destruction of the city and the devastation of the temple. (SJ *War* 5.194, from additional passages)

This passage is not written by Josephus, as it claims that an inscription in the Temple states that Jesus was crucified by the Jews after he foretold the destruction of the Temple. The claim is similar to the gospels' claim that Jesus foretold the destruction of the Temple and Jerusalem (Matthew 24 and Mark 13).

Passage 11: The Torn Veil of the Holy of Holies

Until this generation this veil was intact, for the people were pious. But now it was pitiful to look at it, for it had been suddenly rent from top to bottom when [the] benefactor, man and by his actions not man, was for reward handed over to be killed. And they tell of many other signs that happened then; they said that after his killing and burial he was not found in the tomb. For some claimed he had risen, but others that he was stolen away by his friends. I do not know who speak more correctly. For a dead man cannot rise by himself unless aided by the prayer of another righteous man. Except he be an angel or one of the heavenly powers, or God himself appear as a man and do what he wants—and go among people and fall and lie and rise as is his will. And others said that it could not be possible to steal him away; for they posted guards around his tomb; one thousand Romans and one thousand Jews. Such is what is said about this veil and as to the reason for it being torn. (SJ *War* 5.214, from additional passages)

In the Greek edition of *War* Josephus describes the veil at the time of the Jewish war (66–70) (*War* 5.212–214). This Slavonic Josephus passage attributes the torn veil to the death of the wonder worker, similar to Mark's account of the veil that is torn when Jesus breathes his last (Mark 15:37–38).

There is also a discussion of whether the wonder worker is stolen or resurrected. The passage leans toward resurrection and is similar to the account in Matthew (27:62–66; 28:11–15). Perhaps the Christian interpolator copied the Matthew story, but possibly this interpolation was simply a well-known story in circulation at the time.

Passage 12: The Star Prophecy

But now, what did most elevate them in undertaking this war, was an *ambiguous oracle* that was also found in their sacred writings, how, "about that time, *one from their country should become governor of the habitable earth.*" The Jews took this prediction to belong to themselves in particular and many of the wise men were thereby deceived in their determination. Now, *this oracle certainly denoted the government of Vespasian,* who was appointed emperor in Judea. (*War* 6.312–313) (Emphasis mine)

But they were impelled to [make] war by an *ambiguous prediction* found in the sacred books, saying that in those times *someone from the Judean land would be reigning over the whole world.* For this there are various explanations. *For some thought it [meant] Herod, others the crucified miracle worker, [Jesus], others Vespasian.* (SJ *War* 6.312–313, from additional passages) (Emphasis mine)

The Star Prophecy is mentioned in the Slavonic Josephus Star of Bethlehem story. This prophecy states that a ruler will come from Israel (Numbers 24:17). In both the Greek and Slavonic Josephus versions of *War,* this oracle is said to be ambiguous. In the Greek version Josephus proclaims that the ruler is certainly Vespasian, understandable considering that his work (*War*) is pro-Vespasian and pro-Titus. However, the Slavonic Josephus version gives several possibilities for the prophesied ruler, one being Vespasian but also possibly Herod or the miracle worker. If many believed that the miracle worker was the promised ruler, then these disciples would not have left Jerusalem in the so-called Pella flight. They would have fought and died in Jerusalem.

This passage may have been written by Josephus. If the Slavonic Josephus *War* is the earlier version, written for the Jews, this emphasis on the Star Prophecy being attributed to the miracle worker may well be authentic. It may also be the earliest stratum, written by a Jewish "Christian," consistent with the Star of Bethlehem story. Either way, it presents a Jewish Jesus Movement believing that Jesus—not the Romans—would rule. This belief, in the midst of the war with Rome, places the Jesus Movement in Jerusalem at the bitter end. The story must be very early, since it goes against the grain of orthodox Christianity, which claims the Christians left for Pella before the war began.

Passage 13: Eleazar, the Grandson of Judas the Galilean

It was one Eleazar, a potent man, and the commander of these Sicarii, that had seized upon it [Masada]. He was a *descendant from that Judas* who had *persuaded* abundance of the Jews, as we have formerly related, *not to submit to the taxation* when Cyrenius was sent into Judea to make one. (*War* 7.253) (Emphasis mine)

Their commander was Eleazar, a powerful man, *grandson of Judas,* concerning whom we have told how he *deceived* the Jews so that they *would not submit to Caesar.* (SJ *War* 7.253) (Emphasis mine)

The Slavonic Josephus version states that Eleazar is the grandson of Judas, which is more specific than *War*'s use of the term *descendant*. Also, the Slavonic Josephus version says that Judas *deceived* the Jews, a word with a stronger negative connotation than the word *persuaded,* as used in the *War*. Josephus believes that wonder workers are actually deceivers of the Jewish people (*War* 2.258–260). So the word *deceiver* is often used by Josephus as a stand-in for *wonder worker*. In addition, the Slavonic Josephus version states that the followers of Judas would not submit to Caesar. By contrast, *War* only refers back to the census tax, but from *Antiquities* we know that Judas's movement is much more than a protest against the census tax (*Antiquities* 18.4–10).

THE SLAVONIC JOSEPHUS VERSUS *ANTIQUITIES*

The time line on page 338 compares the "Christian" Slavonic Josephus passages to the corresponding passages in *Antiquities*. This is very important, as the author of these Slavonic verses creates his version of events to accord with Josephus's *Antiquities*. Since *Antiquities* was not published until 93 CE, the Slavonic "Christianized" verses were not added to the *War* text until after that date. The letters (A–F) on the time line correspond to the list on pages 338–39 and the numbers (2, 3, etc.) represent the passage number as identified at the beginning of the chapter (see pages 320–37).

TIME LINE OF THE SLAVONIC JOSEPHUS'S *WAR* (TOP) VERSUS JOSEPHUS'S *ANTIQUITIES**

A. (2) Story of the Star of Bethlehem	B. (3) Story of Judas's brothers and mother	C. (5) John the Baptist introduced		D. (7) John dies	E. (8) Jesus dies	F. (9) Church persecuted
25	4 BCE	6 CE	19	34	36	44–48
Sons of Baba (last of the Maccabees) murdered by Herod	Matthias and Judas cleanse the temple	Judas and Sadduc (John the Baptist) begins their ministry	Jesus dies		John dies	Theudas and sons of Judas crucified

*The letters (A–F) correspond to the list below and the numbers (2, 3, etc.) represent the passage number as identified at the beginning of the chapter (see pages 320–37).

The following points should be noted:

A. The Star of Bethlehem story is not in Josephus's *Antiquities,* but Josephus does relate a story about Herod killing the last of the Maccabees, the sons of Baba. In both stories sons who are possible threats to his crown are killed.

B. In the Slavonic Josephus *War* the passage about Judas's mother and brothers is inserted after the story of the Golden Eagle Temple Cleansing, an incident mentioned in both the Greek version of *War* and in *Antiquities.*

C. The introduction of John the Baptist is placed at 6 CE in the Slavonic Josephus version, at the same point as Josephus's mention of Judas and Sadduc. John preaches the same nationalistic message as Judas the Galilean in the Slavonic Josephus version.

D. The Slavonic Josephus John is put to death around 36 CE, consistent with the account in *Antiquities.*

E. The death of the wonder worker (Jesus) comes after the death of John the Baptist in the Slavonic Josephus version. This order matches the gospel order but not that of *Antiquities.* In *Antiquities,* Jesus dies before John. Perhaps all "Christians" after a certain date (40–90 CE?) try to diminish the role of John. The Slavonic Josephus author may have just followed a version of events differing from that of Josephus. But if the TF (the Jesus passage in *Antiquities*) is an interpolation, then why doesn't the author of this interpolation place Jesus's death after John's? The answer may be because the interpolation in *Antiquities* is a replacement passage for the missing death of Judas the Galilean while the Slavonic Josephus verse is inserted into the text as desired by the redactor.

F. The Slavonic Josephus story of the church's dealings under Fadus and Tiberius Alexander matches *Antiquities*'s stories of the deaths of Theudas and the sons of Judas the Galilean.

THE SLAVONIC JOSEPHUS VERSUS THE GOSPELS

The time line on page 340 compares the Slavonic Josephus events to those same events in the gospels. Many similarities exist between the two sources, but the differences are most striking, an important reason why scholars have long neglected the Slavonic Josephus and have universally focused on the gospel time line. To even admit that the Slavonic Josephus may have merit is to undermine their method of investigation. Perhaps scholars have failed to find Jesus in the gospel time line because he did not live within those parameters. The letters (A–F) on the time line correspond to the list below and the numbers (2, 3, etc.) represent the passage number as identified at the beginning of the chapter (see pages 320–37).

A. The Slavonic Josephus Star of Bethlehem account is placed around 25 BCE, near the beginning of Herod the Great's reign. The gospel Star of Bethlehem story is placed at the end of Herod's life, or around 4 BCE. Both stories are similar, in that Herod wants to kill the Messiah, but the dating is off by twenty years.

B. The important event in 4 BCE, according to both Josephus and the Slavonic Josephus version, is the Golden Eagle Temple Cleansing, where Judas the Galilean and Matthias are first introduced. Note

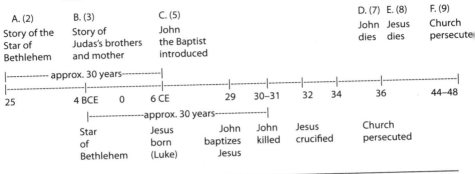

TIME LINE OF THE SLAVONIC JOSEPHUS (TOP) VERSUS THE GOSPELS (BOTTOM)*

A. (2)	B. (3)	C. (5)					D. (7)	E. (8)	F. (9)
Story of the Star of Bethlehem	Story of Judas's brothers and mother	John the Baptist introduced					John dies	Jesus dies	Church persecute

------------ approx. 30 years-----------
25	4 BCE	0	6 CE	29	30–31	32	34	36	44–48

|----------------approx. 30 years---------------|

| | Star of Bethlehem | Jesus born (Luke) | John baptizes Jesus | John killed | Jesus crucified | Church persecuted |

*The letters (A–F) correspond to the list on pages 339–42 and the numbers (2, 3, etc.) represent the passage number as identified at the beginning of the chapter (see pages 320–37).

that the Slavonic Josephus version also emphasizes the importance of brothers and a mother. In Matthew, Jesus is born in the Star of Bethlehem story. Later, his mother and brothers are not full supporters of his mission (Mark 3:20–21). Thus, the positive influence of family reported in the Slavonic Josephus is turned into a negative in the gospels, deemphasizing Jesus's familial relationships. Not only the Jews, but even Jesus's own family do not believe in him.

Also, Luke introduces the birth of Jesus in 6 CE, a good ten to twelve years after Matthew's Star of Bethlehem, a date that coincides with the second great episode in Judas the Galilean's life—the census revolt. Is it just coincidence that Matthew and Luke introduce the baby Jesus at the exact times when Josephus relates the greatest exploits of Judas the Galilean?

C. The Slavonic Josephus introduces John the Baptist in 6 CE, right before the mention of Judas the Galilean. In the Slavonic Josephus, John preaches the same nationalistic message as Judas and Sadduc (the stand-in for John the Baptist in *Antiquities*). In fact this John *is* Sadduc, the teacher who assists Judas the Galilean in his ministry. In the gospels John baptizes at the Jordan around 29 CE, a good twenty-three years after the Slavonic Josephus dating.

Also, thirty years elapse from the Slavonic Josephus Star of Bethlehem account (25 BCE) to the introduction of John (6 CE). Luke claims that Jesus is thirty years old when John begins preaching at the Jordan (Luke 3:23), even though he asserts that Jesus is born at the census (6 CE) and John begins preaching in 29 CE, a span of only twenty-three years.

D. In the Slavonic Josephus version John preaches for thirty years, beginning in 6 CE and ending in 36 CE, the ending date corroborated by *Antiquities* (18.116–119). In the gospels John arrives in 29 CE and only ministers for a short time before he is beheaded by Herod Antipas, sometime between 29 and 32 CE. So not only are the dates different, but the length of John's ministry is much shorter in the gospel account. Interestingly the Mandaeans, a group believing that John the Baptist is the Messiah, hold that John's ministry lasts forty-two years. John's ministry totaled thirty years under the Fourth Philosophy starting at the Census in 6 CE, and perhaps he begins his ministry even sooner after the death of Matthias in 4 BCE. So the forty-two-year claim may be much closer to the truth than the one- to three-year claim put forth by the gospels.

E. In both the Slavonic Josephus *War* and the gospels, John the Baptist dies *before* Jesus. The Slavonic Josephus version has John dying around 36 CE, consistent with his death in *Antiquities,* while the gospels have John dying soon after his introduction, somewhere between 30 and 32 CE, followed in both accounts by the death of Jesus. Possibly the downplaying of John's role can be traced to a very early source. Certainly Josephus does not know of such an agenda; he just positions the original "Jesus passage" (not the interpolated TF) before the death of John. Since "Jesus" really dies first, John is a much more powerful figure in *Antiquities,* someone who controls the crowds. In the Slavonic Josephus version and the gospels, John's power is much less prominent. So, even though both sources differ from Josephus's *Antiquities,* they may have received their rewrites of history from an early Jewish source.

F. The stories of Theudas and Judas the Galilean are introduced in

Acts by Gamaliel, sometime around 35 CE. We are to believe that Theudas and Judas both precede Gamaliel. Certainly Judas the Galilean does predate the famous rabbi, but Theudas does not. Christian apologists for the account in Acts claim that Gamaliel must have been speaking about an earlier Theudas, not mentioned in Josephus's history of the Jewish nation. That, however, is very improbable. According to Josephus, Theudas is beheaded in 45 CE and the sons of Judas the Galilean are crucified shortly thereafter (*Antiquities* 20.97–102). Perhaps the author of Acts mistakes Judas the Galilean for the sons of Judas the Galilean (either accidentally or on purpose), which may help date Acts no earlier than 93 CE, the date of Josephus's *Antiquities*.[5]

The Slavonic Josephus places its church persecution during the time of Fadus and Tiberius Alexander, consistent with the history of Josephus, which states that Theudas is beheaded during the governorship of Fadus while the sons of Judas the Galilean are crucified under the governorship of Tiberius Alexander. As such the Slavonic Josephus history, in this particular case, is more accurate than the story of Acts.

OTHER OPINIONS ON
THE SLAVONIC JOSEPHUS

Most scholars have dismissed the Slavonic Josephus as a grand forgery, primarily because the Slavonic Josephus version's time line does not accord with that of the gospels and Acts. In their eyes the New Testament's time line must be golden, never mind the apparent contradictions, such as the inconsistent birth narratives dated at 6–4 BCE and 6 CE. Most scholars dismiss Luke's birth date, following Matthew's earlier Star of Bethlehem date. If Luke's birth date is in error, though, should we blindly accept his date for John's arrival in 29 CE, the very foundation of the traditional Christian time line? That question has not been seriously addressed by these scholars.

However, several scholars have considered the Slavonic Josephus version of *War* as an important source. The first is Robert Eisler, who, in the 1930s, used it to support his theory that the Slavonic Josephus version is derived from either an Aramaic or a Greek prototype of the existing Greek version.[6] If so, then Josephus views Jesus as a nationalistic Messiah figure pitted against Rome. His theory is denounced by most and the source of his conclusions, the Slavonic Josephus, is universally rejected. Eisler's main problem is that he does not adjust the time line, as outlined in the Slavonic Josephus version. His focus is on the message of John and the wonder worker—rebellion against Rome.

In the mid-1960s S. G. F. Brandon published *Jesus and the Zealots*. Using the traditional time line and various passages from the gospels, Brandon ties Jesus and his disciples to the Zealot movement. He never claims that Jesus is Judas the Galilean, only that Jesus and his disciples are very close to the Zealots. Concerning the Slavonic Josephus, Brandon only comments upon the wonder-worker passage. He states: "The non-committal attitude toward the Wonder-worker, which is clearly evident in the passage, is certainly remarkable. It is impossible to tell whether the author approved or disapproved of him."[7] Brandon can see no agenda, whether positive or negative, concerning this wonder worker. As to who wrote the Slavonic Josephus version, Brandon cannot say for sure, commenting, "If it does not reflect what Josephus originally wrote, we can only wonder at the identity and purpose of him who wrote the account."[8] So, instead of dismissing the Slavonic Josephus without examination, Brandon considers it a remarkable puzzle. Even though it contradicts the traditional concept of Jesus, he thinks that the Slavonic Josephus should be further studied.

Thirty years later Robert Eisenman published *James the Brother of Jesus*. He considers the Slavonic Josephus version as a possible credible source: "Though generally held in low esteem by most scholars, all materials of this kind should be treated equally according to the same methodological approach. Talmudic materials are not usually on a much higher level, nor the gospels themselves—nor, for that matter, the early part of the book of Acts."[9] He then states that sources deviating from orthodoxy can sometimes represent an earlier stratum.

AUTHOR'S OPINION ON
THE SLAVONIC JOSEPHUS

Two parts of the Slavonic Josephus exist—one written by Josephus and passages inserted into the text by a later "Christian." Even though the entire Slavonic Josephus text can be traced to the eleventh or twelfth century, the majority of the text is certainly based on Josephus's works. According to Eisler, the "Slavonic version [was] derived from either an Aramaic or a Greek prototype of the extant Greek version of Josephus' *Jewish War*."[10] Brandon states that nothing in the Slavonic version points toward the original Semitic version or to a shorter Greek text, but that the ultimate dependence was upon the fuller Greek text.[11] Note that each scholar, although differing in opinion as to the ultimate source, does believe that the Slavonic Josephus text is a product of some version of Josephus's *Jewish War*. After perusing the synoptic account published in English by Leeming and Leeming, there is no doubt that Josephus's *Jewish War* is the basis for the Slavonic version.[12]

When some scholars argue that the Slavonic Josephus is a forgery and not to be trusted, they are confusing the main text with the inserted Christianized verses, passages itemized on pages 320–37 (1–3, 5, and 7–12). (Note that passages 4, 6, and 13 are just slightly different versions of Josephus's Greek text and related to Herod and Judas the Galilean). The best proof that these verses are the work of a Christian redactor comes from passage 7, where the Christianized passage confuses the childless Philip with Herod, called Philip, a mistake that would not have been made by Josephus.

So when were these Christianized passages inserted into the text and who wrote them? Clearly, the Christianized passages were inserted into *War* to match existing passages in *Antiquities* (see the time line comparing the two sources on page 338). Since *Antiquities* was written in 93 CE, these Christianized verses must have been written *after* 93 CE.

In addition, some materials contained in the Slavonic Christianized passages have much in common with Matthew. Both have Star of Bethlehem stories that differ on the birth date of the Messiah.* The Slavonic Josephus version includes the mother and brothers of the Messiah, as does Matthew and Mark. However, the Slavonic mother and brothers are part of the ministry (passage 3), while in the synoptic gospels they are either opposed to Jesus or just fail to support him.† In passage 8, Pilate's wife is introduced as the source of Pilate's belief in the wonder worker's innocence. This theme is repeated by Matthew when Pilate's wife suffers from a dream because of that innocent man (Jesus) (Matthew 27:19). Passage 8 also claims that the wonder worker is released and that the chief priests pay thirty talents to Pilate, not Judas Iscariot.‡ In addition, Pilate gives the Jews full authority to do with the wonder worker as they wish. And the Jews kill him. This is repeated in Matthew, with Pilate washing his hands of all responsibility, placing full blame for the death of Jesus on the Jewish people (Matthew 27:24–26). Finally, passage 11 claims that the Temple veil is torn because of the wonder worker's death and that a guard is posted at the tomb, claims also made by Matthew.§ The Christianized Slavonic Josephus passages contain a different interpretation than Matthew concerning the Star of Bethlehem, the brothers and mother of the Messiah, Pilate's wife, the prisoner release, the thirty pieces of silver, the shifting of responsibility from Pilate to the Jews, the torn Temple veil, and the tomb's guard. It appears as if the Slavonic Josephus uses some of the same materials as Matthew, but gives a different time line and a much different meaning, making it doubtful that the Slavonic Christianized verses would have been written long after the release of Matthew and its wider

---

*In Matthew's account (Matthew 2:1–12) Jesus is born near the end of Herod the Great's reign, or around 5 BCE. The Slavonic Josephus version (passage 2) places the Star of Bethlehem event near the beginning of Herod's reign, or around 25 BCE.

†See Mark 3:20–21; Matthew 12:46–50; and Matthew 13:55–58. Supposedly, Jesus says, "Only in his hometown and in *his own house* is a prophet without honor."

‡Matthew 26:13–16 concerns Judas Iscariot and the thirty pieces of silver, and Matthew 27:20–26 speaks to the release of Barabbas instead of Jesus.

§Matthew 27:51 tells of the Temple's veil being torn while Matthew 27:62–66 relates the story of the guard at the tomb.

dissemination. In my opinion the Slavonic Josephus's Christianized passages were written from the same source material used by Matthew, placing the date of original composition after *Antiquities* and near the release of Matthew, sometime between 93 and 120 CE.

Certain parts of the wonder-worker passage (passage 8) were interpolated at a much later date, after the late third century. In *Antiquities* the *Testimonium Flavianum,* as quoted by Eusebius, is not original. Certainly the text claiming that Jesus is more than a man is not from the pen of Josephus and is not quoted by the earliest of church historians. Interestingly the Slavonic Josephus passage also claims that the wonder worker is more than a man. This was probably added by a well-meaning Christian to make the Slavonic Josephus *War* accord with the interpolated TF.

Who would have written the Slavonic Josephus's Christianized passages? Like Matthew this author would have had access to very early Jewish Jesus Movement records (either oral or written). But it is questionable whether this person was Jewish, as he, like Matthew, places the blame for the wonder worker's death on the Jews and not on Pilate (Rome). However, this author does present a more historically accurate account of the wonder worker and John the Baptist, in that they are wildly popular among the crowds, who wish for independence from Rome, a sentiment totally absent in Matthew.

The Slavonic Josephus has been ignored by scholars primarily because its accounts of John the Baptist and Jesus are at odds with the gospel accounts. In particular the time line differs by a generation from Luke, and the nationalist cry for independence from Rome is more in line with Judas the Galilean than with Jesus of Nazareth.

Can the dating of the Slavonic Josephus be trusted? Better put, is it any less reliable than the time line offered by Luke? According to Luke, John the Baptist arrives in 28–29 CE and all other dating has been assigned based on that starting date. But most scholars agree that Luke's birth date for Jesus is in error by ten to twelve years, assuming Matthew's date is correct. In addition, if Luke wrote Acts, then his historical accuracy can certainly be called into question, since many of the events described in that book are anachronistic.[13] As such the Slavonic Josephus should be treated much as we treat the gospels and Acts. Place it next to Josephus, use some common sense, and allow the Slavonic Josephus's Christianized passages to help unravel the "Jesus" mystery.

Notes

CHAPTER 1. HELLENISTIC AND ROMAN INFLUENCES

1. Grant, *History of Ancient Israel*, 210.
2. Ibid., 216.
3. Ibid.
4. Ibid., 218.

CHAPTER 2. PRIMARY TEXT REFERENCES TO JESUS

1. Whiston, *Works of Josephus*, 815.
2. Bettenson, *Documents of the Christian Church*, 2; Suetonius, "Claudius," in *Twelve Caesars*, xxv.4.
3. Bettenson, *Documents of the Christian Church*, 2–3; Suetonius, "Nero," in *Twelve Caesars*, xvi.
4. Unterbrink, *Three Messiahs*, 192–95.
5. Tacitus, *Annals*, xv.44.
6. Suetonius, "Nero," in *Twelve Caesars*, 38.
7. Bettenson, *Documents of the Christian Church*, 1–2; Tacitus, *Annals*, xv.44.
8. Gibbon, *History of the Decline and Fall of the Roman Empire*, vol. 1, 530–31.
9. Bettenson, "Pliny Epp. X (Letter to Trajan)," *Documents of the Christian Church*, 3–4, xcvi.
10. Wise, Abegg, and Cook, *Dead Sea Scrolls*, 24.
11. Ibid., 25.
12. Ibid., 26.
13. Ibid., 32.

14. Unterbrink, *Judas the Galilean*, 82–97.
15. Wise, Abegg, and Cook, *Dead Sea Scrolls*, 33.
16. Ibid.
17. Eisenman, *New Testament Code*, 40–57.
18. Ibid., 297.

CHAPTER 3. TRADITIONAL VERSUS HISTORICAL PAUL

1. Eisenman, *James the Brother of Jesus*, 411–65.
2. Barclay, *The Letter to the Romans*, vol.1, *Daily Study Bible*, 213.
3. Eisenman, *James the Brother of Jesus*, 52.
4. Maccoby, *Mythmaker*, 65.
5. Ibid., 67.

CHAPTER 4. JAMES THE JUST AND PAUL THE LIAR

1. Pseudoclementine *Recognitions*, 1.70.

CHAPTER 5. PAUL'S FAMILY TIES

1. *Antiquities*, 18.130–42; and Eisenman, *James the Brother of Jesus*, 968–69.
2. Philo, "On the Embassy to Gaius," in *The Works of Philo*, 276–326. See also Graves, *Claudius the God*, 282–83.
3. Suetonius, "Claudius," in *Twelve Caesars*, 25.
4. Graves, *Claudius the God*, 324. See also *Antiquities*, 19.338–42.
5. Unterbrink, *Three Messiahs*, 140–43.
6. Whiston, *Against Apion*, 1.51–52, in *The Works of Josephus*; Eisenman, *James the Brother of Jesus*, 968–969. Eisenman has created the Herodian family tree, suggesting that Paul is Saul and that Julius Archelaus is Saul's nephew.

CHAPTER 6. PAUL'S MOTIVATION

1. Pseudoclementine *Recognitions*, 1.70–71.

CHAPTER 7. FOUNDATION LEGENDS

1. Clement of Rome, *First Epistle to the Corinthians*, chapter 5.
2. Irenaeus, *Against Heresies*, I.xxvi and I.2, in Bettenson, *Documents of the Christian Church*.

3. Eusebius, "Tiberius to Nero," in *History of the Church*, 2.25.

4. Ibid.

5. St. Augustine, "Sermon 295."

6. Mack, *Who Wrote the New Testament?*, 153.

7. Ibid. Also see Eusebius, *History of the Church*, 3.39.

8. Eusebius, "Vespasian to Trajan," *History of the Church*, 3.5.

9. Irenaeus, *Against Heresies*, I.xxvi and I.2, in Bettenson, *Documents of the Christian Church*.

10. Brandon, *Jesus and the Zealots*, 217. Brandon clearly states that the Ebionites showed continuity with the Jewish Jesus Movement.

11. Ibid., 209; Brandon, *Fall of Jerusalem*, 168–73 and 263–64.

12. Eusebius, "Vespasian to Trajan," *History of the Church*, 3.11.

13. Ibid., 3.32.

14. Brandon, *Jesus and the Zealots*, 213–14.

15. Ibid.

16. Eusebius, "Vespasian to Trajan," *History of the Church*, 3.12.

17. Ibid., 3.19.

18. Whiston, *The Life of Flavius Josephus* in *The Works of Josephus*, 22–24.

19. Severus, *Chronica*, 2.30.6–8. The translation is from Eric Laupot, who argues that the quote was originally from Tacitus's *Histories*, book 5. For his arguments, see infidels.org/library/modern/eric_laupot/nazoreans.html.

20. Gibbon, *History of the Decline and Fall of the Roman Empire*, vol. 1, 530–31.

21. Unterbrink, *Three Messiahs*, 94–103.

CHAPTER 8. THE GOSPEL OF MARK

1. Mack, *Who Wrote the New Testament?*, 154.

2. Ibid., 160.

3. Brandon, *Jesus and the Zealots*, 8.

4. Brandon, *Trial of Jesus of Nazareth*, 67.

5. Brandon, *Jesus and the Zealots*, 88–92.

6. Irenaeus, *Against Heresies*, I.xxvi and I.2, in Bettenson, *Documents of the Christian Church*.

7. Gospel of Peter, verse 59.

8. Unterbrink, *Three Messiahs*, 171–75.

9. Mack, *Who Wrote the New Testament?*, 154–55.

10. Unterbrink, *Three Messiahs,* 196–206.
11. Irenaeus, *Against Heresies,* I.xxvi and I.2, in Bettenson, *Documents of the Christian Church.*
12. Mack, *Who Wrote the New Testament?,* 159.
13. Brandon, *Jesus and the Zealots,* 78.

CHAPTER 9. THE GOSPEL OF MATTHEW

1. Barclay, *Gospel of Matthew,* vol. 1, *Daily Study Bible,* 2.
2. Ibid., 5.
3. Irenaeus, *Against Heresies,* I.xxvi and I.2, in Bettenson, *Documents of the Christian Church.*
4. Barclay, *Gospel of Matthew,* vol. 1, *Daily Study Bible,* 4.
5. Ibid., 6.
6. Barclay, *Gospel of Matthew,* vol. 1, *Daily Study Bible,* 73.
7. Irenaeus, *Against Heresies,* I.xxvi and I.2, in Bettenson, *Documents of the Christian Church.*
8. Brandon, *Jesus and the Zealots,* 295.
9. Brown and Comfort, *New Greek-English Interlinear New Testament,* 38–39.
10. Irenaeus, *Against Heresies,* I.xxvi and I.2, in Bettenson, *Documents of the Christian Church.*
11. Maccoby, *Revolution in Judaea,* 160.
12. Barclay, *Gospel of Matthew,* vol.1, *Daily Study Bible,* 2.

CHAPTER 10. THE GOSPEL OF LUKE

1. Barclay, *Gospel of Matthew,* vol. 1, *Daily Study Bible,* 2.
2. Robertson, *Pagan Christs,* 120.
3. Ibid., 122.
4. Pseudoclementine *Recognitions,* 1.54.
5. Eisenman, *James the Brother of Jesus,* 114–15.
6. Farrer, "On Dispensing with Q," in Nineham, ed., *Studies in the Gospels,* 55–88.
7. Brandon, *Jesus and the Zealots,* 285.
8. Freke and Gandy, *The Jesus Mysteries,* 46.
9. Brandon, *Jesus and the Zealots,* 290; Mack, *Who Wrote the New Testament?,* 172.

CHAPTER 11. THE ACTS OF THE APOSTLES

1. *Halley's Bible Handbook,* 558–59.
2. Irenaeus, *Against Heresies,* I.xxvi and I.2, in Bettenson, *Documents of the Christian Church.*

CHAPTER 12. THE GOSPEL OF JOHN

1. Mack, *Who Wrote the New Testament?,* 177–78. Mack claims that the Gospel of John closely follows Mark's account of the trial and crucifixion of Jesus. In addition, of the "seven signs" in John, five are included in Mark.
2. www.greekmythology.com/Other_Gods/Dionysus/dionysus.html.
3. Barclay, *Gospel of John,* vol. 1, *Daily Study Bible,* 6–8.
4. Bettenson, *Documents of the Christian Church,* 35.

CONCLUSION. THE REAL JESUS OF NAZARETH

1. Pseudoclementine *Recognitions,* 1.53–54.
2. Crossan and Reed, *Excavating Jesus,* 18.
3. Gibbon, *History of the Decline and Fall of the Roman Empire,* vol. 1, 530–31.
4. www.margaretstarbird.net/mary_called_magdalene.html.
5. Maccoby, *Revolution in Judaea,* 19 and 222 (note 3).
6. Williamson and Smallwood, *Josephus: The Jewish War,* 461.
7. Crossan and Reed, *Excavating Jesus,* 174.
8. Bettenson, "Pliny Epp. X (Letter to Trajan)," in *Documents of the Christian Church,* xcvi.

APPENDIX B. JOHN THE BAPTIST

1. Barclay, *Daily Study Bible,* Gospel of Mark. 16.
2. Eisenman, *James the Brother of Jesus,* 17.
3. Pseudoclementine *Recognitions,* 1.53–54.
4. Pseudoclementine *Recognitions,* 1.54.
5. Unterbrink, *Judas the Galilean,* 83.
6. Eisenman, *James the Brother of Jesus,* 154–84.
7. Ibid., 467. Eisenman quotes Epiphanius (Haeres 78.13.2 and 14.5) and notes that the death of Jesus would be 38 CE, the approximate year of John the Baptist's death, per Josephus. Eisenman has not accounted for

the leadership of John after the death of "Jesus." In fact, James leads the Jewish Jesus Movement for twenty-four years, from the death of John the Baptist to 62 CE.

APPENDIX C. PONTIUS PILATE

1. Eusebius, *History of the Church,* Book 1.9.

APPENDIX D. THE SLAVONIC JOSEPHUS

1. Leeming and Leeming, *Josephus' Jewish War and its Slavonic Version.*
2. Eisenman, *James the Brother of Jesus,* 44. Eisenman believes that Judas Sepphoris (the Judas of the Golden Eagle Temple Cleansing) is probably identical to Judas the Galilean, thus linking one person to the 4 BCE Temple cleansing and the 6 CE Census tax revolt.
3. Whiston, *Works of Josephus,* on *War* 1.3, 543 note b.
4. Unterbrink, *Three Messiahs,* 323–32.
5. Ibid., 17–25.
6. Brandon, *Jesus and the Zealots,* 364.
7. Ibid., 367.
8. Ibid., 368.
9. Eisenman, *James the Brother of Jesus,* 403.
10. Brandon, *Jesus and the Zealots,* 364.
11. Ibid., 365–66.
12. Leeming and Leeming, *Josephus' Jewish War and its Slavonic Version,* 43–47. It was found that the old Russian translation derived "from the generally accepted Greek texts," as some Greek words were left untranslated in the text.
13. Unterbrink, *Three Messiahs,* 242–92. This is a verse-by-verse analysis of Acts.

Bibliography

Barclay, William. *The Daily Study Bible*. Philadelphia: The Westminster Press, 1978.

Bettenson, Henry. *Documents of the Christian Church*. New York: Oxford University Press, 1979.

Brandon, S. G. F. *The Fall of Jerusalem and the Christian Church*. Eugene, Oreg.: Wipf & Stock, 2010.

———. *Jesus and the Zealots*. New York: Charles Scribner's Sons, 1967.

———. *The Trial of Jesus of Nazareth*. New York: Dorset Press, 1968.

Brown, Robert K. and Philip W. Comfort. *The New Greek-English Interlinear New Testament*. Wheaton, Ill.: Tyndale House Publishers, 1990.

Clement of Rome. "First Epistle, Letter to the Corinthians." www.ccel.org/ccel/schaff/anf01.toc.html.

Crossan, John Dominic and Jonathan L. Reed. *Excavating Jesus*. San Francisco: HarperSanFrancisco, 2001.

Dio Cassius. *Roman History*. www.fordham.edu/halsall/ancient/diocassius-nero1.asp.

Ehrman, Bart D. *Did Jesus Exist?* New York: HarperOne, 2012.

Eisenman, Robert. *James the Brother of Jesus*. New York: Penguin Books, 1997.

———. *The New Testament Code*. London: Watkins Publishing, 2006.

Ellegard, Alvar. *Jesus One Hundred Years before Christ*. New York: The Overlook Press, 1999.

Eusebius. *The History of the Church*. Translated by G. A. Williamson. New York: Dorset Press, 1984.

Farrer, Austin M. "On Dispensing with Q." In D. E. Nineham, ed., *Studies in the Gospels: Essays in Memory of R. H. Lightfoot*. Oxford, UK:

Blackwell, 1955; http://NTGateway.com/synoptic-problem-and-q/ books-and-articles.

Freke, Timothy and Peter Gandy. *The Jesus Mysteries.* New York: Harmony Books, 1999.

Gibbon, Edward. *The History of the Decline and Fall of the Roman Empire,* vol. 1. New York: Penguin Books, 1994.

Grant, Michael. *The History of Ancient Israel.* New York: Charles Scribner's Sons, 1984.

Graves, Robert. *Claudius the God.* New York: Vintage International, 1989.

Halley, Henry H. *Halley's Bible Handbook,* 24th ed. Grand Rapids, Mich.: Zondervan, 1965.

Johnson, Paul. *Civilizations of the Holy Land.* New York: Atheneum, 1979.

Leeming, H. and K. Leeming. *Josephus' Jewish War and its Slavonic Version.* Leiden, Holland: Brill, 2003.

Maccoby, Hyam. *Revolution in Judaea.* New York: Taplinger Publishing Company, 1980.

———. *The Mythmaker.* New York: Harper and Row Publishers, 1986.

Mack, Burton L., *Who Wrote the New Testament?* San Francisco: HarperSanFrancisco, 1995.

Philo. *The Works of Philo.* Translated by C. D. Yonge. Peabody, Mass.: Hendrickson Publishers, Inc., 2002.

Pseudoclementine *Recognitions.* www.ccel.org.

Robertson, J. M. *Pagan Christs.* New York: Dorset Press, 1987.

Severus, Sulpicius. *Chronica.* infidels.org/library/modern/eric_laupot/ nazoreans.html.

Slavonic Josephus. *War.* sacred-texts.com.

St. Augustine. "Sermon 295." www.crossroadsinitiative.com/library_ article/151/Peter_and_Paul___St._Augustine.html.

Starbird, Margaret. www.margaretstarbird.net/mary_called_magdalene .html.

Suetonius. *The Twelve Caesars.* Translated by Robert Graves; revised by Michael Grant. London: Penguin Books, 1979.

Tacitus. *The Annals and the Histories.* Translated by Alfred John Church and William Jackson Brodribb. Chicago: Encyclopedia Britannica, Inc., 1952.

Unterbrink, Daniel T. *Judas the Galilean: The Flesh and Blood Jesus.* New York: iUniverse, Inc., 2004.

————. *The Three Messiahs*. New York: iUniverse, Inc., 2010.

Vermes, Geza. *The Complete Dead Sea Scrolls in English*. New York: Allen Lane, The Penguin Press, 1997.

Whiston, William, trans. *The Works of Josephus*. Peabody, Mass.: Hendrickson Publishers, 1984.

Williamson, G. A. and Mary Smallwood. *Josephus: The Jewish War*. New York: Penguin Books, 1981.

Wilson, Barrie. *How Jesus Became Christian*. New York: St. Martin's Press, 2008.

Wise, Michael, Martin Abegg Jr., and Edward Cook. *The Dead Sea Scrolls: A New Translation*. San Francisco: HarperSanFrancisco, 1996.

Index

BOOKS OF RELATED INTEREST

Judas and Jesus
Two Faces of a Single Revelation
by Jean-Yves Leloup

The Gospel of Mary Magdalene
by Jean-Yves Leloup

The Gospel of Thomas
The Gnostic Wisdom of Jesus
by Jean-Yves Leloup

The Gospel of Philip
Jesus, Mary Magdalene, and the Gnosis of Sacred Union
by Jean-Yves Leloup

The Brother of Jesus and the Lost Teachings of Christianity
by Jeffrey J. Bütz

Jesus the Wicked Priest
How Christianity Was Born of an Essene Schism
by Marvin Vining

The Mysteries of John the Baptist
His Legacy in Gnosticism, Paganism, and Freemasonry
by Tobias Churton

The Woman with the Alabaster Jar
Mary Magdalen and the Holy Grail
by Margaret Starbird

INNER TRADITIONS • BEAR & COMPANY
P.O. Box 388
Rochester, VT 05767
1-800-246-8648
www.InnerTraditions.com

Or contact your local bookseller